Constantius II

Constantius II

Usurpers, Eunuchs and the Antichrist

By Peter Crawford

Pen & Sword
MILITARY

First published in Great Britain in 2016 by
Pen & Sword Military
an imprint of
Pen & Sword Books Ltd
47 Church Street
Barnsley
South Yorkshire
S70 2AS

ISBN 978 1 78340 055 3

A CIP catalogue record for this book is
available from the British Library.

Typeset in Ehrhardt by
Replika Press Pvt Ltd, India
Printed and bound in England
by CPI Group (UK) Ltd, Croydon, CRO 4YY

Pen & Sword Books Ltd incorporates the Imprints of Pen & Sword Aviation,
Pen & Sword Family History, Pen & Sword Maritime, Pen & Sword Military,
Pen & Sword Discovery, Pen & Sword Politics, Pen & Sword Atlas,
Pen & Sword Archaeology, Wharncliffe Local History, Wharncliffe
True Crime, Wharncliffe Transport, Pen & Sword Select, Pen & Sword
Military Classics, Leo Cooper, The Praetorian Press, Claymore Press,
Remember When, Seaforth Publishing and Frontline Publishing.

For a complete list of Pen & Sword titles please contact
PEN & SWORD BOOKS LIMITED
47 Church Street, Barnsley, South Yorkshire, S70 2AS, England
E-mail: enquiries@pen-and-sword.co.uk
Website: www.pen-and-sword.co.uk

What difference does it make by what pains each seeks the truth? We cannot attain to so great a secret by one road...
— Quintus Aurelius Symmachus, *Relationes* III.10

My words should and can be brief, lest by dwelling on your great deeds
— 'Laudatio Turiae' *ILS* 8393

Contents

Acknowledgements

I would like to give thanks to those who have contributed in some way to the production and publication of this work:

To Phil Sidnell and *Pen & Sword* for once again placing their trust in me.

To Matt Jones and his team, who have done a tremendous job again in bringing together the words, pictures and maps that I jumbled together and threw in their general direction.

To those artists and photographers, amateur and professional, whose images have been used to add depth and colour to what would otherwise be a solid block of uninterrupted text; specifically, to Noble Numismatics for giving me access to their excellent archive of coins once more and to my sister, Faye, who has again lent her graphic prowess to produce the tremendous maps and tactical diagrams found within.

To John Curran for not only having time to offer advice and provide the opportunities to continue in ancient history through teaching and our newly founded Classical Association in Northern Ireland, the latest step in my "perpetual studentship", but also for taking the time to read the section on Athanasius and offer his thoughts and expertise.

To all the staff, past and present, at Queen's University, Belfast and Dalriada School, Ballymoney for all the time and effort you have put in to help me get this far.

To all my predecessors and peers whose works have been consulted, digested and cited within. I hope to have done you all justice.

To all my family and friends for continuing to put up with and feigning interest in my dropping of ancient history anecdotes and facts into conversations where they were barely warranted.

Last, but by no means least, my mum for being a sounding board for a list of ideas and complaints...

gratias vobis ago

Acknowledgments

List of Plates

1. Constantius II: Bust from Museum of Archaeology, University of Pennsylvania; Mary Harrsch © 2005.
2. Constantius II: In the porch of St John Lateran, Rome, this was once thought to be Constantine I but is instead Constantius II; © TcfkaPanairjdde.
3. Missorium of Kerch: Depicting Constantius II on horseback with a spear, accompanied by a guardsman and preceded by Victory; public domain.
4. Constantius II: Depicted dispensing largesse in a Renaissance copy of a Carolingian copy of the *Chronograph of 354*, Barberini Museum, Rome; public domain.
5. Constantine I: Head of colossal marble statue, Musei Capitolini, Rome; Jean-Pol Grandmont © 2011.
6. Constantius Gallus: Bust in Archaelogical Museum, Aquileia; Wolfgang Sauber © 2011.
7. Gallus: Constantius Gallus holding Victory in a Renaissance copy of a Carolingian copy of the *Chronograph of 354*, Barberini Museum, Rome; public domain.
8. The Tetrarchs in Porphyry: Plundered from Constantinople during the Fourth Crusade, it now stands on a corner of St Mark's in Venice; Nino Barbieri © 2004.
9. Constans: Marble bust in the Louvre; Jastrow 2005, public domain.
10. Constantine II: Statue on the Cordonata, Rome, Italy; TcfkaPanairjdde © 2009.
11. 'Grigor Illuminator baptises Tiridates III of Armenia': Francesco Zugno (1708–1787); public domain.
12. AmidaGerry Lynch © 2003.
13. Walls of Amida: Brian Dell, 2010, public domain.
14. The Western Wall of Amida: Bjorn Christian Torrisen © 2009.
15. Palace of Sirmium: Marko235 © Mediaportal 2012.
16. Sirmium: A scale model of Sirmium in the Visitor Centre in Srmeska Mitrovica; Marko235 © Mediaportal 2012.
17. Scutum Fidei: Attempted explanation of the Trinity; public domain.

18. Bridge over the Pyramus near Mobsucrenae: © (CC BY 3.0) Klaus–Peter Simon 1996.
19. Priest of Serapis, formerly thought to be Julian: Public domain.
20. Shapur II on the hunt: Arthur M. Sackler Gallery, Washington D.C.; public domain.

Coins

All coins courtesy of Noble Numismatics: www.noble.com.au

21. Coins
CONSTANTIUS II
Gold *solidus*, issued 347–350, Antioch
OBV: diademed, draped and cuirassed bust, FL IVL CONSTAN TIVS PERP AVG
REV: GLORIA REI PVBLICAE, enthroned Roma and Constantinopolis holding shield with VOT XX MULT XXX, in exergue SMANS

CONSTANTIUS II
Gold *solidus*, issued 340–351, Nicomedia
OBV: diademed, draped and cuirassed bust, FL IVL CONSTAN TIVS PERP AVG
REV: GLORIA REI PVBLICAE, enthroned Roma and Constantinopolis holding shield with VOT XX MULT XXX, in exergue SMNS

CONSTANTIUS II
Silver siliqua, issued 340–351, Sirmium
OBV: diademed bust, DN CONSTAN TIVS PF AVG
REV: VOT XXX MVLTIS XXXX within wreath, in exergue PCON

CONSTANTINE II
AE follis, issued 326, Trier
OBV: laureate cuirassed bust, CONSTANTINVS IVN NOB C
REV: turreted camp gate with star, PROVIDEN TIAE CAESS, in exergue STR dotted crescent

CONSTANS
Silver siliqua, issued 337–340, Constantinople
OBV: large plain diademed head to right of Constans, looking upwards,
REV: Victory holding wreath and palm branch, CONSTANS AVGVSTVS, in exergue C I

22. Coins

CONSTANTINE I
AE centenionalis, issued c.320, Aquileia
OBV: helmeted and cuirassed bust, Medusa on breastplate, CONST ANTINVS AVG
REV: two captives seated at base of VOT X X vexillum, flanked by S-F, VIRTVS EXERCIT, in exergue AQP

CONSTANTINE I
Forgery AE follies in gold, Antioch
OBV: pearl rosette draped bust, CONSTANTI NVS MAX AVG
REV: two soldiers holding standards, GLOR IA EXERC ITVS, in exergue SMAND

CRISPUS
AE follis, issued 324–325, London
OBV: laureate draped and cuirassed bust, FL IVL CRISPVS NOB CAES
REV: turreted camp gate with star, PROVIDEN TIAE CAESS, in exergue PLON

FAUSTA
AE follis, c.300–326, Nicomedia
OBV: diademed draped bust, FLAV MAX FAVSTA AVG
REV: Fausta holding Constantine II and Constantius II, SPES REI PVBLICAE, in exergue MNA

CONSTANTIUS I
AE follis, issued 307–310 (posthumous), Rome
OBV: veiled and laureate draped bust, DIVO CONSTANTIO PIO PRINCIP
REV: Constantius seated on curule chair, REQVIES OPTIMOR MERIT, in exergue RQ

23. Coins

CONSTANTIUS I
Silver argentius, issued c.295–297, Rome
OBV: laureate bust, CONSTAN TIVS CAES
REV: tetrarchs sacrifice before turreted open camp gate, VIRTVS MILITVM, in exergue A

HELENA
AE follis, issued 324–325, Arles
OBV: draped bust, FL HELENA AVGVSTA

REV: SECVRITAS REIPVBLICE, Helena standing to left, lowering branch, in exergue T*AR

DIOCLETIAN
Gold aureus, issued 290–292, Antioch and Cyzicus
OBV: laureate bust, DIOCLETIANVS AVGVSTVS
REV: Diocletian holding globe, CONSVL IIII P P PRO COS

MAGNENTIUS
AE double centenionalis, issued 353, Amiens
OBV: draped and cuirassed bust, DN MAGNETIUS PF AVG
REV: large Chi-Rho, between alpha and omega, SALVS DD NN AUG ET CAES, in exergue AMB

VETRANIO
AE centenionalis, issued at Thessalonica
OBV: bearded, diademed, draped and cuirassed, D N VERTAN IO (sic) P F AVG
REV: emperor in military dress holding Chi-Rho banner and shield, VIRTVS EXERCITVM, in exergue TSA

24. Coins

JULIAN
Gold solidus, issued 355–361, Antioch
OBV: draped and cuirassed bust, D N IVLIANV S NOB CAES
REV: Roma and Constantinopolis enthroned holding shield inscribed with star, GLORIA REI PVBLICAE, in exergue SMANZ

JULIAN
AE 3, 361–363, Sirmium
OBV: helmeted, diademed bust holding spear and shield DN FL CL IVLI-ANVS PF AVG
REV: VOT X / MVLT XX in wreath, in exergue ASIRM

CONSTANTIUS GALLUS
AE centenionalis, 351–354, Constantinople
OBV: draped and cuirassed bust, D N FL C L CONSTANTIVS NOB CAES
REV: soldier spearing fallen horseman, FEL TEMP RE PARATIO, **G* and dot above, in exergue CONSI

SHAPUR II
Silver drachm
OBV: bust to right with crown, name in outer margin
REV: fire altar with attendants

SHAPUR II
Gold dinar, Kabul
OBV: bust to right with crown, flowing hair type
REV: fire altar, text around

List of Illustrations

Geographical maps

Map 1: The Roman empire of the fourth century
Map 2: Constantine's proposed Tetrarchy
Map 3: The Pannonian settlement 9 September 337
Map 4: The Sassanid kingdom of Shapur II
Map 5: The new settlement 340–350
Map 6: Gaul, Germany and the Rhine frontier
Map 7: The Danube, Italy and the Balkans
Map 8: The Roman eastern frontier

Tactical diagrams:

The Battle of Strasbourg

A. Initial deployments
B. Repulse and rout of the Roman cavalry
C. Alamanni advance
D. The 'hog's head' breaks through
E. Roman rally

All Maps and Diagrams were drawn by Faye Beedle – www.fayecreative.
designbinder.com

Emperors and Usurpers in the Fourth Century

Name	Reign
Diocletian	*Augustus*: 20 November 284 to 1 May 305
Maximian	*Augustus*: 1 April 286 to 1 May 305; *(usurped)*: late 306 to 11 November 308, summer 310
Constantius I Chlorus	*Caesar*: 1 March 293 to 1 May 305 *Augustus*: 1 May 305 to 25 July 306
Galerius	*Caesar*: 1 March/21 May 293 to 1 May 305 *Augustus*: 1 May 305 to May 311
Severus II	*Caesar*: 1 May 305 to July/August 306 *Augustus*: July/August 306 to March/April 307
Constantine I	*Caesar (initially usurped)*: 25 July 306 to c.308 *Augustus*: c.308 to 337
Maxentius	*undefined (usurped)*: 28 October 306 to c.308 *Augustus (usurped)*: c.308 to 28 October 312
Maximinus Daia	*Caesar*: 1 May 305 to May 311 *Augustus*: May 311 to July/August 313
Licinius I	*Augustus*: 11 November 11 308 to 18 September 324
Valerius Valens	*Augustus*: late 316 to 1 March 317
Martinianus	*Augustus*: July to 18 September 324
Licinius II	*Caesar*: 1 March 317 to 18 September 324
Constantine II	*Caesar*: 1 March 317 to 22 May 337 *Augustus*: 22 May 337 to late 340
Constantius II	*Caesar*: 13 November 324 to 22 May 337 *Augustus*: 22 May 337 to 3 November 361
Constans I	*Caesar*: 25 December 333 to 22 May 337 *Augustus*: 22 May 337 to late January 350
Magnentius	*Augustus (usurped)*: 18 January 350 to 11 August 353
Nepotianus	*Augustus (usurped)*: 3 June to 30 June 350
Vetranio	*Augustus (usurped)*: 1 March to 25 December 350
Decentius	*Caesar (usurped)*: winter 350/351 to 18 August 353
Gallus	*Caesar*: 15 March 351 to October 354

Name	Reign
Julian	*Caesar*: 6 November 355 to February 360 *Augustus (initially usurped)*: February 360 to 26 June 363
Jovian	*Augustus*: 26 June 363 to 17 February 364
Valentinian I	*Augustus*: 26 February 364 to 17 November 375
Valens	*Augustus*: 28 March 364 to 9 August 378
Procopius	*Augustus (usurped)*: 26 September 365 to 27 May 366
Gratian	*Augustus*: 4 August 367 to 25 August 383
Valentinian II	*Augustus*: 17 November 375 to 15 May 392
Theodosius I	*Augustus*: 1 January 379 to 17 January 395

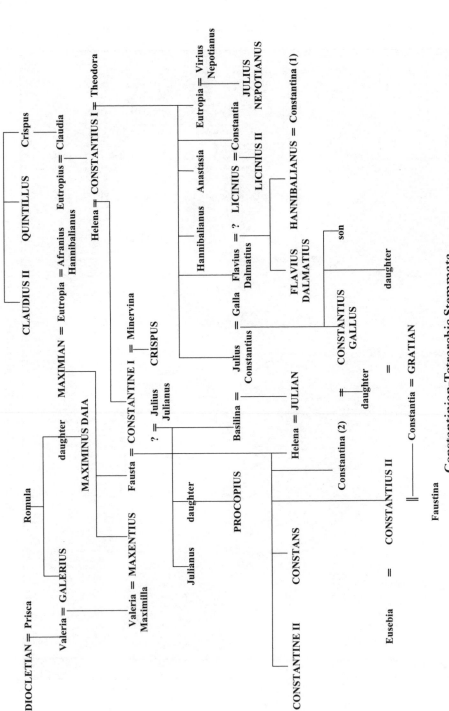

Constantinian-Tetrarchic Stemmata

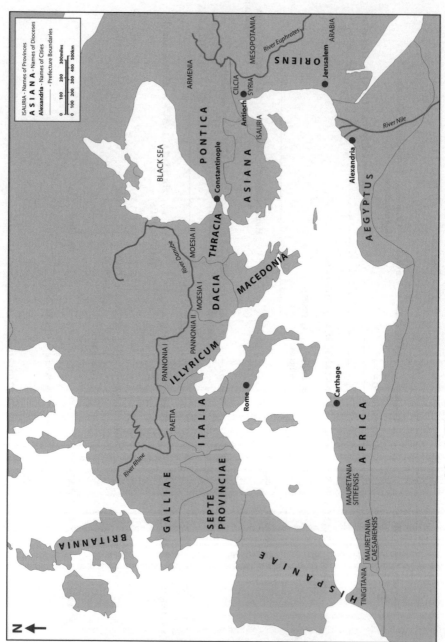

Map 1: The Roman Empire of the Fourth Century

...you need... to reveal not only what was said or done but also in what manner, and... to explain all the reasons, whether they be of chance or intelligence or impetuousness, and also to give not only the achievements of any famous protagonist but also his life and character.

— Cicero, *de orat.* II.15.63

...for history ought not to transcend the truth, and truth is adequate for honourable actions.

— Pliny the Younger, *Ep.* VII.33.10

Introduction

The seed of this work was planted during the researching of my PhD thesis on 'Late Roman Recruiting Practices' at Queen's University, Belfast. In the course of that piece I explored the military developments that took place during the twenty-four year reign of Constantius II, including the development of separate field armies, their growing attachment to specific regions and the increasing protection offered by loyal imperial bodyguards. These developments led to bloody civil war battles such as Mursa, the Save and Frigidus rivers in the second half of the fourth century which encouraged Constantius to initiate a more coherent, even attritional strategy of defence in the east, which would predominate for centuries to come.

And yet, in many works of even the highest standard, I found that the period after the death of Constantine was somewhat glossed over in a subsection with a title such as 'Sons of Constantine'; those twenty-four years relegated to an interim to be gotten through as quickly as possible and the men who sat on the imperial throne mere place-holders between the great Constantine and apostate Julian. The reason behind such oversight is not easy to overcome: the poor state of the sources, which will be discussed below. I am not claiming to have uncovered new knowledge on the life and times of Constantius, but given the aforementioned military developments and the significant number of campaigns, sieges and battles fought between 337 and 361, for there not to be a work in English centred more on Constantius himself seems to be an omission.

Therefore, originally, this work was conceived as an attempt to partially rectify that oversight with a straightforward military biography of Constantius II, focusing on his battles and campaigns against numerous foes within and without the empire. However, throughout the planning stage, I found it necessary to look beyond Constantius' own military career. To focus solely to his personal engagements at Narasara, Singara, Mursa, Mons Seleucus and Bezabde, and the campaigns he led against the Alamanni, Sarmatians, Limigantes and Magnentius would not only do Constantius an injustice as an emperor given that the challenges he faced were not just military in nature but would also have led to an extremely short book due to the paucity of material on those conflicts: of his personal commands only Singara, Bezabde and against the Limigantes are preserved in any detail.

This led to the inclusion of all the other military deployments that took place during Constantius' reign, with varying amounts of involvement from the emperor; whether it be his overall strategic command of the cat-and-mouse games with the long-lived Persian king, Shapur II, during the 330s and 340s, including the three sieges of Nisibis, or his almost complete detachment from the Persian front in the 350s, which saw the Persians capture Singara, Bezabde and Amida, and from Julian's campaigns along the Rhine, punctuated by the Battle of Strasbourg. Due to the lack of detailed information about many of these conflicts, the coverage offered by Ammianus in contrast to the rather slim pickings in the description of other battles of the period demands that the Battle of Strasbourg in 357 and the Siege of Amida in 359 be treated as military centrepieces. Constantius may have had no direct involvement, but Roman imperial tradition would claim that they took place under his auspices as *Augustus* and were therefore his victories.

So far, so military, but as my reading continued, I discovered T. D. Barnes' excellent *Athanasius and Constantius: Theology and Politics in the Constantinian Empire*. It was his extremely useful appendix on 'Imperial Residences and Journeys, 337–361' that was my initial focus as it provides the primary sources documenting the movements of all five members of the Constantinian family to hold legitimate power during that period (Constantius II, Constantine II, Constans, Gallus and Julian); however, as I explored more, I found that it would be doing the reign of Constantius a further disservice if I stuck to a military-political approach. While Constantius is perhaps best known as a son of Constantine, and for his civil wars and defensive strategy against the Persians, it is his religious policies that contribute the most to his poor reputation in many of the sources. His refusal to condemn Arianism and attempts to force doctrinal orthodoxy on the Christian Church through the Homoean Creed in opposition to the Nicene party championed by Athanasius of Alexandria proved unpopular, especially given the eventual triumph of the pro-Nicene party under Theodosius. These religious disputes not only impacted the reception and depiction of Constantius and the religious direction of the empire but would also interfere in the politics of the 340s as fraternal emperors took opposing sides in the growing dispute, almost leading to conflict.

Therefore, while this book will largely follow the chronological progression of Constantius' life and reign from birth to death, certain chapters will be restricted to specific geographical areas such as Gaul, the east or the Danube or over-arching subjects such as religious politics or civil war. And yet, even with the moving away from a strict military presentation and looking at various subjects around the empire, some even within Constantius barely involved, there could have been so much more explored within these pages. Beyond the smattering of religious politics imbued in Constantius' showdowns with Athanasius, more depth could have been presented on the numerous church councils, the burgeoning 'Age of Gold' and their social and religious implications for the empire and neighbouring (and soon to be occupying) tribes. More detail could have been sought on specific regions and their problems, such as Africa and the Donatists or Athanasius' Egypt and their contests with schismatics, heretics and imperial authorities. A closer inspection of those who served Constantius might have uncovered more about his imperial court, military hierarchies and and the women who served as wives for himself, Gallus and Julian. A more intricate survey of Constantius' entries in the *Codex Theodosianus* could have shown the social, economic, military and religious problems he and his colleagues faced while more could have been made of the attempts to reconstruct the make up of the Roman army of Constantius with the *Notitia* and other sources. However, given the constraints of a word limit and the want of keeping this piece accessible to the majority of readers, such depth has been set aside for another day and/or the works of others.

Hopefully though, despite leaving aside such in-depth discussions and having some overlap in time through brief usages of thematic and geographical approaches, the narrative and accompanying analysis remains coherent and allows the reign of Constantius II to come across as one of great military adventure, hardship and revolt against the backdrop of a Roman Empire facing restless and hostile neighbours, whilst attempting to work the kinks out of its new military, political and religious infrastructures; attempts that would see numerous cases of internal strife.

Sources

By far the most important source for the reign of Constantius II is the history of Ammianus Marcellinus. Born in Antioch, Ammianus was an officer in the Roman army, serving as a *protector* for the *magister* Ursicinus across the empire and took part in Julian's Persian expedition. This provides the unusual spectacle of the historian appearing within his own narrative as not only the companion of a high ranking general but also as an eye-witness and participant in the suppression of the revolt of Silvanus and the Siege of Amida in 359. His work was composed of thirty-two books chronicling Roman history from the reign of Nerva (96–98) until the Battle of Adrianople and its immediate aftermath in 378, but the first thirteen books have not survived. Due to this loss and the lack of another secular historian of his skill to fill the gaps, the narrative of the reign of Constantius and consequently this book is divided into two sections: pre-353 without Ammianus and 353–361 with "a full and detailed narrative by a well-informed contemporary... great historian, a man of penetrating intelligence and of remarkable fairness."[1]

However, while the most authoritative study of Ammianus, Matthews (1989), is willing to take the historian at his word, more recent studies such as Barnes (1998) have taken a more sceptical approach, warning any student that the Roman world presented in Ammianus' history could be as much a depiction of his imagination as of reality. Chief amongst those criticisms is that for an historian noted for his neutrality, Ammianus does show some bias, whether it be his failure to focus more on Constantius instead of his favourites, Julian and Ursicinus or his veiled criticisms of Christianity. Ammianus allows his closeness to Ursicinus, admiration for Julian and dislike of eunuchs to cloud his overall presentation of Constantius, who, while "accorded a fair amount of praise, the overall impression is unfavourable... [as] commendation is often qualified whereas the criticism is more rhetorically developed".[2] The eunuchs in particular come in for increasing vitriol as if Ammianus saw them as having "an emphatic part to play in the decline of Rome, and the destruction of its heroes",[3] which raises the question of whether this dislike came from their ill-treatment of Julian and Ursicinus or as a scapegoat for the failures of Ammianus' favourites.

Furthermore, he makes little or no effort to understand or even record Christian theological disputes or councils despite their impact on imperial politics, although Rohrbacher (2005) suggests some hidden insights into Ammianus' knowledge of the non-pagan religions of his time. Kelly (2008) presents a third option – between full embrace and criticism – viewing Ammianus as adhering to the conventions of the classicising literary genre complete with all of its positives and negatives. Other works such as Crump (1973, 1975) and the collection of articles edited by Drijvers and Hunt (1999) provide analyses and interpretations of more specific sections of Ammianus' work. While such accusations of bias or novelisation of events need to be taken seriously, there can be no underestimating the importance of Ammianus' survival of the sack of Amida to the historical record. Without his good fortune, the study of the mid fourth century would be in a far worse state than it already is.

Indeed, without Ammianus, the record of 353–378 would have suffered the same "surprisingly poor documentation"[4] as the first half of the fourth century. There are surviving secular histories from men who lived through parts of the reign of Constantius. Eutropius accompanied Julian on his

Persian expedition and served in various political positions including *magister epistularum, magister memoriae, proconsul Asiae* and by 380 was praetorian prefect in Illyricum; Aurelius Victor was governor of Pannonia II under Julian and later urban prefect of Rome and Festus was a *consularis Syria, magister memoriae* and *proconsul Asiae* in the late 360s/early 370s. Despite their lofty positions within the imperial hierarchy and their writings providing some useful information, they remain scant on detail and analysis of the events for which we do not have Ammianus.

This leads to an over-reliance on chronologically detached historians, compilers and epitomisers, whether it is the late fifth/early sixth century work of Zosimus, the eighth century compilation of Theophanes Confessor or the twelfth century chronicle of Zonaras. While such works can often provide confusing testimony and lack chronological accuracy and critical insight, they should not be ignored. Each of them used more contemporary sources now lost such as Dexippus for the third century and Eunapius for the fourth to bring together their own narratives. While this can be a welcome boon, it can also lead to further trouble as in the case of Zosimus who relied so slavishly on the histories of Dexippus, Eunapius and Olympiodorus that his work suffers from rather dramatic shifts in style, tone and even opinion. While not affecting the period of Constantius, the most obvious example of this potential problem is Zosimus' depiction of the *magister militum*, Stilicho, which veers from the negative pre-404, when he was using Eunapius, to a favourable position post-407, when Olympiodorus became his source. Even more worrying is Zosimus' treatment of history when he has no source with the 404–407 gap between the accounts of Eunapius and Olympiodorus being a garbled mess.[5]

The preserving of contemporary fragments is not the only positive to be found in such non-contemporaries. While falling well short of his claim to be providing a mirror image of Polybius' account of the growth of the Roman Empire by describing its decline and fall, the reason Zosmius states for the collapse – her abandoning of her pagan past and the ancestral rites that came with it – positions him as a useful counterweight to the emergent Christian panegyrists and historians. The late fourth/early fifth century ecclesiastical histories of Socrates, Sozomen and Theodoret are "fulsome in their own concerns"[6] but can be problematic when used for something more. The 'Great' Christian emperors Constantine and Theodosius receive more praise than perhaps they warrant, whilst Diocletian is blamed for the empire's woes by Lactantius, despite being the architect of much of its revival, while Constantius II receives a dire reputation from the victorious Nicene Catholic sources due to his supposed Arianism.

The most prominent of those pro-Nicene clergy was Athanasius of Alexandria, whose writings provide a useful source of information not just on the church matters he was involved in but also on the whereabouts of Constantius and some political and religious matters. However, it must always be remembered that much of his work was to promote his own cause or designed to save his own skin from imperial wrath and therefore must be treated with a cynical eye. On top of allowing their faith to colour the depiction of individuals, the ecclesiastical sources cloud their own narrative potential to varying degrees by attributing events – military victory, political manoeuvrings, imperial actions – to divine interventions rather than recording the actions of the individuals involved in any detail. Therefore, despite the sheer abundance of such Christian material, when joined together with other sources, it provides a barely adequate substitute for the lack of an extended secular history. It must be noted though that without the writings of Theodoret, Ephraem and Jerome, however problematic, the record of various events during the 340s would be in even worse state than it already is.

Another genre of writing that survives for the reign of Constantius is that of panegyric, which can be useful in painting a picture of their target at their best; however, that one of its purveyors, the emperor Julian, could suggest that panegyric "had already come to incur grave suspicion on account of those who have embarked on it improperly, and is now held to be base flattery rather than a true testimony to noble deeds"[7] raises questions about its accuracy and usefulness. Indeed, so close does Themistius, a pagan philosopher who enjoyed imperial favour, veer towards the kind of flattery that Julian warned of in presenting Constantius as the model of a philanthropic, philosopher-king that he has been referred to as the "chief spin-doctor"[8] rather than a panegyrist. His claims to impartiality are therefore to be taken with a pinch of salt. Libanius, a pagan professor of rhetoric at Constantinople, Nicomedia and Antioch, also bears some of the hallmarks of parroting imperial propaganda in his speeches, although at times he is so subtle about it that the listener/reader might not even notice that it is happening; perhaps it is so subtle because it is not actually there?[9]

Julian the panegyrist was in a different position compared to Themistius and Libanius: he was not just an employee of Constantius, he was family and by the time of the composition of his speeches to the emperor, he had been elevated to *Caesar*. The fate of his brother still fresh in his mind, Julian toed the same party line as Themistius and Libanius, two men he was in contact with,[10] and while there are some hints of sarcasm and irony in later sections, this may again be a case of looking for something that is not there. Would Julian have risked everything just for a barely detectable poke at the emperor?[11] However, Julian the writer of letters and the *Misopognon* was in a different position from the panegyrist. Many of these were composed during or after his confrontation with the forces of Constantius in 361. He could therefore be far more open with his negative thoughts about the emperor, even when those thoughts were not popular with some of his audience.

Governmental documents can also provide information on the mid fourth century. Over two hundred and sixty laws of Constantius are preserved within the vast archive that is the *Codex Theodosianus*, published in 438 under the auspices of Theodosius II and then reordered, amended and republished as the *Codex Iustinianus* in 534 for Justinian. However, these codes must also be used with discretion. While they can record where Constantius was on a precise date and how he proposed to deal with problems, the repetition of laws and severe punishments could suggest that the will of the emperor was not fully respected. It is also not known how widespread the implementation of many of these laws was supposed to be. Laws promulgated in the east might not have had much bearing on the west and may never have meant to. However, the most discretion is needed with regard to the truncated nature of the vast majority of this legislation, with much of the introductory information that highlights the circumstances of a law's issue having been removed.[12] Another construct of the late fourth/early fifth century, in listing the senior civilian and military officials of the Empire along with the staff and units under their command, the *Notitia Dignitatum* can provide useful information about the deployments, organisation and make up of the Roman army. However, its use is limited as it does not provide a full snapshot of the entire empire at any one time and it is chronologically detached from Constantius.[13]

Straddling the boundary between literary and physical material are the surviving papyrus documents, from the deserts of Egypt and the Levant and even Ravenna in Italy. The correspondence of officers such as Flavius Abinnaeus, *praefectus* of *Ala Praelectorum V* stationed at Dionysias in Egypt sheds light on the day-to-day lives of soldiers and veterans and their involvement in collecting the recruiting tax and enforcing obligatory military service during the reign of Constantius. While not as plentiful as under the Principate, the corpus of epigraphic evidence remains large and varied for the fourth century, documenting events not thought to be important by literary sources: soldier's epitaphs, troop movements, career progression, fortifications and the general funding of the individual or the army as a whole.

The funding of the army is also seen in the numismatic record. Coins were principally issued by the government to pay its soldiers, therefore their circulation implies how well the Roman military economy was operating, while a large amount of coins in a particular area is a good indication of a strong military presence at a particular time. As well as providing an insight into imperial propaganda, they can also elucidate on the relationship between the emperor and his soldiers. Knowing where and when a coin was minted and what it was made from can highlight the state of imperial finances at a given time. *Roman Imperial Coinage* remains the most useful collection for Roman numismatics, with Volume IX by Sutherland and Carson (1981) focusing on *The Family of Constantine I (337–364)* . General archaeology can also provide information – who was building what and where at any specific time, who was being buried, causes of death, and so forth – but even such contemporary physical evidence is limited in its usefulness even if it can be dated to the reign of Constantius. While it can provide specific information about a particular time, event, person or geographical location, they afford very little regarding their historical context.[14]

While large sections of the life and reign of Constantius are clouded and what does survive leads to a constant balancing act between those hostile to Constantius for various reasons and those panegyrics that fawn over him, it should be remembered that it could have been much, much worse. Looking at modern compilations such as the *Prosopography of the Late Roman Empire*, Dodgeon and Lieu (1993) or Lieu and Monserrat (1996), this combination of narrative, panegyric, epistolary, ecclesiastic and physical evidence, while scattered and of varied importance and usefulness, has left a far richer description for Constantius than for other contemporaries. Indeed, the modern student must only try to investigate the thirteen-year reign of Constans to recognise how fortunate we have been with regard to Constantius. Without these various sources of information, despite his twenty-four years as *Augustus*, Constantius could have been as "shadowy and elusive [a] figure"[15] as his younger brother.

Spelling and Nomenclature

Given the various languages and forms that sources regarding the fourth century were written in – Latin, Greek, Armenian, Syriac, Middle Persian and Arabic – it becomes important for the sake of clarity as well as presentation to establish conventions on spelling and place names. As I admit to having only the most fleeting knowledge of some of these languages, instead of attempting to apply any sort of linguistic convention, I have endeavoured to maintain a consistency in my choices, which hopefully does not create any difficulty in the identification of the individual or place.

The more traditional Latinised form of Roman names has been retained, except when a prominent individual is more well known by a somewhat

Anglicised version so it will be Diocletian, Constantine and Julian instead of Diocletianus, Constantinus and Julianus. Persian and Armenian names present a trickier problem as the transmission of many of these names can provide numerous spellings, which can include several accents to further confuse the matter. For the main period of time explored by this book, there are very few Persian names to be dealt with given the prominence and extended reign of Shapur II, a spelling that will be preferred over Sapor.

As for cities and regions, the ancient name of an existing town or city prevails in the text, such as Constantinople over Istanbul, Antioch over Antakya and Gaul over France, although on many occasions, the first instance of a less well known place name will be accompanied with its more modern equivalent or a more famous location which it is near to aid in its identification.

Of course, any remaining mistakes, resulting confusion or failure to live up to the demands of Cicero and Pliny recorded above are my responsibility alone.

Chapter I

Crisis and Renewal: The Third Century and the Tetrarchy

Be harmonious, enrich the soldiers, and scorn all other men
— Cassius Dio LXXVII.15.2 on Septimius Severus' advice to
his sons

The Third Century Crises

The third century CE had not been the Roman Empire's best. Indeed, the fact that any mention of it is accompanied by the epithet "crisis" suggests that it had been one of its worst. The origins of this crisis were in the last decade of the second century as the Roman world erupted into a four-way civil war on the murders of the emperors Commodus and Pertinax in 193. The commanders of the legions in Syria, Britain and on the Danube vied for control with each other and the Praetorian Guard, which was backing Didius Julianus, the highest bidder in an auctioning of the imperial throne. Through some clever manipulation of his opponents and the benefit of being closest to the centre of the Empire, the Danubian general, Septimius Severus emerged victorious and established a dynasty that was to last for forty years.

However, in achieving this stability, Severus set a disastrous political and military precedent. He made no attempt to hide that his power derived from the army, casting aside the illusion that the emperor ruled by popular consent – the first amongst equals. This might not have been a problem had his successors continued to lead the army in person as they had done for much of the second century;[1] however, with Severus' death, his son Caracalla shrank away from his military duties, although he made sure to buy the loyalty of the soldiers with a 50 per cent pay increase.[2] This hands off and increasingly debauched approach to imperial government was copied and even expanded upon by Elagabalus while Alexander Severus lived in the shadow of his mother and advisors, allowing the army to grow accustomed to their new found status as imperial power brokers. Such rule by proxy undermined imperial authority and emboldened military commanders and when Alexander showed a willingness to buy off enemies and let his mother talk him out of leading the army in person, it sparked mutiny.

The subsequent murder of Alexander at Moguntiacum, modern Mainz in Germany, in 235 brought the Severan dynasty to an end and inaugurated an almost complete military meltdown as every commander of any modicum of success felt the need to claim the imperial title. The increasing feebleness of the central government to project power and stability saw various territories slip out of the imperial orbit. At one stage during the 260s, with the secessionist movements of the Gallic and Palmyrene Empires in the west and east respectively and the frontiers crumbling under the weight of barbarian invasion, the Roman Empire was reduced to just Italy, North Africa and parts of the Balkans.

In the period of fifty years between 235 and 285, twenty-one men were recognised as *Augustus* of the Roman world[3] and that figure does not take into account the innumerable attempted usurpers and breakaway rulers. Of those twenty-one, only one – Claudius II – would be afforded a natural death, probably of smallpox, at Sirmium in 270.[4] Every other emperor either died in battle or was murdered by his own men, while Valerian died as a prisoner of the Persian king. The only other possible exception was the emperor Carus, who after defeating the Persians and capturing their capital at Ctesiphon died in the summer of 283 after his tent was struck by lightning; however, it could be that that 'lightning bolt' was wielded by angry troops, Aper (the Praetorian commander), or Diocles (the commander of the imperial bodyguard). Other explanations are also recorded such as disease or a battle wound, while the lack of immediate opposition to the accession of his son Numerian might suggest a more natural death.[5]

However, the importance of Carus' demise lies less in its suspicious manner and more in the overall circumstances surrounding it. That he had died in Persian territory demonstrates that by the early 280s, the Roman state was enjoying something of a resurgence of fortune. Even at the height of the military and political merry-go-round of the mid-third century, the Roman army remained capable of defeating separatists, usurpers, barbarians and the Persians, allowing skilled men such as Aurelian and Probus to restore the integrity of the Empire. Yet, despite the military successes that such emperors were able to achieve, there was still one set of hurdles that none of these men had proven capable overcoming – the fickleness of the soldiery and the bad faith of ambitious subordinates, which had seen numerous worthy emperors cut down in their prime, their reigns measured in months, weeks and even days rather than years or decades.

Such intrigue had not yet been swept away by the time that Numerian succeeded his father and another episode played out on the journey home from Ctesiphon in 284. At some stage, Numerian contracted an eye infection and had to be carried in a litter. When the column reached Nicomedia in late November, alerted by an awful smell, it was discovered that Numerian had been dead for quite some time. The exact cause of death, infection or murder, is not known for certain but Diocles jumped at the opportunity and before the congregation of the army accused Aper of having killed the emperor. Without being given the chance to defend himself, Aper was disposed of, perhaps even executed by Diocles himself before that very military assembly, which now hailed Diocles as emperor, from then on to be known as Diocletian.

Contemporaries will have been forgiven for thinking that this was just going to be another episode in the anarchy that had dogged the Empire for half a century. However, Diocletian was to confound expectations by not only reigning for twenty years but also bringing about a period of military and political stability and reform. That is not to say that his accession was a smooth transition; far from it. Indeed, there was good reason to think that Diocletian would not last long on the throne for while Carus and Numerian were both dead, Carus' eldest son, Carinus, was still alive and in control of the western provinces. In July 285, the armies of the two emperors met on the banks of the Margus River, the modern Morava near Belgrade. Having the larger army, Carinus gained the upper hand and may even have won the battle; however, it seems that his unpopularity amongst his own officers came back to haunt him. He is accused of mistreating the Senate and seducing the wives of his supporters and just when it seemed he might ascend to supreme power, Carinus was killed by his own men, leaving Diocletian to assume the mantle of sole *Augustus*.

The New Model Empire and its Army

And yet within days of his ultimate victory at the Margus, Diocletian was to relinquish that title of sole emperor by elevating one of his senior officers, Maximian, to the position of *Caesar*, with a promotion to *Augustus* following on 2 April 286. Several reasons for this have been suggested. Despite his charisma and leadership, Diocletian realised that the Roman Empire was too big a job for one man. There were numerous threats along the frontier that were not going to wait for him to defeat them one at a time. He may also have thought that Margus had proven that he himself was at best a mediocre general and that he needed a more skilled man by his side. Diocletian may also have been wary that he as yet had no male heir and so turned to a trusted friend to secure the succession. Diocletian and Maximian both took religious names as part of their imperial title, the former *Iovius* and the latter *Herculius*. This not only helped solidify the esteem with which the *Augusti* were held, it also highlighted that Diocletian remained the dominant partner as the godly Jupiter while Maximian was to be Hercules, the task-completing demigod.[6]

And Maximian did complete a lot of tasks. While Diocletian campaigned against the Sarmatians along the Lower Danube, politicked with the Persian king and reorganised parts of the Roman east, Maximian campaigned throughout Gaul against *bagaudae* rebels, along the Rhine against Germanic tribes and in the English Channel against pirates. While not always plain sailing, these operations were successful until he found that his admiral, Carausius, was skimming imperial spoils. Maximian ordered his arrest prompting Carausius to abscond with the Roman fleet and set himself up as *Augustus* in Britain. Distracted by barbarian raids and neutered by the loss of his fleet, Maximian could do little to undermine the leader of the new *Imperium Britanniarum*.

By 293, the list of barbarian tribes defeated by the *Augusti* was extensive – Saxons, Franks, Alamanni, Frisii, Chamavi, Burgundians, Heruli, Chaibones, Sarmatians – but even then the troubles showed little sign of abating. The Rhine and Danube remained troublesome, Carausius still ruled Britain and now Egypt, Africa and the Arab tribes were becoming restless. This led Diocletian to view two emperors as insufficient to manage the military needs of the Empire so he extended the imperial college into what would become known as the Tetrarchy – Rule of Four – by promoting two more Illyrian officers, Galerius and Constantius, to the rank of *Caesar*, the former to serve under Diocletian in the east and the latter to serve under Maximian in the west. While not immediate, success was forthcoming. Constantius ejected Carausius from the continent and then defeated his successor, Allectus, in 296, reincorporating Britain before again defeating the Franks, while Maximian focused on the Saharan nomads harassing Africa. Over the next decade, Diocletian and Galerius took turns in campaigning along the Danube against the Sarmatians and the Carpi and creating a strong defensive line called the *Ripa Sarmatica*. They also took turns in suppressing revolt in Egypt, with Diocletian defeating the usurper, Domitianus, and his regime by 298.

The biggest war of the Tetrarchs, however, was with the old enemy, Persia. Wishing to follow in the footsteps of his father, Shapur I, the Persian king, Narseh struck west in around 295, meeting with great success, conquering Armenia and then defeating Galerius near Carrhae in 296. Such was the extent of the defeat that Diocletian forced Galerius to walk alongside the imperial carriage in humiliation. However, within two years, the humbled *Caesar* made amends. Gathering a large force from the eastern half of the empire, Galerius marched into Mesopotamia in early 298. Narseh retreated into Armenia, preventing Galerius from moving on Ctesiphon by threatening his supply lines; although when Galerius instead turned north, Narseh was trapped on unfavourable ground amongst unfriendly locals with nowhere to run. In two successive battles, the second at Satala, Galerius crushed the Persian army and seized the king's camp, treasury, harem and wife. The victorious *Caesar* then advanced south, defeating whatever meagre forces Narseh could scramble together, retaking Nisibis and sacking Ctesiphon before 298 was out. The subsequent Peace of Nisibis confirmed the Roman annexation of northern Mesopotamia, including major cities such as Nisibis itself and Singara, and the extension of Roman influence into Armenia, Iberia and even across the Tigris into Corduene and Zabdicene.[7]

While the determination and martial prowess of Gallienus, Aurelian, Probus and now the Tetrarchs had saved and reunited the Empire, the financial, structural and military problems had yet to be addressed. Therefore, Diocletian set out on a wide range of reforms in order to recast the Roman Empire.[8] He checked the power of governors and tightened local government through a "policy of giving officers carefully defined, more manageable areas of responsibility, and of avoiding wide discretionary powers".[9] This was achieved through a process of subdivision, stratification and separation. The number of provinces was doubled by the division of existing ones, with each of these smaller provinces having a civilian and military governor. These provinces were then grouped together into one of twelve *dioceses* under the command of a *vicarius*, while a group of *dioceses* made up a prefecture run by one of the four Praetorian Prefects, who served at the imperial residences at Trier, Milan, Sirmium and Nicomedia. As each governor now oversaw a smaller area and four prefectural capitals allowed closer imperial supervision, local administration was made more effective, tax collecting made more efficient and the chances of large scale military revolt were seemingly diminished.[10]

Diocletian also recast the frontiers with a mixture of aggression, rationalisation and deterrence. The aforementioned campaigns deterred opposition in Europe, Africa and Asia, but Diocletian was not above utilizing strategic withdrawals. No attempts were made to reconquer Dacia or the *Agri Decumates* abandoned in the 270s, while the Egyptian frontier was withdrawn to the first cataract of the Nile.[11] To strengthen what he did retain, Diocletian embarked on an extensive building programme, placing strategic roads and fortresses all around the fringes of his empire to the extent that it was exclaimed "who can count the numbers of forts of cavalry and infantry that have been rebuilt along the whole length of the Rhine, the Danube and the Euphrates."[12]

The building of so many roads and fortresses has caused great debate on their proposed use in a defensive system. This should not be viewed as a preclusive strategy of "keep them out", but nor should it be seen as defence-in-depth. Instead, a combination of perimeter defence built on new style permanent fortresses supported by small mobile armies behind the frontiers is more likely with the overall idea being that local forces and barbarian allies would repel small-scale raids and hold up a larger invasion long enough for the main armies to arrive, while these fortifications and supply lines would allow for punitive raids and large scale offensives.[13]

As well as overhauling the political and administrative hierarchies of the empire, Diocletian also introduced numerous reforms in the Roman army. After fifty years of repeated fighting, many of the units inherited from the third century were mere shells of their former selves, while "many units must have been lost and many new formations raised."[14] Some of the old units were restored through rigorous recruiting in the Danubian provinces, which had become prevalent in providing soldiers during the third century, best highlighted by virtually all emperors from the mid third century until the elevation of Theodosius in 379 being of Danubian origin, including the Constantinian family.[15]

These reformed units were still insufficient to defend the Empire, leading to the formation of new legions. While there is no real consensus on just how many were raised,[16] it might be expected that any increase of units will have included an increase in overall numbers. However, that is not necessarily the case. The use of detachments called *vexillationes* shows how more units might not mean more men. Many of these detachments were taken on an expedition, never to return to their parent unit. This is seen with the *vexillationes* of V *Macedonica* and XIII *Gemina*, which were taken from the Danube as part of Diocletian's Egyptian expedition in the 290s and were still there a century later.[17] Such detachments became identified as units in their own right but neither they nor their parents were brought up to traditional strength. On top of that is the sheer implausibility of the figures for 50–70 full strength 'classical' legions, which would require a 50–100 per cent increase on the Severan army, which was no larger than 400,000. This suggests that legions of the fourth century were smaller than their predecessors, with 1,000 being conjectured as the norm, but even this is to go beyond the evidence and impose a stricter format than was perhaps the case.[18] It is more likely that "size-regulations had given way to a wider range of big and little regiments [with an] almost entire lack of consistency",[19] suggesting that any reforms Diocletian had made to the size of the legion were not all-encompassing.[20]

Such a transitional period makes it difficult to ascertain the number of legionaries and auxiliaries, which usually served at a ratio of 1:1. That absurd figures up to one million or Lactantius' misleading claim that Diocletian quadrupled the army[21] – he divided the army into four – cannot be discounted is a testament to the poor state of the evidence, with only sixth century sources putting forward a figure for Diocletian's army. Agathias suggested 645,000 while John Lydus recorded 389,704 plus 45,562 in the navy, although the former is thought to be too high and cannot be attributed to Diocletian while the latter raises suspicion from its unusual accuracy, although it could have come from an official document.[22] Due to the many unknown variables, modern estimates vary from 400,000 to 1,000,000. Such vast increases involved in the latter end of that spectrum over just twenty years would have required rampant conscription; something that the sources would have commented on more than a fleeting mention in an anti-Diocletian polemic. Therefore, if the army of Diocletian was bigger than its predecessor, it was not significantly so with a more feasible increase of around 25 per cent bringing the total to around 500,000.[23]

Diocletian's military reforms were not restricted to the size of his army. He also implemented changes in its make up. Infantry remained the backbone but due to the mixture of static and mobile forces, a division within the infantry began to appear. Mobile legions and new crack *auxilia* units such as the *Ioviani, Herculiani, Diocletiana* and *Maximiana* were incorporated into the field armies[24] while a second class was made up of frontier troops. However, infantry no longer provided all the offensive power. Many different types of cavalry were now deployed such as the traditional *equites*, the heavier *contarii*, *cataphractarii* and *clibanarii* plus mounted archers and skirmishers. These cavalry contingents were 500 strong, enabling them to work independently, in concert with the legions or deployed at strategic points.[25] In doing so, Diocletian was incorporating a development from the nadir of Roman fortunes in the 260s. The sheer number of incursions along the 4,000 kilometres of the Rhine-Danube frontier created a "necessity for rapid movement",[26] leading Gallienus to form an independent cavalry wing made up of Mauri and Dalmatians from within the empire and Sarmatians and Alans from without.[27] Together with several *vexillationes*, II *Parthica* and the Praetorian Guard, this force enabled Gallienus to maintain the Italian core of the empire.

While he learned some lessons from it, Diocletian seems to have dispersed any remnant of this force along the frontiers and rather than have a permanent field force relied instead on forming an expeditionary army in the normal manner of assembling units from across the empire.[28] However, Diocletian did expand the *comitatus*,[29] which is seen as the forerunner of Constantine's *comitatenses* field army. Crack infantry units such as the *Ioviani, Herculiani, Diocletiana, Maximiana* and the *lanciarii* and elite cavalry like the *equites Mauri, equites Dalmatae, equites promoti, schola gentilium* and *scholae Scutariorum* all served in the Diocletianic *comitatus*. Another major part of the *comitatus* was the *protectores*. While originally a distinction given to "men of military experience who had a close bond with the emperor",[30] by the time of Diocletian, they had grown large enough to be organised into a corps, which acted much like an officer training school, with Diocletian himself having been the commander of Carus' *protectores domestici*.[31] The role of the *comitatus* under Diocletian was therefore varied. It could serve as an imperial bodyguard, while the *protectores* provided skilled generals and on occasion future emperors. It could act as a small but elite field army or as the nucleus of an expeditionary force. It also included representatives of the imperial bureaucracy and the personal household of the emperor, giving it the look of a "peripatetic court of a medieval king".[32]

One important but often overlooked task facing Diocletian and his successors was, having reformed and expanded the army, how were they to fill these spots? With replacement rates ranging from 5 to 20 per cent, anywhere between 25,000 and 100,000 new recruits would be needed just to maintain numbers.[33] Diocletian will not have been worried by those put off by the harsh discipline and constant training of the Roman military as that kind of man were not wanted in the army anyway.[34] However, it was those willing to serve but put off by poor pay and conditions that were a serious concern. Army pay in particular had become problematic for Roman emperors. Despite a six-fold increase over the previous two centuries, this *stipendium* had ceased to be anything more than nominal as it "had not kept pace with inflation".[35] While Julian's complaints that his men had not received their annual pay in years suggest that the *stipendium* was still valued, the fact that these men had survived without it suggests that not receiving it was not seriously detrimental.[36] This depreciation meant that the soldiers needed other sources of income. These were provided by the *annona* (rations and uniform in kind) and the *donativum* (an occasional payment in gold and silver). However, as the former remained an insignificant amount, it was incumbent upon the latter to keep the soldiers provisioned.[37]

Such *donativa* had been used to reward, bribe and even buy the imperial title in the past[38] but by the fourth century, it was an integral part of military pay. Its distribution was associated with the anniversaries of an imperial birth or accession with a standard rate of 2,500 *denarii*, meaning that with two emperors serving, an *Augustus* and a *Caesar*, a soldier might expect a flat rate of 10,000 *denarii* a year.[39] The formal accession of a new emperor was also accompanied with another donative of "five *solidi* and a pound of silver",[40] with the five *solidi* alone worth perhaps 5,000 *denarii*. The size of these *donativa* made them vital to the ordinary soldier, "increasing the moral dependence and loyalty of the troops to the emperor".[41] While these sums sound significant and soldiers are recorded keeping slaves and attendants, the continued depreciation of the *denarius* throughout the fourth century saw it become worthless by the 350s.[42] Diocletian had protested that due to price rises "a soldier is sometimes by a single purchase robbed of his *stipendium* and *donativum*"[43] and attempted to tackle it through a fixing of maximum prices.[44] This collapse of the silver coinage forced salaries to be paid largely in kind; a system that "was bound to be unreliable, clumsy and extremely burdensome",[45] while leaving the soldier to feel out of pocket and unrewarded. Therefore, it could be suggested that the main reason that successive fourth century emperors faced frequent revolts and problems recruiting was simply that they "paid [the soldiery] rather badly".[46]

As his attempts at fixing prices proved unable to alleviate the financial plight of the soldiery, Diocletian was also forced to overhaul the recruiting system by invoking the obligation of citizens and subjects to serve in the military. This was enshrined in a "new and drastic system of conscription"[47] under two general headings: conscription by family and conscription by taxation. The first was achieved by Diocletian's forcing of the sons of soldiers to follow their fathers' profession.[48] The rationale was that a good percentage of soldier's sons would be of similar fighting skill to their father. However, there was "no regular machinery for enforcing the rule"[49] and the promulgating of numerous laws may suggest that the sons of veterans were shirking their responsibility, with some so intent in avoiding military service that they cut off a finger.[50] Conscription by taxation was accomplished by linking the obligation of service to the *capitus* tax.[51] An individual's land was assessed and then equated to the value of a recruit and as only the largest landowners would be assessed at one or more whole recruits, smaller landowners were grouped together to provide one soldier. In each group, landowners took it in turns to provide the recruit, which was a considerable burden, although a payment in cash or kind – *aurum tironicum* – could be exacted instead.[52]

There were still specific requirements that needed to be passed in order for a recruit to be enrolled: age, legal status and physical fitness were measured. In 326, a recruit had to be at least twenty years old, although this was reduced to "their nineteenth year" by 353.[53] An upper age limit of around thirty-five may also have been established.[54] Aside from being fit, the only other physical requirement was height, which under the Tetrarchy was set at five feet ten inches, although this was also later reduced.[55]

A lack of Roman citizenship was supposed to disbar a man from service in the legions with non-citizens serving alongside the Roman army as auxiliaries rather than in it. However, this had changed over the previous centuries with *auxilia* units becoming permanent fixtures and when Caracalla's *Constitutio Antoniniana* of 212 extended citizenship to all inhabitants of the Empire, the establishment had to look to barbarian communities to comprise the *auxilia* and even the legions as citizen enthusiasm for military service waned. The same pay and living conditions that Roman citizens abhorred "must have seemed luxurious [to many barbarians], with ample food and fine clothes and equipment and arms, and occasional payments of gold and silver coins".[56] Barbarian prisoners of war, hostages and *dediticii* became a valuable source of manpower, no longer to be wasted as slaves or gladiators. Levies of soldiers were also imposed on defeated enemies, either as a one-off measure or as an annual obligation.[57]

Another category of barbarians was the *laeti*. This was the settling of barbarian families within the Empire, who were liable for military service. "Originally the *laeti* may have been prisoners of the tribesmen brought back into the Empire",[58] but the system evolved into plantations of tribal groups.[59] This was not a great breakthrough, merely the next step in the Empire's Romanising of barbarians.[60] It was well established by 296 and became far more systematic thereafter with land – *terrae laeticae* – set aside for them,[61] while settling them on the frontiers opposite their countrymen could ease external pressures and alleviate land desertion.[62] Gradually, they became integrated with the Gallic provincials as the barriers between Germanic and Roman culture began to blur.

Through this wide range of reforms, Diocletian set the Empire back on track. He initiated the final phases of the transition towards an emphasis on movement and punitive strikes to deter enemies rather than vast, unwieldy campaigns of conquests. The army was expanded to include more cavalry and mobile infantry while the frontiers were reorganised with a combination of perimeter defences and strategically placed battle groups. However, his attempts to regularise recruitment met with little success. His *Edict on Maximum Prices* failed to halt the inflation crippling army pay and even led to the growth of the black market and hoarding, while non-Romans served in ever increasing numbers as the fourth century progressed, demonstrating that he had been unable to reverse or even arrest the growing apathy for military service amongst large sections of the Roman citizenry.

Imperial Multiplicity and the Great Persecution

Despite a marked lack of success in some areas, Diocletian's reforms were working as the new model army won sufficient victories to quiet the frontiers by the turn of the fourth century.[63] This period of relative peace and security saw the imperial government look inward for potential opposition. The spotlight fell on Christianity. Diocletian had maintained the tolerant approach to Christians that had prevailed since Gallienus, allowing Christians to grow in confidence and for Roman society to become more at ease with some of their more peculiar practices and beliefs. This is shown by the presence of a Christian Church opposite Diocletian's own imperial palace at Nicomedia and the appearance of Christians in the higher echelons of the political hierarchy.[64] As the pagan pantheon was not filled with jealous deities such as the Jewish Yahweh or the Christian God, who demanded singular worship, Romans had little problem integrating Christians into the state.[65] It could be argued though that the speed with which this tacit acceptance turned into rapid persecution suggests that such tolerance was born more out of necessity during the worst of the third century crises rather than any real acceptance of Christianity.

The spark of persecution is said to have been interference in a public sacrifice in the presence of both Diocletian and Galerius. Supposedly, some Christians crossed themselves to ward of evil demons and in so doing profaned the sacrifices.[66] Having imbued the Tetrarchy and new army units with religious terminology and symbolism, Diocletian was furious at this perceived intrusion; after demanding that all military commanders and members of his palace sacrifice on pain of a beating or dismissal, it was left at that. This lull has been used to play down Diocletian's role in the persecution with Lactantius and Eusebius depicting Galerius, who was in a strong position following his victories over Persia, as instrumental in orchestrating the persecution;[67] however, as senior *Augustus* and the man whose force of will and charisma was keeping the Tetrarchy together, Diocletian must have had a hand in it.[68]

Over the course of the winter 302/303, Diocletian and Galerius conversed at Nicomedia on the religious future of the empire, with the latter championing "the necessity for a rigorous persecution of the Christians".[69] The result was an edict of 23 February 303 that forbade any Christian meetings, ordered the destruction of any building used for such meetings and the surrender and burning of Christian scriptures and texts. More worrying was the removal of any and all privileges of status, class or citizenry from Christians, placing them outside the protection of common law.[70] The pressure was ramped up following a fire at the imperial palace, which was blamed on Christians, although Lactantius points the finger at Galerius in a false flag operation to further discredit the Christians in the eyes of Diocletian.[71] Rumours of unrest in Syria and Melitene being stirred up by Christians only served to further raise the imperial ire, leading to edicts calling for the imprisonment of all clergy, who would only be released if they sacrificed.[72] Some agreed, some relented under intense bullying and torture, some were martyred.

With the Great Persecution in full swing in the east, Diocletian visited Rome, perhaps for the first time, for a joint celebration of his twentieth year as *Augustus* – his *vicennalia* – on 20 November 303, the tenth year of the Tetrarchy – *decennalia* – and a triumph for the victory over the Persians. Not only did the Romans refuse to treat the *Augustus* with the deference he felt he deserved, on his way back east or perhaps on campaign against the Carpi, Diocletian fell ill and was reported to have died on 13 December 304 at Nicomedia. While such rumours proved to be exaggerations, Diocletian was not the same man. Lactantius would have it that Galerius now swooped in to pressurise the weakened Diocletian to retire and hand over the reins of authority to him, although it is also suggested that Diocletian had already organised at least part of his dynastic plans with Maximian in Rome in late 303.[73] On 1 May 305, both *Augusti* retired, with Constantius and Galerius becoming *Augusti*. Although overshadowed by Constantine the Great and his reputation sullied by the Great Persecution and the partial failure of his reforms, the achievements of Diocletian should not be overlooked. It was he who introduced the political, military and administrative reforms, which tackled many of the problems that had beset the Roman state for half a century and given it over twenty years of strong rule, the longest reign since Antoninus Pius died in 161. The years following his retirement were to demonstrate just how much of the new stability had relied on his charisma and skill.

This dual retirement was not the only surprise. The new *Caesares* were not the expected duo of the sons of Constantius and Maximian; instead, they were Maximinus Daia and Severus, both experienced officers with links to Galerius, the former a nephew and the latter a friend. It seems that Galerius had indeed managed to exert some influence over the ailing Diocletian, which was to have dramatic religious and political consequences.[74] Finding a willing persecutory partner in Daia, Galerius took a firm grasp of the government's anti-Christian legislation, which was bolstered by an edict ordering all men, women and children to sacrifice and offer libation on pain of death.[75] With people flocking to altars to perform their sacrifices, Daia and Galerius must have felt that their plan was working but this is only a regional snapshot and gives no impression of what was happening across the empire.

Indeed, "the severity of the persecution differed very greatly".[76] In Britain and Gaul, Constantius limited his 'persecution' to destroying some churches and while the Christian sources paint this as sympathy for the Christians from the father of Constantine,[77] it may just have been that as still the most active of the tetrarchs against Franks, Saxons and Picts, Constantius did not have the time to focus on the very small numbers of Christians in his realm. Maximian did enforce the edicts of Diocletian and Galerius in Italy, Spain and Africa, although only for a year at most, but even this limited timeframe of persecution could have a lasting impact. In Africa those who acquiesced to the demand to handover scriptures for destruction – *traditores* – were not welcomed back into the church by a significant proportion of the Christian population, leading to the Donatist schism.[78] It is significant that those regions that showed the most resistance to the Great Persecution, Africa and Egypt, would be the regions to cause the early Christian emperors the most persistent doctrinal problems through Donatism, Melitanism and the Arian controversy.

While the Tetrarchy was creating problems for the future, it had also created problems for itself in the present by failing to foresee or to address two issues: Maximian's reluctance to give up imperial power and the disinherited sons of tetrarchs. The first of these disinherited sons to make a move is by far the most famous, Constantius Chlorus' eldest son, Constantine. Serving on the staff of Diocletian at the time of abdication, it was later put about that Constantine fled the court of Galerius, who sought to eliminate him after having engineered his passing over for *Caesar*. However, it is far more likely that Constantius asked for his son to join him upon his accession to *Augustus*. In allowing Constantine to join his father, Diocletian and Galerius were giving tacit acknowledgement to Constantine's right to succeed his father and because of that, they likely extracted an agreement from Constantine that while he would become *Caesar* on his father's death, he would recognise Severus as the western *Augustus*.[79]

If there was no such arrangement and Diocletian and Galerius hoped to raise another of their Illyrian officers to *Caesar* on the death of Constantius, they had underestimated the popularity of Constantine. On the expected death of Chlorus at York on 25 July 306, Constantine was proclaimed emperor by his father's soldiers. Faced with a plan coming to fruition or a *fait accompli*, Galerius recognised Constantine as *Caesar* in the west.[80] With an *Augustus* and a *Caesar* each ruling in the east and west, it seemed that the Tetrarchy had been renewed. It lasted three months.

Before 306 ended, the other disinherited heir, Maxentius son of Maximian, was proclaimed emperor by the people of Rome and the remnant of the Praetorian Guard. Public discontent at taxes and seeming relegation from importance saw most of Italy, North Africa and the islands of Corsica, Sardinia and Sicily side with Maxentius, providing him with what seemed like a strong bargaining position. Despite the territory he had gained, Maxentius remained weak though as none of his lands contained sizeable garrisons or field forces. Galerius and Severus recognised this and the latter marched south from Milan to crush this upstart. However, Maxentius still had cards left to play. Recognising his own military weakness, he coaxed his father out of retirement, investing Maximian with imperial authority once more. Severus' men therefore found themselves marching against the man with whom many of them had served for years. Coupled with Maxentius' adroit deployment of the wealth of his African provinces, the conflicted troops deserted Severus *en masse*, the western *Augustus* becoming a prisoner of the father and son duo.

The position of Maxentius and Maximian was further enhanced by a diplomatic coup in mid-307. Ever the opportunist, Constantine married Maximian's daughter Fausta, who would give birth to Constantius II some ten years later. Unwilling to accept this usurpation of imperial authority, Galerius himself led an army into northern Italy but his men too failed to resist the bribes of Maxentius and it was only with great difficulty that he escaped with some semblance of his force intact. However, much like Diocletian three years previously, Maxentius underestimated his father's want to be in control. In April 308, Maximian attempted to usurp his son's position at Rome and when that failed, he fled north to the court of his new son-in-law, Constantine.

In an attempt to rectify this mess, Diocletian was dragged out of retirement to preside over a conference at Carnuntum in late 308. Rather than fix the Tetrarchy, the conference sealed its fate. Instead of promoting either Constantine or Daia to *Augustus* to replace the now deceased Severus, murdered upon Galerius' invasion of Italy, Galerius' senior commander Licinius, was plucked from political obscurity to become *Augustus* in the west. This irked both *Caesares* and they were soon claiming the title of *Augustus*. Carnuntum also failed to deal with the problems overlooked by the abdication of 305: the ambitions of Maxentius and Maximian, the former ignored as a usurper and the latter forced to relinquish his imperial titles for the second time.

Milvian Bridge, Tzirallum and the End of the Tetrarchy

While Licinius made slow progress against the positions of Maxentius in northern Italy throughout 309 and Maxentius himself was distracted by a rebellion in his African provinces, Maximian played the part of father-in-law and adviser at Constantine's court at Trier but all the while brooding over his loss of power. Then in 310, when Constantine was fighting the Franks along the Lower Rhine, Maximian struck once more. Stealing away to Arles, he announced that Constantine was dead and proclaimed himself *Augustus* for the third time. Without any military support, it was a foolhardy move and having detached himself from the Rhine, Constantine was soon on his tail. He caught up to his father-in-law at Marseilles, where it is recorded that Maximian received no help from the locals and was soon given up, although given Maximian's popularity amongst the soldiery and the treasury funds he had lifted from Constantine, it is possible that Constantine's siege of Marseilles was far less successful than suggested. Perhaps the two emperors came to an arrangement, only for Constantine to go back on his word or for Maximian to be caught plotting Constantine's demise. Whatever the events, by August 310, Maximian was dead, either executed or by his own hand.[81]

He was joined in the afterlife the following year by Galerius, whose last illness had been horrendous. Perhaps a combination of bowel cancer and gangrene, his doctors were "unable to endure the overpowering and extraordinary stench"[82] of rotting flesh. Such a pitiful end was seen by Christians as God's retribution on the real mastermind of the Great Persecution and by his final days, Galerius seems to have agreed, rescinding all of his previous anti-Christian legislation before dying in early May 311.[83] When the aged Diocletian also passed away on 3 December the same year, the first iteration of the Tetrarchy was gone and any stabilising influence they still had went with them. While there were once again four emperors, they were by no means a picture of Tetrarchic unity. Instead, they were at each other's throats.

In the west, the death of Maximian sparked a propaganda war between Constantine and Maxentius, with both claiming legitimacy through descent from not just their Tetrarchic fathers but also past emperors, with Maxentius cultivating a link to the *gens* of Valerian and Gallienus, while Constantine fabricated a connection to Claudius II.[84] When the war of words turned to the questioning of parentage, actual war was inevitable and in early 312, Constantine crossed the Alps into Italy. Victories at Segusium, modern Susa in Italy, and then on the approaches to Augusta Taurinorum, modern Turin, saw Milan and several other northern Italian cities fall to Constantine. Constantine then struck at Brescia and Verona, where Maxentius' praetorian prefect, Ruricius Pompeianus, was positioned with a significant force. Bottling up the Verona garrison, Constantine led a risky surprise attack on approaching Maxentian reinforcements, which saw the death of Pompeianus. When Verona surrendered soon after, Aquileia, Modena and Ravenna all followed suit without a fight.

Maxentius had made preparations for a siege of Rome in the face of the opposition of Severus, Galerius and Licinius and now with Constantine approaching, he put many of them into action. He still had a vast force, his grain stores were well stocked and the Aurelian Walls provided a strong defensive position. However, what he did not have was the support of the Roman citizenry. In the face of Diocletian and the Tetrarchs, Maxentius had set himself up as a man of the Italian people, willing to shelter them from taxation whilst thrusting them back to prominence. Now, after six years of increasing taxation and Maxentius' brutal subjugation of any protestors, the citizenry had had enough. The loss of popular support undermined Maxentius' plan to resist Constantine from behind the Aurelian Walls as he could no longer guarantee his own safety. Therefore, early on 28 October 312, after consulting the Sibylline Books, which in ambiguous fashion told him that "on that same day, the enemy of the Romans should perish",[85] Maxentius led his men out of Rome, across a bridge of boats beside the destroyed Milvian Bridge, to square up to Constantine.

Constantine's army arrived before the Milvian Bridge with a strange symbol emblazoned on their standards and shields, made of a large X and a large P. These were the Greek letters *Chi* and *Rho*, which represented the first two letters of the Greek word Χριστος, meaning Christ. Different versions of how Constantine came to give this symbol such a prominent position are recorded,[86] but whatever the reason, it was enough for Constantine to attribute his subsequent victory to the support of the Christian God. And it was a crushing victory. Despite their superior numbers, Maxentius' cavalry and infantry proved incapable of resisting Constantine's opening charge. Streaming back across the Tiber, the bridge collapsed under the weight of so many, with thousands drowned including Maxentius.[87]

While Constantine's victory at Milvian Bridge secured his primacy in the west, it had not been a fight for mastery of the entire empire. The eastern provinces were still controlled by Maximinus Daia, while the Balkans belonged to Licinius. As the emperors in Europe had descended into political manoeuvring and war in the aftermath of Carnuntum, Daia returned to his eastern provinces nursing a great deal of disappointment at having not been elevated to *Augustus*. He took it out on the Christians, with Palestine and Egypt faced with another brutal repression.[88] The use of the death penalty seems to have been relaxed after 307 but a sentence of deportation "to the mines, having first blinded them in one eye and severed the tendons of one foot"[89] hardly seems much better. So bad was this oppression that many pagans began to show reticence at the treatment of Christians. Galerius' deathbed rescinding of all anti-Christian legislation stayed Daia's hand but any Christian joy at the change of heart of Galerius or even gloating of his gruesome end was to be short-lived. Within six months, Daia had restarted his persecution, banishing Christians from large sections of the east and initiating a large-scale propaganda campaign, including the publication of the apocryphal *Acts of Pilate*, which contained many outrageous stories about the conduct of Jesus.[90]

Following the death of Galerius, Daia now had other things on his mind. He had managed to extend his influence into Asia Minor and almost came to blows with Licinus in mid 311. Now in 313, with the success of Constantine at the Milvian Bridge, it did not take much for Licinius and Daia to square up to each other again. Daia may even have heard of the marriage of Licinius to Constantine's half-sister, Constantia, sounding alarm bells that he might soon be the target of the other two *Augusti*. He therefore launched an attack across the Bosphorus, capturing Byzantium and Heraclea after short sieges. But these short sieges were enough to give Licinius time to race back from his nuptials, mobilise his forces and intercept the invader on the banks of the River Ergenus near the town of Tzirallum, modern Çorlu in European Turkey. On 30 April 313, the vast army of Daia squared off against the much smaller force of Licinius.[91]

Rather than due to mass prayer, Licinius' superior leadership and tactics and an early attack won the battle. That Licinius was able to incorporate some of Daia's men into his force in the aftermath might also suggest that Licinius had made contact with some of the contingents within his opponent's force or that Daia himself was not popular with his men.[92] Retreating back across the Bosphorus dressed as a slave, his army in ruins, Daia hoped that the rugged terrain of the Taurus Mountains would slow Licinius' men long enough for him to rebuild his military position. He was mistaken and by mid-summer, Daia was trapped in Tarsus, besieged by land and sea. Rather than surrender, he decided to end his own life. To the undisguised glee of Lactantius, he chose a poison that proved slow-acting and painful. Only after being driven mad by four days of torture, "amidst the groans, like those of one burnt alive, did he breath out his guilty soul in the most horrible kind of death".[93]

With the passing of Daia, the Great Persecution came to an end. It had left an indelible stain on the reputations of Diocletian, Galerius and Daia, which supersedes their skills in leading the army and ruling the empire. This was due to the unexpected boon that Christianity received at Milvian Bridge, Constantine and Licinius' joint declaration of religious tolerance in the *Edict of Milan* and the Christianisation of the imperial family and then the Empire as a whole. This progression of Christianity shows that the Great Persecution was an almost complete failure. It failed to eradicate Christianity and may have encouraged its continued growth by providing Christians with a unifying cause and propaganda tools to blow "out of all proportion to its actual severity".[94] In its aims, the Great Persecution was at least forty years too late for since the attempts by Decius and Valerian, the ordinary Roman citizen had become used to Christianity and recognised that it posed no insidious threat to the well-being of the empire. It was perhaps that lack of public support for persecution that was as much to do with its ultimate failure as it was the expansion and resistance of Christianity. That said, the hangover of the Great Persecution in the form of schisms and doctrinal controversy was to cause many a headache for Constantine, Constantius II and other emperors for much of the fourth century.

With the death of the last persecutor, Licinius incorporated the eastern provinces into his realm and then celebrated that triumph by purging any remaining threats to his rule, with sons of Galerius, Severus, Daia and even the daughter of Diocletian all put to the sword. Despite this un-Christian bloodshed, the alliance of Constantine and Licinius had finished the Tetrarchy but in so doing had brought peace to the empire. Or so it seemed.

Chapter II

Preparation for the Purple: Constantius' Upbringing and Accession

The one who benefits from a crime is the one who committed it.

– Seneca, *Medea* 500

Pannonian Home

Flavius Julius Constantius was born at Sirmium in the province of Pannonia, now Sremska Mitrovica in Serbia, on 7 August 317. He was the third son of Constantine the Great, and second by his second wife Fausta, the daughter of Maximian. The location of Constantius' birth demonstrates that it was not only Constantine's family that had been expanding in the four years since Daia's death. In 313, Sirmium and the entire region of Pannonia had been part of the realm of Licinius and yet now Constantine had been well enough established there to allow his latest child to be born there. The peace won at Milvian Bridge and Tzirallum had not lasted long at all.

Despite the attempts of Christian sources to say otherwise, the outbreak of war in 316 was Constantine's doing. The birth of Licinius II in around 315 and the accepted idea that he would become *Caesar* led Constantine to formulate a *casus belli* by proposing that his brother-in-law, Bassianus, be elevated to *Caesar* in Italy. When Licinius refused, Constantine marched into Pannonia in autumn 316, defeating Licinius' forces at the Battle of Cibalae on 8 October.[1] Licinian forces regrouped near Adrianople under Valens, a Danubian commander who Licinius invested with imperial power, and a second battle took place at Campus Ardiensis, possibly modern Harmanli in Bulgaria. This time the outcome was far less clear and Constantine had to settle for the removal of Valens and the annexation of Pannonia and Moesia rather than the entire Balkans. He also agreed to recognise Licinius II as *Caesar* alongside his sons, Crispus and Constantine II.

While the entire Balkans had not fallen to him, it was obvious that Constantine was not happy to share the empire and over the next six years he worked to orchestrate another reason for war. He found it in the growth of his Christianity and the mission he felt was his to perform in protecting Christians from oppression. Licinius had remained tolerant of Christianity as per the *Edict of Milan*, but as Constantine promoted himself as the champion of all Christians, the eastern emperor came to believe that the Christians within his realm were acting as fifth columnists in favour of Constantine. He dismissed them from his administration and the army and when he went as far to execute bishops who had displayed disloyalty, he brought a vengeful Constantinian torrent down upon himself. The vast field army of Constantine struck into Thrace and won a decisive victory at Adrianople on 3 July 324. A brilliant naval victory by Crispus in the Battle of the Hellespont later the same month allowed Constantine to cross to Asia Minor and inflict a final, crushing defeat on Licinius at Chrysopolis on 18 September, with the defeated *Augustus* and his nine-year-old son being executed in spring the following year, despite being promised the life of private citizens.

Constantius II therefore spent much of his earliest years in an empire on the verge or in the midst of armed conflict with itself and barbarian tribes, foreshadowing what much of his own career would involve. However, despite the political importance of this period, very little is known for certain about the earlier life of Constantius. Aside from his elevation to *Caesar* at the age of seven on 13 November 324 in celebration of the unification of the Roman Empire at Chrysopolis, only a few inferences regarding his upbringing and potential education can be made. Following the first settlement with Licinius after Campus Ardiensis in 317, Constantine took up residence at Sirmium perhaps to recruit men from the surrounding area and to campaign against the restless Sarmatians and Goths along the Danube, all the while continuing to cast a covetous eye upon Licinius' territory.

This may have enabled Constantine to be present more often in the earliest days of Constantius' life than he had been for his two elder sons. Crispus had been entrusted to his grandmother, Helena, as Constantine left Diocletian's court at Nicomedia in 306; Constantine II had been born in early 316 at Arles, while Constantine was squaring off against Licinius in the Balkans. Constantine is recorded as a loving father and he does seem to have made up for lost time in connecting with Crispus in Gaul. Now, in late summer 317, the emperor might even have been on hand for the birth of his third son at Sirmium and even with operations along the Danube, he may have made time to bond with Constantius and Constantine II, who was eighteen months older.[2] However well-settled Constantius' earliest years might have been, Constantine's campaigning along the Danube and against Licinius will have interrupted the time shared between father and son. This may have had some detrimental effect on Constantius' psyche, but perhaps no worse than any other child faced with a parent who works away from home.

Much of Constantius' upbringing will have been in the looming shadow of his father, both figuratively as emperor and Christian reformer and literally in person and through vast statues across the empire. That Constantius is considered by Julian to be a very similar emperor to Constantine[3] might hint at the father having a strong influence on his son, who would go to great lengths to safeguard the future of his family, to the extent of pathological paranoia. However, such speculation can be dangerous and such an idea of fatherly impressions could be twisted to apply to Constantine II as well for as will be seen, he took his position of being Constantine's eldest heir very seriously and would not be satisfied with a portion of the Roman Empire, much as his father post-313. Equally suspect is seeing Constantius making a good impression on his father with his eventual choice as Constantine's representative on the all-important eastern frontier ahead of Constantine II. Perhaps Constantine had seen some of the hot-headedness that would lead to Constantine II's downfall in 340 or the level-headedness in Constantius that could be vital when facing the Persians. Or perhaps Constantius was just the next in line for a command. Constans was still too young to be delegated such an important military command while Constantine II was well established in Gaul, where he or his generals won a substantial enough victory for him to take the title of *Alamannicus* before September 337.[4]

Early Trauma and Constantius' Personality

This talk of Constantius' eventual promotion to command in the east and Constantine II being placed in Gaul begs one important question: where was Constantine's first son Crispus in all of this? The answer arises in the form of a scandal that rocked the imperial family in 326, one that may have left an indelible mark on Constantius for the rest of his life. As already mentioned, Crispus had played an important role in the final defeat of Licinius and Constantine had honoured his eldest son with consulships, military commands and his depiction on coins, statues, mosaics and cameos, making Crispus seem every bit Constantine's heir. But in 326, out of the blue and after a brief show trial at Pola, Crispus was stripped of his position and executed. Even more shocking was that not long after, Constantine's wife and mother of Constantius, Fausta, was also executed. The unexpectedness of these deaths and the lack of information caused by the subsequent damning of their memories, which saw the attempted removal of any mention of them from various historical and physical records, has led to speculation about what happened to provoke such a violent outburst from Constantine.

Perhaps the more believable suggestion, given the intricacies of imperial politics, is that Fausta, who had already played a major role in the death of her father, Maximian was also behind the orchestration of Crispus' downfall. Perhaps she was jealous of Crispus' prominent position in the Constantinian regime compared to her own sons,[5] going as far as to attempt to ensnare Crispus in a honey pot trap. When Crispus recoiled in shock at the suggestion of an illicit affair with his step-mother and left the imperial palace, Fausta then used this departure as part of a concoction in which she accused him of attempting to rape her and then fleeing in disgrace. Believing her, Constantine allowed his temper to get the better of him, leading to the brief trial and execution of Crispus. That Fausta followed Crispus into the afterlife shortly after might suggest that Constantine found out the truth regarding the potential innocence of his son. Perhaps he caught Fausta in a lie or she was caught out by spies belonging to Constantine's mother, Helena.

The method chosen for the execution of Fausta – an overheated bath – has raised further questions and perhaps an alternative explanation for the events of 326. It is possible that Constantine may not have wanted to spill the blood of the mother of his surviving children but overheating in a bath was not a known method of execution. What it was known as was a technique for inducing a miscarriage. Perhaps Fausta was trying to rid herself of an incriminating pregnancy either by way of a servant or even Crispus, forced or consensual, and was therefore not executed by Constantine at all.[6] Even if it was an accidental suicide, Fausta had still committed an egregious sin in the eyes of Constantine for as with Crispus, she found herself the victim of a *damnatio memoriae* (the erasing of her name from statues, records, and so forth). That the *damnationes* on Fausta and Crispus were not lifted by either Constantine or any of his sons suggests that it was the belief of the Constantinian family that there was at least some truth to some of the rumours surrounding their executions, even if Constantine's reticence of removing the damnation of Crispus was as much to do with not wanting to admit a catastrophic error in judgement in listening to Fausta's lies.

It is difficult to determine how these events might have affected the then nine-year-old Constantius. While it is difficult to gauge how close he was to either his half-brother or his mother, Crispus was stationed in Gaul for the vast majority of Constantius' life up until then, although his settled life in Sirmium might have seen him enjoy a close relationship to his mother, their killings on the order of his father cannot have helped his development. The idea that no one was safe within the Constantinian family may have influenced the untrusting, paranoid nature that the future emperor is accused of exhibiting in his adulthood, traits that rebellion and usurpation will have no doubt exacerbated.

It is perhaps these accusations of paranoia that are the most stand-out of the supposed traits of Constantius. For Ammianus to claim that he "easily surpassed the savagery of Caligula, Domitian, and Commodus"[7] if he should be confronted by even an inkling of another aspiring to supreme power is obvious hyperbole; but the root of such an accusation is a want to maintain the dignity of his office, something for which Ammianus also praises him[8] and was drilled into Constantius by his father as part of his political education. Of course, it must be asked whether this paranoia was bred of repeated usurpations against his family and then him personally or did his paranoid behaviour spark these usurpations? While impossible to answer with certainty, as with many such questions, it is likely that the answer lies somewhere in between: paranoia was sparked by previous usurpations, revolts and familial plotting, which along with his military reputation and brand of justice, led to further instances of disloyalty. Constantian paranoia, punishment and revolt may have been repeating parts of the same vicious cycle.

A more direct inheritance from his father than reverence for the imperial position, and one that will have encouraged a poor reputation, was the same fiery temper that had seen Constantine order the execution of Crispus. Constantius is recorded as being milder than his father,[9] but there are numerous examples of him letting his temper get the better of him, in the face of supporters of rebels, people he viewed as heretics or who were going against his imperial decrees.[10] Perhaps due to a personal recognition of this short fuse, Constantius "made a special effort to be considered just and merciful,"[11] as well as philanthropic, a trait that several of those who wrote to and about Constantius picked up on. Others commented that composure, self-control and mercy were the hallmarks of Constantius' character,[12] with the dealing with Vetranio in 350 seen as Constantius at his best displaying not just mercy, composure, self-control but even charisma; although as will be seen later, it may have been an example of cunning and orchestration.[13] What Ammianus made of the case of Vetranio in his missing book is an intriguing question. Bribery? Bullying through superior force? Manipulation? Or pointing out that while this was a positive occasion, his bouts of bitterness, suspicion and willingness to overlook injustice overshadowed any efforts at being just and merciful?[14]

While cynicism about Ammianus' approach to Constantius is difficult to set aside, the historian was capable of praising elements of Constantius' personality.[15] He commended his prudent and temperate way of life, how his eating and drinking in moderation allowed him to enjoy rude health, even if he suggested that a lack of luxury left Constantius susceptible to grave illness. That not even a rumour of dissolute private behaviour was uttered by Ammianus suggests that Constantius was indeed a model of chastity behind closed doors.[16] One of Ammianus' stranger 'praises' of Constantius was that as "long as he lived he never tasted fruit,"[17] although why such an abstention would be a positive is not elaborated upon. It has been suggested that instead of praise, this was an attempt by Ammianus to use anti-Manichaean Christian propaganda to take a jab at Constantius.[18] In his running of the state, Ammianus agreed with Constantius' maintaining of the separation of civil and military authorities, even if it did not stop usurpations, while he heaped praise on him for propagating the majesty of his imperial position – "no one ever saw him wipe his mouth or nose"[19] – and never appealing to popular support to enhance his position, all the while keeping the army in check by not over-promoting its commanders.

Even when Ammianus criticises Constantius' use of violence, merciless judges and torture, there are some hints that the historian understood that at times even a good or "medium quality"[20] emperor had to do harsh things, even if Constantius overstepped the mark. In highlighting the deeds of Marcus Aurelius, Caesar, Manlius, the philosophy of Heraclitus the Ephesian and even the situation faced by Gallienus, Ammianus seems to state that Constantius might have had some justification for his brand of justice so long as there was room for clemency at certain times to aid the emperor's reputation and perhaps to prevent other revolts.

Even the unscrupulousness and corruption of his tax-collectors, which contributed to his unpopularity in the provinces, particularly Gaul, could be explained, although not excused, due to a need for cash for the constant wars along the Rhine, Danube, in Mesopotamia or against usurpers. There is also some suggestion of historical insensitivity with his celebrating of civil war victories with triumphs and even triumphal arches in Gaul and Pannonia "commemorating the ruin of the provinces",[21] although as will be seen later, Constantius went out of his way to portray those victories as victories over a barbarian invader, showing a keen understanding of sensitivities and propaganda.

Constantius is also panned for his poor choices in courtiers. While he received praise for his choices of military commanders, making sure they were tried and tested before appointing them, he appears far less competent in his selection of those he had closest to him.[22] Not even his panegyrists do a good job in covering up these poor selections, instead speaking of how Constantius was slow to trust but once he did he would be a loyal friend.[23] While this might seem like a conscientious approach, when coupled to a reputation for poor selections, it became disastrous as it could leave Constantius surrounded by incompetents, flatterers and overtly ambitious men to whom he was too loyal to get rid of even if they proved detrimental to his standing and the empire as a whole.

When it comes to his education, Constantius and his brothers represent a crossroads in imperial history as they were the first emperors to receive a Christian education, with Lactantius being employed by Constantine as a tutor for Crispus. While the name of any Christian tutor for Constantius is not recorded, he was brought up a Christian from the very outset. It is difficult to discern Constantius' Christian beliefs as the majority of sources are so determined to portray him and his religion in a negative light. Even the pagan Ammianus talks about Constantius' polluting of Christianity with superstition and arousing of controversies, although he may be allowing not just his anti-Constantian bias to shine through once more but also reflecting the Christian opinion of the time when he was writing, as Constantius' Homoeanism had been defeated under Theodosius.[24] Constantius demonstrated veneration for Christianity in his building works, especially in the Church of the Holy Apostles in Constantinople,[25] and while "his repeated disputes with Athanasius of Alexandria provoke much comment, naturally unfavourable",[26] it must be noted that in the earliest exchanges with Athanasius, Constantius was backing a faction in the church that was welcoming more doctrinal discourse rather than championing Arianism. This might place Constantius' personal beliefs in a far more moderate position than his opponents would have it be remembered, even if it was claimed that he was rigid in doctrinal matters: "the sentence which has once been passed ought not to be revoked."[27]

When it came to confronting such obstinacy, Constantius revealed that perhaps his beliefs in the primacy of the Roman emperor outstripped that of the church, another consequence of the majesty of the emperor instilled in him by his father. While Constantine is recorded as being far less interfering, Constantius took a far more heavy-handed approach and in so doing shows, much like every emperor and king who attempted to arbitrate church disputes over the coming centuries, that he did not understand the inherent independence of the Christian Church. It is his more direct interference in church councils and attempting to force unity through threats and manipulation that deserves ridicule rather than his doctrinal beliefs. Such belief in imperial leadership of the church was not limited to Constantius. His brother Constans also took an active role in attempting to enforce his side of the doctrinal dispute, which would lead to threats of war with Constantius.

Despite the growing importance of Christianity and it playing a central role in Constantius' education, it should be noted that the classics remained a vital part of an education in the fourth century. When Constantine employed Lactantius to tutor Crispus, he was not just employing a zealous Christian convert but also a rhetorician and imparting his knowledge of such a discipline must have been part of his lessons. Again, while there are no names attached to Constantius as a tutor, mention is made of the kind of education he received in relation to his success or failure at mastering them. Ammianus suggests that despite his pretensions, a "dullness of mind"[28] made Constantius a poor poet and rhetorician, although the historian does suggest that this was more to do with a lack of the necessary creativity than a lack of intelligence. Libanius backs up Ammianus in recording that Constantius was educated in rhetoric, as well as administration and argument, although he suggests that the emperor had no formal training in oratory, even if his ability to perhaps talk around Vetranio and his army might show at least some skill in public speaking.[29] Themistius was keen to portray Constantius as a philosopher through action and deed rather than education, similar to how Plutarch portrayed Alexander the Great. However, enthusiasm for education and philosophy does not necessarily demonstrate a good education, while the identification of 'education' as the acquisition of skills and experience in practice rather than pure learning could be an attempt at disguising a lack of learning on the part of Constantius.[30] It could be that being born at such a period of transition between a classical and Christian education saw Constantius end up with a lesser version of both.

Constantine saw to it that his sons received training in to how to rule, perhaps even teaching them himself in the administration of the empire and justice, which included the distinction between the need for anger or mildness, tyranny or clemency.[31] However, as Constantius came of an age to embark on a public career, Constantine provided him with a man of experience from whom to learn in a more hands-on way, the highest non-imperial official in the empire, Flavius Ablabius. Born a pagan of the most humble origins in Crete,[32] Ablabius converted to Christianity and worked his way up through the offices of the governor of the island before leaving for Constantinople perhaps in the earliest days of the new capital. There, he acquired a fortune and became a leading member of the new Constantinopolitan Senate. He was serving as *vicarius* of Asiana by 326 before being promoted to praetorian prefect in the east in 329, a position he held until 337.[33] He was held in high enough regard by Constantine to be awarded the consulship in 331 and for the emperor to organise the marriage of Constans to Ablabius' daughter, Olympias, although this match did not take place. Upon taking up this role of accompanying Constantius to the east in 335, Constantine hoped for Ablabius to teach Constantius the finer details of governing, although as will be seen, the situation Constantius and Ablabius found in the east in 335 left little time for lessons in governance and Constantius himself does not seem to have been fond of his tutor, getting rid of him at the first convenience.

Even though he dispatched Ablabius with him, that Constantine felt confident enough in Constantius to send him to Syria to oversee the preparations for war with Persia could suggest that his second surviving son had made a good impression in terms of his leadership qualities. Constantine's residence in Sirmium in 316 meant that while Constantius will have been brought up in the halls of the imperial palace, he was also close to the Pannonians whose military abilities had played such a major role in the revival of the Roman Empire in the second half of the third century. This will have seen Constantius educated from an early age in military drill and skills, both of which his physical and mental attributes will have helped him in. His sharp-sighted, bulging eyes, a Constantinian trait, made him a superb archer[34] while his long trunk of a torso and short bowed legs made him a good runner and jumper. These physical strengths also provided him with a sturdy disposition, which, along with his chastity and abstinence, allowed him to endure the nomadic, austere life of a soldier, which in turn made him popular with his troops.

His deployment in the east was not the first time that Constantius had been entrusted with a prominent position. In 331/332, while Constantine II was campaigning with their father along the Danube against the Goths, the still teenaged Constantius was sent to Trier in Gaul to act as the figurehead of the Constantinian dynasty. When Constantine II returned to Gaul, Constantius perhaps took his place at their father's side against the Sarmatians in 334, who had managed to capture Campona, modern Nagytétény near Budapest in Hungary, forcing Constantine to relocate to Siscia. It was his subsequent victories that saw Constantine supposedly settle 300,000 Sarmatians in parts of Thrace, Macedonia, Italy and Gaul, as well as taking the title of *Sarmaticus* for the second time, while possibly allowing Constantius to take it for the first, although this is disputed.[35]

While Constantine expected to move east in due course to oversee the Roman war effort and had furnished his son with a skilled court led by Ablabius, for him to entrust Constantius with leading the initial responses to Shapur's attacks in 335 demonstrates some faith in the abilities of Constantius; although again, to see this as Constantine seeing a more level-headed approach from Constantius compared to Constantine II is to go beyond the evidence. Perhaps this was one of the occasions when being the middle child paid some kind of dividend. However it came about, this was seen as a great honour for Constantius as the Roman east was the richest part of the Empire and with the presence of the Persian Kingdom, it was seen as a place to win military glory. However, Constantine was placing a heavy burden upon the young and inexperienced shoulders of Constantius and had he known of the long-running quagmire that he was being thrust into with Shapur II, it is doubtful that the nineteen-year-old *Caesar* will have thanked his father for such a 'reward'.

The Death of Constantine: Purging the Family and Dividing the Spoils

Having made his arrangements with Constantine II in Gaul and Constantius and Ablabius holding the Persians at bay in Mesopotamia and Armenia throughout 335 and 336, Constantine set out from Constantinople to take charge of the eastern frontier with his full entourage and military retinue in the spring of 337. Not long after leaving the city, the emperor fell ill. It is even possible that he was already unwell when he left the city and was intending to travel to the hot baths at Helenopolis, a city in Bithynia he had renamed for his saintly mother.[36] After praying at the church Helena had had built for the martyr, Lucian of Antioch, Constantine determined to travel on to Nicomedia. However, the combination of prayer and hot baths did not stem the illness and by the time he reached the imperial villa of Achyron, just outside Nicomedia,[37] Constantine recognised that his end was near.

He therefore called together a group of bishops to receive his baptism, despite his prior wish to be baptised in the Jordan river as Jesus of Nazareth had been.[38] Baptism and confession in the early fourth century were very different to more modern times. Instead of being performed on young children, "the sacrament of baptism was the culmination of a course of instruction lasting up to three years."[39] Constantine was either fast-tracked through such a course or allowed to forego it altogether. There were also several other reasons why Constantine should have been disqualified from receiving baptism: his holding of public office, dispensing of capital justice and service in the Roman army.[40] It is understandable why the Christian hierarchy agreed to forsake some of their own rules for the man who had promoted their faith from just another in a vast pantheon to the religion of the imperial family.

Unlike the regular confession of sin that is part of many modern Christian faiths, during Constantine's time, it was a once in a lifetime occurrence that was not supposed to be repeated. Therefore, it almost always preceded death, or at the very least the death of a former self and was a major part of baptism. So when Constantine asked to be baptised, it was clear evidence that he expected to die soon. With his claim that he had confessed his sins at Helenopolis in martyrium of Lucian of Antioch accepted by the bishops, Constantine then underwent the baptismal procedure: exorcism, triple immersion in water and the laying on of hands. Reborn in the light of God, the emperor then caste aside his imperial purple garments and wore robes of white. So dressed, he met with the officers and leaders of his army and then "proceeded to complete the needful arrangement of his affairs"[41] before passing away on the last day of Pentecost, calculated as 22 May 337.

The news of Constantine's illness was sent to Constantius and the wording of the message must have been sufficiently gloomy as both the *Caesar* and his praetorian prefect set off for Nicomedia immediately. However, despite the relative rapidity of the *cursus publicus* (the imperial message service), Constantine had been dead a few days before word of his illness reached Constantius and Ablabius at Antioch. Constantine II received news of his father's death at Trier before 17 June 337 and despite his exact whereabouts in the summer of 337 not being recorded,[42] Constans will have heard of his father's passing anything up to a week before his eldest brother. This left Constantius to oversee not just Constantine's funeral in Constantinople, but also the imperial succession.

On the surface, the succession to Constantine would seem rather straightforward. He had three surviving sons, all of whom had been raised to *Caesar* and given a region to oversee; Constantine II in Gaul, Constantius II in the east and Constans in the central provinces. However, the 330s had seen developments that challenged this straightforward succession, specifically the restoration to favour of Constantius Chlorus' children from his second marriage to Theodora.[43] Allowed to move to Constantinople in the early 330s after something of a nomadic existence, Constantine's half brothers, Flavius Dalmatius and Julius Constantius, and their families were thrust into the reckoning for imperial power. It has even been suggested that "the reinstatement of the descendants of Theodora, therefore, may be read as a dynastic coup",[44] orchestrated by court factions in opposition to Constantine II and Constantius. Such an idea would see the great Constantine cast in a position of being manipulated with his age being taken into account; he was in his sixties by the mid 330s.

If such a manipulation was taking place, it was bearing fruit for not only were Flavius Dalmatius and Julius Constantius awarded consulships in 333 and 335 respectively, the former's sons, Flavius Dalmatius the Younger and Hannibalianus, were set to receive part of Constantine's inheritance. In 335, the younger Dalmatius was elevated to *Caesar* with control over the dioceses of Thrace and Macedonia, while Hannibalianus was proclaimed "King of Kings and the Pontic Peoples" and married to Constantine's daughter, Constantina.[45] Perhaps Constantine had been convinced that Diocletian had been right – one man trying to rule the empire alone was folly – and was looking to reinstitute some form of the Tetrarchy that he had done so much to undermine, although

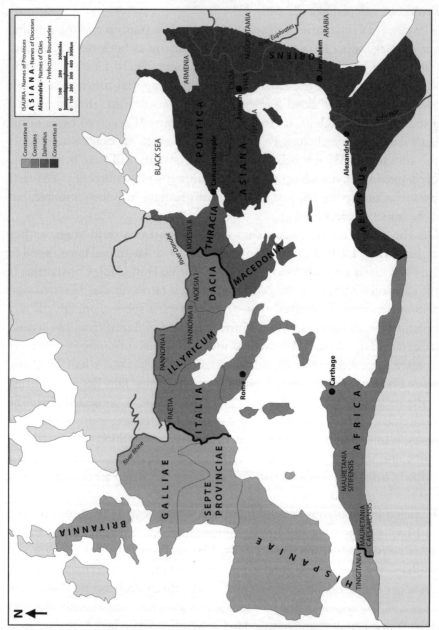

Map 2: Constantine's Proposed Tetrarchy

such a system would have seen Constans relegated to a position below his brothers.[46] Whatever his plans, Constantine did not explain them or they were suppressed by his sons and their supporters and any thought of the brothers sharing power with any other relatives was put to rest by their one trump card: the army.

Egged on by rumours that Constantine had always meant for his sons to inherit the empire alone and even that Dalmatius and Hannibalianus had poisoned the departed emperor,[47] the soldiery perpetrated a massacre of all those who stood in the way of the tripartite succession of the sons of Constantine. Flavius Dalmatius the Elder, Hannibalianus, Dalmatius *Caesar*, Julius Constantius, his unnamed eldest son and perhaps more all perished in the purge in or near Constantinople. Of the Constantinian family, only the young sons of Julius Constantius, Gallus and Julian, and the son of Eutropia, Julius Nepotianus, were left alive on account of their youth along with Constantine II, Constantius II and Constans.

As the only beneficiary of the massacre to be on hand in Constantinople, suspicion fell on Constantius. Julian blamed him for the massacre; Zosimus suggests he orchestrated the whole matter, while Ammianus held the purge of 337 against Constantius for having "destroyed root and branch all who were related to him by blood and race".[48] However, there is a lack of consistency from the sources over what role Constantius had in the massacre. While he suggests that Constantius was directly involved, Julian also records that under pressure from mutinous soldiers and "forced by circumstances [Constantius]… reluctantly failed to prevent others from doing wrong", an inactivity he had since come to regret and that Julian linked to his childlessness and failure against the Persians.[49] It is possible that Julian did not accept such a capitulation by Constantius as that was not the confident and experienced emperor that he knew. However, in mid-337, Constantius was not yet out of his teens and while this does not preclude his involvement, along with his current deployment against the Persians, it reduces the likelihood that Constantius was behind the orchestration of the massacre.

Perhaps this lack of clarity over the events of mid-337 and the level of Constantius' involvement in them is another symptom of the hostility of the sources towards Constantius. The purge of the imperial family may have left them in a quandary for to blame Constantius and portray him as a monster would be to also accept that he had the cunning to mastermind the removal of his opponents through the skilful manipulation of the army and its loyalty to Constantine the Great. Perhaps some of those hostile sources decided that the portrayal of a helpless *Caesar* overcome by events and forced by his own weakness to accept something he had no control over was preferable to a cunning mastermind.

That said, it has been argued that a massacre prompted by Constantius "is consistent with all the evidence",[50] as well as motive, opportunity and that the confusion in the sources is born out of an ever-changing imperial narrative. The sons of Constantine had been far from happy at the dilution of their power and the loss of territory that the promotion of Dalmatius and Hannibalianus involved, seen with the failure of their prestige coinage, "those intended particularly for imperial payments to the army and the civil service",[51] from Trier, Rome and Antioch to depict Dalmatius *Caesar* between 335 and 337. This simultaneous imperial snubbing also suggests that the three brothers were in communication and of a similar mind regarding the interlopers in what was their birthright. The issuing of coins depicting Theodora from the brothers' mints after the massacre appears to be a transparent attempt to distance themselves from the massacre.[52]

That the brothers did not take the title of *Augustus* until perhaps 9 September suggests that any idea of Constantine meaning for them to inherit solely, even through a deathbed proclamation should be discounted. Without such a claim the question must be asked why would the army target a portion of the imperial family to overthrow the succession planned by Constantine two years before his death? "That was *maiestas*, plain and simple, on a scale unparalleled in Roman history."[53] And if they did commit such an act of treason without orders from on high, there would have been extensive reprisals, instead of the promotion of two generals, Flavius Ursus and Flavius Polemius, to the consulship of 338.[54] The sparing of all female descendants of Theodora and little idea of casualties outside of targeted members of the imperial family and their supporters do not seem like the actions of a mutinous army. They seem to be part of a coordinated assault on specific dynastic targets.

"The weakness of the official explanation"[55] is also demonstrated in the attempted *damnationes* of the deceased male descendants of Theodora and the exile of the survivors, Gallus and Julian. Neither of these moves makes any sense if the massacre was the result of a mutinous army attacking innocent members of the imperial family. *Damnationes memoriae* suggest that the descendants of Theodora were removed as enemies of the state rather than by the mutinous soldiers and if they were *hostis*, why is there no mention of what they were charged with to justify their erasure from public memory apart from some rumours of poisoning Constantine? The only reason to exile Gallus and Julian was due to continued hostility towards the descendants of Theodora.

It therefore seems that someone had to have been responsible for guiding the actions of the army and perhaps spreading rumours to encourage and then explain their actions. As the only beneficiary on hand, the finger points to Constantius. If there was some inkling that the family of Theodora had been restored to favour in the early 330s in an attempt to undermine the brothers' position as imperial heirs through the manipulation of Constantine by officials, perhaps even Ablabius,[56] then "pragmatically and politically, Constantius' actions are completely understandable and explicable"[57] should he have orchestrated the elimination of such opponents. And while his brothers may not have had a direct hand in the massacre, they do not seem to have borne any ill will towards Constantius because of it and as suggested by the simultaneous issuing of similar coinage on more than one occasion, the brothers were capable of coordinating their political aims.

While it has been suggested that Constantine had passed on his skills in constructing legitimacy to his sons,[58] the purge of 337 and the attempts to ignore, explain and cover it up do not show them applying these lessons particularly well. The inconsistencies in the sources show how "the official version of events evolved over time",[59] perhaps as other evidence made the current version untenable. It began with a silent *damnatio* of those removed before moving on to placing blame on mutinous soldiers and praising Constantius for managing to hold them in some sort of check. This then devolved into Constantius being a helpless bystander, forced into a tacit acceptance of the mutineers' actions before the veil slips completely and Constantius is revealed as having orchestrated the entire massacre, seeking repentance and viewing his personal and professional failures as a karmic balancing for his destruction of much of his family. However, even if they were far from competent in the manufacturing of the story surrounding the pruning of the family tree at the time, the brothers' efforts and those of the sources over the years have managed to muddy the waters sufficiently that it is difficult to state with any certainty either what happened in the months following Constantine's death or what the imperial brothers wanted people to think had happened.

It seems though that the simplest explanation – Constantius did it – is the correct one. Arriving in Constantinople to oversee his father's funeral in late May/early June, Constantius likely had a confrontation with his extended family present in the city over how the succession was going to play out, particularly over the proposed positions of Dalmatius, Hannibalianus and even Constans. Taking advantage of the proximity of so many potential opponents as well as the army, Constantius employed the soldiers to assassinate Dalmatius *Caesar*, Hannibalianus, Flavius Dalmatius, Julius Constantius and others, securing the accession of himself and his brothers. The rapidity of

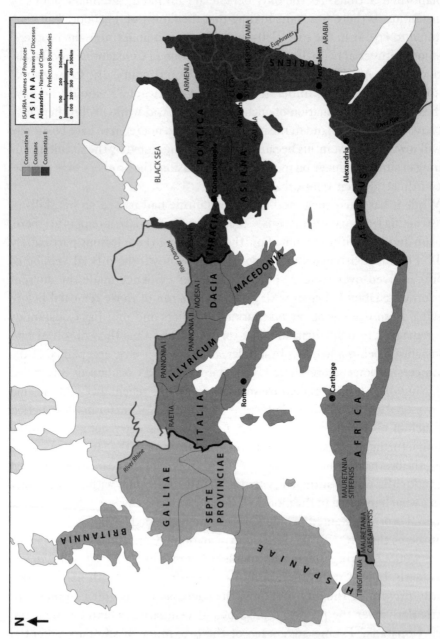

Map 3: The Pannonian Settlement 9 September 337

this massacre, the implementation of diplomatic and numismatic propaganda and the calling of the meeting in Pannonia may suggest that there was some underlying agreement between the brothers to remove their dynastic opponents. Constantius then distanced himself from the fall out by absenting himself to the Danube to campaign against the Sarmatians, perhaps even alongside Constans. He then met Athanasius at Viminacium at the end of July and then moved to Sirmium for negotiations over the division of the empire with Constantine II and Constans and the final overthrow of their father's succession plan of 335.[60]

At this Pannonian conference, each brother was confirmed in the territorial position to which they had been assigned during the reign of their father: Constantine II got the western provinces of Gaul, Spain and Britain; Constans received those of Italy, Africa, Illyricum and Dacia; Constantius received all of the Asian provinces and Egypt.[61] The only real territorial negotiations would have been on the division of the realms set aside for Dalmatius and Hannibalianus. The latter's "kingdom" would seem to have been planned to be carved out of conquests made at the expense of Persians, Armenians and Caucasian tribes, although there may have been some trimming of land from the territory of Constantius in Anatolia. Any such inherent ideas of expansion were set aside. The realm of Dalmatius though was well defined as the dioceses of Macedonia and Thrace with its own army and so needed to be dealt with. The decision reached was simple and effective: Constans would take Macedonia and Constantius would receive Thrace. With this division agreed, all three brothers were declared *Augustus* by 9 September 337.[62]

Despite this seemingly straightforward territorial division, the negotiations do not seem to have been amicable. Rather than any disgust towards Constantius over the massacre or from Constans over their father's plan to relegate him to a junior partner, the enmity seems to have originated from Constantine II. Not only had he been allotted the least fashionable and probably poorest provinces of the empire, Constantine seems to have maintained that his age afforded him some form of seniority in the imperial college and even guardianship over the still minor Constans. Some tacit acceptance of his primacy as the eldest may have been given by the representatives of Constans and perhaps from Constantius too as the latter was keen to extricate himself from the conference in order to deal with reports of another Persian invasion. However, it would soon become clear that a tacit acknowledgement of his seniority was not going to placate Constantine.

Constantius' Martial Inheritance: The Reforms of Constantine and their Consequences

While there would be political ramifications within three years, the most important fall out from the Pannonian conference in terms of immediacy was the fate of the army. Understanding Constantine's reforms is "rendered difficult… [by] the unsatisfactory nature of the surviving literary evidence",[63] leading some sources to "give the impression that the late Roman army sprang up, instantly operational, on the morning after the battle of the Milvian Bridge".[64] However, as a product of the Tetrarchy, Constantine's reforms marked a continuation of those of Diocletian. Building on the expansion of the *comitatus* and the increasing need for movement, as well as his need to defend his Rhine frontier, Constantine launched his strike against Maxentius with a reduced field force of about 40,000. The success of this elite strike force in northern Italy and at Milvian Bridge led Constantine to expand further upon that idea, collecting a large central field army around his person. Under his direct command, this force allowed for "occasional aggressive pre-emptive defence across the frontiers".[65]

Cautious use of the *Notitia Dignitatum* suggests that Constantinian field armies consisted of smaller-sized legions, *cunei equitum* cavalry and infantry *auxilia*. The latter was a new form of non-Roman auxiliary unit, while the *cunei* replaced the cavalry *vexillationes*.[66] Despite the presence of more cavalry, the core of Constantine's new *comitatenses* field army remained infantry and was therefore no more mobile than its predecessors. That this army was capable of winning victories over Maxentius and Licinius and that there was little in the way of frontier trouble from barbarian tribes or the Persians may give a false impression of how successful this new field army was.[67]

The most regular criticism of this central field army was that Constantine stripped the frontiers to create it. A high proportion of the forces used in 312 came from Britain and Gaul, suggesting that many had been on frontier duty, with several field units sharing names with frontier units.[68] However, "archaeological evidence… [shows] that the army maintained a strong presence along the rivers throughout the fourth century",[69] suggesting that while Constantine did remove soldiers, he and his successors were far from negligent with the frontiers. Constantine is also criticised for establishing the status gap between the field armies and *limitanei* and *ripenses*.[70] If the *comitatenses* did all the serious fighting, relegating the *limitanei* and *ripenses* to more of a regional police force that was not expected to defeat the enemy, then would they not avoid battle altogether? However, this outlook is unnecessarily bleak. The adoption of *limitanei* into the field armies and continued payments in cash, kind and land suggests that they were still more than useful.[71] Indeed, "at least one emperor between Constantine and Justinian would have noticed and applied some thought to the matter"[72] if the *limitanei* were in any way useless.

This does not exonerate Constantine. There is considerable reason to believe that his reforms and strategies contained defects, particularly with regard to his plan for the succession. The multiplication of emperors would have placed an increasing strain on the forces and bureaucracy of the empire for each member of his projected Tetrarchic system – Constantine II, Constantius II, Constans and Dalmatius – and perhaps Hannibalianus will have had their own *comitatus*, military and civilian hierarchies. In a way, the overthrow of Constantine's succession plan may have lessened the burden on the empire but even the tripartite division of territory, resources and the army will have stretched imperial logistics. The three brothers likely divided Constantine's field army as evenly as possible, although some allowance for the origins of some of the troops may have been made; those Gauls, Germans and Britons who had come east after 312 may have gone back west with Constantine II while those forces that had been part of the Balkan and eastern forces of Severus II, Galerius, Daia and Licinius could have returned to their respective homelands with either Constans or Constantius.

The poor source material means only speculations are possible on the size and make up of the forces each brother ended up with. Constantine is reported to have had a military establishment of about 100,000 in 312 from which he picked his field force of under 40,000 to lead against Maxentius. His victory at Milvian Bridge brought the entire western armed forces under his command, perhaps 286,000 men.[73] With such newfound wealth and manpower, Constantine could now augment the field army formula he had stumbled upon, with it suggested that his recruiting of *auxilia* increased the military establishment, although at a level "well under 25 per cent".[74] This may have allowed him to produce a field force of up to 120,000 infantry and 10,000 cavalry for his war with Licinius, While this seems like an exaggeration, it would not be beyond the realms of possibility for the mechanisms to be in place to allow Constantine to bring together a single field force of such size, but it would be a huge logistical challenge that would undermine the security of large parts of realm.[75] It should also be noted that Constantine is recorded as only having commanded 20,000 men at Cibalae.[76]

It was perhaps such a vast force, brought together for the Persian campaign, which was to be divided between Constantine II, Constantius II and Constans in September 337. However, while Constantine had gathered a significant force around his person, this cannot have been the only field force he deployed not just due to the aforementioned lack of speed for one army to defend all frontiers but also due to the deployment of his sons as regional commanders. Constantine would hardly have left Crispus, Constantine II, Constantius II, Constans, Dalmatius and even Hannibalianus without some kind of *comitatus* capable of protecting their lives and serving as the core of any campaigning army.

It is likely then that Constantine's personal field army in 337 was not of some monstrous magnitude the order of 100,000, but it is possible that as it will have been expanded to form an expeditionary force capable of taking on the Persians, it will have been in the high tens of thousands. Perhaps therefore each of the brothers had their military strength bolstered by up to 20,000 men. The sizes of the regional field armies that were to emerge in the years after this division at around 20,000 (and up to 40,000 for those in the presence of an emperor) might suggest that the brothers were influenced by Constantine's early *comitatenses* deployed against Maxentius and Licinius.

While Constantine's military reforms could be vaguely summed up as encompassing a policy of centralisation, the tripartite succession of his sons initiated an increasing regionalisation of the army and the empire as a whole. Even before Constantine's death, the division of the empire into west, centre and east was already underway with the areas of influence doled out to the three brothers. After the massacre and their formal imperial accession on 9 September 337, the forces the brothers inherited and divided between them became attached to their respective regions: Gaul, Illyricum and Syria. The limiting of the field armies to geographic areas and the division of the empire saw each brother somewhat short on resources; Constantius in particular would struggle to find sufficient troops to fight the Persians, which would influence his strategic choices.[77] Therefore, while regionalisation may have minimised the risk of heavy losses caused by war on two fronts, it could have reduced the imperial capacity for offence. More drastically, this regionalisation increased the possibility of usurpation as it became necessary to appoint non-imperial individuals such as Magnentius and Vetranio to these powerful, independent positions as there were insufficient imperial personages to defend all of the flashpoints on the frontiers. When coupled to the potential for an emperor to be seen favouring one region over another, seen in the Gallic opposition to Constans and Constantius, this regionalisation and command of a single powerful individual meant that such regional disgruntlement had a military outlet: usurpation and civil war. It was somewhat fortunate then that Constantius would prove so adept at fighting civil wars, even if that commendation was meant as an indictment.[78]

But even then, Constantine's reforms, along with those of Diocletian, changed the kind of civil war that Constantius would have to face. The rise of field armies and their command by non-imperial generals saw to it that the emperor needed to be seen sharing the military burden of his men to maintain loyalty;[79] this in turn amplified the need for an effective and loyal bodyguard to protect the emperor as he exposed himself to such dangers. Under the reforms of Constantine, this protection was to be provided by the *scholae palatinae*, in place of the disbanded Praetorian Guard. These were units of elite barbarian soldiers and *commendabiles*, young men recommended by their father's reputation.[80] Aside from the emperor himself, the *scholae* had no single commander, removing the threat of a powerful individual in close proximity to the emperor. While such personal loyalty coupled with the meritocracy fostered by Diocletian and Constantine made assassination less likely,[81] that protection could be extended to someone other than the ruling emperor and could have drastic consequences on the battlefield. Protection by his own *scholae* and the ability to exploit regional tensions provoked by an emperor favouring one over another meant that a usurper would have to be defeated in the field rather than by an assassin's blade or rebel troops. And with such regional factionalism involved, armies were more likely to fight to the end, meaning that fourth century civil wars were fought to a sanguinary conclusion. This would be demonstrated for Constantius at Mursa in 351: two armies loyal to their well-protected emperor and wary that defeat might mean a demotion in prevalence for their regions fighting to the bloody end.

Such bloody conflicts, at home and abroad, put further strain on the recruiting systems of the empire. Due to a lack of evidence to the contrary, it is assumed that the Diocletianic system of conscription by taxation and hereditary service coped with the losses incurred during wars of the fourth century. However, the recruiting practices of Constantine and his successors suggest otherwise. Several laws indicate trouble finding recruits and forcing individuals to fulfil their obligations with tax exemptions for veterans and their families, local senators – *decurions* – illegally joining the army or potential recruits flocking to take holy orders after Constantine gave "immunity from curial charges to all clergy".[82] That such laws continued to be promulgated not just in the reign of Constantius II but also throughout the fourth century and beyond suggests that the mechanisms for citizen recruiting were not working.

In light of such a potential failure of the citizenry to enrol, it is unsurprising that Constantine and his sons turned to other sources of manpower. Non-Romans had always formed part of the Roman army but Constantine seems to have increased their numbers and "did more than anyone else to advance the already existing tendency to appoint German generals".[83] Such large numbers undermined the ability of the empire to integrate these new batches of barbarians as part of society.[84] Had the recruiting system of Diocletian been working, Constantine would not have needed to use an army that relied upon barbarians. Perhaps therefore through necessity, recruiting non-Romans became a much more viable avenue of manpower under Constantine, whether it was Franks, Goths, Sarmatians, Arabs, African nomads or eastern tribes.[85] Furthermore, Constantine was not alone in his barbarian recruiting. While Constantius found useful recruits in Thrace and Isauria, he hoped to use the Limigantes as recruits, found reliable cavalry and bowmen in Armenia, took barbarian *laeti* and *dediticii* for his *scholae*, likely settled Gothic Christians in Moesia in return for military service, while he promoted various non-Romans to high office.[86] Even Julian, who so decried Constantine as a "destroyer of hallowed laws and traditions"[87] for his recruiting policies, found himself unable or unwilling to reverse these practices.

The army of the fourth century had been initially the work of Diocletian but it was Constantine and the succession of his three sons that completed the development of the regional field armies supplemented by frontier garrisons, which were to characterise the Roman military in some form until perhaps the mid seventh century and maybe even beyond. However, in late 337, it is clear that, despite the Roman Empire now being on a firmer footing, the sons of Constantine had inherited an empire in a state of military, administrative and religious transition; a position further complicated by the failure of the Pannonian conference to address the concerns of all parties. Within a year, these problems were causing friction, although the material and military problems were to rear their heads far sooner. Before the ink on any agreement signed at the conference was dry, the newly enthroned Constantius *Augustus* quickly removed himself and his forces back to Antioch. The east had not been quiet as he and his brothers manipulated the intended inheritance of their father. Indeed, the eastern frontier would prove far more resistant to the brand of political machination and military massacre that Constantius had used against his relatives.

Chapter III

The Sins of the Father: Constantius' War with Shapur II

For it yields very little and uses up vast sums.
– Cassius Dio LXXV.3.3 on Roman conflict over Mesopotamia

Romans versus Persians: The First Century

While the imperial purge and Pannonian conference had settled some of the political disputes caused by the inheritance left by Constantine I, there was one such legacy left to Constantius that was not to be fixed with a simple redrawing of the map or a dagger in the ribs: war with the Persian Empire. By the time Constantine turned his attention to the eastern frontier in 335, the Romans and Persians had been at each other's throats on and off for over a century. In fact, the Romans had been duelling with the owners of the Iranian plateau for the best part of four hundred years.

For the first three of those centuries, the occupant of Iran had been the Arsacid kingdom of the Parthians, a confederacy of Iranian tribes from the Central Asian steppe. Warfare with the Parthians began rather inauspiciously for the Romans, punctuated by the calamitous defeats of successive triumvirs, the plutocrat Crassus at Carrhae in 53BCE and the Cleopatra-obsessed Marcus Antonius in 36BCE. Taking advantage of these defeats and Roman in-fighting, the Parthians briefly controlled large parts of Syria and Palestine before being forced to retreat. The conflict then switched its focus to the position of Armenia with both wanting to exert influence over this quasi-buffer state. On several occasions, the armies of these two great empires came face to face only to thrash out a peaceful accommodation and when such overtures failed or one side jumped the gun and placed their own candidate on the Armenian throne, any fighting was inconclusive, leading Armenia to resume its role as a no man's land.

However, the third and final century of Romano-Parthian conflict saw the Romans become dominant on the battlefield. The first step in this turn-around came from the emperor Trajan, who, fed up with political posturing and military indecisiveness, announced the annexation of Armenia. He then proved that his talk was not cheap with an invasion in 114 that confirmed the conquest of Armenia, overran Mesopotamia and captured the Parthian capital at Ctesiphon. Buoyed by these victories and standing on the shore of the Persian Gulf, Trajan looked to make these conquests permanent but numerous rebellions convinced his successor Hadrian that these new lands were less easily governed than conquered, leading him to relinquish them for the sake of forty years of peace and stability.

When war again broke out again in the 160s, the Parthians showed that they were still capable of taking the offensive, but the Roman counterattack not only retrieved the situation in Armenia and Syria but saw Ctesiphon sacked again by Avidius Cassius in 165. The Parthian capital suffered another scourge by the legions in 198 under the command of the emperor Septimius Severus, who achieved a more permanent annexation of Northern Mesopotamia, including cities such as Nisibis and Singara. Despite this string of Roman victories throughout the second century CE, rather poetically, the final Romano-Parthian battle at Nisibis in 217 was both bloody and inconclusive, with both sides happy to accept a stalemate.

This bloody draw had more long term consequences than the loss of thousands of men on either side. While the Romans were fast approaching the crises of the third century, the Parthians were to find out that that spark of resurgence glimpsed at Nisibis was a mirage. Holding off the Roman invasion of 217 was their last hurrah as a century of civil war and lying prostrate before a succession of Roman attacks had fatally undermined the Parthian kingdom. For many of their subjects, enough was enough. It was time for change; a change that was to have far reaching consequences for not just the Middle East, but for the Roman Empire as well.

The source of this change was the Parthian subkingdom of Persis, equating to the modern day Iranian province of Fars. Home of the Achaemenid Persian Empire, which had stretched from Greece and Libya to India and Central Asia but now, over five hundred years after its fall, Persis was to produce another imperial dynasty. While the late second century Parthian king, Vologaeses IV, had already faced a revolt of "Medes and Persians,"[1] it was his warring grandsons, Vologaeses VI and Artabanus V, who were to face the tempest that those dark clouds had threatened.[2]

This storm was focused around the descendants of a fire priest of the temple of Anahita at Istakhr called Sasan. First his son Papak used the influence accorded by his father's position to overthrow the local pro-Parthian dynast and then his grandson, Ardashir, after defeating his brother for control of Persis, stepped into the struggle between Vologaeses and Artabanus to make it a three-way contest for the title of King of Kings. Of similar Aryan stock to their Parthian overlords, these Sassanids claimed descent from the Achaemenids. While there is no evidence of a direct familial connection, their shared Persian homeland and similar language – the Latinised form of Ardashir was 'Artaxerxes,' a name used by three Achaemenid Kings – suggests that it would not be a big leap for the Sassanids to be descended from a group of Achaemenid Persians who resisted the infusion of Hellenism that accompanied the conquests of Alexander the Great.[3]

The specific dates of Ardashir's rise to power are difficult to nail down but it would seem that by the Roman invasion of 216, Persis had achieved some form of independence from the Parthian state and Ardashir was making a start in using his superior charisma and charm to bring other subkingdoms over to his side. This rebel alliance then attacked and defeated the Parthians on three occasions, with the decisive victory and death of Artabanus V coming at Hormizdagan in around 224. While there were still other petty kingdoms to subdue and another Parthian king at large, the result of Hormizdagan was clear: Ardashir was now the most powerful man on the Iranian plateau.[4]

The subjugation of the Parthians and expansion into Bahrain and the Kushan Empire to the east enabled Ardashir and his son, Shapur I, to mould their army into a considerable fighting force, not just through additional recruits from the vast array of conquered peoples but through the experience gained on various battlefields and terrains.[5] The lack of reliable testimony makes gauging the size of the Sassanid military at almost any stage during its first three centuries difficult, although their ability to hold their own against the Romans suggests that they could raise significant forces and as will be seen, a successful king like Shapur II could bring together large enough armies to defeat vast Roman armies, capture well defended cities and endure enormous casualties without breaking up.

There is also limited information about the make-up of the Sassanid force, although what has survived does suggest that it resembled the traditional Iranian force of the Achaemenids and the Parthians. Commanded by the King of Kings, a member of the royal family or a leading noble, the backbone of the armies of both Shapur I and Shapur II was heavily armoured aristocratic cavalry. While armed with a variety of weaponry for different attacks – swords, axes or clubs for a melee or pursuit, lances for a shock charge or armour piercing, reflex composite bows at range[6] – both man and horse would also be encased in mail or scale armour.[7] This is reflected in the names given to such heavy cavalry. The Graeco-Romans knew them either as cataphracts, meaning 'covered over,' or *clibanarii*, which was either a derivation from the Persian *grivpan*, meaning 'warrior' or the Latin name for a field oven, *clibanus*, in a joking reference to how these troopers must have sweltered in the desert heat.

From amongst these walking ovens were chosen an elite corps of bodyguards, the Immortals, a throwback to the Achaemenid Persian unit that broke against the Spartans at Thermopylae.

This heavy cavalry was supplemented by lighter cavalry raised from the minor nobility and the numerous peoples that inhabited and surrounded the Persian Empire: Arabs, Kushans, Chionitae and Armenians. Most of these were light-armed skirmishers armed with javelins and bows and would be deployed to harass an enemy formation with a shower of arrows but rarely to engage in melee fighting as their lack of substantial armour made them vulnerable. Another armoured beast in the Persian ranks was the elephant corps, capable of inspiring "almost unbearable fear [in men, while their] noise, smell and strange appearance terrified horses even more".[8] While these mammoths could provide a decisive strike, they also provided a threat to their own side should they be shocked or injured enough to run amok. For this eventuality, the elephant rider was prepared to kill his mount by driving a blade or stake into the beast's neck.

Despite the importance of its mounted forces, the vast majority of the Sassanid army was made up of infantry. Sassanid archers, protected by long, curved shields of wickerwork and hide and armed with composite bows, were held in high regard, although the peasant levies of light armed troops were a source of ridicule, being of limited use on the battlefield and were therefore relegated to guard duty.[9] However, it was the deployment of such infantry in siege works that was to provide the Romans with perhaps the biggest shock from this new Persian army. Unlike the Parthians, the Sassanids proved proficient in capturing even the largest of well-defended settlements, perhaps learning the techniques of siege craft from Roman prisoners of war.[10]

That there were enough prisoners of war to provide the Sassanids with a technological boost is due to their successes on the battlefield throughout the mid-third century. In overthrowing the Parthians, Ardashir had not just assumed control of their territories but also their economic, social, cultural and foreign policies; many of which could not be overturned so ingrained were they in Iranian customs. But most importantly, this Parthian legacy gave Ardashir and his successors the role of challenging Roman superiority in the Middle East and as a new, confident empire, Sassanid Persia was not going to shirk that responsibility. For so long Roman emperors had seen the lands of Iran and Mesopotamia as a target for glory. Now, the rulers of those lands began to view the Roman territories in Syria with equal relish.

As soon as the last Arsacid king had been dispatched, Ardashir was leading raids into Roman Mesopotamia, Syria and Armenia in 230, seemingly demanding the cession of all territories that had once belonged to the

Achaemenids, a rallying cry that the Sassanids would use for propaganda purposes rather than any real thoughts of reclaiming so much territory. The Roman response to this new threat suffered from ill-discipline and over-confidence, although was successful in forcing Ardashir back.[11] This kind of back and forth would characterise the first generation of Romano-Persian warfare. Arashir's second invasion in 238–240 saw him conquer cities such as Hatra, Carrhae and Nisibis only for the Romans to recapture them after the victory of Timesitheus over Shapur I at Resaena in 243. However, any thoughts that such a victory would lead to the easy capture of Ctesiphon, which had become almost customary in the second century, were expunged the following year when the Romans were defeated at Misiche.[12]

The treaty that followed Misiche held for the best part of a decade, but instead of taking advantage of this interim to firm up their eastern defences, the Romans descended further into chaotic in-fighting in the face of Germanic invasions. When Shapur I launched his next invasion, he won a stunning victory at Barbalissus in 253, annihilating a large part of a 60,000 strong Roman army, opening the Roman east to Persian depredations. Armenia and its king fell to Shapur; the frontier city Dura-Europus was destroyed after a brutal siege in 256; Antioch was sacked twice in seven years and dozens of other cities and settlements faced a similar fate. It was not until a second Persian invasion in 260 that the Romans were able to get another large army into the field and it was to meet with even greater catastrophe. Between Edessa and Carrhae, this huge Roman force of up to 70,000 was defeated by Shapur and the Roman emperor, Valerian, was taken prisoner with thousands of others to live out his days as a stool for Shapur to mount his horse before being skinned and stuffed after his death, to serve as a warning to the Romans.[13]

Despite these extensive victories, Shapur's attempts to make such gains permanent were frustrated by the remaining Roman forces under Ballista and the growing power of Septimius Odenathus, the ruler of the caravan emporium of Palmyra. The combination of a holding action in the Taurus Mountains by the former and an attack by the latter saw Palmyrene forces camp outside Ctesiphon and was enough to reverse many of the gains made by Shapur during the 250s.[14] After such a dramatic decade, the Romano-Persian border was quiet during the 260s and 270s, with both sides dealing with internal problems: the Sassanids with the deaths of Shapur and his sons Hormizd I and Bahram I within four years and the Romans with secession in both the east and west of their empire, as well as continued Germanic incursions along the Danube. The closest hostilities came to breaking out again was in 273 when the emperor Aurelian moved against Palmyra, which had expanded to take control of Syria and Egypt, and its queen Zenobia asked Bahram I for aid. The Persian king sent a force, which may have fought against the emperor, but with the dissolution of the Palmyrene Empire, emperor and king were happy to accept a continuation of the peace.[15]

That peace prevailed until Narseh's attack in 295, only punctuated by the aforementioned opportunistic sack of Ctesiphon by Carus in 283 and a brief stand off over Armenia in 286–287.[16] By the time Narseh launched his attack, the Roman Empire was in a much better state and when the dust had settled, Galerius had made amends for his humbling at Carrhae with victory at Satala and Ctesiphon. The terms of the Peace of Nisibis then re-established Roman superiority in the east and would hold for the next forty years.

Crowned *in utero*: The Rise of Shapur II and Religious Conflict

That this Peace of Nisibis held for so long is surprising. The Sassanids were unhappy with the loss of territory and influence that it entailed while the expectation might be that the multiplication of *Augusti* or *Caesares* with the Tetrarchy would have increased the chances of the Romans looking to build further on their dominant position. However, the internal distractions of both parties put war in Mesopotamia on the back burner. While the Tetrarchy collapsed under the weight of its second generation, the Persian court was rocked again by short-lived reigns and the jostling for power of the nobility and priesthood.

Broken by his humiliations at the hands of Galerius on the battlefield and Diocletian at the negotiating table, the reign of Narseh came to an end in 302. He was succeeded by his son Hormizd II, who in turn was killed in 309 fighting against Arab raiders. The Persian nobility and priesthood took this opportunity to increase their hold over the throne by not just murdering the new king, Adhur-Narseh, but also neutralising several of his family, including blinding an unnamed brother and imprisoning a second brother, Hormisdas, who managed to escape and flee into exile at Constantinople.[17] The nobles and priests were then free to choose their own successor to the Persian throne. Their choice was to be a good one as Shapur II was to go down as one of the best Sassanid kings, providing a long period of stability and success. However, their timing was off. When he was proclaimed King of Kings in 309, Shapur II was not yet a man. He was not yet a boy. He had not even been born yet! In what must have been a bizarre scene, a crown was placed upon his mother's belly, leading to the suggestion that Shapur was the only king in history to be crowned *in utero*. That the Persian state could afford to crown Shapur while he was still in his mother's womb and then survive his long minority suggests that early fourth century Persia was more stable than the series of short-lived kings might otherwise suggest.[18] That said, it must have been considered too risky to take advantage of the in-fighting that marred the end of the Tetrarchy, leading to the Peace of Nisibis holding through the first three decades of the fourth century.

While the Romano-Persian frontier was quiet through these years, there were important religious developments taking place, which were to affect the political landscape in the fourth century. As with their Achaemenid and Parthian predecessors, the Sassanids were Zoroastrians, which was centred on the dualism of good and evil and striking a balance between these two aspects of the supreme deity, Ahura Mazda. However, by the time of the Parthians, something more apocalyptic had developed with good and evil now in a struggle for supremacy with the world as their battleground. Man was seen as the only being capable of choice and could therefore influence the final battle. Due to such teachings of "individual judgment, Heaven and Hell, the future resurrection of the body, the general Last Judgment, and life everlasting for the reunited soul and body"[19] becoming integral parts of the Abrahamic religions of Judaism, Christianity and Islam, Zoroastrianism may have had "more influence on mankind, directly and indirectly, than any other single faith".[20]

The position of Zoroastrianism was augmented by its close association with the Sassanid family. Sasan, Papak and Ardashir had all held some position within the priesthood and used those connections to jump-start their overthrow of the Parthians. Therefore, once in power, the Sassanids took special care to associate their regime with Zoroastrianism, basing much of their legitimacy on a divine right to rule through their "propitious relationship with the gods".[21] However, Zoroastrianism was far more than a religion in Sassanid Persia; its ethics provided the legal framework of the empire, meaning that the clergy were not only responsible for its religious well-being but also the dispensing of justice. This made the priesthood a powerful entity, more than capable of challenging the influence of the military classes. While the strength of these two power blocks could be beneficial for the Persians, it also represented one of their greatest weaknesses as these military and priestly nobilities were continually at each other's throats, trying to impose their own supremacy. Only the most skilful and powerful of the Sassanid kings could impose his will on both parties.

While Zoroastrianism was the dominant faith in Sassanid Persia, there were numerous religious minorities within its borders; Jews, Buddhists, Hindus, Nazarenes and Manicheans are all mentioned but the most important for the outbreak of Romano-Persian war in the fourth century were Christians. There had long been a Christian presence in Iran and in the main the Sassanids tolerated such minorities, going as far to integrate them into their tax and trade systems.[22] The successes of Shapur I and sporadic Roman persecutions increased the numbers of Christians in Persian territory through prisoners of war and fugitives, who brought with them new techniques in siege craft, textiles, craftwork, medicine and building works, with the dam bridge at Shushtar and the city of Bishapur built by such captives.[23] Despite their religious tolerance, by the 330s, this growing Christian community raised some concern in Persia as a potential 'fifth column' prepared to undermine the Sassanid state by passing information to the Romans or aiding any incursion.[24] The brief persecution of Persian Christians by Bahram II,[25] decades before the conversion of Constantine, could also have been seen as an avenue for Christian Roman emperors to create divisions within the Persian state and even use it as a pretext for war.

The growth of Christianity in the east and its influence on Romano–Persian relations was further demonstrated by the conversion of the Armenian king, Tiridates III, by St. Gregory the Illuminator in 301. This added yet another aspect to the already complex position of Armenia between Rome and Persia. The expulsion of the Arsacids from Iran had seen their survivors establish themselves as the royal family of Armenia making the buffer state a more natural enemy of the Sassanids, a position only reinforced by the Peace of Nisibis, which forced the recognition of Armenia as a Roman vassal. The conversion of Tiridates when coupled with the subsequent conversion of Constantine cemented Armenia's position as a pro-Roman state. However, these conversions also bolstered support for the Sassanids as a significant portion of the Armenian population remained Zoroastrian and should they think themselves under any sort of pressure to follow the conversion of their king, they would find a willing ally in the Sassanid court, who remained committed to overturning the Peace of Nisibis.[26]

Outbreak: The Battle of Narasara and the First Siege of Nisibis

While the death of Hormizd II in 309 and then the extended minority of Shapur II meant that there was no immediate move to capitalise on any growing political and religious insecurity in Armenia, the situation continued to deteriorate throughout the 310s and 320s. Fresh from his conversion and final unification of the empire in 324, Constantine appeared to be in no mood to accept any challenge to his divinely ordained authority. A letter to Shapur from Constantine shows the Roman emperor in a pious but aggressive light as he proclaimed himself as God's temporal representative and the protector of all Christians, even those in Persia.[27] This letter is likely fictional or at least its

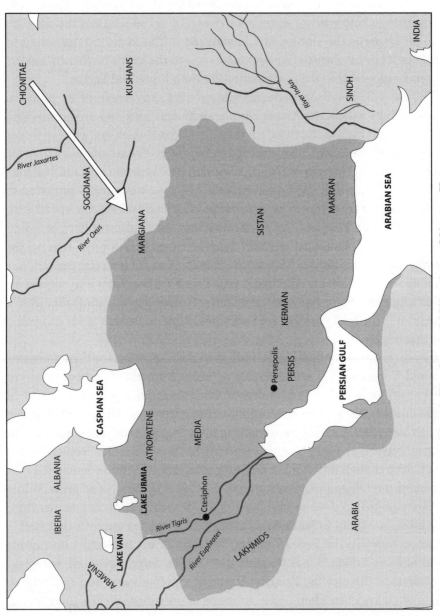

Map 4: The Sassanid Kingdom of Shapur II

exact contents are but could reflect the religious dimension of Constantine's justification for aggression towards the Persians. By the time of this letter, Shapur had entered his seniority and was himself fresh from avenging the death of his father with a defeat of a combination of Arab tribes. Buoyed, the young Persian king was not going to be cowed by veiled religious threats even from an emperor the stature of Constantine.[28] The reported poisoning of Tiridates III by his Zoroastrian opponents upped the stakes further by leaving Armenia vulnerable to the machinations of both Rome and Persia.[29]

The early 330s on the eastern frontier were characterised by political manoeuvrings within the Armenian hierarchy and back and forth raids into the territory of each of the three participants. Both Roman and Persian forces were gradually mobilised during this period for when Constantine signalled his intentions towards his eastern frontier with his proclamation of Hannibalianus as "King of Kings and the Pontic Peoples," Shapur was already prepared to retaliate against what he saw as a declaration of war. Indeed, the speed with which the young Persian king put armies into the field capable of invading both Roman and Armenian territory has been suggested as proof that he was the instigator of Constantine's eastern preparations.[30] However, the military build up was likely mutual and had reached such a point that it only required a single action to trigger war, and Constantine's elevation of Hannibalianus to a somewhat ill-defined position, making some claim on Persian lands and titles, was that trigger.[31]

Part of that military build up had involved the dispatch of the then nineteen-year-old Constantius II and Ablabius to Antioch to take initial command of the war effort in 335.[32] Any thoughts that Constantine might have had of Constantius being a place-holding figurehead were quickly dispelled as the young *Caesar* and Ablabius were confronted by the rapid advance of the Persian general, Narses, possibly Shapur's younger brother. That this Sassanid force struck deep enough into Roman territory as to capture Amida demanded that Constantius retaliate and he was soon in the field at the head of an army. While the Romans suffered some initial setbacks, probably in cavalry skirmishes, they brought Narses to battle at a place called Narasara and inflicted such a defeat on him that the Persian general lay dead on the field and Constantius could reclaim Amida.[33] It is possible that Narses' force was small, launched by Shapur to distract the Romans from their preparations and the Persian king's offensives elsewhere, only to make opportunistic, even unexpected gains in the face of limited resistance. Around the same time as Constantius was dealing with Narses or perhaps somewhat earlier, the Persians had also invaded Armenia, which was successful enough for Shapur to set up Arsaces II as King of Armenia, after capturing the previous king.[34] Nevertheless, this should not detract from how in his first campaign in command, Constantius had defended northern Mesopotamia and defeated and killed a Persian general.

It was in the aftermath of this victory at Narasara that Constantius and Ablabius received word of Constantine's final illness and the *Caesar* left the eastern front. By the time he returned to Antioch in the winter of 337/338,[35] Constantius had massacred a large part of his family and had his authority as *Augustus* over the eastern provinces and Thrace confirmed. However, while this was a step up politically, the six months away from the east had damaged Constantius' position both personally and militarily. The imperial purge had opened him to character assassination and while the murders provided him with Thracian resources and prevented him from having to share the eastern frontier with Hannibalianus, Constantius was left fighting Shapur with the resources of only a third of the empire. The break up of his father's massive field army meant that there was to be no large scale reinforcement of the eastern provinces as Constantine II and Constans retreated to their territories to deal with their own local and personal problems. Indeed, that Constantine II would later think that marching east to help Constantius would be enough of a pretext to enter the territory of Constans in 340 could suggest that Constantius had been asking for assistance or that it was obvious he would need it to defeat Shapur.

Constantius and his advisers recognised the potential manpower and resource problems in the east even before the death of Constantine and made a conscious effort to reorganise the defences of Mesopotamia. Amida was expanded in size and strength with vast circuit walls, large defensive towers, numerous artillery batteries and an extensive armoury, seeing it become a bastion against future Persian attacks and a safe haven for local populations.[36] A further stronghold was built at a place called Antinopolis and when brought together with already existing fortresses and heavily defended cities of varying size, such as Reman, Busan, Singara and Nisibis, it would seem that Constantius was already instituting a shift in Roman defensive policies in the east.[37] He would have reason to test this seeming "preference for achieving results without unnecessary expenditure of manpower"[38] as soon as he returned to the east in late 337 for Shapur had launched another attack on Roman Mesopotamia and was camped before the walls of Nisibis.

Situated at the foot of the Tur Abdin hills in what is now the Mardin province of Turkey on the border of Syria, Nisibis occupied an important position along the routes across northern Mesopotamia and was the only site where official Romano–Persian trade could take place. Such a position meant that the city was one that the Persians knew well.[39] Since its initial conquest by the Romans in 165 through numerous changes of ownership throughout the third century until the Peace of Nisibis, the city had elevated to "the strongest bulwark in the east";[40] a reputation that it would earn and justify over the next thirteen years. Under the reorganisations of Diocletian, Nisibis became the capital of Mesopotamia Provincia, which ran from the Tigris to the Khabur and the headquarters of the *dux Mesopotamia*, a forward base for the *magister militum per Orientem* and in all likelihood the seat of the provincial governor.[41]

Given the lack of archaeological survey and the paucity of visible remains, the lay out of Nisibis is unknown and is not helped by the sources, which fail even to agree on the position of the city in relation to the river Mygdonius. Some sources claim that it flowed alongside the city and others that it ran through the city. It is possible that these sources record different stages in the development of Nisibis with it growing to establish a foothold on the far bank of the Mygdonius in the form of poor suburban and temporary buildings.[42] However, it is with the position of the Mygdonius that a major problem with one of the more extensive sources for the sieges of Nisibis emerges: the Christian theologian, bishop and writer, Theodoret. Not only does he give conflicting information about the Mygdonius flowing through or past Nisibis depending on which of his works is consulted, Theodoret has either conflated the first and third sieges of Nisibis into a single account or has failed to provide enough of an indication about which siege he is commenting on. This presents difficulty in ascribing many of the actions he records to either 338 or 350 with any certainty.[43] Furthermore, without Theodoret's account to ascribe to 338, the record this first siege of Nisibis is largely blank.

While information about the defences and dispositions of Roman Mesopotamia is scant, it would be logical to assume given its importance, its position opposite Rome's greatest enemy and its subsequent resistance to Shapur that Nisibis contained a sizeable garrison. In later years, there are several legions recorded in Mesopotamia stationed at cities and fortresses such as Amida, Singara and Bezabde so Nisibis probably had at least one legion defending its walls, with support from *auxilia* or local, indigenous units.[44] Those sources that survive regarding this first siege of Nisibis would suggest that the most important part of the Roman defences in the city was not its garrison or the strength of the walls and towers but a certain Jacob, the first recorded bishop of the city. These fanciful tales regarding Jacob mean that the record of the siege must be treated with even greater care. While the bishop may have played a role in bolstering the city's morale through his displays of piety, prayer and courage, the attempts to attribute the survival of Nisibis to him is going too far.

Against whatever garrison forces Nisibis had, Shapur came with a vast force of infantry, cavalry and elephants; a force that included a number of

Armenians.[45] Having likely asked the city to surrender and received a negative reply, the Persian king will have set about surrounding Nisibis and placing a wide array of siege engines: likely towers, palisades, embankments, catapults, *ballistae*, battering rams and sappers to undermine the walls. Numerous attempts will have been made over the course of two months but all met with failure in the face of what must have been desperate defence from the men on, and perhaps under the walls, whether they were inspired by Jacob's exhortations or not.[46] Disconcerted by this failure and seeing his army weakened through casualties, tiredness and even disease, rumours of Constantius' return to the eastern theatre at the head of part of his father's field army induced Shapur to cut his losses and retreat from Nisibis.[47] This successful repelling of the Persians by Nisibis provided further proof to Constantius that strong fixed point defences could blunt the aggressive moves of the Persian king and make up his shortages in military resources.

Constantius was also confronted with the growing mess in Armenia. The Persian puppet, Arsaces II, had proven more popular with the Armenian people than the pro-Roman/anti-Persian factions. In keeping with his growing unwillingness to risk resources and demonstrating his burgeoning shrewdness in political matters, instead of looking to bully Arsaces into a Roman alliance through threats and violence, Constantius lavished gifts and offered pardons to any who had taken up arms against the Romans in return for Arsaces and Armenia defecting to the Roman side. This political gambit was a complete success. There can be no doubt that Constantius' bargaining position was aided by Shapur's failure to take Nisibis as well as rumours of Shapur's ill-treatment of the members of the Arsacid family who had fallen into his hands. In taking advantage of that, the emperor had scored a considerable diplomatic and strategic victory as Arsaces would remain a valuable ally for the remainder of Constantius' reign.[48]

As Constantius gained a new ally, he disposed of another. Having perhaps rankled under the guardianship and advice of Ablabius, now that he was established as *Augustus* and out from under his father's shadow, Constantius dismissed the praetorian prefect from the imperial court. Ablabius retired to his estates in Bithynia but was soon followed by accusations of ambitions for the imperial throne, drawing upon rumours of a prophecy stated by his mother at the time of his birth. Tricked or coerced into acting upon these accusations, Ablabius was executed.[49] It is possible that this was one of the first examples of Constantius being willing to believe the worst of even close associates when it came to the imperial throne; a trait that would be further exposed or exaggerated by Ammianus Marcellinus in years to come. However, any involvement of Ablabius in the machinations surrounding the succession in the last years of Constantine's reign may also have played a significant role in Constantius first neutralising and then ridding himself of a significant political threat.

Unpopular Success: The Battle(s) of Singara

The same source problems that plague the record for Constantius' first forays into the eastern theatre persist for the next fifteen years. Until the surviving books of Ammianus pick up the narrative in late 353, the period between the deaths of Constantine and Magnentius is dimly illuminated by exaggerated Christian works or fawning panegyrics. That said, there is sufficient information from historiographic, legal and archaeological sources to build an outline of Constantius' movements during this period, which suggests that he rarely left the eastern frontier in the thirteen years after the Pannonian conference in 337. He established his imperial court at Antioch and spent several extended periods of time there, although both Hierapolis and Edessa were visited on several occasions, suggesting that these strategic positions were where Constantius stationed concentrations of his field forces and perhaps where he commanded his forces from when he was not leading them in person.[50]

Worried by the rapid successes of Narses and Shapur in 335–338, Constantius set about maximising the revenue his lands produced and training his forces to high levels of "endurance, energy, and military experience".[51] The most overt change that Constantius implemented was the development of a heavy cavalry arm to deal with the excellent Persian cataphracts. Bringing the Armenian king back into his camp paid dividends here as the Armenians produced hardy cavalry as well as archers.[52] Satisfied with these improvements, Constantius was eager to test his army in the field; however, following their ejection from Armenia and Mesopotamia, the Persians were far less eager to take the field again, resorting instead to raids. From his bases at Hierapolis and Edessa, Constantius responded by sending his own raiding parties across the Tigris. Such mutual raids likely became the predominant form of warfare throughout the early 340s, although on one such raid, Roman forces are said to have captured a Persian city. The identity of this city is not recorded but as there were few major settlements within striking distance of the Middle Tigris, it has been suggested that this 'city' was instead the ancient ruins of Nineveh and that the capture of this "important city of Adiabene"[53] and the raids were the origin of Constantius' victory title of *Adiabenicus Maximus*.[54]

The mess of the historical sources for the 340s is perhaps best seen in the account of the Battle of Singara. Not even the date of this, the biggest confrontation between Constantius and Shapur, is certain, with 343, 344 and 348 all mentioned. Indeed, it has been suggested that there were two separate battles at Singara in the 340s, perhaps even with different names, Singara and Hileia.[55] Despite this, it is possible to reproduce something of an outline of battle, if not when or where it took place. In response to Constantius' raids across the Tigris, Shapur gathered a significant force for a strike into Mesopotamia, possibly aiming to capture Singara. Informed of this attack, Constantius ordered his frontier forces not to engage the Persian column and perhaps to congregate at a rendezvous point as the emperor marched his field army to intercept Shapur. This might look like Constantius abandoning his growing reliance on city defences in favour of a tilt at military glory but perhaps the emperor felt it necessary to protect Singara or that he was yet to fully commit to a more low-intensity defensive system. Perhaps it was the outcome of Singara that was to encourage him to do so.

The Persians seemingly reached Singara and even breached one of its round towers before Constantius and his army arrived on the scene. Aelianus, the future commander at Amida, is recorded leading a successful sally of the *Praeventores* and the *Superventores* from Singara against Sassanid forces at an earlier siege,[56] although it is difficult to give a definitive date to these events. Bloodied by the Singaran garrison and now aware of Constantius' approach, Shapur fell back from his siege works, although he did not retreat completely. Instead, the Persian king took up a defensive position and had fortifications built and placed archers and javelinmen in the surrounding high ground to cover the core of his army, which was deployed in front of the defences.

Given these deployments, it seems that the Persian king's plan was to force Constantius into an uphill attack against the crossfire of his archers and the charge of his cataphracts. To further induce such an attack, Shapur sent a detachment against the Roman position. With the Romans committed to action in order to repel this initial attack, the Persian detachment broke off and retreated back towards their camp, their opponent in pursuit. It must be noted that Constantius would not have taken this decision to advance lightly for it would appear that not only had Shapur had time to pick and fortify his position, there was a distance of between eleven and seventeen miles between the armies when Constantius' men began their pursuit. This would account for the approach of nightfall by the time the Romans reached the Persian position despite having taken the field before noon.[57]

If he had not already, faced with the fortified Persian position, Constantius will have recognised the role that the Persian bait division was attempting to play and managed to keep control of his men. However, frustrated at being held back after hours of pursuit and having their blood up, the soldiers proved immune to the sensible orders of their emperor and launched themselves uphill at the entrenched Persians. This rash, foolhardy attack was successful as the Romans brushed aside the Persian infantry and even the cataphracts to burst through the wall, wreaking havoc in the camp and killing Shapur's heir along with his entire escort.[58] But then, when it looked like the Persians were about to rout, the reasons for Constantius' reticence in attacking were proven correct. The combination of a long day's march, with its incumbent thirst and tiredness, the uphill struggle, the Persian defences, the covering fire from the archers and the growing darkness began to tell as the Roman attack lost coherence and organisation, allowing Shapur to snatch a bloody draw with a nocturnal counterattack.[59]

The casualties and unpredictability of battle near Singara may have had an effect on Constantius, encouraging him to shy away from such encounters and rely more on strong, hard point fortifications in the future. Of course, this perspective on Constantius' employment of overall strategy changes somewhat depending on when this encounter with Shapur took place. If it was in 343/344, then the draw at Singara and all it encompassed may have played a significant role in encouraging Constantius' reliance on walled cities and forts. If in 348, Constantius is likely to have already established his eastern strategy on a wide scale only to allow himself to be swayed onto the offensive by the need to save Singara and perhaps the criticism he was receiving for having employed a low-intensity, almost passive defence against Rome's greatest foe. Whatever the timeline of its establishment and regardless of whether or not Constantius could point to its success, it is clear that Constantius' overall strategy in the east was unpopular; it was un-Roman in its defensiveness.[60] But then what else could he do? From 337 to 353, Constantius had to face down the most bellicose and skilled of Persian kings with what amounted to a third of the Empire's resources and little help from his brothers.

Diverting Shapur's energies into expensive and unproductive sieges was the best way to make use of his meagre resources. Furthermore, eastern warfare had often been as defensive as it was offensive and the use of cities and forts in a frontier system was not a new development.[61] And yet with so little room for offence, Constantius still managed to raid across the Tigris on numerous occasions while his forces fought up to nine major battles with those of Shapur. And while not always successful on the battlefield, Constantius took the best that the Persian kingdom could offer without incurring any decisive losses of territory or manpower. His immediate successor would not be so successful when abandoning this more defensive approach.[62]

Amongst the proposed dates for the Battle of Singara, Shapur also launched another attack on Nisibis in 346; unfortunately, the sources for this second siege are scant even by the wretched standards of the 340s. In something of an ironic turn from Singara, all that is known about the Second Siege of Nisibis is its date and that it held out for seventy-eight days before Shapur again cut his losses. This second Persian failure could be used as more evidence that Constantius' system was working and it may well be pertinent that Constantius visited Nisibis the previous summer. Perhaps he made a survey of the defences to make sure any damage done in 338 had been repaired or even made moves to strengthen those defences and the garrison. Constantius may well have been impressed enough by the Nisibean garrison and its defences to believe that it would hold out against another Persian attack without him having to come to its aid in 346 or 350.[63]

It must be pointed out though that Constantius was far from an absentee commander. While he may not have been at the very forefront of military activity such as Nisibis or Singara for extended periods of time, when he was not at Antioch, he is recorded at his forward bases of Edessa and Hierapolis on several occasions. Indeed, from his return to the eastern theatre in mid 338, there is evidence for him leaving Syria/Mesopotamia on only three occasions before 350: a brief visit to Constantinople in early 342 to remove the usurping bishop Paul, a proposed return to the imperial capital in October/November 343 to celebrate his *vicennalia* and he is recorded at Ancyra in 8 March 347.[64] And yet, despite his successes in maintaining control of Roman Mesopotamia without risking large casualties and in recruiting Armenians, Goths, Arabs and others,[65] the perception remained negative. There can be no denying that by making no real attempt to relieve Nisibis on two occasions and rarely challenging the Persians in the field Constantius had damaged his reputation by 350. However, before that year was out, the emperor was to have another opportunity to right the 'wrongs' of 338 and 346 for Shapur was about to confront his bête noire once more.

Third Time's the Charm? Shapur II's Third Siege of Nisibis

The third siege of Nisibis is illuminated by more sources than either of the previous Persian attempts on the city. However, despite being more numerous, these sources remain problematic, whether it is the aforementioned contradictions and possible conflations of Theodoret, the religious poetry of Ephraem, an eye-witness to the siege, the non-contemporary accounts of the *Chronicon Paschale* and Zonaras or the panegyric of Julian, which "does not give a full and coherent narrative".[66] None of these sources give any indication of the strength of either the Persian attackers or the Nisibean defenders. The best that can be done is to comment again that Shapur brought numerous infantry, archers, cavalry, elephants and siege engines to bear against the legionaries, *auxilia* and local units holed up within Nisibis; the only addition is the recording of the identity of the garrison commander, with this Lucillianus being either *dux Mesopotamiae* or *comes rei militaris* and the future father-in-law of the emperor Jovian.[67]

With the defence of the city left in the hands of Lucillianus, this hints that Constantius had no real intention to make good on his 'wrongs' of 338 and 346 and had not made any move to place one of his senior commanders such as the *magister equitum per Orientem*, Ursicinus in command. However, while Ephraem complained about the emperor's absence from Nisibis, the majority of the sources recognised that developments in Europe in early 350 more than explain not only Constantius' absence at Nisibis but also his unwillingness to send a relief force. Despite him making preparations to march west to confront the murderers of his brother, it should also be noted that Constantius chose to stay in the east until the siege of Nisibis ended, not arriving in Europe until the last fortnight of 350. His exact whereabouts are not known during the siege but he is recorded at Edessa and Antioch during 350, marshalling troops for his inevitable advance against Magnentius, although his remaining in the east until the winter may also suggest that he was prepared to march against Shapur should the Persian king be successful at Nisibis.[68]

Shapur invaded Mesopotamia in early spring, which would seem to preclude any suggestion that word of Magnentius' usurpation had played a role in his plans for 350, as he would need more than a few weeks to organise and bring together the vast army he would take against Nisibis. The usurpation of Magnentius and its incumbent distraction for Constantius should therefore be seen as a useful addendum to Shapur's attack rather than a vital part of the initial planning.[69] Arriving before Nisibis once more, Shapur again approached the garrison with an offer to capitulate and having again been rebuffed, he initiated the investiture of the city, perhaps becoming aware of the situation in Europe and the likelihood that Constantius was not going to make a move to relieve Nisibis. The eventual length of time that Shapur stayed before Nisibis – recorded as either one hundred days or four months[70] – may also show that the Persian king recognised that time was on his side.

Having surrounded the city in ditches, palisades, camps and earthworks, Shapur had his siege engines and artillery brought to bear against Nisibis, as well as sending sappers to undermine the walls in a "battle under the earth".[71] All of these attempts to capture the city through conventional measures once again failed as Lucillianus and his men demonstrated the strength of Roman arms and the defences of Nisibis. Shapur then looked at more inventive ways of undermining the walls, ordering his men to dam the Mygdonius. It is here that attention must return to the problems with the dating of Theodoret. Even if he was conflating his accounts, any of Theodoret's information on the Persian preparations in 338 could mirror that of 350 considering it will have likely been a similar lay out. Indeed, if the record of Shapur's redirecting the Mygdonius belongs in 338, that does not preclude a similar episode in 350. After all, the plan had been shown to work as the river brought down part of the walls so there is some expectation that Shapur could attempt it again.[72] However, given the weight of the sources talking about the use of the Mygdonius in 350 – Ephraem alone references the 'flood' twenty-three times –[73] Theodoret's account probably belongs to the siege of 350.

Shapur may have initially diverted the river to deprive Nisibis of water but when he learned that there were springs within the city, the Persian king then unleashed the river against the walls. This seems the plausible progression but it would include two redirections of the river and the building of a dam in a short period of time, although it is far from the most spectacular feat of engineering attributed to the siege.[74] Julian takes the story of Shapur's manipulation of the Mygdonius to a whole new level of incredulity by stating that the earthwork mounds doubled as dykes to let the river form "a lake with Nisibis standing in its midst as an island",[75] allowing for ships bearing siege towers to sail right up to the walls. While such an ambitious project would highlight Shapur's increasing desperation to take the city that had already foiled him twice, this is Julian presenting the siege as an epic fit for the lines of Homer rather than factual history. A Christian writer such as Ephraem or Theodoret would have incorporated references to biblical events such as Noah and the Ark in the face of such a spectacle, especially given the miraculous salvation of Nisibis.[76]

Ignoring Julian's dykes and lake building, it still seems from the sources that having strengthened its banks and allowed the waters to build up behind the dam, the release of the Mydonius was a watery battering ram smashing into the city walls. Such a harnessing of the power of a river to knock down walls would seem beyond not just the time available to Shapur but also classical technology. However, the exaggeration of the sources does not mean that the whole episode should be discarded. Manipulation of rivers was not a new concept and as will be seen later, men in the service of Julian would redirect a river and use floating siege towers at the Siege of Aquileia in 361. Furthermore, a drop of only a few feet in the level of the river and then surge may have been enough to undermine the dry, sandy ground that Nisibis was built upon and thereby cause a collapse in the masonry. It is therefore feasible that a manipulation of the waters of the Mygdonius took place, just not on the epic scale recorded.[77]

With the collapse of a section of the walls,[78] Shapur launched everything he had at this breach but it seems that his forces were victims of their own machinations. Ditches, earthworks, fallen masonry and dead bodies made the approaches awkward enough but the footfall of thousands of men and beasts on the Mydonius-sodden ground churned it up into a muddy, bloody quagmire. There are even claims that the elephants sank into the mud after being targeted by the Nisibean artillery.[79] Another obstacle to this initial Persian assault was perhaps a makeshift wall that the defenders were able to throw up across the breach, although this would involve an unlikely delay between the collapse of the wall and Shapur's attack.[80] This makeshift wall could have been constructed during a lull in the fighting and even through the night the initial Persian attack had been repelled by the combination of mud, artillery and the sheer determination of Lucillianus and his men.

Poor weather may also have contributed to the failure of the Persian siege, which will have seemed like divine actions to the Christian sources. Other supernatural aid was claimed in the inventions of St. Jacob, who interceded with God on behalf of the city, despite having died sometime in the interim between the first and third sieges.[81] A modern audience may well scoff at such tales of divine aid but the Romans were becoming aware of "the latent ability of Christianity to act as a steadying influence on the minds of beleaguered and hard-pressed forces"[82] and while the religiosity and faith involved in such acts might be doubted, the affect is clear to see. There was another intercession on the behalf of Nisibis, which will have appeared as a sign of God's protection as Jacob's prayers were reportedly answered with an outbreak of plague in the Sassanid camp. Given the presence of so many horses, elephants and men in close quarters during the hot summer months in a region infamous for large clouds of insects, it would not be surprising if some kind of pestilence affected the Sassanid ranks at Nisibis.[83]

Beset by failure, casualties, disease, poor weather, the stubbornness of the defenders and perhaps growing reports of problems on his own eastern frontier, when confronted by the rebuilt wall, Shapur decided to cut his losses, destroying his equipment and lifting the siege. The suggestion that Constantius visited Nisibis in the wake of the siege before he headed to Europe could raise the idea that he had set out for the city before the siege had ended and that his approach had also contributed to Shapur's decision to retreat, although that is speculative. But whatever the combination of reasons, Nisibis had once again proven beyond the Persian king.[84]

There can be no mistake that "the raising of the siege represents a humiliating defeat for the Persians".[85] Despite the favourable circumstances of Constantius' distraction with Magnentius, his vast army and the massive undertaking of redirecting the Mygdonius, Shapur had once again failed to break the physical and mental will of the Nisibean garrison. This third repulse did not end Shapur's designs in Mesopotamia but it might have affected his future plans, such as implementing a fast dash to the Euphrates or bringing together far larger forces. However, as will be seen later, there were still several immense sieges to be fought between Roman garrisons and the monstrous armies of Shapur in the 350s. It should be noted though that on each occasion he crossed the Tigris in force, Shapur would not attempt to besiege Nisibis, choosing to blockade it.

As for Constantius, the retreat of the Persians from Roman territory without extensive casualties to the eastern field forces should have seen the vindication of his more low-intensity, hard point defence strategy in Mesopotamia, with even Julian praising his work in the east, given how there was a civil war on the horizon.[86] While having not defeated the Persians in the field like a good Roman emperor should, Constantius had blunted every attack Shapur had launched with few casualties not just at the muddy, mosquito-infested surroundings of Nisibis in 350 but throughout the thirteen years since his father's death in 337, with perhaps the losing control of his blood-thirsty troops at Singara the only real blemish.

But this job well done was not enough for many Romans, who could look back to the previous century and see that even when at their lowest ebb, they had brushed aside Persian forces, blitzed their way through Mesopotamia and sacked the Sassanid capital with seeming ease. For them, everything was the exact opposite. The drawn battle at Singara was the one shining light in a dark decade of hit-and-run raids, cowering in fear behind the walls of major cities and not rushing to the rescue of those Roman citizens and soldiers fighting for their lives against the Persian invaders. Regardless of its success and the freedom it gave Constantius to focus on other problems, to such people who refused to see the big picture, his strategy was a betrayal of what it meant to be Roman.

As well as the unwillingness of many Romans to recognise it as such, the potential importance of the third siege of Nisibis as vindication for Constantius and humiliation for Shapur was overshadowed by the events at either end of the known world that had encouraged both rulers to extricate themselves from Mesopotamia. Defeated by the immovable object of Nisibis, Shapur turned to find an irresistible force from the steppe of Central Asia in the form of the horsemen of the Chionitae bursting into his eastern holdings.[87] It would be the best part of ten years before the Persian king regained enough control of that situation to once again turn his attention to Mesopotamia. But even with Shapur engaged elsewhere, Constantius had little time to catch his breath for while he had been overseeing Rome's defence of her eastern extremities time had not stood still in Europe. Civil war and usurpation had seen to it that what little remained of the Constantinian family after the purge of 337 had been reduced even further, leaving Constantius as the only man in a position to continue his illustrious father's imperial legacy. Therefore, soon after visiting Nisibis, Constantius set out west from Antioch, arriving at Serdica via Heraclea in the last week of 350.[88] There was usurpers' blood to shed, a brother to avenge and an empire to reunite.

Chapter IV

Fraternal Civil War and the Usurpation of Magnentius

> Hail, king! for so thou art: behold, where stands
> The usurper's cursed head: the time is free...
> — MacDuff (William Shakespeare, *Macbeth* Act V
> Scene VIII Lines 56–57)

Brother versus Brother and the Reign of Constans

The division of the empire agreed at the Pannonian conference of late 337, Constantius headed east to deal with Shapur, while Constantine II and Constans returned to their assigned realms. The historical record for Europe over the next seventeen years is just as bad as it was for Constantius' conflict with the Persians and at times it is only possible to form the most skeletal of timelines. What is known is that while there were issues on the Rhine, Danube and Tigris frontiers, the most pressing was to come from within the imperial family itself. As the Persians invested Nisibis for the first time and the court of Constans was busy establishing its regency over the central provinces of the Empire, Constantine II grumbled over his share of their father's inheritance. Even after returning to Trier and spending the campaigning season of 338 fighting the restless Alamanni tribes of the Rhine and Upper Danube,[1] Constantine continued to maintain that a great injustice had been done to him. Such a perception will only have been heightened in the months after the Pannonian division as it became clear how little influence he had at the court of Constans.[2]

By early 339, Constantine was attempting to use one of the peculiarities of the Diocletianic provincial reorganisation to expand his sphere of influence. The westernmost province of Roman North Africa, Mauretania Tingitana, equating largely to modern Morocco, was detached from the diocese of Africa and attached to the diocese of Hispaniae and therefore as of 337 came under the purview of Constantine II, while the rest of north western Africa belonged to Constans. Using this foothold in Africa, Constantine looked to bully his way east, going as far as to issue an edict to the proconsul of Africa at Carthage in early 339.[3] Such overstepping of his boundaries shows that Constantine presumed some authority over Constans and his territories. This was met with resistance from Constans' officials, who likely informed Constantine that they were prepared to take a hard line approach to his interference. However, they must have been shocked at the drastic action that Constantine himself took in order "to assert his fragile theoretical primacy in the imperial college".[4] In late 340, Constantine led his field army into northern Italy.

The lack of information means that the exact motives of Constantine cannot be established but while he claimed to be bringing aid to Constantius, Constans and his officials were not buying it. They saw this move by Constantine for what it was: an aggressive invasion to exert authority over the territories of Constans. At the time of this attack, the youngest *Augustus* and the bulk of his army were stationed in Dacia, perhaps dealing with Sarmatians, although the speed with which his forces reacted might suggest that there was some sort of contingency in place for just such a sneak attack, with a force of battle-hardened Illyrian troops intercepting Constantine near Aquileia. The position of this engagement does not elucidate much on Constantine's true intentions. Aquileia was the starting point of several important roads linking Italy to the northern and eastern provinces, which could support either claim of marching to Constantius' aid or cutting off Constans from Italy or using the roads to march against him in Illyria, Pannonia and Dacia. As Fate would have it though, it need not have mattered much what Constantine had planned as any thoughts of a prolonged fraternal civil conflict were ended by this Aquileian ambush. Constantine II was killed by Constans' Illyrians, leaving the latter to take control of the former's territory without any real bloodshed.[5]

Constantius' reaction to this war between his brothers is not known but so distracted was he with Shapur that even if he had felt the need to challenge the new political arrangement emerging from the ambush at Aquileia, he was in no position to do so. That Constantius followed Constans' *damnatio memoriae* of their latest dead brother – "the public's enemy and our own"[6] – and did not reverse it once he later became sole *Augustus* suggests that he either cared very little about the situation or backed his younger brother against the aggression of Constantine II.[7] However, tacit agreement between the two remaining brothers could not mask the fact that in just under three years the house of Constantine had descended into internecine warfare. It would not be the last time.

The poor sources hinder the study of Constans' administration of two-thirds of the Roman Empire throughout the 340s but it appears that he relied on a small group of supporters, whom he remained loyal to even in the midst of scurrilous rumours and accusations against them. It is worth noting that for

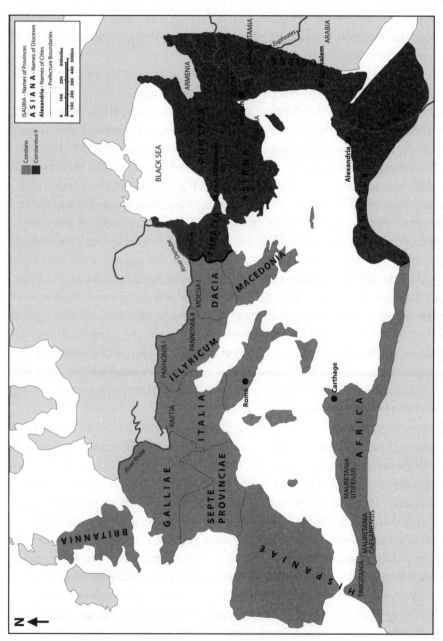

Map 5: The New Settlement 340–350

a large part of the first three years of his reign as *Augustus*, Constans was still a minor and would have been under the sway of those courtiers whom his father had positioned around him. Even when Constantine II launched his invasion, Constans was at most seventeen years old, having been born sometime in 323, so while he was now considered to be of age, he will have still taken a lot of guidance from those around him.

Such trust is seen in the extended tenures of several of his officials. Fabius Titianus, a senior administrator under Constantine, consul in 337 and grandfather of the last defenders of paganism, Quintus Aurelius Symmachus, was promoted to praetorian prefect for Gaul in 341 and perhaps served until switching his allegiance to Magnentius suspiciously easily in 350. The trust that Constans had in one Flavius Eugenius is not just shown in his service as *magister officiorum* for the majority of the 340s but also in the presence of a statue of him in the Forum of Trajan in Rome. Such long tenures "annoyed and frustrated other aspirants to high office",[8] leading to allegations of corruption, with Eugenius himself accused of being involved in corruption even though Constans stood by him.[9] The reputation of Constans' court cannot have been helped by the presence of men such as Eusebius Mattyocopa and Marcellinus. Not only does the former's nickname suggest he was a glutton – 'Mattyocopa' means 'cut of delicacies' – both of these men were involved in schemes against men of the highest rank; Eusebius plotted against the supposed usurper Silvanus while Marcellinus would instigate the plot that brought down Constans himself. That officials of extended tenure such as Titianus and Marcellinus would turn against Constans could hint that the emperor intended to remove them from their positions.[10]

There may also have been some regional feeling in the growing dislike of Constans. The emperor, "reared as a child in Constantinople and the east, may have had a personal preference for the Greek world",[11] and may have let this leak into his appointments. His first choice of newly created praetorian prefecture of Illyricum in around 345 was Anatolius of Beiruit; his choice for Roman prefect in 347 fell on Ulpius Limenius, a former proconsul of Constantinople, who was also appointed praetorian prefect of Italy and replaced on his death in 349, by another easterner, Hermogenes. Constans may have had good reason for such favouritism, but in "hoping perhaps to break the control of western elites over government posts, he had relied too much on outsiders and a small core of trusted advisers and administrators."[12] That there was some feeling of impediment to advancement in the west under Constans, through prolonged tenures and cultural favouritism, is suggested by a number of westerners travelling east to take up positions under Constantius.[13] Such willingness of the

Augusti to use officials of opposing origin might suggest a failure to recognise or care about any east-west divide within the empire.

Constans also managed to make himself unpopular at Rome. The independent urban citizenry did not take kindly to him interfering in the running of the city and its elections, even if his imposing of his own prefects was an attempt to bring order. The catalyst or at least an accelerant to that disorder may have been Constans' religious policies. Despite the Christianisation of the imperial family and the Roman Empire, the senatorial elite remained a bastion of paganism, and would do so for decades to come. Therefore, it would be no surprise if these pagan elements within the city were in uproar over not just Constans' interference in the city's elections but also his dropping of the title of *pontifex maximus* from his imperial titulature in the early 340s, reiterating a ban on sacrifice and initiating the confiscation of temple treasures.[14]

Regional favouritism may also have raised ire in the army with Gallic forces feeling that Constans showed preference towards his Danubian and *palatini* forces. As will be seen, the Danubian legions would not accept the usurpation that ousted Constans and it would not be surprising for the emperor had spent the vast majority of his life amongst his fellow Danubians, although he hardly shunned the Gallic forces. Constans visited his western provinces on several occasions, campaigning against Franks and Alamanni along the Rhine and even crossing to Britain to defend it from Pictish raiders. However, there must have been disaffection amongst some army personnel for the Gallic forces to turn against Constans in 350, with the most likely explanation being financial. Constans or his officials may have failed in their obligations to the army, either in pay, supplies or reward for the fighting they undertook in his name, which saw to it that Constans was accused of being "passionate in his greed and his contempt for the soldiers".[15] The empire was going through financial difficulties by the end of the 340s, as seen with Magnentius' early steps to raise funds through a 50 per cent property tax and debasing the coinage. The personnel involved in the plot that ousted Constans may also add credence to financial problems in the west, with Marcellinus being a prominent financial official and choosing Autun to proclaim Magnentius as *Augustus*, a city that was not a strong military centre but was home to several weapons factories, which were under the control of the finance ministers.[16]

Other allegations include Constans causing no fear amongst the barbarians and that after an energetic start, he slipped into decadence and lethargy;[17] however, both of these are disprovable. The scant descriptions of Constans do portray him in a positive military light: a warrior of tremendous strength, endurance and daring, willing to ride off with a small cadre of picked men to get to a flash point with the best possible speed, while barbarian tribes are recorded as being afraid of the very name of Constans.[18] Furthermore, the skeletal record of Constans' movements during his thirteen-year reign shows him as rarely inactive, squaring up to various barbarian tribes. After leaving the Pannonian conference in September 337, and perhaps establishing his base at Naissus, Constans began an exhausting tour of his central realm. He was in Thessalonica by the end of the year before returning north to Viminacium and Sirmium for mid 338 and perhaps then campaigning against the Sarmatians on into 339 as he is seen at Savaria, modern Szombathely in Hungary, in April of that year. The importance of such a rigorous criss-crossing of his new domain was that it galvanised support for his regime by giving the people a sight of their ruler and the soldiers a view of their paymaster.

Constans may then have spent the winter of 339/340 at Naissus before making for Dacia, presumably to deal with further barbarian raiding. It is either here or in the earlier 338/339 campaign that Constans assumed the victory title of *Sarmaticus*. It was also while in Dacia that he heard of Constantine's invasion of Italy.[19] Sending his Illyrian forces on ahead, Constans was not slow to follow, again suggesting that he was a man of action who had no problem with putting himself at risk. With his rebellious eldest brother dead and before 341 was out, Constans had moved through Aquileia, Milan, Lauriacum, modern Enns in Austria, and perhaps even Rome before moving on to Gaul. Distributing his imperial patronage here was even more important than it had been in the Balkans as the western provinces had been under the command of the now deceased and damned Constantine II since the execution of Crispus. The Gallic forces that had seen their emperor die before the walls of Aquileia needed to feel like they were not going to be left out in the cold so not only did Constans go to them in Gaul, he likely took a sizeable portion of them against the Franks in late 341/early 342. Upon settling some of these defeated barbarians in Toxandria, Constans spent part of the summer of 342 at Trier before then returning to Milan where he interviewed Athanasius, the displaced bishop of Alexandria, in the autumn.[20]

However, any thoughts of a quiet winter at Milan were quickly upset as Constans found himself at Bononia, modern Boulogne in northern France, by 25 January 343. The reason for this wintery race north is not mentioned in the sources but will have been Pictish raiders across Hadrian's Wall or perhaps even the Scots from across the Irish Sea; whatever the reason, it was troublesome enough for Constans to make a hazardous winter crossing of the Channel. Further information about this British campaign is again lacking but it would seem that Constans himself played little direct part in any fighting for he was back in Gaul before the end of spring and in Trier by 30 June, when he again met with Athanasius.[21]

As will be seen later, it was this series of meetings with the bishop of Alexandria that led to Constans acting belligerently towards Constantius over the growing religious disputes across the empire, particularly over the restoration of Paul of Constantinople and Athanasius of Alexandria to their respective sees. Why Constans would threaten civil war over such an issue is impossible to answer; was it fervent religious conviction in anti-Arianism or was he using this religious problem to make a political and military point to his elder brother that he would not be pushed around? Or was Constans perhaps looking to distract or even blackmail Constantius into giving up those recruit-rich Thracian lands that had fallen to the elder emperor at the Pannonian conference? Regardless of the reason, that Constans would go as far as to threaten civil war might suggest that he had not yet lost interest in running the empire, although it could also hint at prominent churchmen becoming important at the imperial court, further alienating the political and military elites in the west. For this game of brinkmanship, Constans had moved back to the Balkans where he was in Pannonia for the autumn of 344 before receiving an embassy from Constantius at Poetovio, modern Ptuj in Slovenia, early in 345 and then meeting with Athanasius again at Aquileia on 7 April.[22]

For the first five years of his reign over two thirds of the empire, rather than a lethargic emperor who played favourites, Constans had shown himself to be energetic and willing to traverse a large part of his domain and lead the army in campaigns against barbarians. Even now in 345, after leaving Aquileia, he again returned to the Rhine frontier, visiting Cologne and Trier, where he met Athanasius for the last time before the restoration to Alexandria, which Constans' brinkmanship towards Constantius had facilitated.[23] However, according to the surviving material, this was to be Constans' last visit to Gaul for the next five years after he returned to the central provinces of his domain.[24] And as there is no record of him leading his army in battle during this period, it is possible to see where such accusations of neglect and descent into decadence have spawned from. It must be noted though that as the record is so incomplete for Constans' reign, it is dangerous to try to associate those silences with periods of lethargy and inactivity.

Also, even though Constans is not recorded leading troops on campaign during the later half of the 340s does not mean that his forces were inactive. Indeed, to write off this period would be to overlook another example of Constans being willing to militarise religious disagreements: the Donatist dispute in Africa. Donatism was born from the Great Persecution, with Donatists being far less forgiving of those who in the face of imperial pressure had allowed their faith to lapse or handed over holy books for destruction; hence their name of *traditores*, meaning "those who handed over". Some priests and bishops had even cooperated with persecuting officials only to be restored to favour by Constantine. Donatus, bishop of Carthage,[25] and his followers proclaimed that any sacrament celebrated by such rehabilitated clergy was invalid. This saw the church in Africa split into two camps: Donatists and Catholics. Constantine and the Council of Arles in 314 had sided against the hard-line Donatists and spent the next seven years attempting to browbeat them into compliance through further laws and military pressure. This "merely succeeded in creating heroic Donatist martyrs instead of subservient new Catholics"[26] and by 321, the emperor conceded defeat and rescinded the anti-Donatist laws.[27]

For the next twenty-five years, Donatists lived alongside Catholics able to spread their message beyond Africa. However, the increasing confidence that such freedom brought was to end the extended period of state non-interference. In 346, Donatus appealed to Constans to be recognised as the senior bishop in Africa. Constans sought the counsel of his father's theological advisor, Hosius of Cordoba, and got the same advice as Constantine received: heresy is not to be tolerated and Church unity is fundamental. Therefore, following in his father's footsteps, Constans dispatched a military force under the *notarii* Paul and Macarius ostensibly to investigate the situation and help the needy on both sides but really to harass the Donatists in to accepting the decisions of Arles. This led Donatus to utter his famous rebuke to a demand for unity, "What has the church to do with the Emperor?"[28]

In such a tense atmosphere, a single spark could ignite something far more unsavoury and it came in the face of a third religious group making its presence felt in North Africa. Better known as the Circumcellions, the Agonistici sought to redress what they saw as the social imbalance of property, slavery and debt; these admirable beliefs are tempered by their extreme belief in martyrdom, which led them to seek eternal release in attacking Roman soldiers and travellers across Africa. Congregating under another Donatus, bishop of Bagai, these Agonistici awaited a delegation from Paul and Macarius under guard from soldiers provided by Sylvester, *comes Africae*, but when the delegation arrived, they attacked them and their escort. Enraged by such an attack, the soldiers returned in greater numbers, leading to a massacre at Bagai.[29] This has been seen as the beginning of a persecution of Donatists, with the forces of Paul, Macarius and Sylvester forcing those who would not renounce Donatism to take refuge in Numidia, face banishment like Donatus himself did to Gaul or martyrdom like Donatus of Bagai. This repression would continue until Julian allowed Donatist exiles to return to Africa in 362.[30] That Constans had authorised force against religious dissidents shows again that he was more than willing to use the military might of the Empire to enforce the unity of the Church and as will be seen, this was a willingness that his remaining elder brother also shared as this was not the last time that the Constantinian dynasty would be dragged into theological issues.

Unlike Constantius though, Constans' private life provided a significant amount of ridicule. He came under egregious assault from various sources for his perceived homosexuality, which was 'proven' by his failure to marry and his "unduly favouring good-looking members of his barbarian bodyguard".[31] Aurelius Victor perhaps even suggests that Constans was a paedophile, only happy in his dealings with barbarian tribes when he received the best looking boys as hostages, although the historian harboured homophobic tendencies as well as having soured on Constans after he failed to celebrate the 1100th anniversary of Rome's foundation in 348.[32]

The negative stories of Constans' reign and perceptions of his private life do not prove that he was a poor or unpopular emperor. His forces were active in virtually all parts of his realm with the emperor visiting much of it in person, which would seem to put paid to the most prominent accusations of lethargy and favouritism, while he was more than willing to threaten war for what he saw as the religious good of the empire and its church. It must be said though that there is some evidence of a slow down in Constans' activities in the second half of the 340s, although perhaps instead of lethargy, Constans was suffering from exhaustion. However, what the perceptions of Constans do suggest is that he had made enemies amongst influential people, whether it was regional army commanders, political and financial officials, the pagan senatorial elite of Rome or historians like Aurelius Victor.

Usurping the Usurper: Magnentius, Nepotianus and the Curious Case of Vetranio

Whatever the origins of the enmity towards Constans, it was enough for a plot to emerge in early 350. On 18 January, at a dinner party at Autun, Flavius Magnus Magnentius, commander of the *Herculiani* and *Ioviani* imperial guard units, was proclaimed emperor by the *comes rei privitae*, Marcellinus, and a small cadre of military and civilian supporters.[33] The selection of Magnentius as *Augustus* may also betray something of a panicked usurpation for while he was a successful general, he was not the best choice for the highest, most regal office in the land. Not only was he a common soldier, he was reportedly the son of a British father and a Frankish mother.[34] His *nomen* Flavius, which was also the family name of the Constantinian dynasty, might also suggest that his family owed their citizenship to a member of the ruling dynasty within the last half century. Such origins would normally remove a man from consideration as emperor. However, the suspicion is that Constantian propaganda played up Magnentius' barbarous, pagan heritage and perhaps even invented parts of it to besmirch his reputation, making it difficult to believe anything that is recorded about the usurper. Julian the panegyrist shows this imperial propaganda, depicting Magnentius as a barbarian invader rather than a usurper, with Constantius fighting to save the west from barbarian depredations and to avenge his brother.[35]

The spectacular and rapid success of this plot in ousting the most powerful man in Europe makes it seem far-reaching, intricate and orchestrated against an unpopular emperor, who was abandoned by his army. However, instead this plot was much more a desperate move of mounted by a small group of disgruntled political officials, in fear of losing their positions. The main Gallic army was barely involved, with only those troops billeted at Autun for the winter in any position to take part in the revolt. Their success stems more from fortunate timing for while the plotters were launching their coup at the dinner table, Constans was on a hunting trip in the foothills of the Pyrenees, detached from the safety of his armed forces. Rather than running away after his army sided with the usurper, Constans was intercepted, cornered and killed at Helena, modern Elne near Perpignan in southern France by an assassination squad led by Gaiso and including a tribune called Laniogaesus, the last man to see Constans alive.[36] The actions of the Illyrian forces in the face of the usurper and the report by Julian that Magnentius had to kill several of Constans' generals to claim control of the Gallic army would also suggest that any idea of Constans being removed because he was unpopular with the army should be dispensed with. Instead, the usurpation of Magnentius should be seen as "the result of a private grudge on the part of an apprehensive official and not the outcome of widespread discontent among the military or the wider population".[37]

With the emperor disposed of, Magnentius moved to assert his newfound authority. By 27 February, Fabius Titianus, who as already mentioned had defected to the usurper suspiciously quickly, was installed as *praefectus urbi* at Rome, demonstrating just how rapidly the usurper had advanced into the Italian heartland of the empire. From there, Magnentian forces under Valens and Clementius secured Africa while Magnentius himself moved east through Aquileia and Emona to seize the passes through the Julian Alps that link Italy to Illyricum.[38] This was as far as Magnentius' initial wave of success was to take him. Upon probing the lands of Illyricum in March, the usurper found substantial obstacles in his way. Not only were the Illyrian field forces unwilling to accept the murderer of Constans as their emperor, they had gone a step further and proclaimed their own usurper. The man they had chosen was an experienced soldier from Moesia serving as *magister peditum* called Flavius Vetranio. One of the main movers behind this usurpation was Constantina, a sister of Constantius, who encouraged Vetranio's usurpation on 1 March 350, in order to protect herself and her family following the murder of Constans. This would not be the last time that Constantina would play a leading role in the power politics of the Roman Empire.[39]

Vetranio set about concentrating the forces loyal to him under his personal command, bringing them up to battle strength through rigorous recruiting and increasing the immunity of his men to bribery by issuing an accession donative paid from coins minted at Thessalonica and Siscia. With the significant Illyrian forces arrayed against him, Magnentius was faced with a costly military engagement if he was to gain access to those valuable recruiting grounds in the Balkans; however, before he could make any move against Vetranio, Magnentius' attention was drawn away from his Illyrian frontier towards the city of Rome, where another of Constantius' relatives was playing kingmaker.

The least powerful of the three usurpers to appear in 350 was the only one to be a member of the imperial family. Flavius Julius Popilius Nepotianus Constantinus was the son of Eutropia, a half-sister of Constantine I, making Nepotianus a grandson of Constantius I and a half-cousin of Constantius II. Much like Gallus and Julian, Nepotianus was considered too young to be a threat and therefore survived the purge of 337, although it may have claimed the life of his father, Virius Nepotianus, consul in 336. Very little is known of Nepotianus before he was proclaimed *Augustus* on 3 June 350. Together with his mother and their senatorial supporters, Nepotianus gathered a force of gladiators and fought a brutal battle with another cobbled together force of Roman citizens under Titianus. With the streets of the city soaked in blood, control of the western imperial capital fell to this imperial usurper.[40]

The use of gladiators and the senatorial origins of his father could suggest that Nepotianus was a pagan. Gladiatorial contests had long been linked to pagan sacrifices and had been outlawed by Constantine in 315, although the staging of contests during the 330s suggests that the ban was not widely enforced, not even by Constantine himself and especially not in Rome, which remained a bastion of paganism.[41] However, Nepotianus likely set aside religious considerations when looking for allies and welcomed support from wherever he could find it: pagan or Christian, elite or lowest strata.

Constantius' reaction to this usurpation is unknown and it is difficult to come to any firm conclusions about what he might have thought. His later responses to Gallus and Julian might suggest that he will not have taken kindly to this assumption of imperial power by one of his relatives even if it was providing a potential distraction for the much more dangerous threat of Magnentius. However, as will be seen with Vetranio, Constantius was more than capable of being pragmatic in the face of claimants to imperial authority. Regardless of how he would have reacted, Constantius was as yet in no position to intervene in events in Europe as Shapur's third siege of Nisibis played out.

Furthermore, if Constantius held any hope that Nepotianus and his Roman supporters would distract Magnentius for an extended period, it was quickly dispelled. Gladiators and senators were not enough for Nepotianus and without military support from Constantius, Vetranio or any other Constantinian loyalists, his insurrection was doomed once Magnentius was able to bring his regular forces to bear on Rome. And so it proved when Magnentius' *magister militium*, Marcellinus, arrived in central Italy at the head of an armed detachment in late June. Nepotianus and his gladiators proved no match for these professional troops and the usurper was killed on 30 June 350, his head paraded around the city on a spike. He had 'ruled' for twenty-eight days. Following Nepotianus to an early grave was his mother Eutropia and a sizeable number of those senators who had supported the short-lived reign.[42]

Despite being so brief, the usurpation of Nepotianus, along with that of Vetranio, had a substantial effect on Magnentius' overall objectives. In the initial months of his usurpation he had gone to great lengths to portray himself as a potential partner for Constantius rather than an opponent. His most overt measure was the presence of Constantius on his coinage as the senior *Augustus*. Therefore, it is possible that in attempting to seize all of Constans' lands, Magnentius was not only attempting to strengthen his military position for a conflict, but also to secure a strong bargaining position from which to garner recognition from Constantius. The brutality displayed in Rome by Nepotianus and the failure to displace Vetranio through military, diplomatic or subversive means saw hopes of such an accommodation fade throughout the summer of 350. They were then quashed by Constantius who not only rejected Magnentius' proposal of a marriage alliance – Constantius would have married Magnentius' daughter and Magnentius would have married Constantina – but refused to broker any kind of accommodation with the murderer of his younger brother.[43]

Therefore, by mid-350, Magnentius "no longer aspired to join the Constantinian dynasty, but to supplant it".[44] Magnus Decentius, likely Magnentius' brother, may have been proclaimed *Caesar* at Milan around this time while Constantius no longer appeared on the usurper's coinage, which now featured slogans such as 'liberator of the Roman world', 'restorer of liberty and the state' and 'preserver of the soldiers and the provincials' to promote claims that Magnentius had replaced a corrupt and incompetent regime.[45] This completing of the break from Constantius did not prevent Magnentius from attempting to add legitimacy to his own rule. Indeed, it made such legitimacy more important. To that end, Magnentius married a woman called Justina, who had some link to the Constantinian family. It might be incorrect to call Justina a woman as sources suggest that she was too young to have children at the time she was married to Magnentius. On top of that, her exact connection to the imperial dynasty is disputed with it suggested that she was descended from Constantius Chlorus through Julius Constantius or from Constantine through her father, Justus, the son of Crispus' daughter and Vettius Justus, consul in 328.[46]

As a man attempting to usurp the imperial throne and deprived of Illyrian forces and resources, Magnentius also needed to find additional support wherever he could and this involved both sides of the religious divide. Despite the rhetoric regarding his barbaric paganism and tyranny following his death, Magnentius was a Christian, but was willing to look to pagans for aid.[47] As a concession to the pagan senators in Rome, he rescinded Constans' ban on pagan sacrifice as Constantius would later re-establish the ban on "the nocturnal sacrifices allowed on the authority of Magnentius".[48] Conversely, the usurper even likened himself to Constantine, associating his own political and military successes with his conversion to Christianity.[49] His overtures to religious dissidents in the east provoked the murder of the exiled Paul of Constantinople, while Athanasius had to defend himself from accusations of collusion with Magnentius when the usurper sent envoys to Alexandria. A letter would later appear from Athanasius to Magnentius, which the bishop claimed as a forgery. It is possible that Magnentius was replying to Athanasius' request for help from Constans and was looking to take advantage of the less than cordial relationship between Athanasius and Constantius to detach Egypt from the eastern *Augustus* or at least provide a distraction. As will be seen later, Constantius showed that even in his dealings with Athanasius, he was capable of being pragmatic in the face of revolt and moved to quell any potential eastern in-roads Magnentius might have made.[50]

With both Magnentius and Vetranio making sure to bolster their own forces as much as possible, a confrontation between these two usurpers over control of Europe seemed to be in the offing. But before they could come face to face, things got even more muddled. In late 350, with Shapur retreating from Nisibis, Constantius arrived at Serdica at the head of the eastern field army.[51] Vetranio moved to intercept this new threat and it appeared the first major confrontation in this year of usurpers would be between the field forces of the east and Illyricum. However, something peculiar happened instead. On Christmas Day, 350, rather than meeting in a bloody battle, Constantius and Vetranio appeared together in front of the assembled troops and the latter agreed to abdicate his position and surrender all of his forces in return for a quiet life in Bithynia, living off a pension until his death in 356.[52]

The suddenness of this capitulation, the timing of the revolt, the involvement of Constantina and the treatment of Vetranio upon his abdication has led to suggestions that the whole usurpation was a loyalist revolt orchestrated by the *magister peditum*, Constantina and even Constantius to keep Illyricum out of the hands of Magnentius or another local usurper. Both Constantina and Vetranio sent letters to Constantius during 350, professing their continued loyalty to the emperor and asking for financial and military aid. That Constantius briefly recognised Vetranio, giving him full command of the Danubian forces and sending funds and even a diadem, may suggest that at the very least, if he was not involved in its planning, Constantius recognised the potential benefits of this usurpation. That Vetranio moved to meet the emperor at Serdica perhaps even without his army instead of waiting at Naissus may also indicate collusion.

However, it is unlikely that Constantius was involved in the planning of any such strategic usurpation. While the emperor had and would continue to prove himself a skilled political operator, such a flagrant manipulation of the imperial title would seem beyond a man who held it in such high esteem. Time will also have been a factor in the removal of Constantius from the planning stages of any such strategic usurpation. There had been little over six weeks from the death of Constans to the proclamation of Vetranio so by the time Constantius heard of his brother's murder, Magnentius was already probing Illyricum and Vetranio may already have been proclaimed. Therefore, the story behind Vetranio's brief stint as emperor is somewhere in the middle of a stage-managed usurpation and out-and-out rebellion. As a man who had served under both Constantine and Constans, Vetranio was likely a Constantinian loyalist and intended to stay loyal to Constantius but was forced to assume an imperial title by circumstances beyond his control: the advance and attempts at bribery by Magnentius, potential rumours of usurpation within his own ranks and pressure from the scheming Constantina, who revelled in being a member of the imperial family and looked to exert her influence wherever she could.

Hearing of this usurpation by another general from the letters of the usurper and his sister, having already confronted the machinations of Magnentius in the east with Paul and Athanasius but unable to extricate himself from the eastern frontier, Constantius accepted Vetranio's elevation as a *fait accompli*. Then through continued communications made the best of what could have been a bad situation in getting Vetranio to give up the purple. Of course, it is likely that Vetranio did envisage wielding his usurped imperial authority in the long run only for his dreams to be crushed by Constantius' quick arrival. Faced with the imperial legitimacy of a son of the great Constantine and a large, battle-hardened force under the command of an emperor with a strong military reputation, Vetranio set aside his imperial aspirations for a comfortable retirement on the Black Sea coast.

However it happened, by the turn of 351 the abdication of Vetranio left Constantius in control of not just his own field army but also the Illyrian forces of the deceased Constans. The reinforced emperor now established himself and his court at Sirmium, which had thrived in the years since Constantius' birth, first through the patronage of Constantine and then Constans, who had also used it as his Balkan base throughout the 340s. Not only was Sirmium now an increasingly important military position in the prefecture of Illyricum, the extended presence of emperors had seen the construction of many of the buildings required for an imperial residence: imperial and public palaces, mint, circus, arena, aqueduct, churches and villas. Indeed, so well-polished had Sirmium become that the hard-to-please Ammianus called it "a populous and famous metropolis".[53] With such an extensive building programme, it is not surprising that Constantius chose it as his base for much of the next eighteen months during the struggle with Magnentius.

The Price of Reunification: The Bloody Battle of Mursa

While two of the three usurpers of 350 had been dealt with almost bloodlessly, dealing with the last remaining aspirant to imperial power was to prove a chaotic and damaging affair for the Roman Empire. An outline for the campaign of 351 in Pannonia can be reconstructed, although it lacks detail.[54] Perhaps because of that, it appears that there was a long lull in the action between Vetranio's abdication in the last week of 350 and the eventual battle at Mursa in September 351. There is some suggestion that Constantius' generals attempted to break into Italy in the spring but were repulsed due to Magnentius' control of the mountain passes. The usurper took advantage of this victory, moving forward to capture Siscia and its mint.[55] Buoyed by these successes, Magnentius then accepted the challenge of the regrouping Constantian forces, gathered his men and took to the field. The two forces drew up opposite each other in mid September 351 at Mursa, modern Osijek in Croatia, in the valley of the Drava River, a tributary of the Danube.

As the two forces stood eyeballing each other, Constantius sent an embassy to Magnentius under his eastern praetorian prefect, Flavius Philippus, who was taken to the usurper by Marcellinus. On the surface, it was an attempt to negotiate some kind of withdrawal by Magnentius or even a settlement similar to that that had seen Vetranio retire; however, it is more likely that Philippus travelled to Magnentius' camp in order to gather information about the size and composition of the rebel army and to spread disaffection, perhaps even to engineer the defection of officers.[56] The information Philippus brought back to Constantius may have emboldened the emperor. Not only was there to be defection from Magnentius' ranks, Philippus may also have confirmed what Constantius' scouts will have suggested: there was a vast disparity in the size of the two armies. No contemporary sources survive for the size of the forces involved at Mursa but one later historian who may have had access to mid-fourth century material suggests that while Magnentius had just 36,000 men, Constantius had up to 60,000.[57]

That such forces were arrayed suggests that perhaps much of the nine months since Vetranio retired had been taken up with intense recruiting. Constantius in particular seems to have been concerned about the potential military strength and abilities of Magnentius and his forces – or he was worried or even paranoid about the strength and loyalty of his own men – as he employed every recruiting technique in the book to ensure that he had a substantial numerical advantage over his opponent. As well as bringing a large section of the eastern field forces with him and incorporating Vetranio's army, Constantius is thought to have brought the heavy cavalry he had raised to fight Shapur with him to Europe.

Constantius also went to some lengths to portray his conflict with Magnentius as a religious struggle between the virtuous Christian emperor and the barbarous, pagan usurper. Through Valens, bishop of Mursa, angels would be given credit for bringing word of the victory at Mursa while Constantius made sure to invoke his illustrious father by having *HOC SIGNO VICTOR ERIS* printed on his coinage.[58] It is unlikely though that there was any religious element to this conflict. Not only was Magnentius a Christian, Constantius enjoyed a poor reputation amongst Christians due to his efforts to force doctrinal unity on the church. It should also be mentioned that despite the great strides that Christianity had made in the last fifty years, its adherents remained a minority in the Empire and therefore of limited recruiting use. However, as Constantius ruled over the eastern provinces, where Christianity was the strongest, and Magnentius controlled the western provinces where the new monotheistic religion had made the shortest strides, it is possible to see how and indeed why Constantian spin could concoct such a Christian/pagan veneer to the war against the 'barbarous pagan', Magnentius. Such propaganda would have adverse consequences for Constantius in the long run as it made it seem as though he was waging war on Gaul and he would not enjoy the best reputation there throughout the last decade of his reign.

As well as attempting to bolster his own forces, Constantius also worked to undermine Magnentius' strength. Perhaps through Philippus' visit to the Magnentian camp, contact was made with Claudius Silvanus, the Frankish commander of Magnentius' *schola armaturarum* who was persuaded to defect in return for a promotion. It is possible that Silvanus already held some reticence at siding with Magnentius due to links between his family and that of Constantius. His father, Bonitus, had been an ally of Constantine I during the latter's war with Licinius and was trusted with high military office.[59] Such lingering connections might also explain how Constantius was able to contact Silvanus with the offer of a promotion in return for the Frank's defection.

Whilst bribery may not be the most ethical of practices, another of the strategies Constantius is accused of employing to undermine Magnentius was far more dubious. The emperor is said to have encouraged the restless Alamanni tribes of the Upper Rhine and Danube to invade Gaul. Despite being detrimental to Roman territory, this had the sound premise of forcing Magnentius to either split his forces, preventing the usurper from bringing his full military might to the inevitable confrontation or leave the Rhine undermanned, opening Magnentius to propagandist ridicule.[60]

As he wintered behind his defensive positions in the Julian Alps, Magnentius was not idle in his attempts to recruit forces but he faced a difficult proposition in bringing his full military strength to bear on Constantius. Despite regional usurpations "sucking troops out of the periphery",[61] the disparate nature of Magnentius' half of the empire made it more difficult for him to gather together his forces, particularly as Constans dispersed the field army of Constantine II in 340 rather than maintain a single unified force in Gaul. He might have brought the British legions across to Gaul to either bolster the Rhine defences under Decentius or join his personal army but he would not have done the same to Africa due to its importance while Spain and Italy had little in the way of garrison forces worth siphoning off. That Magnentius also saw fit to leave a sizeable force in Gaul under Decentius and thereby reduce the forces he could bring to Mursa could suggest that in spite of being ethically dubious, Constantius' encouragment of the Alamanni to raid Gaul was a success.

Despite these obstacles, Magnentius did manage to recruit more men raising at least two new legions in Gaul, the *Magnentiaci* and *Decentiaci*, and hiring significant numbers of Frank and Saxon auxiliaries. He also seems to have removed men from the frontier garrisons along the Rhine, which later attracted ridicule and could be construed as evidence that Magnentius had trouble raising troops in general if he had to resort to *limitanei*.[62] It would therefore appear that Magnentius' army in the Julian Alps was mostly made up of the Gallic field and frontier forces he had brought together, supported by whatever German mercenaries he had hired. Having left behind Decentius to defend Gaul and only being able to call upon the constituent parts of a dispersed field army, it is unsurprising that Magnentius would find himself outnumbered by an emperor who could call upon the manpower of the two remaining field armies. However, this should not overlook that Magnentius still had a sizeable force at his disposal; one that could do significant damage in the broken ground of the foothills and river basins of the Julian Alps.

And it was to prove as the subsequent Battle of Mursa on 28 September 351 was one of the bloodiest battles in Roman history; although even with such a status, information about the battle remains scant. Magnentius is said to have lost two-thirds of his force in this slogging match while the victorious Constantius lost half of his, equating to perhaps more than 50,000 casualties.[63] As both Constantius and Magnentius had sizeable barbarian contingents within their ranks, the internal manpower supplies of the Roman Empire will not have had to suffer the full weight of such a colossal bloodbath; but even with barbarian troops taking the lion's share of the burden, Mursa still saw the empire suffer tens of thousands of casualties that "would have been adequate for any number of outside wars and could have won many triumphs and brought peace".[64]

Constantius himself was reportedly not even at the battlefield to witness the carnage that unfolded along the banks of the Drava, or at least left it, receiving news of his victory at the tomb of a Christian martyr nearby from the bishop of Mursa, Valens and his angels. It is difficult to put full trust in such reports. Anti-Constantian sources jumped on this as evidence of a lack of courage and that Constantius was gullible in religious matters.[65] Magnentius' position at Mursa is unknown but with the casualties suffered and the death of his closest ally, Marcellinus, in the course of the fighting,[66] the usurper was likely in the thick of things.

With such carnage and with perhaps half of Magnentius' forces still in Gaul, where the usurper retreated back to without much in the way of a pursuit, Mursa could almost be classed as a Pyrrhic victory for the emperor; another one like it would lead to his and the empire's ruin. The shock of such casualties would best explain the lack of an immediate chase of the defeated. It would in fact be upwards of two years before Constantius and Magnentius met in battle again, suggesting that Mursa had been so bloody as to dissuade Constantius from advancing west before recouping his losses and retaking control of towns claimed by Magnentius such as Siscia.[67] It has also been suggested that post-Mursa, Constantius campaigned against the Sarmatians once more. This could have been an attempt to find a new source of recruits but given how troublesome the Danubian tribes had been, Constantius' forces were likely deployed in a punitive or even defensive campaign.[68]

Eventually, by mid summer 352, a full ten months after the bloodbath at Mursa, Constantius was ready to move west. As his forces entered Italy, it was clear that Magnentius had chosen not to defend the peninsula, leaving it to submit with little fighting; although it should be noted that Italy had not completely abandoned the usurper. There is evidence of a continued Magnentian presence in Aquileia as late as 28 July 352 and it was not until 26 September that Constantius was in firm enough control of Rome to see his nominee, Gallus' maternal uncle, Naeratius Cerealis, appointed *praefectus urbi*.[69]

Establishing himself at Milan for the winter of 352 through the summer of 353,[70] Constantius gathered his strength for a final confrontation with Magnentius. As little information that survives for the Battle of Mursa, there is even less for the climactic campaign in southern Gaul and the final battle at Mons Seleucus. No exact date is preserved and little reliable information can be garnered from the surviving material, while several of the laws that place Constantius at certain locations at certain times have had the year of their publication questioned. Nor is there any information on the size and make up of the forces involved. It might be expected that Magnentius will have called together all of the forces from his domain to confront the imperial invader, but it is possible that they would have refused to answer any call to arms as Mursa suggested that they had backed the wrong horse and did not want to further taint themselves in the eyes of the soon-to-be victorious Constantius.

Even when it came to the final campaign, Magnentius still failed to bring together those forces he had, most crucially those of Decentius. That the army of the western *Caesar* did not arrive in time to aid in the defence against Constantius may be a result of the emperor's conmn tinued machinations. As the Alamannic king, Chnodomarius had won a victory over Decentius in 352,[71] it is possible that Decentius was tied up with the Alamanni or the Franks at the time of Mons Seleucus. This was not the only distraction for Decentius. In the summer of 353 as Constantius was beginning his crossing of the Alps, Trier shut its gates to the *Caesar* at the instigation of a certain Poemenius.[72] As with Vetranio's usurpation, the timing of Poemenius' show of loyalty to Constantius is somewhat suspicious and raises similar questions about the potential involvement of the emperor in orchestrating the revolt. Again though, the distances involved make it unlikely but as with the boost to his manpower the loyalty of the Illyrian army had shown him, Constantius benefitted for this combination of frontier trouble and revolt at Trier prevented Decentius and a sizeable force from joining Magnentius.

After perhaps leaving Milan early in July,[73] Constantius moved into southern Gaul to force battle with Magnentius. There is some suggestion that the usurper was "defeated in several battles",[74] implying a series of skirmishes in the run up to Mons Seleucus and perhaps even some stalling by the usurper to allow enough time for Decentius to arrive with the reinforcements. Alas, it was all in vain. Decentius did not make it and in August 353, in the modern French commune of La Bâtie-Montsaleon in the Hautes-Alpes department in south eastern France, Magnentius was defeated at the Battle of Mons Seleucus. The usurper again escaped the battlefield but recognising the futility of continued resistance, he "put an end to his life at Lyons, in the third year and seventh month of his reign"[75] (10 August 353). Upon hearing of his brother's suicide, Decentius hanged himself at Senones just eight days later.[76] The usurpation was over. The Roman Empire had been united under a single *Augustus* once more.

The First Bloody Assizes

The civil war between Constantius and Magnentius perhaps represents the best example of the trauma that the reforms of Diocletian and Constantine along with the division of the empire in 337 could cause. Personal loyalty amongst the *scholae* and the regionalisation of the field armies saw the Roman Empire inflict horrendous damage upon itself at a time when it could ill-afford the losses. How Constantius was to make up these awful casualties is not recorded, with the assumption being that Diocletian's conscription by taxation, hereditary service and employment of specialised foreigners coped with these losses; as mentioned earlier, this would seem to be a faulty assumption and there is evidence to suggest the opposite. That Constantius felt the need to reiterate the age limit for military service at eighteen and remind his prefects to ensure that men had not falsely assumed the rank of *decurion* to escape the draft suggests that there were problems fulfilling the recruiting quotas.[77] Julian would also come up against a recruiting and tax system under tremendous strain in Gaul post-Mursa due to the over-taxing of the citizenry and various forms of corruption and misuse of the recruiting laws.[78] The defeat and deaths of Magnentius and Decentius did not just put all things right with the Roman world overnight.

Successful at Mons Seleucus, the now sole emperor moved to Lyons from where he issued a law repealing the legislation of the 'tyrant' Magnentius before moving south to Arles for the winter, where he celebrated his *tricennalia*, the thirtieth year of his reign on 8 November 353.[79] Constantius would then spend much of 354 and early 355 attempting to bring law and order to Gaul and campaigning against the Alamanni who might have started their raids on Constantius' say so, but refused to relent when ordered. Part of Constantius' plan was to weed out the supporters of Magnentius, which on the surface seems identifiable as justice. However, several courtiers soon played on the emperor's pathological hatred of dissent and his fiery temper to further their own agendas.[80] This saw numerous treason trials undermining military and political structures in the western provinces as anyone suspected of connivance with Magnentius was banished or executed.

While there were some convicted on the flimsiest of evidence and hearsay, it must be said that many of the fears attributed to Constantius were not entirely irrational or imagined. The recent revolt of the western provinces and the "growing doubts as to the intentions of Gallus *Caesar*"[81] provide some vindication of the emperor's suspicions. Therefore, to link him to the unjustified treason trials that were rife under Tiberius, Caligula, Domitian and Commodus is to go too far.[82] However, any ideas of vindicating Constantius for his post-Magnentius actions must be tempered by his deputising of a *notarius* named Paul to investigate disloyalty. A native of Spain, Paul proved that he not only had "an extraordinary capacity for scenting hidden perils"[83] but also in embellishing and even inventing threats to the emperor. Worse still, having frequently trumped up charges, Paul demonstrated a ruthlessness and cruelty towards the accused that can only have been born of a sadistic love of inflicting pain and misery.

Dispatched to Britain in 353 to investigate the island's support of Magnentius, Paul earned the nickname *Catena*, meaning 'the Chain' perhaps in reference to a proclivity for chaining up the accused or his ability in weaving an inescapable web of intrigue. While ordered to focus on British military officers thought to have supported the dead usurper, Paul the Chain saw fit to target anyone under the remotest suspicion and did so with such gusto and repeated injustice that it drew the intervention of the *vicarius*, Flavius Martinus. Despite being a loyal Constantian official, Martinus was horrified at the refusal of Paul to release innocent men and threatened to resign in the hope that the disruption it would cause would curtail the rampaging *notarius*. Instead, Paul turned on Martinus, accusing him and other loyal officers of treason and threatening to drag them in chains before the emperor. Fearing for his life, desperation took hold of the *vicarius* as he drew his sword and attacked Paul. However, "the weakness of his hand prevented him from dealing a fatal blow"[84] and well aware of the dire position his failed gambit had left him in, Martinus plunged his blade into his own side to save himself from the ignominy of torture and execution. Such a personal attack on the *notarius* and resultant suicide made Martinus seem guilty and strengthened Paul's hand in continuing to root out 'opposition' to Constantius. Indeed, this episode in Britain was far from the only time Paul's particular brand of justice would be inflicted upon the Roman populace. Constantius' sole rule of the Roman Empire was not off to the most just of starts and developments in the east were to make sure that it was not to get any prettier any time soon.

Chapter V

Drunk with Power: The Rise and Fall of Constantius Gallus

Power tends to corrupt, and absolute power corrupts absolutely.
– John Emerich Edward Dalberg Acton, first Baron Acton (1834–1902)

The Elevation of Gallus

Despite having come to some kind of mutual but un-negotiated agreement with Shapur that allowed both to detach themselves from the Mesopotamian front to face threats on the other side of their respective empires, Constantius was not comfortable with leaving the east without an imperial presence when he was facing down Vetranio and Magnentius. With the death of his last remaining brother and the danger involved in leading his army against usurpers, as well as continued trouble from the Persians and barbarian tribes of the Rhine and Danube, Constantius' mind will have drifted to the future of the Constantinian dynasty. Despite having been married to a daughter of Julius Constantius since 335–336,[1] Constantius was still without issue, leaving the imperial succession in some jeopardy. Therefore, in his preparations for war against Magnentius in 351, Constantius decided to promote a *Caesar* to serve as an imperial figurehead, distributing imperial patronage across the east and to perpetuate the Constantinian family should the worst happen against the European usurpers.

The question though was who to choose. With two non-imperial usurpers challenging his authority, Constantius will have been wary of giving power to another general even from amongst his current crop of *magistri*, such as Arbitio and Ursicinus, not to mention not wanting to promote such outsiders into the Constantinian dynasty. Therefore, the emperor sought to bind his new *Caesar* more closely to him by looking to his own family. Such a decision left Constantius with very few options as the 337 purge, civil war and usurpations had reduced the number of Constantinian men to just two besides the emperor himself: the youngest sons of Julius Constantius who had survived the "dynastic bloodbath"[2] because of their age in 337, Gallus and his half-brother,

Julian.[3] As the eldest – he was probably twenty-six by 351 – the choice fell upon Gallus.

Born in Massa Veternensis in Etruria, now part of Tuscany in Italy, in around 325–326, Gallus' earliest years were not spent surrounded by the imperial court despite being a grandson of Constantius Chlorus. The suggestion is that Helena, Chlorus' second wife and mother of Constantine, had Julius Constantius and his wife, Galla, sent to various residences throughout the empire – Tolosa in Spain, Etruria in Italy and Corinth in Greece[4] – because she saw the first family of her husband as a threat to the established power of her own son. The suggestion that the restoration of the descendants of Theodora was part of a political plot might prove Helena correct in her suspicions and it was only after Helena's death that Constantine welcomed his half-brother and his family to Constantinople. Julius Constantius was appointed *patricius* in 330 and then served as consul with Caius Caeionius Rufus Albinus in 335.[5] Together with Gallus and an older but unnamed son and daughter – the latter would be Constantius II's first wife – Julius Constantius also brought with him a new wife, Basilina, who gave birth to Julian in Constantinople in the summer of 331 or 332.

However, such seeming harmony between the branches of the Constantinian family tree was not to last and Julius Constantius and his eldest son fell victim to the murderous purge of 337.[6] Along with Julian and Nepotianus, Gallus was saved from slaughter by his youth, although it is also recorded that he was so ill at the time that he was not expected to survive anyway.[7] There is some debate over where Gallus was housed after the murder of his father. It has been assumed that he joined Julian under the care of Eusebius of Nicomedia with the boys following their tutor back to Constantinople from Nicomedia when he became bishop of Constantinople in 340. When Eusebius died soon after, Gallus may have accompanied Julian to a remote imperial palace at Macellum in Cappadocia, where for six years they were isolated under the care of another bishop, George of Cappadocia, who later succeeded Athanasius as bishop of Alexandria. However, there is some suggestion of Gallus being sent to Ephesus or Tralles, modern Aydin in Turkey, before his arrival in Macellum.[8]

There are also conflicting accounts of the brothers' time at Macellum. Christian sources paint a picture of scholarly retreat in the Cappadocian mountains complete with philosophical and religious discourse, whereas Julian depicts a far less idyllic experience more in line with house arrest in a remote location. Julian even suggests that some of Gallus' less flattering attributes, particularly his violent temper were due to their imprisonment and isolation at Macellum.[9] The murder of his father and brother and the death of his mother can also not have helped his psychological development. Because of this lack of definitive knowledge about how long the two half brothers lived together and where, it is difficult to ascribe a similar education and upbringing to Gallus to that which Julian received from the likes of George and Mardonius. Despite this and his exile, as a member of the ruling imperial family, Gallus will have received an extensive education not just in Christianity but also perhaps in preparing him for public office, although it is doubtful that any education will have been in preparation for the position that was thrust upon him in 351.

Having been called from his mountain retreat, Gallus was elevated to the rank of *Caesar* by Constantius at Sirmium on 15 March 351. He was also imbued with the name 'Constantius' and married to Constantius' eldest sister and recently made *Augusta*, Constantina. There has been some speculation about Constantius' motives in arranging this match. The most obvious is that the emperor looked to use his sister to solidify Gallus' loyalty and to aid or even control the inexperienced *Caesar*. However, there is also a possibility that Constantius was hoping as much to control his sister as his new heir. Constantina was not only the daughter of the great Constantine and the widow of the 'King of Kings and Ruler of the Pontic Tribes,' Hannibalianus, she had also been instrumental in the usurpation of Vetranio and regardless of whether or not it had been a tactical revolt in favour of Constantius, it demonstrated that she could be a force to be reckoned with. An embassy from the west enquiring about a marriage between Magnentius and Constantina may also have prompted Constantius to engineer a match with Gallus to prevent his sister from entering into any treasonous scheming. Events in the east would prove that any such suspicions held by Constantius were not far from the mark.

There is also some suggestion of Constantina herself being the originator of the plan for her marriage to Gallus and it is not difficult to see why she would suggest such a move. Given the problems Constantius was having with producing offspring and the danger he was about to be subjected to in Europe, Constantina could see the potential for her to become empress. On top of his political credentials, if Ammianus' description is anything to go by, Gallus also had other attributes that will have attracted Constantina to his cause, being "a man of remarkably good looks, with a fine frame and well-proportioned limbs. His hair was blond and soft, and his beard, though at first delicate down, gave him a look of authority beyond his years."[10] This union seemingly produced a daughter, whose name and fate are unknown. Therefore, politically and physically, Constantina had again landed a prize catch. However, within four years, both she and her husband would be dead.[11]

Gallus versus the Peoples of the East

With the dynastic arrangements complete and with a few choice words of advice whispered in his ear from Constantius, Gallus and his new bride were packed off to Antioch to rule the east in the emperor's absence. Along the way Gallus met with Julian at Nicomedia; a meeting that would later be used as evidence of connivance between the two against Constantius.[12] Arriving by 7 May, the new *Caesar* was greeted not only by the appearance of a cross in the sky across the east,[13] but also a considerable cadre of experienced politicians, much as Constantine had provided Constantius with in 336: Thalassius as praetorian prefect, Montius as *quaestor sacri palatii*, Ursicinus as *magister equitum* and Theophilius as *consularis Syriae* and a mediator between Gallus and Constantius.[14]

It has been asserted that during his tenure as *Caesar* Gallus faced down Persian activity in Mesopotamia with a show of military force and even won victories in the field. However, this conjecture comes from one poorly transmitted source and does not tabulate with what is known from other more trusted sources of the period. The source, Philostorgius, survives only as a chapter in the epitome of Photius, who may not accurately preserve Philostorgius' point. That other sources who derive their detail from Philostorgius (*Passio Artemii*) or who follow Eunapius the same way as Philostorgius did (Zosimus) do not record any victories over the Persians by Gallus may further suggest that Photius has misrepresented Philostorgius.[15]

And while there may be some information in the first thirteen missing books of his *Res Gestae*, in those that do survive Ammianus does not go out of his way to present Gallus as a successful commander. When he is claiming to know the root of Gallus' swollen pride, there is no mention of military action, except for the suggestion that the only reason he had not marched against Constantius was due to a "lack of strength".[16] Even when Gallus did take the field in around March 354, and headed towards Hierapolis, the historian recorded it as an attempt "to give at least the appearance of taking part in a campaign",[17] suggesting that not only was he not doing so now in 354, he had not done so at all during his reign. Such obvious contempt for Gallus, who "differed as much from the disciplined character of his brother Julian as did Domitian, son of Vespasian, from his brother Titus",[18] likely stems from the *Caesar*'s treatment of the people of Antioch and the historian's attempts to excuse Ursicinus for his role in the troubles of Gallus' reign. Therefore, Ammianus' credibility on the actions and temperament of the *Caesar* should be called into question, with the suggestion that he went out of his way to denigrate or play down any military action undertaken by Gallus.

Despite any downplaying of Gallus' military credentials, Ammianus does record an attempted Persian strike into Roman territory in 354. Having been given orders by Shapur "to invade Mesopotamia whenever occasion offered",[19] the Persian commander in Mesopotamia, known by his title 'Nohodares', looked to take advantage of any opportunity. Finding Roman Mesopotamia well-defended, with the presence of both Ursicinus and Lucillianus, he turned instead to Osrhoene, where he attempted "a novel and all but unprecedented manoeuvre; and if he had succeeded he would have devastated the whole region like a thunderbolt".[20] His target, the town of Batnae, was situated along the routes to crossings of the Euphrates and contained a large number of wealthy merchants; a number only increased by an annual festival. Nohodares planned to use the distraction of this festival to sneak his men across the wilderness and the Abora river and fall upon the town unnoticed. However, it seems that some of his men defected to the Romans to escape punishment and roused the Batnae garrison to the Persian plan. Without the element of surprise, Nohodares withdrew without making an attempt to capture the town.

Attempting to find a direct connection between Gallus' move to Hierapolis and Nohodares' attempt on Batnae is undermined by the placing of the former in March and the later in early September;[21] however, the proximity of these two towns cannot be overlooked. Despite its failure, the Persian strike at Batnae and Gallus' march to Hierapolis, whether a mere show of force or part of an actual engagement, could suggest not only on-going Romano-Persian operations but also a widening of the focus of the theatre to include Osrhoene. That at least some kind of military campaign was planned for 354 might be highlighted by the shortage of supplies that dogged Antioch at this time, with resources being diverted to the frontiers and army bases.[22]

The movements of Ursicinus could shed further light on any significant Persian activity that needed Gallus to lead men in the field. Appointed to this prominent position in the east in 349 after having begun his military career under Constantine,[23] Ursicinus was to become a major figure in the last decade of Constantius' reign, not just because of his military credentials but also because he had one Ammianus Marcellinus serving on his staff as a *protector domestici*. As Constantius departed the eastern front for Europe in the autumn of 350, Ursicinus had been redeployed from Mesopotamia to Palestine. While this move hints at the beginnings of trouble amongst the Jews, that the senior military figure in the east would be sent to deal with what was a local revolt, even one as dangerous as the Jews, might suggest the extent to which military operations in Mesopotamia had been shut down in the wake of Shapur's retreat from Nisibis. However, Ursicinus would be back at Nisibis both before and after presiding over Gallus' treason trials. While the *magister* may have wanted to find any excuse to remove himself from the turmoil around Gallus in Antioch, his return to Mesopotamia may betray some military need for his presence. Furthermore, despite the suspicions of Ammianus, Constantius' summoning of Ursicinus to Milan to discuss the Persian threat, rather than a pretext to removing both the *magister* and Gallus, may have been genuine and suggests continued military action on the eastern frontier.[24]

Even if the reporting of Gallus' campaigning in person in Mesopotamia was misplaced, embellished or incorrect, it would be naïve to think that the eastern frontier had been shut down upon Constantius' departure. Shapur's orders to Nohodares to keep up pressure on the Roman frontier would suggest that mutual border raids were the norm. So while Gallus may not have won a grand victory over the Persians, it is possible that under his auspices Ursicinus, Lucillianus or other regional commanders did inflict casualties on the Persians. Indeed, there are some who have claimed that Gallus has been underrated as a commander due to a poor record and some Ammian manipulation of the record.[25]

These continued problems with the Persians and the usurpations of Magnentius and Vetranio were perhaps not the only military reasons behind the timing of Constantius' promotion and dispatch of Gallus to the east. The redeployment of Ursicinus suggests that the emperor had reports before he departed for Europe of growing tensions amongst local populations. The first of these was a revolt amongst several Jewish populations in Galilee. The Roman psyche contained something of an inferiority complex with regards to the ancient roots of the Jews. This led them to treat Judaism with a strange mixture of respect and fear, although when it came to Jewish revolt, such psychological hurdles were overcome by brutal but clinical rage. And while not as famous or widespread as the 66–73 conflict that saw the destruction of the Temple in Jerusalem and the mass suicide at Masada or quite as vicious as the Kitos War of 115–117 or the Bar Kokhba uprising of 132–135, this Jewish revolt of the early 350s saw another episode of that clinical brutality that the Romans could deal so well in.

The reason for this brutality was not just Roman dislike of rebellion or their inherent fear of Jewish ethno-religious nationalism but also because of an extra religious dimension to this revolt that piqued Roman anger. While the temporal leader of the revolt was Isaac of Diocaesarea, there was also a spiritual leader in the figure of a certain Patricius, also known as Natrona, who made certain messianic claims. Numerous Jewish leaders had claimed to be the Messiah in the past, with the pagan Romans ignoring the religious connotations of such a claim. However, by the fourth century, with Christianity now ensconced as the official religion of the empire, such a claim attacked one of the main tenets of Christianity – that Jesus of Nazareth was the one true Messiah – and will have enraged Christian Romans.

Extensive information about the revolt, even its exact date, is lacking but it appears to have begun with an attack on the Roman garrison of Diocaesarea in either 350 or 351. With the arms appropriated from the garrison, Isaac, Patricius and their followers massacred large numbers of the Greek and Samaritan populations in surrounding towns; a massacre that will also have encouraged the vicious Roman reaction under Ursicinus. It is not certain if any sort of battle took place between the rebels and the Roman forces sent against them, although the destruction wrought on the cities of Diocaesarea, Diopolis and Tiberias could suggest a series of sieges. Avoiding pitched battle against professional troops and taking advantage of urban defences would be in keeping with the limited resources available to Isaac and Patricius. Whatever type of fighting took place, fuelled by religious and vengeful outrage, Ursicinus and his men crushed the insurrection and punished the towns that helped the rebels, although the complete destruction of Diocaesarea was caused by an earthquake in 363 rather than Roman retaliation in around 351/352.

While some of the sources state that "Gallus suppressed the Jews",[26] it would appear that this was an inference that these operations took place under Gallus' auspices rather than his direct involvement in the Roman reaction to the Jewish revolt. Such a lack of involvement should have seen the blame for the supposed massacre of thousands of rebels passed from Gallus onto his commanders but there is some suggestion that Ursicinus was ordered to resort to overt brutality in Palestine and there were few who could have issued such an order to a *magister*; Constantius was more than capable of such ruthlessness but was too distant, leaving Gallus as the only other candidate. This begs the question of whether or not Ursicinus would have listened to such an order from a figurehead. Ursicinus and his commanders likely were responsible for the harsh exactions post-revolt, with or without imperial order, but as it took place under his regime and when put with his own actions at Antioch, the repression of the Jews helped earn Gallus a reputation for cruelty.[27]

The Jews were not the only people in the Levant causing trouble for Gallus and his commanders: the perennial frontier menace that was the Arab tribes were also "ranging up and down the country".[28] While Ammianus does not name an exact target for this round of Arab raids in the 350s or any Roman reprisals for such actions, it would not be surprising to find that the focus of any Romano-Arab skirmishes was the *Strata Diocletiana*. This 'road of Diocletian' was a fortified highway that ran from the Euphrates through the northern reaches of the Syrian Desert towards north-eastern Arabia, a region known to the Romans as the *limes Arabicus*. That Diocletian felt the need to build such a road, lined with numerous rectangular forts a day's march apart, shows just how chronic Arab raiding had become. One moment they could be serving the Empire, the next they could be hampering it through raids or even serving in the Persian army, where one of their number may have killed Julian in 363.[29]

Another people giving grief to Gallus who had also seen Diocletian take administrative action against them were the Isaurians. Resistant to Romanisation in their mountainous abodes in Cilicia, the Isaurians developed into a "profound security threat"[30] through various daring raids by land and water. Repeated Roman attempts to deal with them were frustrated by the combination of their skill as hardy guerrilla fighters and the strength of their mountain redoubts. By the turn of the fourth century, their raids had become so problematic that Diocletian formed all Isaurian territory into a separate province complete with sizeable garrison forces. Even with this administrative and military mobilisation, the Isaurians continued their raiding to such an extent that southern Anatolia was transformed "into a militarized zone that regularly diverted imperial troops and attention".[31]

As Gallus was settling into his role of *Caesar* in the early 350s, the Isaurians were launching daring raids, stealing boats to raid the southern coast of Asia Minor, plundering towns and butchering their populations. Local militias and garrisons attempted to stop them but were cut down as the raiders retreated to higher ground and concentrated their superior numbers upon them. Learning their lesson, the Roman soldiers refused to follow the Isaurians into the mountains, hoping to force the raiders into more conventional pitched battle. Hemmed in by the Roman refusal to fight in mountainous terrain, the Isaurians drove west towards Pamphylia, a region as yet unmolested by their raids. They found that the Romans were ready for them, having posted strong garrisons and flying columns of cavalry and fleet-footed infantry around the region. Trapped in the hills, the Isaurian raiders were then confronted by three Diocletianic legions emerging from their winter quarters at Side. By interlocking their shields on the bank of the Melas river, the legions blocked the Isaurian advance, forcing them to fall back to the town of Laranda, modern Karaman in Turkey.

The Isaurians were getting desperate and "distressed by severe hunger"[32] and turned to even more daring attacks. This suggests that their raids were not always those of plundering pirates but those of desperate men looking to feed their families. They launched an attack on the fortified Roman supply depot at Palaea, which proved futile in the face of its defences and was called off after three days. In one last effort, they called together their full strength and aimed a lightning strike at the provincial capital at Seleucia, where the *comes* Castricius was stationed with three veteran legions. Informed by scouts of the impending arrival of a large Isaurian host, Castricius led his men out to intercept them beyond a bridge of the Calycadnus river. Despite drawing up for battle, Castricius chose to retreat back to the safety of Seleucia and its walls, leaving the Isaurians to surround and besiege the city. In response, Gallus hoped to send Ursicinus to relieve Seleucia but he was still dealing with the Jews. Therefore, he charged the *comes Orientis*, Nebridius, with the job. Nebridius gathered a force sufficient enough to scare off the Isaurians from before Seleucia without a fight, rescuing "this great and strategically important city from danger".[33]

While the question remains as to how much direct involvement Gallus had in the military activities that took place between 350 and 354, there is no denying that those activities were successful. And as Constantius and every emperor since Augustus almost four hundred years previous had done, Gallus reaped the reward of these successes taking place under his auspices, even if he had not taken any direct role in the campaigns. However, it would appear that the *Caesar* allowed these successes to go to his head.

"The many fearful misdeeds of the *Caesar* Gallus"[34]

It was not just the restless tribal and religious populations in and around the eastern provinces that Gallus found himself at odds with during his tenure in Antioch. He "forgot that Constantius intended him to be a mere figurehead, necessary for political and dynastic reasons, but with the real power vested in experienced administrators whom he himself had appointed".[35] This led to bitter conflicts not only with these officials but also with the people of Antioch. The military successes carried out in his name may have increased Gallus' "notoriously swollen pride"[36] but this alone cannot explain the actions of the *Caesar*. The circumstances of his upbringing – transient formative years punctuated by the death of his mother, the remarrying of his father and then the murder of a large proportion of his family before being held under house arrest for a decade – cannot have helped his mental state. The sudden change in his fortunes must also have played a part, with Gallus settling into his role as the heir to the throne, encouraging him to think he was untouchable and to go "beyond the limits of the authority granted to him".[37] Ammianus also lays a lot of blame for Gallus' increasing ruthless behaviour on that "Fury in mortal form",[38] Constantina. The historian credits her with a bloodlust that complemented that of her husband and a thirst for intrigue and rumour that would see many an innocent person thrown to the wolves.[39] "It should have been her part to bring him by feminine mildness and sensible advice back to the paths of truth and kindness… [instead she pushed] her husband headlong to destruction."[40]

If there was one specific event to have shunted Gallus towards despotism, it may have been the uncovering of an assassination plot early in his time in Antioch. The suggestion is that this plot originated with Magnentius, who was looking to destabilise Constantius' regime any way he could. The assassin gathered a group of conspirators around him, perhaps highlighting that Gallus had already angered some, ready to strike at the palace, only to be betrayed by their hostess, who supposedly was too old to hear or understand what they were planning. Constantina jumped on this plot, showering the old woman with praise, hoping that this might encourage others to betray conspiracies. This might seem like a good idea but it only encouraged the exaggeration and invention of supposed plots and the punishment of innocents: "what had been a just constitutional government was transformed into a bloody despotism."[41]

Suspicion became rife with spies employed to report anything approaching a slight. Gallus himself was so eager to hear any slight against him that supposedly he went out at night in Antioch disguised with a band of followers to ask random people what they thought of the *Caesar*. In such a climate, trials became redundant as Gallus accepted a bribe to issue a death warrant against the innocent Clematius of Alexandria. This started a new wave of false accusations and condemnations with many put to death, exiled or had their property confiscated.[42] Libanius, his mentor Zenobius and his uncle Phasganius all fell foul of such whispers and although acquitted or not even charged, this encouraged Libanius to leave Antioch for Thrace.[43] Even those accusations that did make it to trial were not beyond ridicule. The former *dux Phoeniciae*, Serenianus, was brought up on charges of treason stemming from his failure to prevent the sacking of the city of Celse in Phoenicia and of using magical enchanting and prophecy. Ammianus records this as an open and shut case with Serenianus' guilt being obvious and yet he was acquitted in another example of Gallus' willingness to take a bribe. However, if Gallus thought that he might have bought a friend in Serenianus, he would be mistaken.[44]

If such an atmosphere of intrigue and fear was not bad enough, Gallus then fell foul of the Antiochene upper classes when the combination of military action and a poor harvest led to trouble with the food supply in Antioch. When Gallus' attempts to resolve this crisis by reducing or freezing the price of grain were met with disdain, the *Caesar* gave free rein to his anger, ordering the execution of all the leading members of the Antiochene senate. They were saved from a grizzly fate by the intervention of the then *comes Orientis*,

Honoratius.[45] In response to the growing anger of the people, Gallus served up Theophilius, claiming that there could only be a famine if the *consularis Syriae* wanted there to be one. Theophilius was set upon by the mob, beaten and torn to shreds. Before their bloodlust subsided, the mob turned on the *decurion*, Eubulus, but not finding him or his son, they burned their house down.[46] There is some suggestion that Gallus recognised his plummeting popularity as he spent large amounts of time in the Hippodrome and Circus throwing games and races for the people. However, it is here that his bloodlust shone through the most as he took great delight in watching fights to the death.

Dismayed by these events, Thalassius wrote to Constantius to inform him of the two-headed monster he had unleashed in the east. The praetorian prefect did little to soothe Gallus' rage; indeed, he is accused of enflaming it by reproaching the *Caesar* in private and in public.[47] With such information of his *Caesar*'s behaviour, Constantius realised that he had made a bad choice and may even have feared that Gallus would spark rebellion. Therefore, while writing to Gallus in glowing terms, the emperor began to orchestrate his removal by withdrawing important military and civilian resources from his direct control. When Thalassius died of natural causes in 353,[48] Constantius sent Domitianus to replace him and to encourage Gallus to visit Italy; instead, Domitianus took this as a cue to undermine Gallus and embellished his reports to Constantius. The one time that the prefect met with Gallus, he used an insolent tone and threatened the *Caesar* with: "Depart, *Caesar*, and know that, if you delay, I shall at once order your supplies and those of your palace to be cut off."[49] While this might seem like Domitianus was overstepping his bounds, given the attitude of Constantius, it is unlikely that the new prefect would have acted in such an adroit manner had the emperor not authorised it or at least made it seem like it would not be punished.

Outraged by such insolence, Gallus ordered his guards to arrest Domitianus. The *quaestor*, Montius, encouraged restraint and pointed out that acting against the prefect would be tantamount to rebellion against Constantius. After Constantina reportedly dragged Montius from his official seat with her own hands, Gallus ordered all troops to muster and spoke before them pleading his case.

I need your help, my brave men, in a danger which is threatening us all. Montius, with unprecedented arrogance, has made a speech which amounts to an accusation that I am a rebel in revolt against the majesty of the emperor, he is angered, no doubt, because to teach him a lesson, I have ordered the arrest of an insolent prefect who pretends not to know what protocol requires.[50]

Further incited by a *curator urbis* called Luscus, who was later burned to death as punishment, the soldiers attacked both Montius and Domitianus, bringing them both bound before Gallus. After a desultory judgement, both men were then dragged through the streets and dismembered, their remains thrown in the Orontes river like criminals. Numerous arrests followed with anyone with any link to the deceased *quaestor* and prefect clapped in irons. Epigonus of Cilicia and Eusebius Pittacus were accused of connections to Montius but this seems to have been a case of mistaken identity. Instead of these two orators, Montius had connections to two *tribuni fabricarum*, officers of the state arms factories, "who had promised arms in case a revolution should be set on foot".[51] Domitianus' son-in-law and *cura palatii*, Apollinaris, was also arrested after looking for evidence of potential rebellion from Gallus amongst the troops in Mesopotamia. When it was found that an imperial robe had been made in Tyre, where the governor was Apollinaris' father of same name, Gallus had all the pieces he needed to construct the framework of a plot against him and "all justice vanished from the courts".[52]

To preside over this kangaroo court, Gallus turned to the one major official who had yet to turn against him: Ursicinus. Ammianus maybe argues a little too strongly in trying to point out that the *magister* was serving under duress, hoping to distance Ursicinus from the 'justice' that his court was meting out. And why the historian might want to cover up any direct involvement from Ursicinus is soon clear: instead of court cases, these were a series of brutal torture sessions, during which Epigonus broke and admitted to crimes he had not committed while Eusebius Pittacus proclaimed his innocence even when virtually eviscerated and even tore out his own tongue rather than admit guilt for something he had not done. Taking such stubbornness as insolence, Gallus had Eusebius and Epigonus executed regardless of the lack of evidence. In the case of the Apollinares and the imperial robe, a lack of evidence seemed to have saved them as they were merely exiled but as they reached their villa at Craterae, they too were executed. These were not the only treason trials in the aftermath of the deaths of Domitianus and Montius. Shocked by the complete breakdown of law and order precipitated by the *Caesar*'s temper and worried that he might be next due to the arbitrary nature of the killing, Ursicinus wrote to Constantius, asking the emperor to intervene.[53]

The Removal of Gallus

These communiqués from Thalassius, Domitianus and Ursicinus regarding Gallus' increasingly brutal and arbitrary rule reached Constantius as he continued the mopping up operations in the aftermath of the defeat of

Magnentius. Having spent the winter of 353–354 at Arles, Constantius set out for Valentia to face up to one of the problems that had been dogging Gaul for years; a problem that he was responsible for enflaming: the Alamanni. This campaign did not get off to the best of starts as spring rains hampered the arrival of supplies, leading to the army congregating at Châlon-sur-Saône to grow restless. Constantius then sent his praetorian prefect for Gaul, Rufinus, to explain the problems to the troops. It is suggested that this was a plot to remove Rufinus, the maternal uncle of Gallus, by placing him before restless and hungry soldiers, although the head chamberlain, Eusebius was also soon sent to abate the trouble long enough for the supplies to arrive by distributing gold.[54]

Adequately provisioned and with the emperor himself now present, the army moved towards the Rhine. Upon reaching Augusta Rauricorum, modern Augst in Switzerland, the Romans found a large Alamannic force under Gundomadus and Vadomarius in position to dispute any attempted river crossing. This left Constantius with two options: a risky crossing or retreat. The imperial army was saved from further atrophy by the appearance of a local informant, who revealed the existence of a shallow section of the river that would allow the Romans to cross unseen. However, before Constantius could use this information, the Roman plan to use these shallows were revealed to the Alamanni, who took measures to defend against it. Worse for Constantius was that the source of this information was suspected as being a leak from high-ranking soldiers of Alamannic origin: Latinus, a *comes domesticorum*, Agilo, the *tribunus stabuli* and Scudilo, the commander of the *Scutarii*.

Despite this horrendous breach of loyalty, Constantius did not go on the kind of witch hunt that had accompanied his defeat of Magnentius. Perhaps this was due to the unresolved issue of the Alamanni and the coming to a head of the problem of Gallus. But if Constantius was worried by these conundrums, he need not have been. Despite blocking the emperor's crossing of the Rhine, the Alamanni were having second thoughts about confronting Constantius in battle. Not only was the emperor's reputation undermining their confidence, poor auspices from their holy men discouraged any further action. Therefore, Gundomadus and Vadomarius sent envoys to Constantius, seeking peace and pardon for their crimes against Gaul. This presented the emperor with a decision to make. Could he withdraw having not defeated his opponent or even fought a battle without tarnishing his reputation? At length, Constantius and his advisers decided that he could and the emperor appeared before his army to inform them of the decision to disengage.[55] Constantius might have feared a negative response from the soldiers at having their chance for revenge against the Alamanni taken away but not having to cross into enemy territory was enough for the army to accept the withdrawal. With more of a hint of his dislike of Constantius, Ammianus claims that the real reason for the soldiers' willingness to accept peace was "the conviction, which they had formed from frequent campaigns, that his [Constantius'] fortune washed over him only in civil troubles, but that when foreign wars were undertaken, they had often ended disastrously".[56]

With the army's agreement, Constantius concluded a peace treaty with the Alamanni and returned to Milan. It is doubtful that the army would have complained whatever Constantius had decided. But the Constantian propaganda machine still went into overdrive in order to present yet another opponent of the emperor being cowed by his imperial majesty and reputation without bloodshed: first Vetranio and now the Alamanni. And it was not long before another name could be added to that list.

Re-established in Milan, Constantius could now give fuller attention to the increasingly distressing reports he had been receiving about Gallus. Worried that the *Caesar* might rebel or cause a rebellion, Constantius and his advisers decided to lure Gallus into letting his guard down. There were dissenters from this plan such as Arbitio and Eusebius, because they feared Ursicinus, who might use his position within the eastern army for his own ends; such rumour was spread by several of Constantius' eunuch attendants and embellished with claims that Ursicinus' sons hoped for imperial power, just because they were young, popular and gifted. They also claimed that Gallus had been manipulated into his misdeeds by those who wished to see Ursicinus and his sons on the imperial throne.[57] Whether Constantius believed these rumours or not, Ursicinus was instructed to travel to Milan to converse with the emperor on the preparations for the inevitable rekindling of war with the Persians, leaving the *comes* Prosper to replace Ursicinus as military commander in the east.

With the *magister* removed, Constantius then targeted the other powerful figure within Gallus' regime: Constantina. The emperor sent word to Antioch asking her to come to Milan as he had not seen her in so long. Despite being wary of the machinations of her brother, Constantina hoped to placate Constantius before he moved against her husband and so set out west. However, by the time she had reached Bithynia, she had developed a fever from which she failed to recover, dying a short while later.[58] This sudden death of his wife removed the one remaining connection between Gallus and the emperor. The *Caesar* realised it and is reported to have considered rebelling against Constantius, only to think better of it due to his own unpopularity and the emperor's reputation in civil conflict.[59] Even if Gallus did harbour worries about what Constantius had planned for him, the emperor found that one thing that was to override those thoughts: the temptation of power. Through his agents, including Scudilo, a member of Gallus' *Scutarii*, the rumour was put about that Constantius intended to elevate Gallus to the rank of *Augustus* with command of the Rhine frontier. Gallus allowed himself to be taken in by such a possibility and departed Antioch for Milan in early September 354. So taken in by this ruse was Gallus that when he arrived in Constantinople, he celebrated with little restraint.

Meanwhile, the emperor was putting his plan to remove Gallus into full swing. Any troops stationed along the route that the *Caesar* would take across the Balkans were removed and numerous dignitaries including Leontius, a *quaestor* and later urban prefect of Rome, Lucillianus, a *comes domesticorum*, and a *Scutarii* called Bainobaudes were sent to meet Gallus along the way, ostensibly to deliver updates and business due to a *Caesar* but in reality to prevent any plotting. These dignitaries prevented Gallus from making contact with some Theban legionaries who were wintering near Adrianople and were perhaps looking to warn Gallus about what lay ahead for him. The game was almost given away by the insolence of Taurus, the *quaestor* of Armenia, who failed to show Gallus due deference for a man of his rank, despite Constantius' order to do so.

However, once Gallus reached Poetovio in Pannonia, modern Ptuj in Slovenia, all pretence was dropped. The *comes* Barbatio, a former bodyguard of Gallus, and Apodemius, an *agent in rebus*,[60] arrived at the head of a force of soldiers loyal to Constantius and arrested Gallus, stripping him of his rank but also promising that he would not be harmed. Gallus was then taken to Histria, near Pola, where Crispus had met his end twenty-eight years previously, to face an interview from Eusebius, the *notarius* Pentadius and Mallobaudes, *tribunus armaturarum*, regarding the killings at Antioch. When the deposed *Caesar* tried to blame Constantina for his reign of terror, the emperor had had enough. Serenianus, Pentadius and Apodemius were sent to condemn Gallus to death. Bound like a common criminal, Gallus was beheaded, "his head and face were mutilated, and the man who so short a time before had been an object of dread to cities and provinces was left lying a hideous corpse upon the ground".[61] Apodemius brought word of Gallus' death to Constantius at Milan, bringing the dead *Caesar*'s shoes as proof.

Constantian 'Justice'

With another threat done away with, the imperial court descended into flattery towards Constantius for having carried out the elimination of rebels such as Vetranio and Gallus without having to resort to fighting; the former was defeated through might, persuasive oratory and generosity and the latter through careful planning and the loyalty he inspired. That this headed off a potential civil war may be to believe Constantius' propaganda, although the testament of Ammianus is enough to suggest that Gallus was capable of causing trouble. Constantius allowed himself to be taken in by such flattery,[62] although this did not stop him from continuing to take the field against military threats.

Having already scared a peace treaty out of Gundomadus and Vadomarius, Constantius was now faced with the raids of the Alamannic Lentienses into Raetia.[63] In response, he marched from Milan to Campi Carini, near modern Bellinzona in Switzerland, with Arbitio taking a stronger force on ahead to Lake Constance. In his haste, Arbitio failed to take adequate precautions, charging headlong into a trap along the lake shore, his force soon put to flight. Buoyed by this success, the Lentienses attacked the Roman camp where the survivors were attempting to reform the following day. Here, they met far more stubborn resistance and were fought to a standstill by the *Scutarii*. Fearful of a repeat of the debacle at Lake Constance, Arbitio hesitated in rejoining battle, leaving three tribunes – Arintheus of a bodyguard unit, Seniachus of the household cavalry and Bappo of the veteran *Promoti* – to take the initiative and lead their men to the rescue of the embattled *Scutarii*. Together, these four units broke the Alamannic assault and forced the barbarians into retreat. It was only then that the rest of the army sallied forth to turn what was a successful defence into a victorious rout. With the Lentienses dealt with, regardless of the fortune involved, Constantius returned to Milan in time to oversee the elevation of a new *Caesar* on 6 November 355.

The aftermath of Gallus' removal was not taken up with just military action. Another wave of accusations spread across the empire as Constantius began targeting any supporters that Gallus might have had, again proving himself willing to listen to any accusation no matter how unfounded or disprovable. This allowed the rumours surrounding Ursicinus and the imperial yearnings of his sons to gain an audience and saw the *magister* abandoned by the majority of his friends; not Ammianus though, which serves as a warning about the presentation of this "high-souled hero."[64] Arbitio appears as Ursicinus' worst enemy, professing to be his friend in public but laying the foundations of his discrediting in private. Constantius may have gone as far as to order the execution of Ursicinus without trial in the aftermath of the downfall of Gallus only to then change his mind.

Having been foiled in their initial attempts to remove a powerful and popular general, the intriguers turned their attention to the emperor's last remaining male relative; Gallus' half-brother, Julian. These men accused Julian of conspiring with the deposed *Caesar*, pointing to their meeting at Nicomedia in

351 as Gallus was travelling to Antioch. Constantius was persuaded enough by these spurious charges as Julian was called to the imperial court to answer them and despite being able to refute the accusations, it is alleged that the future emperor was only spared the same fate as Gallus through the intervention of the new empress, Eusebia. After a brief but frightening stay at Comum, near Milan, Julian was allowed to travel to Greece to continue his studies.

It was not only Ammianus' heroes who were targeted for Constantian 'justice'. Eusebius and Arbitio dealt with those soldiers accused of carrying out the worst of Gallus' actions. Without examining evidence or conducting any sort of investigation, they doled out torture, banishments, demotions and even death however they saw fit. And yet, demonstrating just how arbitrary Constantius' justice could be, Gallus' head chamberlain, Gorgonius, was acquitted despite his knowledge, collusion and even instigation of many of the *Caesar*'s ill-deeds. It would seem that the imperial court looked after their own but for a price. With Constantius again proving himself susceptible to rumour, slanderous accusations again began to be thrown about at almost all levels of the military and political hierarchies, with Paul the Chain and a new partner in crime, Mercurius, known as the 'Count of Dreams' prominent in the dishing out of such arbitrary 'justice' and making sure that even the most insignificant charges came to the attention of the emperor.[65]

The kind of accusations flying about the imperial court is highlighted by a group of men being brought to trial for uttering anti-Constantian words whilst drunk and supposing that the emperor's reign might not have long left at a party held by Africanus, the governor of Pannonia II. Gaudentius, an *agent in rebus*, was present and reported the conversation to Rufinus, chief steward of the Illyrian prefecture. Keen to win promotion, Rufinus informed Constantius and in a rage, the emperor ordered the arrest of all those present by his bodyguard, Teutomeres. On their way to face trial at Milan, the man accused of starting the conversation, a tribune called Marinus, committed suicide in a tavern in Aquileia. The rest were tortured until they admitted their roles in the drunken conversations and were condemned to exile, although Arbitio secured them a pardon, for something in return.[66] These were not the last instances of this brand of torture and exaggeration infiltrating the imperial justice system; and the potential problems of such arbitrary justice, court intrigue and how they could turn loyal soldiers into desperate and deadly opponents were soon to be laid bare in the part of the empire that felt it had been overlooked, even abandoned, by the imperial authorities over the previous decade. The focus now switched to Gaul. But before that, it is important to look at another on-going distraction for Constantius: the religious politics of his newly Christian Roman Empire.

Chapter VI

"This Turbulent Priest": Constantius, Athanasius and Religious Politics

If you want the Logos Doctrine, I can serve hot and hot. God begat Him, and before he was begotten, he was not.
— A paraphrasing of Arius' jingle by Sayers (1951), 119

"If the Father begat the Son...": Athanasius and the Arian Controversy

While conflict with the Persian king, barbarian tribes, imperial usurpers and members of his own family are forefront in the reign of Constantius, it is arguable that the most important crises he faced were in the religious sphere. Here, Constantius was faced with the fallout of another decision taken by Constantine: the embracing of Christianity. The various disputes that arose over Christian thought, faith, Christology and imperial attempts to force doctrinal unity would bring the Roman Empire to the brink of a second civil war between sons of Constantine. While being far from the only religious thorn in Constantius' side, the most prominent obstacle and the instigator of this second bout of brotherly enmity was the bishop of Alexandria, Athanasius.

Born in the late third century,[1] over the course of almost half a century, Athanasius would demonstrate "an unerring political instinct, an unfailing judgement in knowing when to resist the emperor and when to yield for future advantage... [while] conspicuously lacking in the Christian virtues of meekness and humility".[2] Athanasius' background is somewhat obscure, although he was likely of urban Alexandrian origins. Such low-class origins not only saw Athanasius stuck with the quarrelsome and poorly educated stereotype of Egyptian priests in the fourth century, they may also explain his populist leanings and lack of inhibition in the face of opposition and authority.[3] This low status also led to suggestions of Coptic origins as the urban working classes in Alexandria were a mixture of Greek and Coptic. However, it is more likely that Athanasius was an Alexandrian Greek who was later appropriated by Coptic

Christians as there is no suggestion that he knew Coptic in the way that he learned Latin during his prolonged western exile.[4]

His religious doctrine was inherited from his mentor, bishop Alexander of Alexandria. As with most early fourth century priests, Alexander was influenced by the Great Persecution and his own mentor and predecessor, Peter, was martyred in late November 311. This date played an important role in Athanasius' calling as Alexander first met the young Athanasius on the anniversary of Peter's martyrdom and taking this as an omen, the bishop brought Athanasius into his household. There, Athanasius received a religious education, although his writing and debating skills demonstrate some familiarity with more classical techniques. The young Athanasius excelled and was soon promoted to deacon and as Alexander's personal assistant, he travelled to the Council of Nicaea in 325. While it had a long agenda to address, the most important issue faced by this Council for the career of Athanasius, the reputation of Constantius and the doctrinal disputes for the rest of the century was the Arian Controversy.[5]

Soon after Alexander became Bishop in 313,[6] a man of Libyan origin called Arius rose to prominence in Alexandria through his radical theological teachings. The exact nature of those teachings is difficult to determine as Arius modified his beliefs over time and hostile interpretations moved the perception of 'Arianism' away from its original form. Extensive work has been done in trying to uncover this original form but a consensus is unlikely.[7] Rather than go into the full extent of these arguments, it will suffice to focus on the central controversy of Arius' teachings: the subjugation of Jesus to God.

If the Father begat the Son, he that was begotten had a beginning of existence: and from this it is evident, that there was a time when the Son was not. It therefore necessarily follows, that he had his substance from nothing... [and] possessing free will, he was capable of vice and virtue.[8]

These ideas sparked debate within the Alexandrian hierarchy before Alexander "declared himself in favour of those who affirmed that the Son was consubstantial and co-eternal with the Father"[9] and had Arius deposed and excommunicated. However, the bishop had been too slow as the Arian doctrine had taken root and soon claimed the support of many leading eastern churchmen, including Eusebius of Nicomedia.[10] This allowed Arius to portray his excommunication as being extended to men of similar beliefs. Local ecclesiastical councils were called in Palestine and Bithynia to discuss the implications of Arianism, with many more coming out in support, allowing Arius to return to Alexandria, although not without violence.[11]

If not for the hardening of attitudes caused by the Great Persecution and the recent activities of Melitius, who would cross paths with Athanasius on several occasions,[12] Arius may have faced less vehement opposition from the Alexandrian authorities. As it was, Alexander, Athanasius and their allies saw this subjugation of the Son as an anathema to be excised from the church. However, the terms 'Arian' and 'Arianism' must be treated with great caution. So vehement was their opposition that Athanasius and his allies deployed these terms in a pervasive and derogatory manner towards anyone they considered an enemy, whether it was Constantius who backed a Christology that differed from that of Athanasius and had the temerity to not persecute known Arians or leading churchmen like Eusebius of Caesarea who, despite not agreeing with Arius, were willing to listen to and engage him in philosophical debate.[13]

So entrenched were these opinions that another council of Alexandria, intervention from Hosius of Cordoba and a letter from Constantine urging Alexander and Arius "not to quarrel, since they differed only on esoteric points of theology and philosophy, not over the central tenets of divine law",[14] failed to break the deadlock. This led to the inclusion of the Arian controversy on the agenda at Nicaea and in the presence of the emperor, numerous prominent bishops, Arius and Athanasius, the Council promulgated a creed that was accepted by all but the most ardent Arians, who followed Arius into exile.[15] But this seeming victory of the Nicene Creed and its supporters was far from the end of the matter. Arianism continued to gain support throughout the east, especially in Syria and Palestine. And when Eusebius of Caesarea deposed several anti-Arian bishops at a council of Antioch in 327,[16] Arius petitioned Constantine, who welcomed him back into the church through a council at Nicomedia. Alexander was not so forgiving, refusing to attend Nicomedia or "to admit Arius to communion with himself or the church of Egypt",[17] Even an intervention from Constantine fell on deaf ears.

The sudden death of Alexander in the spring of 328 provided an opportunity to resolve this deadlock as a conclave met to find a compromise candidate to satisfy the supporters of Alexander, Arius and Melitius. However, Athanasius forced himself into the spotlight. He was not in Alexandria at the time of his mentor's death, having been sent to deliver a letter to the imperial court. Perturbed by the idea of compromise with those he considered heretics and schismatics, he rushed back to the city to have himself elected bishop by a small group of allies on 8th June 328. Despite the questionable nature of his consecration, the new bishop refused to bow to pressure to readmit Arius and his followers. He then went further by using force against the Melitians, driving them into an alliance with Eusebius of Nicomedia. This alliance brought various charges against Athanasius throughout the remainder of Constantine's reign including extortion, bribery, uncanonical election, destruction of church property and even the murder of Arsenius, bishop of Hypsele, who was still alive.[18]

Such scurrilous accusations led Constantine to call a council at Tyre for 335, where "all interested parties were to attend, whether they wished to do so or not".[19] Again Athanasius was faced with various accusations and the Tyrian council sent a commission to Egypt to investigate.[20] Despite obstruction from Athanasian allies, the commission found evidence of the destruction of the chalice of a priest called Ischyras. On hearing this, the Council of Tyre deposed Athanasius,[21] who fled to Constantinople where he met Constantine and pleaded for protection from such charges. By the time the bishops arrived from Tyre, they found that imperial suspicion had fallen on their impartiality, essentially voiding their findings.[22]

This led to a showdown between Eusebius of Nicomedia and Athanasius in the presence of the emperor, with the former claiming that the latter had threatened to interrupt the flow of grain from Egypt to Constantinople. Much like the 'murder' of Arsenius, this charge was nonsense but its seriousness obliged Constantine to investigate. The argument came down to whether Athanasius was the poor ascetic he claimed to be or the unscrupulous churchman who manipulated his position to become rich and powerful. In the heat of this argument, Athanasius lost his composure and told Constantine that it would be God who judged between them. In the face of such insolence, the emperor exiled him to Trier, although he did not depose Athanasius and declared that further investigation would take place.[23] While many of these charges were trumped up and Constantine refused to depose him, it does seem clear that "Athanasius exercised power and protected his position in Alexandria by the systematic use of violence and intimidation."[24]

It was not until after the death of Constantine that Athanasius' Gallic exile, along with that of all other bishops exiled by the deceased emperor, was overturned. Athanasius claimed that it was a joint pronouncement by all three surviving sons, although it appears instead to have been the initiative of Constantine II, who was likely influenced by the man resident at his capital, Athanasius himself.[25] While Constantine II was behind his restoration, as an Egyptian bishop, Athanasius was under the jurisdiction of Constantius. This raises the question of why would Constantine II restore Athanasius? Given his short tenure as emperor and the damnation of his memory by his brothers, it is difficult to come to any firm conclusions about the second Constantine. Perhaps he believed in Athanasius' innocence or had been manipulated by the Alexandrian bishop. A more sinister motive and one that is not all that difficult to believe given his actions towards Constans in 340 would be that Constantine

II was hoping to use the upheaval that Athanasius' return to Egypt might cause to distract Constantius. Of course, he might just have been looking to rid himself of a religious troublemaker. One could well imagine Athanasius petitioning Constantine II to the extent that he would have done anything to rid himself of such a nuisance. For his part, Athanasius claimed that Constantine I had intended to recall him, having only really 'exiled' him for his own safety.[26]

Getting Off on the Wrong Foot

On his journey home, Athanasius met Constantius at Viminacium, near modern Kostolac in Serbia, shortly before the three brothers met to divide the empire.[27] Nothing is known of this interview save that it took place, although it can be envisioned that Constantius encouraged Athanasius not to stir up religious problems at a transitional time for the empire and war in the east. Such a warning might help explain Constantius' outrage at the contested election for the new bishop of Constantinople and Athanasius' role in it. This trouble spawned from the anti-Arian, Paul, armed with the recommendation of the deceased bishop, having himself consecrated without a consensus or the required approval of adjacent sees.[28] The suggestion is that when passing through the capital, Athanasius encouraged and even took part in Paul's consecration. Wishing to hasten east, Constantius was furious, and called a council, which deposed and exiled Paul to Pontus. Eusebius of Nicomedia was then elected as bishop of Constantinople. Athanasius also found time "to intervene in ecclesiastical matters in Syria, Phoenice, and Palestine",[29] taking any opportunity to promote anti-Arianism, which no doubt further angered Constantius.

Athanasius continued to show that he had not been chastened by his time in exile or the warnings of the emperor when he arrived home in Alexandria and his opponents were soon attempting to depose him, calling a council at Antioch in late 337/early 338. In response, Athanasius called his own council at Alexandria for 338. Needless to say, these two meetings achieved nothing other than mutual recriminations. However, Antioch made one thing clear to Athanasius: Constantius had taken up against him. The emperor sent a letter to Athanasius expressing his backing for the Antiochene council and reproaching the bishop for embezzlement. This imperial missive also included a summons to the imperial court at Cappadocian Caesarea. This was not something that Athanasius could ignore but he was determined to defend himself and was successful in nullifying the pronouncements against him as he was back in Alexandria overseeing the visit of the ascetic, Antony the Great, before the end of summer 338.[30]

Such an event would seem to demonstrate the continued popularity of Athanasius, but instead it highlighted the tenuousness of his position. The stage-managed spectacle of Antony emerging from the desert to lend his prestige to Athanasius was an overt attempt to shore up his support in the face of further attempts to unseat him. Indeed, Antony's visit might have been sparked by the replacing of the pro-Athanasian prefect of Egypt, Theodorus, with a certain Philagrius, who had played a major role in the commission of the Council of Tyre and was considered a reliable pair of hands to carry out the expected deposition of the bishop.[31] This change of Egyptian prefect must have been a plan by Constantius.

With this new prefect in place, another council met at Antioch in late 338/early 339 with Constantius once more present. Again the charges of destruction of church property were levied at Athanasius as was his conduct on his return journey to Alexandria and his use of violence against his opponents. Given the weight of evidence and the make up of the council and its imperial convenor, the outcome was inevitable; Athanasius was deposed, with a Cappadocian called Gregory installed as bishop of Alexandria on 22nd March 339. Rather than face justice, Athanasius fled the city on 16th April 339,[32] although he did not go quietly, complaining of his mistreatment by heretical bishops and how Philagrius had employed armed bands of pagans and Jews, while depicting the arrival of Gregory more in terms of a sack by a military conqueror: rape, pillage, plunder and the defiling of Alexandrian churches on Easter Sunday. To Athanasius, this was an attack on the Christian Church, on a greater scale even than that seen during the Great Persecution.[33]

Such fiery rhetoric was sure to incite his allies and other anti-Arians but in the meantime, Athanasius needed somewhere safe to hide, somewhere he could either lay low or enjoy support from the local clergy and authorities. This meant that he had to remove himself from the territory of Constantius altogether. The support of Constantine II made Trier an option but in the months prior to his deposition another western ally had emerged: Julius, the bishop of Rome. The pope had shown his dislike for the manipulation of councils, calling for a church-wide meeting to deal with the disputes involved. And so upon slipping out of Alexandria, the deposed Athanasius travelled to Italy to be closer not just to a more favourable emperor but also to a powerful religious ally.

Imperial politics soon intervened. Not long after arriving in Rome, Athanasius wrote to both Constantine II and Constans for aid against his imperial and ecclesiastical detractors. This was innocent enough but the events of 340 introduced a hint of intrigue. The letter to Constantine now looked like an encouragement to invade the territory of his brother. Even if such rumours were untrue, Athanasius' personal acquaintance with the defeated, dead and damned Constantine saw him frozen out of politics, even though his later works reflected Constantine's *damnatio memoriae* with the removal of his name.[34] Constantius offered no help and Constans was distracted by the ramifications of his overthrow of his treacherous eldest brother. Therefore, Athanasius focused on the ideological issues involving Arianism, which he claimed "represented an attack on the doctrinal orthodoxy of the whole church".[35] There is propagandist posturing in such a pronouncement but it was not without its purpose with Athanasius realising "that ultimate success in his own struggle depended on producing proof that more was at stake than the restitution of a single proud prelate".[36]

Julius again looked to call a church-wide council but the Constantian Council of Antioch replied with a thinly veiled rebuke, stating that while his position as pope accorded Julius significant prestige, it did not give him the right to interfere with the decisions of a canonical council. It also threatened to remove the recognition of Julius' see by eastern bishops should he continue to support Athanasius.[37] Julius defended his guests using the decisions of other councils, particularly the original condemnation of Arius, to highlight the error and indeed hypocrisy of the Antiochene council. He also demanded that the eastern bishops cease what he saw as the persecution of those who were following the findings of Nicaea. The pope then held a council of fifty western bishops to give his response a canonical veneer but such grandstanding had done nothing for the exiled bishops or doctrinal unity.[38]

Instead, the number of exiles increased as Paul of Constantinople arrived in the west having been displaced once more from the imperial capital. Paul had returned to Constantinople from his first exile in Pontus in the aftermath of the death of Eusebius of Nicomedia in mid-341,[39] hoping to regain the see from the newly elected successor, Macedonius. By resorting to violence, Paul briefly succeeded forcing Constantius to send his *magister militum*, Hermogenes, to expel the usurping bishop once more. This only enflamed the situation and Hermogenes was soon lynched by Paul's supporters. Such an outrage roused Constantius from his winter quarters at Antioch to deal with this in person. The emperor regained control and once again expelled Paul. He also punished the city itself by halving its free grain dole.[40] Such decisive action against an anti-Arian contributed to the depiction of Constantius as having Arian beliefs; however, this is untrue as the emperor's demand that law and order were preserved and respected will have spurred him to act against anyone. Had Macedonius' supporters resorted to such violence and lynched a *magister*, it is certain that Macedonius will have faced a similar punishment to that of Paul.

Civil War and Exile

The exile of Paul exacerbated things for rather than join the increasing cadre of exiles residing with Julius and perhaps highlighting the failure of religious dialogue, Paul instead travelled to the court of Constans at Trier. The combination of Paul, the bishop of Trier, Maximinus, Julius and Athanasius convinced Constans "that their deposition imperilled Christian orthodoxy".[41] This alliance saw Athanasius meet with Constans on perhaps four occasions during the first half of the 340s: Milan in autumn 342, Trier in summer 343, Trier again in autumn 345 and Aquileia in 345. While the extent of Athanasius' role in advising Constans is unknown, it is perhaps unsurprising that Constantius would later complain that Athanasius, "not satisfied with the ruin of the older of my brothers, did not cease from inciting the blessed Constans to hatred against me".[42] By mid 342, Constans had demanded that Constantius explain the depositions of Athanasius and Paul, to which Constantius replied by sending four bishops to Trier. Unsatisfied by their answers, Constans upped the rhetoric, hinting at military intervention if Constantius did not accept the return of the exiles. Distracted by the Persian war and unwilling to call his brother's military bluff, Constantius acceded to the idea of a joint council at Serdica in 343.[43]

Both sides sent sizeable delegations but crucially, given the democratic nature of voting in such councils, they were of unequal size: the eastern group was eighty strong, while the western one, containing Athanasius, had ninety.[44] This ensured that the Council of Serdica was a farce. Neither side proved willing to negotiate while the eastern bishops refused to countenance any vote they knew they would lose. Such dead-end talks dragged on for several days until a letter arrived from Constantius that altered the political situation: he had defeated Shapur.[45] The eastern bishops removed themselves from Serdica on the excuse of needing to congratulate their emperor but not before composing a long synodical letter excommunicating Hosius of Cordoba and Julius and denouncing the exiled bishops. The western delegates responded with a similar polemic against the Arian heresy and any who failed to denounce it, complete with a writ of excommunication against any who doubted the singularity of the Trinity. If nothing else, Serdica had proved the intransigence of both sides of the Arian controversy, particularly now that each had the support of an emperor.

That is not to say that there were not attempts to overcome this impasse. On top of their polemic, the western bishops also composed a letter for Constantius' eyes only in which they demonstrated an understanding of the emperor's tendency towards flatterers. They appealed to Constantius' clemency and piety in order to stop the 'persecution' of orthodox priests and to allow them to return to their sees. Indeed, Constantius had already allowed some exiled clergy to return to Egypt.[46] This apparent negotiation roused Stephanus, bishop of Antioch, in an attempt to discredit the two western bishops who had brought the letters to Constantius. To do so, he used priestly intermediaries to hire a prostitute to spend the night with one of the envoys. The plan unravelled and Stephanus' role was uncovered, leading to his deposition.[47] The potential motive of Stephanus of hardening attitudes to the envoys and their letters may be given some credence by the conciliatory air that the 344 Council of Antioch took to the western position. Another embassy of bishops then travelled to Milan to deliver these conciliatory decisions, only for the western response to be rejected by the eastern envoys.

This lack of progress in the re-establishment of exiles saw Constans issue another missive to his brother threatening war if he did not comply. This declaration would later cause trouble for Athanasius as it was believed by Constantius that Athanasius had again encouraged Constans to resort to military brinkmanship.[48] While Constantius would hold a grudge against Athanasius, in the 340s, the eastern emperor was still in a placatory mood. Despite underlying insincerity, Constantius sent to both Constans and Athanasius inviting the exiled bishop to reoccupy the see made vacant by the death of Gregory on 26th June 345.[49] After meeting Constans once more at Trier and then visiting Julius at Rome, Athanasius took ship for Antioch. There, the bishop met Constantius sometime before the summer of 346 with the emperor supposedly swearing never to listen to slanderous accusations about the bishop.[50] Even if this was an exaggeration by Athanasius, Constantius had gone out of his way to reconcile Athanasius and rescind past measures taken against him. And so, on 21st October 346, Athanasius re-entered Alexandria as its bishop once more,[51] but for all its triumphalism his restoration was far from secure. It had only been possible through the perceived weakness of Constantius, whose position was improving with the blunting of Shapur's attacks and the declining popularity of Constans in the west. Therefore, it became clear that the pro-Arian party would soon go after the restored anti-Arian bishops once more.

In the early months of 349, they made their latest move. Restored to Constantinople at the same time Athanasius had been returned to Alexandria, Paul was once again accused, condemned and deposed by a council. This time, Constantius was taking no chances. Paul was seized and brought before the emperor in chains by the praetorian prefect, Flavius Philippus, before being sent into an ignominious exile in the Taurus Mountains.[52] With the fate of Paul and the calling of another Council of Antioch for autumn 349, Athanasius recognised that he had a target on his back.[53] The make-up of the council and its imperial backing meant that there was only one outcome: Athanasius was once again condemned and deposed. However, before Philippus could carry out this deposition, news arrived from the west. Constans was dead.

The usurpation of Magnentius would appear to be a significant blow to Athanasius as it removed his imperial benefactor. Even if Constans had done little to prevent Constantius' actions against the bishops in 349, he had threatened war just four years previously. However, instead, the advent of Magnentius to imperial power presented Athanasius with an opportunity as the usurper looked for any avenue of support and acceptance, especially amongst Constantius' enemies. Recognising this threat, Constantius responded with an almost admirable combination of brutality and pragmatism. Paul of Constantinople was starved in his small mountainous prison cell for six days before being strangled; the report of which reached Athanasius through Philagrius, now serving as *vicarius* in Pontus, in a move that the bishop saw as gloating and perhaps even "chagrin at not being permitted to supervise the murder himself".[54] It was also a warning to Athanasius about the perils of communications with the usurper, an accusation that Athanasius would have to defend himself against. The root of such an accusation lies in the idea that Athanasius sent a letter to Constans pleading for help against the 349 Council of Antioch and that that letter fell into the hands of Magnentius. In replying to it in his own name, the usurper tainted Athanasius in the eyes of Constantius with communication with his imperial opponent.

This seems more like rumour than fact but Magnentius did dispatch an embassy of two bishops, Servatius of Tongres and Maximus, ostensibly to Constantius, but with the purpose of contacting Athanasius. In response, Constantius overturned the decisions of Antioch and wrote to the bishop of Alexandria in benevolent and familiar terms, expressing sorrow over Constans' murder and promising that "in accordance with our wishes, you be bishop in your own place for all time".[55] By moving so quickly, Constantius' letter arrived in Alexandria before Magnentius' envoys, impressing upon Athanasius who could get to him first and despite knowing that Constantius was disingenuous, the bishop of Alexandria was left with very little choice but to turn down the approaches of Magnentius.

If Athanasius hoped for a Magnentian victory, he was to be disappointed as the battles of Mursa and Mons Seleucus left Constantius as sole emperor. Even before the final reckoning with the usurper, he had been putting things in place to force his ecclesiastical politics on the west through the Council of Sirmium to be held in late 351. While the council deposed the bishop of Sirmium, Photinus, its real aim was the removal of Athanasius. What followed was a delicate episode of "diplomatic evasion".[56] Athanasius wrote to Liberius, the new pope, reiterating his innocence and claiming that the bishops at Sirmium had promulgated a heretical creed. In turn, Liberius wrote to Constantius asking for a large, representative council to meet at Aquileia. However, the triumphant emperor was not to be denied. At a council at Arles in winter 353, it was made clear that any bishop who did not ascribe to the pronouncements of Sirmium would be condemned, deposed and exiled. Liberius remained defiant and called once more for a joint council with Constantius relenting and the Council of Milan convening in 355. Due to perceived imperial interference, attendance at Milan was poor, perhaps as low as thirty bishops.

If Athanasius, Liberius and their allies hoped to call the emperor's bluff, they were much mistaken. When several bishops refused to ascribe to the condemnations of Sirmium, Constantius had them deposed. His replacing of Dionysius, bishop of Milan, with the eastern Auxentius hints at an underlying aim of replacing opposition with allies.[57] Pressure was exerted on those who had not attended Milan, particularly Liberius and when the pope again refused to join in the condemnations of Sirmium, Constantius had him arrested by the prefect of Rome and brought before him at Milan.[58] When Liberius again refused to conform, the emperor exiled him to Beroa in Thrace and had an archdeacon called Felix 'elected' as the new bishop of Rome. After some months in exile, in 357, Liberius accepted the condemnations and creed of Sirmium.

However, Constantius refused to wait for the support of the pope or the findings of Milan. An imperial *notarius*, Diogenes, arrived in Alexandria in August 355 to undermine Athanasius. When this proved unsuccessful,[59] Constantius resorted to more direct action. On the Feast of the Epiphany 356, the *dux* Syrianus and another *notarius*, Hilarius, entered Alexandria at the head of troops. Athanasius approached the *dux* for an explanation and having received nothing concrete in reply, asked for imperial arbitration. Syrianus agreed to send for word from Constantius but this was just a show to placate Athanasius' supporters before carrying out the declarations of Sirmium and Milan in deposing the bishop of Alexandria. After twenty-three days of keeping up this pretence, Syrianus launched his attack on the night of 8–9 February 356, declaring Athanasius deposed and occupying many Alexandrian churches. Athanasius again evaded capture as Syrianus set about consolidating his control in preparation for the arrival of George of Cappadocia, the appointed successor of Athanasius. The deposed bishop would later claim that he left Alexandria to plead his case to Constantius but was stopped by the enforcement of the edicts of the Council of Milan, the arrest of Liberius and reports of persecution of bishops across Libya and Egypt.[60]

Despite strong support,[61] Athanasius stayed in hiding for the remainder of Constantius' reign. The upheavals of the imperial crackdown allowed him to remain within the city itself before taking refuge in other parts of Egypt and perhaps beyond as Constantius would address angry letters to the kingdom of Axum south of Roman Egypt. In advising the Axumites against the teachings of Athanasius, Constantius demonstrated a similar belief to his father that the Roman emperor had an obligation to Christian unity and orthodoxy not just within the empire but beyond its boundaries.[62]

A New Controversy

By the end of 356, Constantius might have been forgiven for thinking that he had a handle on the theological direction of the empire. Pope Liberius had accepted the findings of the councils of Sirmium, Arles and Milan, declaring that neither he nor Rome were in communion with Athanasius, who was deposed from the Alexandrian see and on the run. Throughout this next period of exile, 356–362, Athanasius wrote more than at any other time of his life.[63] The vast majority of these works see Athanasius defending himself and recording the viciousness of his Constantian opponents, even to the point of making "the false and barefaced claim that he has never been condemned by an ecclesiastical verdict, only persecuted for his devotion to Christ by imperial fiat".[64] Despite his exile, Athanasius was kept informed of theological discussions across the empire as his *On the Councils of Arminium and Seleucia* demonstrated an understanding of the new controversy to rack the Christian Church in the late 350s, the Homoean Creed.

Buoyed by his successes, Constantius turned his attention to Hosius of Cordoba. Despite being nearly one hundred years old, the Spanish bishop[65] initially withstood imperial threats and flattery, only to be forced to put his name to a statement which "emphasised the uniqueness of God the Father, and hence the subordination of the Son".[66] However, the important issue that emerged from this statement was not Hosius' compliance but rather its suggestion that *-ousia* and *homoousios* should be removed from official creeds because it does not appear in the Bible and was "beyond the knowledge of man, and no one can explain the incarnation of the Son".[67] Just when Arianism had started to run out of steam Constantius and his allies had stumbled into a whole other set of theological problems.

Arianism had focused debate on the relationship between God the Father and God the Son but now it moved on to the primacy of the Father over the Holy Spirit as well as the Son. In this Trinitarian argument, the semantics become even more difficult to distinguish and even Athanasius himself, who had spent the best part of the last three decades arguing over doctrinal minutiae, stated that there was little difference between the terms used in this split – *homoousios* and *homoiousios*[68] – despite preferring the former due to its selection by the Council of Nicaea. Such new theological approaches saw the shattering of the duality of pro- and anti-Arianism with a third doctrine emerging in the late 350s: Anomoeanism.[69] This was the belief that not only was Jesus not of the same nature as God, he was not of a similar nature, rejecting the consubstantial *homoousios* of the Nicene party and the compromise doctrine of *homoiousios*. As they were his theological enemies, Athanasius referred to Anomoeans like Aetius and Eunomius as "Arians"[70] but this must be taken with a pinch of salt. Rather than being Arian, both built upon Arius' questioning of the relationship between Father and Son through logical thinking but they became so radical that they forced Athanasius and his allies to join with their former opponents in an attempt to shutdown this new heresy.

In suggesting the removal of such party-defining words and undermining their creeds in the process, it is unsurprising that Constantius and his allies were faced with an adverse reaction. A small council at Ancyra issued a letter asking why the definitions of Christology needed such a rethink when they had already been formalised by several previous councils and asked Constantius for another great council to settle this dispute before it got out of hand. The emperor acquiesced but under the influence of those who had forced Hosius' hand, instead of one great council he called two: Seleucia Isauria in the east for 27 September 359 and Arminium in July of the same year in the west.[71] The idea of the separate meetings was presumably that they would be more easily controlled.

These councils saw the presentation of a new creed, which had been settled on by a small committee beforehand and was light on technical terms.[72] Rather than appease everyone, the compromise was rejected by the majority at Arminium, which then reaffirmed the Nicene Creed and condemned the promulgators of this Homoean Creed. As a supporter and instigator of the minority opinion, Constantius refused to accept this. Envoys from the Homoean minority were well received at his court while the anti-Homoean majority was fobbed off with excuses and told to wait at Adrianople until he returned from his military campaign against the Sarmatians, Quadi and Limigantes. This delay broke the nerve of the majority envoys and on 10 October 359, they disavowed the findings of Arminium and signed up to a slightly altered Homoean Creed during a meeting at Nike in Thrace. The choice of Nike was no coincidence as the new creed to replace that of the Council of Nicaea could also be called a 'Nicene' creed and it is recorded that the similarity did fool some bishops.[73]

Despite this capitulation, it can hardly be said that the western council had gone smoothly, revealing just how few his anti-Nicene supporters were: only about eighty of the four hundred bishops at Arminium. And forcing its delegation into compliance along with the coercion of Liberius was not going to gain widespread recognition in the west. This did not bode well for the Council of Seleucia and there was trouble on its opening. Not only had several prominent bishops failed to arrive, those present could not agree on the course of the council's deliberation and whether the hearing of the cases or the discussion on theological disputes should occur first.

Even with imperial officials present, both parties failed to reach any agreement and the anti-Nicene minority soon removed itself from deliberations. This left the majority to follow its own agenda and reaffirm the Nicene Creed. Of course, this was opposed by the Homoean faction who pronounced their own creed, which was that of Sirmium with the removal of *homoousia*, *homoiousia* and *anomoios*. Both sides sent envoys to Constantius to present their own findings and again the emperor resorted to delay and threats to undermine Nicene resolve, highlighting that only this Homoean Creed could provide a united front against heresy. "The classic manoeuvre of telling both sets of recalcitrant envoys separately that the other had accepted the homoean creed succeeded"[74] and on the last day of 359, representatives of Arminium and Seleucia subscribed to the new creed.[75]

Armed with this 'acceptance,' Constantius and his allies set about purging their enemies from prominent bishoprics and called a council at Constantinople for 360 to enforce their will. Such imperially sanctioned orthodoxy at the point of a sword proved unacceptable. And once the fall of Amida forced Constantius back east, his new orthodoxy began to fall apart under the attacks of the likes of Hilary of Poitiers. The works of Hilary demonstrate the hardening of attitudes towards Constantius over time as his *To The Emperor Constantius* (written pre-360) "adopts the assumption that Constantius is good, pious, religious – and therefore orthodox",[76] while his later *Against Constantius* is a violent diatribe denouncing the emperor "as a tyrant who does not deserve to rule because he attacks God and persecutes the Christian Church just as much as Nero, Decius, and Galerius ever had".[77] It is Hilary who even goes as far as to call Constantius an Antichrist who had unleashed war, attacked the church and rebelled against the piety of his own father.[78]

Such vitriol might have been extreme in order to shock Constantius away from his Homoean path but if that was the case, it was fruitless hyperbole. The emperor had already proven himself willing to threaten force against churchmen so being warned off it by one of the most prominent opponents of his Homoean orthodoxy was not going to stop him. It was not to come to violence though for, as had happened at various other points, the religious situation of 359/360 was interrupted by military-political developments. Not only had Shapur gone on the warpath again but just weeks after the Council of Constantinople, Julian was declared *Augustus* at Paris.

The Constantian Aftermath

Much like with Magnentius, Julian likely reached out to dissidents such as Hilary and Athanasius when he started formulating his plan for usurpation with the former complaining that Julian had been treated badly by evil men.[79] This could be seen as somewhat hypocritical given Julian's secret paganism but it was a pragmatic acceptance of the religio-political realities of the mid-fourth century. The reach and power of the Christian Church and its adherents could not be ignored, leading Julian to pose "as a champion of religious freedom, specifically of the freedom of western bishops to adhere to the Nicene creed".[80] Regardless of Julian's faith, the opponents of the Homoean Creed will have supported the young upstart as he would be bound by the need to find allies "to abandon Constantius' most unpopular policies".[81]

Julian may have had something to do with a council at Paris led by Hilary that excommunicated the Constantian bishops who disseminated the Homoean Creed beyond allowing it to take place.[82] At some stage he issued an edict that allowed bishops who had been exiled by Constantius to return home. This is dated to after Constantius' death as it arrived in Alexandria on 8 February 362 but will have been issued earlier as restoring troublemakers like Athanasius will have been little use to Julian without Constantius around to be distracted.[83] It is speculative to suggest how the religious side of civil war between Julian and Constantius would have gone had the latter lived. It would have been foolhardy for Julian to reveal his paganism before any defeat of Constantius for even the most fervent anti-Homoean may have sided with the emperor in the face of a pagan usurper, no matter what promises he made. That is not to say that Julian was reticent in his promotion of paganism in the wake of Constantius' death. He restored temples, ordered the army to sacrifice to the old gods and removed the privileges given to Christianity whilst imposing legal disabilities as part of "a systematic attempt to undo the Constantinian reformation".[84] Therefore, it appeared that with Julian's usurpation the future of Roman Christianity was at a crossroads, with either a pagan usurper or a heretical emperor destined to emerge victorious.

However, even with Julian emerging from 361 as sole *Augustus* and a confirmed follower of the old gods, his attempts to turn back the clock were in vain. As the great persecutors had found, the roots of Christian belief ran deep and "harassment or covert persecution was doomed to be ineffectual".[85] The continued obstinacy of Athanasius and Egypt shows the impossible task ahead of Julian. George was lynched, seemingly by pagans, not long after word of Constantius' death arrived and together with Julian's general edict restoring exiles, Athanasius retook his see again on 21 February 362 to continue the fight against the Homoean Creed. Despite perhaps hoping that the likes of Athanasius would disrupt Christianity enough for paganism to take root, Julian realised that such stubborn bishops could not be controlled and in October 362 he banished Athanasius once more, although the bishop removed himself to the Thebaid.[86]

Upon hearing of Julian's death in Mesopotamia a year later, Athanasius returned again to Alexandria and then took himself off to the imperial court for an audience with the newly elected Jovian. This audience at Hierapolis perhaps in October 363 saw Jovian instruct Athanasius to return to his duties in Alexandria.[87] The new emperor also sought a new creed to bring about unity and while his attempt was not successful, his more inclusive approach boded well for the future of Roman Christianity. However, this period of grace for Athanasius and his fellow anti-Homoean allies did not last long as Jovian himself died on 17 February 364, apparently of accidental suffocation.[88]

His replacement in the east, Valens, proved similar to Constantius in his approach to religious and doctrinal politics. This led Athanasius to label Valens as an 'Arian' and the period 365–375 progressed similarly to the 340s and 350s. The major difference was that, unlike Constans, Valens' brother and co-*Augustus*, Valentinian, refused to be drawn into the religious disputes, allowing Valens a freer hand imposing imperial orthodoxy through the Homoean Creed.[89] On 5 May 365, Valens repealed the restoration of exiled bishops which saw Athanasius again go into hiding, supposedly in his father's tomb, where he would remain for a few months until imperial politics again intervened. Worried that disorder would encourage Egypt to side with the usurper Procopius, Valens allowed Athanasius to retake his see in February 366. This would be his last exile and Athanasius was able to live out the last seven years of his life in relative peace, although he remained a champion of the Nicene Creed against imperial interference and heresy until dying in his own bed on 2 May 373.[90]

The peaceful times in Egypt did not last long after Athanasius' death with Valens subjecting the supporters of Peter, Athanasius' successor as bishop, to torture and deportation leading to the flight of the Alexandrian bishop to Rome. Imperial politics again altered the situation with Valens' death amongst the Roman military catastrophe at Adrianople on 9 August 378. Just over five months after Adrianople, the pro-Nicene Theodosius was promoted to

Augustus in the east and under his auspices the Second Ecumenical Council of Constantinople of 381 saw the triumph of Nicene Christianity over the remnant of Arianism, the Homoean Creed and other heresies enshrined in law.[91] Less than a decade after his death, Athanasius had had his final victory over Constantius.

"Let Superstition Cease": Constantius, Paganism and Judaism

Battling various doctrines within Christianity was far from the only interaction that Constantius had with the religions of his empire. While Julian's failed restoration would prove that the dominance of Christianity was not to be broken, it also highlighted that centuries of pagan tradition were not to be swept away in a generation or two and their interactions with paganism seem to bear out that Constantine and Constantius understood this. The former's Christian beliefs developed over the course of his reign and his conversion was by no means a complete *volte face* from paganism; his coinage, buildings and laws continued to demonstrate respect, even reverence for pagan rites and traditions. Sol Invictus – the Unconquered Sun – continued to be held in high regard and remained on Constantinian coinage until 325; pagan cults, shrines and temples were largely left alone, even in his new Christian capital. Early in his reign, he allowed pagans to "celebrate the rites of an outmoded illusion",[92] provided that they did not force Christians to join in. It must be highlighted though that Constantine confiscated a vast amount of the accumulated wealth of the pagan temples in the form of dedications, decorations and land, much of which was to be used in his monetary reforms and in the building of Constantinople.[93]

Constantine's language and actions towards paganism hardened as his reign and personal Christian faith progressed. Restrictions were placed on the "abominable blood and hateful odours"[94] of pagan sacrifices, some temples were closed and something of a blind eye was turned to violence against cult sites. However, this was far from all-encompassing and there was to be no systematic persecution. Many of these restrictions were rarely enforced and many pagan rites and practices were confirmed in law: augurs were still consulted, priests still protected and many state sacrifices still performed.[95] This would suggest that Constantine was taking something of a long term approach to undermining paganism, either through a fear of reprisal or due to an "aura of inevitability"[96] surrounding the death of paganism. Perhaps highlighting the continued minority of Christianity, the focus was more on the expansion and funding of churches and tax breaks for its members than on attacking others.

As Constantius was raised as a Christian from birth, it might be expected that he would show far less respect for ancient pagan rites and build on the foundations of his father. There seems to have been little Christian enthusiasm for a more fervent anti-pagan policy, although Julius Firmicus Maternus, showing all the zeal of a convert, pleaded for the emperor to see to it that paganism was "utterly eradicated",[97] and there are even some accusations that Constantius was under the influence of far more fervent anti-pagans.[98] Constantius did target paganism at various times throughout his reign, issuing bans on sacrifices, shutting down temples, and ending tax relief and subsidies, while also imposing torture and the death penalty on those who consulted soothsayers to divine the future.[99] This would seem like a large quantity of clear legislation aimed at paganism by Constantius; however, the circumstances of these laws need to be taken into account before any suggestion of a more concerted anti-pagan stance can be suggested.

The law of 353 reintroducing a ban on night time sacrifices after Magnentius had permitted them, shows some anti-pagan effort, although the lifting of the ban suggests that there was enough power left in paganism to harvest support, particularly amongst the senatorial families of Italy. Instead, it is a law of 341 that would seem to be more an attack on the "very lifeblood"[100] of paganism. The harshness of such a law has led to much speculation on whether or not this was a general ban and what might have been meant by *superstitio* in the mid fourth century. Could the pagan senators of Italy have given Constantine II support in his attack on Constans, leading the latter along with Constantius to punish them? Was Constantius merely acting in his role as *pontifex maximus* to regulate pagan practices?[101] The law itself requires clarification about its aims and scope, hinting at it having not been thought through or was focused on Italy rather than designed to be disseminated throughout the empire. Indeed, the following year, a follow-up law stated that many temples around Rome should be left alone, while a law of 356 was similarly harsh and has brought up similar questions over its intent.[102]

It is impossible to ascertain how effectively imposed such legislation was, with Ambrose of Milan claiming that pagan sacrifices continued throughout the city of Rome in 384.[103] That such laws were repeated would seem to suggest that they were either not enforced or were ignored by pagan populations; however, an emperor would repeat laws which had been successful so it is difficult to come to any firm conclusions on the effectiveness of Constantius' anti-pagan laws. It was understood by Constantius and his officials that the continued preponderance of pagans at most levels of society meant that such bans would not be widely implemented. Constantius even offered some protection to pagan sites by imposing fines on the desecration of pagan temples, tombs and monuments.[104]

It would therefore seem that despite some vociferous language and legislation, Constantius was happy to be "tolerant in deed, if not always in word"[105] towards paganism. This would not be all that surprising given the threat of pagan backlash and constant distractions of civil, foreign, political and religious strife. This relative moderation of Constantius' actions toward paganism is reflected by the lack of complaint by pagans themselves. The Roman Senate remained on good enough terms with Constantius in spite of the removal of the Altar of Victory in 357 to have him deified after his death.[106]

Because of that, Constantius' anti-pagan policy should be viewed as being much like that of his father: to promote Christianity and enfeeble paganism without resorting to fervent persecution. To that end, rather than disband existing pagan institutions, the erecting of new sites was banned while sacrificing was limited to private meetings, reducing the perceived power of such rites. And while there were as yet no real legal disabilities aimed at pagans, Christian clergy were subjected to various exemptions on compulsory public service, property and tax relief, although a law demanding that Christian prostitutes should only be bought by Christians does not sound very 'Christian' to modern ears.[107] Through such measures, conversion to Christianity was to be made an attractive proposition both in terms of finance, status and spirituality while paganism was to be left intact but as an "empty shell, drained of supernatural power".[108]

Constantius also built upon his father's policies towards the third religion of the Roman world, Judaism. The Constantinian approach to Jews mirrored that towards pagans, possibly for similar reasons; Judaism was an ancient religion worthy of respect but it would die out in the face of Christianity. Constantine again deployed harsh language against the Jews criticising their madness in not seeing the true path and their irredeemable sin as "murderers of the Lord"[109] while issuing laws prohibiting the spread of Judaism through proselytising and introducing penalties for the forced circumcision of slaves.[110] However, at the same time, Jewish religious officials were granted a similar immunity to curial duties as Christian clergy. Constantius did not revoke this privileged status but did increase the legal disabilities of the Jewish population. Forced circumcision of slaves was elevated to a capital offence and Jews were not allowed to own slaves of any other religion.[111] Other Constantian legislation towards the Jews included the confiscation of the property of Christian converts to Judaism and the forcible restoration of weaving women to state factories from Jewish businesses.[112]

This has led to suggestions that Constantius was focused as much on Jewish business being a competitor to state-run businesses than Judaism as competition to Christianity, hoping to provide as much of an advantage to the former as possible by limiting the skilled workers and slaves available to the latter. This idea may be furthered by claims of Constantius resorting to something approaching fiscal extortion of the Jews through excessive levies, which Julian felt the need to reimburse.[113] It is possible that such financial exactions were linked to the Jewish revolt of Isaac and Patricius, either as something of a catalyst or a punishment.

However, despite such financial undermining and some legal disabilities, it seems that the Jews, much like the pagans, were largely left alone by the Constantinian emperors so long as they kept themselves to themselves. If they did not attempt to convert Christians or prove too successful in competing for business and manpower, Constantius was willing to leave the Jews alone. It was only with the accession of Theodosius and his championing of Nicene Catholic orthodoxy that more forceful stances were taken against both paganism and Judaism.

Christian Emperor or Imperial Heretic?

Ultimately, Constantius' reputation in the realm of religion was due to his interaction with the Christian church. In a general sense, he again followed in the footsteps of his father. Constantine had begun the promotion of Christians to high office, which along with the meritocracy fostered by the Tetrarchs explains how a Cretan of humble birth such as Flavius Ablabius could rise to some of the highest positions in the empire. The prevalence of Christian consuls and praetorian prefects in Constantius' section of the empire demonstrates that he continued to promote Christians to high office. Indeed, it seems he appointed only one pagan to the consulship throughout his reign, Lollianus Mavortius.[114] Ablabius' career also shows how Constantius could turn against those who failed to accept his religious policies. Siding with Athanasius against Constantius contributed to Ablabius' dismissal from the imperial court and later his execution. However, the rapidity of these events so soon after the death of Constantine might suggest that Constantius was using such false rumours to rid himself of his tutor.[115]

The most obvious example of Constantius' reaction to intransigence in the face of his will was in the doctrinal disputes that lasted throughout his reign. Imperial interference in church affairs was never popular and with the idea that even the great Constantine as a layman had no direct influence on council votes, it was inevitable that an impasse would be reached between imperial and ecclesiastical spheres of influence. Constantine endured the initial shots in the conflict with the Donatist and Arian controversies and on the surface it appeared that the Council of Nicaea had solved many of these issues. Unfortunately, too many clergy had similar thoughts to those of Donatus – "What has the emperor to do with the church?"[116] – and Nicaea was only the beginning. This left the sons of Constantine to deal with the intractable sides of the doctrinal disputes caused by the theorising of Arius. Constantius viewed such intransigence as a challenge to his authority and once he achieved sole rule over the empire, he attempted to impose doctrinal unity. It took his direct political involvement in the councils of Sirmium, Arminium and Seleucia, "strong-arm tactics and deceit to extort from the bishops an acceptance of the official homoean creed".[117]

It should be noted though that Athanasius and his allies incorrectly painted Constantius as an Arian to further their propagandist aims. Instead, the emperor was acting in a fair and balanced way in refusing to condemn the more philosophical approach that blossomed from the teachings of Arius. Constantius should also receive some *kudos* for trying to find a compromise to the doctrinal impasse with the Homoean Creed rather than trying to bludgeon the malcontents into submission or resorting to persecution. It must also be noted that Constantius was not universally hated by religious sources with Cyril of Jerusalem presenting a positive representation of the emperor and his religious politics. However, the miraculous event reported by Cyril where "an enormous cross of light appeared in the sky"[118] over Jerusalem on 7 May 351, a symbol of divine approval of Constantius, appears more as a self-serving appeal to an emperor prone to rewarding flattery.

It is clear that Constantius did underestimate the depth of feeling and stubbornness that the Great Persecution and the repeated disputes had bred in the clergy. In attempting to take a step back from the doctrinal issues in the hope of becoming more inclusive and portray the contradictions within Christology as a divine mystery that man would never understand, the Homoean Creed was not only superseding the pronouncements of the Council of Nicaea but also encouraging learned, scholarly churchmen, some of whom will have devoted large parts of their lives to such study, to give up investigating a significant area of Christian philosophy. Unsurprisingly, such extortion did not make for a final settlement and the taint of force made the Homoean Creed even less palatable, leading its imperial champion to be depicted "as an 'Arian', a persecutor, a devil incarnate, or even an Antichrist".[119]

With such vehement ecclesiastical opposition and a damaged reputation, it is easy to forget that despite fervent opposition Constantius succeeded in establishing Homoeanism in large sections of the empire. The question then remains of what would have happened had he lived through his illness in 361. As it was expected that he would defeat Julian, Constantius may have found himself again in the position of divinely inspired, military conqueror, free to impose his Homoean orthodoxy. Faced by a victorious emperor who was willing to use force, many holdouts may have acquiesced to this new creed. However, it is possible that the likes of Athanasius will have continued to resist imperial interference in the church, leading to a further round of exiles, executions and perhaps even a general schism regarding the nature of the Trinity.

However, the defeat of Constantius' imperial orthodoxy by Nicene Catholicism had drastic ramifications for the Roman Empire and Europe as a whole. The presence of the Gothic bishop, Ulfila, during some of the negotiations surrounding the promulgation of the Homoean Creed saw to it that that doctrine, recorded as 'Arianism' even though it discarded all of Arius' central tenets, became favoured amongst the Christian Goths, who would over time spread it to their Germanic neighbours: Gepids, Lombards, Burgundians, Suebi, Vandals. As these tribes moved across the frontiers and took control of the western half of the Roman Empire throughout the course of the fifth and sixth centuries, they would cling to this creed not just as their religion but also as a way to differentiate themselves from Nicene Catholic Roman populations.[120]

In his dealings with religion, Constantius had shown himself to be every bit his father's successor with a mixture of legislation to establish who was in control but tolerance and at times even reverence for the ancient rites of paganism and Judaism. It was with his fellow Christians that Constantius found that trying to be somewhat fair to everyone was not going to be tolerated. And the Christian church was quick to demonstrate its power to defy imperial demands, not just on a theological basis but also on a physical one with the likes of Athanasius avoiding imperial justice through the connivance of priestly and lay populations. It will have come as quite a shock to an emperor like Constantius, who prided himself on being the son of the great Constantine, victorious against usurpers and steadfast in defending the empire against its outward enemies that his imperial writ did not extend to his empire's religion, its councils and even provinces such as Egypt.

Chapter VII

From Student to Soldier: The Rise of Julian

The duty of youth is to challenge corruption.

– Kurt Cobain

The Revolt of Silvanus

Despite having resisted Shapur, defeated Magnentius and soon to have dealt with the potential threat of Gallus, Constantius found that reuniting the empire under his sole control did not bring any real measure of peace to the Roman world. While Gallus was holding his kangaroo court, his generals were dealing with Jews, Isaurians and Arabs and Paul was terrorising Britain in the name of 'justice', Constantius himself had to take the field against the Alamanni along the Upper Rhine and Danube. But even this was not all of the empire's troubles in 354. Northern and central Gaul remained open to raids from the barbarians and the *bagaudae*. The origins of these *bagaudae* are murky but the most likely explanation is a reaction amongst the poorer classes to the combination of military confiscations, barbarian raids, harsh taxation and landowner exploitation throughout the third century joined by brigands and deserters. They had been dealt with by Maximian during the mid 280s, but there was enough of a resurgence by 353, spurred on by the degradations of civil war and barbarian incursion, for Constantius to have to send Silvanus to deal with them.[1]

That Silvanus was in a position to take command in northern Gaul demonstrates that Constantius had made good on his promise to promote the Frank to *magister peditum per Galliam* in return for his defection at Mursa. However, it is claimed that this appointment to such an important region was not made for the good of Gaul but because Arbitio saw an opportunity to remove a rival by encouraging Constantius to appoint Silvanus; the idea being that the task was more likely to ruin Silvanus' career than to see him achieve success. Whether part of Arbitio's plan or opportunism fostered by the climate of underhanded competition fermenting under Constantius, almost immediately there were attempts to undermine Silvanus' position even while he was dealing with threats to Roman security. It could even be that the likes of Arbitio were worried that Silvanus was becoming too popular through his successes against the Franks and the *bagaudae*, even if the *magister* made more use of bribery and financial concessions than force, and therefore instigating the plotting against him.

Dynamius, the intendant of the imperial baggage train, obtained Silvanus' signature on several documents only to forge their contents to make it seem as though the *magister* was attempting to place his allies at court to make a play for the imperial throne. This plot was aided by Aedesius, a former *magister memoriae*, the former *comes rei privitae*, Eusebius Mattyocopa and the praetorian prefect of Gaul, Lampadius, whose position allowed him to place these incriminating forgeries into the hands of the emperor. In the atmosphere of growing suspicion, it is unsurprising that Constantius took these letters at face value and ordered the immediate arrest of Silvanus and his supposed courtly allies, Tuscus and Albinus, as well as other individuals named in or to be recipient of the letters.

Fortunately for Silvanus, the commander of the Constantius' *Gentiles*, Malarichus, protested at the unfairness of men who fought for the empire being condemned on the word of cliques who had the most to gain from their removal. Instead, Malarichus asked permission to go to Silvanus and bring him to Milan in order to answer the accusations made against him. So sure was he of Silvanus' innocence that Malarichus offered to leave his relatives and colleague, Mallobaudes, behind as hostages while he fulfilled his mission. He is even thought to have offered himself as a hostage while Mallobaudes went to Silvanus. This might display some unity amongst the non-Romans in imperial service, although Arbitio, another non-Roman, was hardly on their side and felt no barbarian brotherhood when it came to his own personal advancement at the expense of fellow Germans. Instead of either Malarichus or Mallobaudes, Arbitio persuaded Constantius to send the *agent in rebus* Apodemius to Silvanus with a letter of recall. That this was the same Apodemius who had arrested Gallus demonstrates Constantius' thinking towards Silvanus. The *agent in rebus* acted as though the *magister* had already been removed from command as soon as he arrived in northern Gaul.

Meanwhile, Dynamius continued to stir up trouble with his forged letters. He sent one to the armoury at Cremona, addressing its tribune as if he was in on Silvanus' 'plot' and informing him to prepare for what was seemingly the next stage of an attempted coup. Puzzled, having never spoken to Silvanus before, the tribune forwarded it to Malarichus, whose name was also attached, asking for clarification of the letter's meaning. Recognising that there was something afoot, Malarichus gathered together Frankish officers and officials to inform them of the growing conspiracy against him and Silvanus. Supported by this cadre, Malarichus disclosed the details to the imperial court.

The existence of such a group of Frankish officers at court has led to some suggestion that the plot against Silvanus was based in 'anti-Frankism'. However, despite his growing reputation for listening to such whispers, the weight of the Frankish outcry encouraged Constantius to now question the 'evidence' of this plot and ordered an investigation. The judge, Florentius, a deputy of the *magister officiorum*, undertook a thorough examination of these letters, proving that they were forgeries by uncovering the original writing. And yet the four main conspirators were let off largely scot-free. Lampadius was removed from his post of praetorian prefect but along with Aedesius was acquitted of conspiracy, even though Eusebius admitted his role in the plot under torture. The most damning indictment of imperial justice though and perhaps evidence of a more intricate plot against Silvanus was that Dynamius went not only unpunished; he was promoted to *corrector* of Etruria and Umbria.[2]

While this was unfolding, in Cologne Silvanus received word of the increasing opposition to him within the emperor's inner circle. Aware of the fickle nature of Constantius, Silvanus feared that it was only a matter of time before he was faced with execution on trumped up charges. Therefore, he prepared to flee across the Rhine to his fellow Franks but a tribune, Laniogaesus, the man present at the murder of Constans, persuaded the *magister* that the Franks would kill him, ransom him back to the Romans or shelter him long enough for the Romans to offer a sizeable bribe to murder him. Before word could arrive of the success of his allies in defending him at court, suggesting how subsequent developments were a product of a breakdown in communications between Constantius and his general,[3] Silvanus decided that his only option was to fight for his life. In order to galvanise his support amongst the Gallic field army and perhaps amongst the Franks themselves, Silvanus announced his intention to rebel against Constantius by adopting the title of *Augustus* on 11 August 355.

There have been questions over the authenticity of Silvanus' usurpation of imperial office. Mere days before his revolt, Silvanus had paid the soldiers in the name of Constantius, something he would not have done had he planned to rebel.[4] Furthermore, while not a determining factor considering the nearest imperial mint, Trier, closed its gates to him, there have as yet been no coins found bearing his likeness, which is one of the first things that a usurper would do as the best way to promote his accession. A perceived lack of Romanity in Silvanus the Frank has also been pointed to as a potential reason for him not adopting the imperial title. However, much like with Magnentius, his father's lofty position under Constantine saw Silvanus raised within the empire and provided with the best education, so Silvanus and many of this 'Frankish cadre' may have seen themselves as more Roman than Frankish. It could even be suggested that the usurpation as a whole was an invention by the supporters of Constantius to create an excuse for getting rid of a popular general or even by Ammianus to colour the role of his patron, Ursicinus, in the demise of Silvanus.[5]

News of Silvanus' revolt took Constantius by surprise, perhaps so convinced had he been by the work of Malarichus and Florentius. A meeting of the emperor's inner council failed to find an acceptable response, so fearful were they of Silvanus' control of much of the Gallic field forces. The immense casualties suffered in the east and against Magnentius will have made Constantius all the more willing to end such a military crisis without resorting to bloodshed. With things at an impasse, the name of Ursicinus was brought up as an instrument for stopping Silvanus, probably in the hope of removing two targets at the same time. Worried by the situation in Gaul, Constantius welcomed Ursicinus back into the imperial fold, despite having mistrusted the general enough to order his execution before changing his mind.

The plan was that Constantius would play dumb regarding Silvanus' revolt and would send Ursicinus to Cologne to replace Silvanus as *magister peditum* with a congenial letter from the emperor perhaps promising Silvanus a more lucrative command. At the very least it would not have been presented as a demotion. The choice of Ursicinus for such a ploy was a good one as rumours of his being at odds with Constantius' court will have reached Silvanus, making the general more trusted by the rebel. Of course, the question remains that if Ursicinus was mistrusted by the emperor, sending him to meet a rebel, who had been hounded by false accusations much as Ursicinus had, would seem disastrous should the two popular generals find common cause against the imperial court.

Indeed, when this imperial mission arrived in Cologne, Silvanus impressed upon Ursicinus the injustice done to both of them despite their years of loyal service, while less distinguished flatterers were rewarded with imperial favour. Ammianus, who accompanied Ursicinus, suggests that many of the soldiers were eager to march against Constantius in support of their general,[6] forcing Ursicinus to find a more clandestine way of undermining Silvanus. He found it amongst Silvanus' *Bracchiati* and *Cornuti*, who were less than keen to fight an emperor who had already proven himself against various usurpers. With their pockets suitably lined, these troops attacked the palace where Silvanus had taken up residence, killing the guards. They then dragged Silvanus from the seeming sacrosanctity of the Christian chapel he had taken refuge in and butchered the short-lived rebel.

While it was "repeated sword thrusts"[7] that brought about the end of
Silvanus, he had in reality been destroyed by a clique of enemies at court
and the emperor's reputation for listening to unfounded accusations. Despite
being part of the ploy to remove Silvanus, Ammianus compares Constantius'
fear of brave, energetic and popular men to that of Domitian, the first century
emperor renowned for his paranoia.[8] Despite being the son of a loyal servant
of Constantine and having given good service in the settling of northern
Gaul, that Silvanus had already betrayed one emperor probably prayed on
Constantius' mind and provided those at court with an avenue to exploit in
the removal of the Frankish *magister*. Having said that, however ignoble the
actions of Ursicinus, the imperial court and Constantius were, they may have
prevented another destructive civil war between the Gallic and Constantian
field armies.

The successful elimination of yet another usurper, again ascribed to the
emperor's fortune in dealing with internal strife, further enflamed Constantius'
paranoia, leading to another round of proscriptions, with Paul the Chain at
the forefront once more. Anyone connected to the fallen *magister* came under
suspicion with the likes of the *comites* Asclepiodotus, Lutto and Maudio and
most ungratefully, Poemenius, the man who had rebelled against Magnentius
in favour of Constantius, all executed.[9] It is related by Ammianus that even
under the "venomous arts"[10] of Paul, no real evidence for a planned rebellion
by Silvanus could be extracted; a *domesticus* of the fallen general, one Procolus,
defending his action as "not driven on from ambition, but compelled by
necessity".[11] It appears that a valuable and skilled general, sacrificed in the
name of imperial security, had instead been the victim of the petty jealousies
fostered at the imperial court. It would not be the last time.

The Elevation of Julian

Whilst Constantius celebrated the demise of another rebel with "inconceivable
joy",[12] he was not blind to the difficult situation that his empire was facing. The
revolts of Magnentius, Decentius and Silvanus, together with the degradations
of the *baguadae*, Alamanni and Franks had left Gaul in a terrible state,
especially as the death of Silvanus seems to have undone the progress he had
managed against the Franks and *baguadae*. Constantius felt that Gaul required
a strong military and even imperial presence. However, he could not afford
to vacate the central position that Milan provided due to the restlessness of
various peoples along the Lower Danube and throughout the east. The empire
remained too large for a single emperor to rule and redistribute patronage and
despite the behaviour of Gallus, Constantius still saw his family as the main

source of imperial rule. The Constantinian name still carried a lot of weight within and without the empire, especially along the Rhine where Constantius was looking to deploy his new *Caesar*. As neither of the emperor's wives had yet given him an heir, there was only one possible candidate: his cousin, Julian.

Many court officials attempted to deter the emperor from this course of action, resorting to effusive flattery as to how Constantius could manage the empire alone and pointing out the example of Gallus. These men were driven as much by self-preservation as any hope of gaining the promotion for themselves as several had already tried to do away with Julian by linking him to the actions of Gallus and accusing him of aspirations for the highest rank. However, once the empress Eusebia again backed Julian, Constantius' mind was made up. Summoned from his studies in Athens, Julian must have been nervous of what was in store for him as he approached Milan. Constantius had a poor record in how he treated his family and the last time Julian had been called to court had been to answer charges of treason, which he had only just evaded with his life intact. Any such fears were soon proven to be unfounded for when Julian arrived at the imperial court, he was greeted with all the pomp and ceremony accorded to the elevation of an heir apparent. Then on 6 November 355, "surrounded by the eagles and the standards",[13] Constantius declared his desire that Julian share in his *imperium* as *Caesar* in the west, to which the vast military congregation gave their enthusiastic acclaim.[14]

Having clothed Julian in his new purple robes, Constantius then addressed his cousin,[15] asking him "to share in pains and perils, and undertake the charge of defending Gaul"[16] while offering advice and warning about the dangers that that region of the empire would provide for him. Ammianus depicts Constantius' speech in somewhat weary terms as if the emperor was tired with the fighting he had already had to do and was unburdening himself in appointing Julian. On top of that, with the benefit of hindsight it is easy to see at least some hypocrisy given that Julian would see as much danger from the imperial court as he would from the barbarians of the Rhine, which might have been Ammianus' aim in recording these speeches, particularly with the declaration that "I shall not fail you in whatever you undertake".[17] Julian himself seems to have been under no illusion that he was "holding a wolf by the ears",[18] going as far as to whisper a poignant verse from Homer as he was conducted to the imperial palace beside Constantius; "By purple death I am seized and fate supreme."[19]

Within a few days of his elevation, Julian was married to another of Constantius' sisters, Helena.[20] There was little time for nuptial celebration though as the *Augustus* and *Caesar* set out for Gaul on 1 December. Constantius only travelled as far as the staging post at Duriae, modern Dorno in Lombardy, before returning to Milan, leaving Julian to continue on to Turin where he received word of a major development on the Rhine, news that Constantius seems to have suppressed in order to not disturb his arrangements: Cologne had fallen to the Alamanni.[21]

The death of Silvanus and the reprisals wrought on his supporters undermined the Roman military presence in northern Gaul. The emperor or Ursicinus may even have dispersed much of the Gallic field army to prevent it from reacting to the death of their commander. This encouraged the Frankish tribes to break whatever agreement they had come to with Silvanus; the spoils of war being greater than the incentives he had offered them to remain at peace. These tribes may have seen the removal of Silvanus as having nullified their arrangements with him or they feared that the Roman government would not honour any agreement signed by the rebel. It could even have been a different Frankish group that moved against Cologne than those who Silvanus had treated with.

Whatever the background, a Frankish host struck at the fort of Divitia on the right bank of the Rhine opposite Cologne, before then forcing their way across the river to besiege the Roman capital of Germania Secunda. By the end of autumn 355, Cologne had been "taken by storm and destroyed".[22] This was a grievous blow to Roman Gaul, not just through the loss of such an important city but also the lack of movement to relieve the siege will have undermined Gallic confidence in the ability of the Roman army to protect them whilst encouraging the Franks, Alamanni and other tribes that there were easy gains to be made across the Rhine.

The fall of Cologne, coupled with the decades of raids across Gaul, might better explain the warm greeting that Julian received when he entered Vienne. Even though Ammianus attempts to paint the reaction as being to the presence of Julian personally,[23] the populace of Vienne may have reacted in a similar manner to any imperial presence, Constantinian or not, seeing it as a sign that the government was taking an active role in a Gallic recovery. However, it should be noted that Constantius had little intention of Julian acting as a militarily independent *Caesar* as their shared grandfather Constantius Chlorus had been during the Tetrarchy. While his position would appear authoritative, it "was really that of a figurehead"[24] to be used as an overt symbol of Constantius' authority.[25] Much like with Gallus, the military operations and political decisions were instead meant to be exercised by a "carefully selected staff of high officials".[26]

Even when Julian disregarded his figurehead status and took the field in order to restore imperial prestige in the Gallic provinces, he found himself disadvantaged. He later complained that he was furnished with a field army

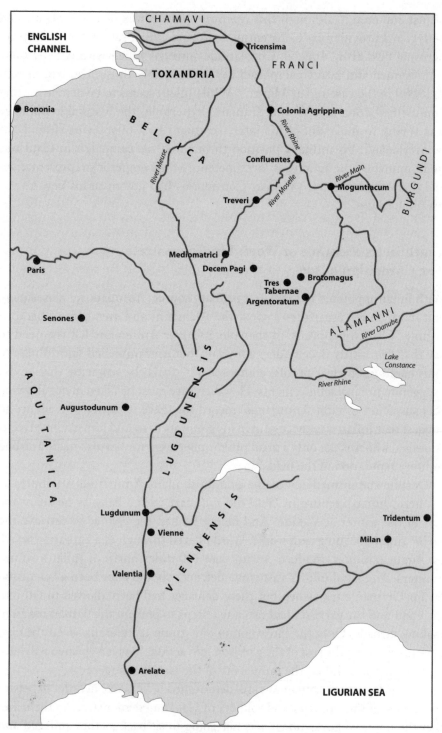

Map 6: Gaul, Germany and the Rhine Frontier

of just 360 men,[27] although this *comitatus parvus* was just the retinue and bodyguard provided by Constantius to defend Julian rather than his entire personal field army. Indeed, Constantius outfitted Julian with elite *ballistae* artillerymen and heavy cataphract cavalry, possibly those who had proven so useful in the east and at Mursa.[28] While Julian seems to be demonstrating "unjustified contempt"[29] and dramatic hyperbole, the justifiable point he was trying to make about his later treatment by Constantius should not be overlooked: his military position throughout his campaign in Gaul was undermined by the actions or incompetence of the emperor's representatives and that contrary to his promise, Constantius had not given his new *Caesar* his full backing.

Youthful Exuberance or Woeful Inexperience: The Campaign of 356

With Julian appointed to Gaul, our primary source, Ammianus, focuses more and more on his escapades against the Alamanni and members of his own regime. That in his praise of the young *Caesar* Ammianus felt the need to say that "no wordy deceit adorns my tale, but untrammelled faithfulness to facts based upon clear proofs, composes it"[30] fuels the suspicion that he did exaggerate Julian's achievements. However, care must be taken in not allowing this suspicion to taint Ammianus' record for there is plenty of evidence to suggest that Julian was successful in his attempts to mould himself on Marcus Aurelius, who was not only a great philosopher emperor but also made a strong military reputation in the field.[31]

Despite the immediacy of the grandiose plans Ammianus attributes to his hero, Julian's tenure in Gaul did not start with a bang as he spent the rest of the winter at Vienne. And before he had the chance to retrieve the Gallic situation, things got worse. Word filtered through of a barbarian attack on Augustodunum, modern Autun, just 100 miles north of Julian's winter quarters. Augustodunum's vast stone defences should have been a bridge too far for Germanic tribesmen but these defences had been allowed to fall into disrepair and the garrison had taken few steps to prevent the barbarians from making inroads. Only the intervention of a group of veterans saved the city, perhaps shaming the rest of the garrison into action. Such an episode will have rammed home to Julian the immensity of the task that he faced.

Despite this shock, Julian was still determined to be active in order to bolster the morale of the citizenry and soldiery of Gaul and demonstrate to the tribes that the imperial government was not going to sit back as they pillaged and plundered Roman territory. Therefore, while he was still at Vienne, Julian ordered the remnant of the Gallic field army, now under the command of the *magister equitum*, Marcellus, to congregate at Rheims with one month's supplies. This was a clear indication that he intended to take the field, a decision that would be met with cheer amongst the rank and file.[32]

However, before Julian could lead the Gallic field army in a counterattack, he would first have to reach Rheims and between his small column at Vienne and Marcellus lay 300 miles of Roman territory that was flooded with barbarian raiding parties and included a large forested area that Ammianus records as the "dark woods".[33] The young *Caesar* was not to be discouraged and set off for Augustodunum, arriving there on 24 June 356. After surveying his options in a council of war, Julian showed the streak of daring that was to colour his military career. Upon hearing that Silvanus had taken a risky shortcut through the woods with a sizeable force, Julian determined to follow the same route with his small force of cataphracts and *ballistae* even if it was against the advice of his council and local guides. This initial instance of Julianic risk-taking proved to be a success as this small Roman escort made the journey from Autun to Auxerre without incident.[34]

The next leg of the journey from Auxerre to Troyes was a different story, with barbarian forces attacking the small column. Julian's cavalry drove off the smaller raiding parties but when larger barbarian forces appeared, the *Caesar* had to rely on the defensive strength and resolve of his men to get him to the safety of Troyes, demonstrating that while he might not have provided Julian with a large escort, Constantius had assigned top quality troops to protect his *Caesar*. So rapid was Julian's advance and so rampant had the barbarian raiding been in the area that the garrison at Troyes initially refused to open their gates to him. After a brief rest, Julian forged on to Rheims to meet up with the Gallic field army and in a war council spelled out to Marcellus and Ursicinus, who had been retained in some sort of military role until the end of the campaign, his intention to take the fight to the Alamanni.

The only decision left to make was where Julian was going to aim his reformed field army. After taking the advice of his commanders, the young *Caesar* decided that rather than mop up the various barbarian raiding parties, he would attempt to re-establish control of the Rhine, cutting of the line of retreat for those barbarians already in Roman territory. This was another instance of Julian's military boldness and the army was more than happy to follow such an aggressive path; however, Julian was also demonstrating his inexperience as he was driving into a region that his opponent knew well and had not been well scouted. This lack of reconnaissance combined with poor weather almost led to disaster.

After making good progress from Rheims through Metz and on to within about 60 miles of the Rhine, Julian blundered straight into an ambush near Decem Pagi, modern Dieuze. The Romans managed to march past a large Alamannic force, which then launched an attack on the two rearguard legions that had lost contact with the main body in the deepening mist. This Roman rearguard was only saved from destruction by the counterattack of the *auxilia*, who heard the uproar caused by the fighting. Ammianus attempts to gloss over this incident by claiming that it made Julian "cautious and deliberate, qualities which are of particular advantage in great generals and often enable them to relieve and preserve their armies".[35] But while this may be true – he does seem to have somewhat tempered his brashness – it does not hide the fact that on his first campaign, Julian had committed an almost fatal blunder.

Even with this setback at Decem Pagi and intelligence that numerous Alamannic warbands had taken up residence along his proposed route, the young commander continued on towards the Rhine. As the Gallic army approached Brotomagus, modern Brumath, a sizeable German force appeared and offered battle. With his soldiers champing at the bit to release months – even years – of pent up frustration and aggression and himself keen to avenge the mess at Decem Pagi, Julian accepted. This was to be his first real test in pitched battle; it was a test that Julian passed. The battle of Brotomagus may not have been a crushing victory but the crescent formation that Julian drew his forces up in together with the discipline of his men blunted the initial Alamanni charge. This allowed the Roman wings to close in and break the barbarian lines, leaving some to be captured, others to be run down in the pursuit and the remainder to be scattered.

This first victory must have buoyed morale and confidence. However, the exact extent to which Julian commanded the army during these movements and fighting must be questioned. It would not be surprising if either Marcellus or Ursicinus were giving the orders. Of course, that would not only nullify the praise meted out to Julian for this advance, it would also absolve him of blame for the near disaster at Decem Pagi. Having said that, responsibility for the outcome of battle was placed on the most senior authority figure and in this case that was Julian. These military manoeuvres had taken place under his auspices as *Caesar* and therefore he received the majority of the *kudos* but also the blame.

Until now, Ammianus had related Julian's movements on the hazardous trek from Vienne to Rheims and the march through the Decem Pagi towards the Rhine almost point to point, but after the victory near Brotomagus, the detail fades perhaps because his source or even Ammianus himself as part of Ursicinus' retinue had been present on the initial march but then left soon after.

This leaves the last stages of Julian's first campaign somewhat unexplained. The lack of recorded action post-Brotomagus might suggest that the arrival of the Gallic field army along the banks of the river under imperial command saw tribal raiding parties shirking any further confrontation, allowing Julian to march unhindered.

The peculiarities of the Germanic tribes of antiquity may also have contributed to the seeming lack of action following Brotomagus. As Julian aimed to retake control of the Rhine, he would be targeting the major settlements along the river: such as Strasbourg, Worms, Mainz and Cologne. Despite the extent of their raids, the Germans rarely attempted to fortify any of the towns or cities that came into their power, viewing them as "tombs surrounded by nets".[36] The Romans had recognised this from their earliest dealings with the Germanic tribes with the great historian Tacitus commenting in the late first century CE that "it is a well-known fact that the peoples of Germany never live in cities and will not even have their houses set close together."[37] Therefore, perhaps the real reason why Ammianus did not go into any real detail about the Roman advance north through territory bordering the Rhine in 356 is because "in many cases, Julian must have done little more than enter the city."[38]

Whatever the reason, it appears that from Brotomagus, Julian advanced north, through the forts of Confluentes and Rigomagum, modern Coblenz and Remagen respectively, without serious hindrance by Alamanni or Franks. The Romans were even allowed to reclaim Cologne without a fight and once they set about rebuilding its defences, a Frankish delegation appeared seeking peace.[39] Despite these successes, Julian and his commanders were wary of getting carried away. The victory near Brotomagus was hardly earth-shattering and the Alamanni and the Franks remained a major problem. Logistical problems also meant that Julian could not yet countenance a strike into enemy territory to deter other raiding parties. He was therefore willing to accept a treaty with the Franks, which likely included provisions for the return of prisoners and providing of supplies for Cologne and other forts along the frontier. Accepting a treaty without a major victory may not seem particularly Roman but this and Julian's mistakes should not take away from the importance of the 356 campaign. The Rhine frontier was a mess of large settlements lost and barbarians penetrating deep into Gaul and while Roman fortunes had not yet been turned around, a good start had been made.

After seeing to the rebuilding of Cologne's defences, Julian withdrew through Trier to winter at Senones, where he was confronted with the troubles of provincial and military management: reintegrating deserters and prisoners of war into garrisons and making sure that the finances and resources of Gaul could support a field army. However, if Julian thought that just because he had retired to his winter quarters that his enemies had too, he was in for a rude awakening. As part of his attempts to lessen the burden on the Gauls, Julian dispersed his army in various towns around north-eastern Gaul and as garrisons along the Rhine. The main body returned to Rheims with Marcellus and only a small escort accompanied Julian to Senones.[40] Word of the *Caesar's* lack of soldiers, in particular the absence of elite troops, was leaked to the Alamanni by deserters and seeing a chance to eliminate an imperial enemy, the barbarians launched a surprise attack on Senones.[41] That they could strike that deeply into Gaul shows just how badly undermined the Rhine defences were but Julian and his commanders also shoulder some of the blame. They failed to appreciate the continued tribal threat and must have neglected their deployment of scouts and spies to allow a sizeable Alamannic force to congregate near an imperial winter quarters some 250 miles from the Rhine.

Julian had undertaken some essential repairs to the walls of Senones, which prevented the Alamanni from storming the town upon their arrival, forcing them to settle in for a siege. His lack of troops left Julian with no option but to wait out the besiegers whilst keeping up the spirits of what few men he had, mingling with them, sharing their burdens and food, in full view of the besieging forces.[42] However, if Julian hoped that relief would come from those Roman troops quartered in nearby settlements, he was in for another surprise. Throughout the month-long siege, Marcellus did nothing to gather together the disparate units and march to the aid of Senones. It was only the combination of putting too much value in reports of the garrison's lack of provisions, fear of a Roman relief army and their own lack of manpower and technological ability to overcome the repaired walls that led to the Alamanni lifting the siege.

In Marcellus' defence, Rheims is 100 miles from Senones and the suddenness of the Alamanni attack may have prevented news reaching the *magister*, but this would only account for a delayed arrival of a Roman relief force, not the complete lack of movement. Ammianus sees the hand of the emperor in this episode, but had Constantius wanted to remove Julian, history suggests that he would have been far more direct and not to mention successful than allowing his winter quarters to be besieged. However, the emperor cannot be absolved of all blame for the inaction of his subordinate and not just because Ammianus has painted the picture of a devious and conniving emperor. If Marcellus had decided to bring about the end of Julian in the winter of 356, he must have done so with the inkling that such actions might have been met with "an unofficial pat on the back".[43]

Despite this toxic atmosphere at the imperial court and the upper echelons of the military hierarchy, Constantius' decisive reaction to Senones removes much of the foundation for the argument that he was behind the whole thing. For having shown "cowardice in the face of the enemy",[44] Marcellus was dishonourably discharged and exiled to his home in Serdica, modern Sofia in Bulgaria. Of course, those looking for conspiracies will just see the emperor removing a pawn in his game to undermine Julian and suggest that Marcellus was not removed for trying to orchestrate Julian's demise but for failing. Unwilling to accept his deposition, Marcellus gained a personal hearing before the emperor to air whatever grievances he had regarding Julian, hoping to play on Constantius' past receptiveness to rumour.[45] Suspecting that the former *magister* would present trumped up charges, Julian sent his eunuch chamberlain, Eutherius, to Milan to defend him.[46] Marcellus accused the *Caesar* of supreme arrogance and aiming for the highest office; however, as he was weaving this tapestry of lies, Eutherius was ushered into the council chamber, where he explained the truth of the siege of Senones: Marcellus had done nothing to help and Julian had staved off defeat through his own visible leadership. Eutherius' eloquence convinced Constantius that there was no case for Julian to answer and the exile of the *magister equitum* was carried out, with a distinguished officer, Severus, promoted as his replacement.

Free from military and political attack for now, Julian remained in Senones to give his men an actual rest while he continued to deal with the problems of provincial and military management throughout the rest of the winter. It is perhaps now that Julian decided to take a keener interest in the taxation of his provinces, even if it was beyond his purview as a figurehead military commander. Leading an austere lifestyle based on the Laws of Lycurgus, the backbone of Spartan society, and Cato the Censor, Julian had little time for corruption and this first winter in Gaul opened his eyes to the extent to which unscrupulous officials manipulated and exaggerated the tax assessment, demanding cash payments rather than military recruits or kind so they could skim the excess. However, such an interest would destroy what had been a cordial relationship between Julian and the praetorian prefect of Gaul, Florentius.[47]

Julian's Gallic Campaign of 357

Despite evidence of good governance, Julian could not hope to deal with Gaul's internal problems before he dealt with the external ones. Therefore, after surviving the siege of Senones and the accusations of Marcellus, Julian prepared to take the offensive again in 357, rejoining the Gallic field army at Rheims early in the new year. Julian was encouraged by Constantius' choice of Severus as Marcellus' replacement, who was seen as "a man neither subordinate nor overbearing but well known for his long excellent record in the army".[48] However, Julian was not to be furnished with such dependable types throughout his tenure in Gaul. While the *Caesar* was moving to Rheims, Barbatio –who had been promoted to take Silvanus' place as *magister peditum* – was sent by Constantius from Italy to Augst with 25,000 men, probably a major part of Constantius' own *comitatus*. The plan seems to have been for Barbatio to first deal with the raids of the Suebi and then join Julian in an advance into Alamanni territory, catching them in something of a pincer movement. It is here that Ammianus records a tribe called the Laeti stealing between the converging Roman forces to raid the countryside and even attack Lyons, leading to the city closing its gates and Julian sending three units of cavalry to incept them.[49]

While not doubting the occurrence of such a raid, Ammianus has either mistaken the name of these tribesmen or has mixed up unconquered tribesmen from outside the empire and those already settled on Roman territory as *laeti*, in return for military service. The system had been used to some success amongst the Franks by Constantius Chlorus, while Constantine made heavy use of *laeti* in his recasting of the Roman *auxilia*.[50] Constantius continued the use of such agreements and while inherent military service is not mentioned, those Gothic Christians allowed to settle at Nicopolis in Moesia in around 348 must have agreed to service in return.[51] He would also hope to settle the Limigantes on imperial territory in 359 to "compel a very strong force of recruits".[52] Despite looking "like the opening move against Gallus",[53] Constantius' later request of troops from Julian betrays a respect for the abilities of these mostly barbarian units.[54] While launching scathing attacks on both Constantine and Constantius for their recruiting, subsidising and promoting of barbarians, Julian himself made wholesale use of barbarian soldiers, valuing the *laeti* and *dediticii* highly. He would think it a huge concession to provide Constantius with *laeti* and he saw *adulescentes laetos* as worthy of service in *palatini* units. Julian was also more than willing to allow the Franks to remain on abandoned Roman land as long as they provided soldiers and produce. Therefore, given the predominance of these settled barbarians, the men who attacked Lyons were likely disgruntled *laeti* rather than a misnamed tribe.[55]

However, the importance of this episode at Lyons lies not in the identity of these attackers or Julian's successful reaction but the lack of cooperation from Barbatio. While Julian's cavalry intercepted the retreating *laeti* and recovered the booty they had taken, one section of the marauders escaped past the forces of Barbatio. This was because the cavalry commanders sent to do the job, Bainobaudes and the future emperor Valentinian, were forbidden from carrying out their task by Cella, a tribune of the *Scutarii*, under orders from Barbatio. When questioned, Cella admitted that what had been done was against Roman interests but the *magister peditum* managed to shift blame from himself onto Cella, Bainobaudes and Valentinian, all of whom were cashiered.

This attack on Lyons distracted the converging Roman armies long enough to give the Alamanni time to block many of the mountainous passes and roads and cease control of crossing points and islands of the Rhine. In order to deal with them, Julian asked Barbatio to send seven ships down the river so he could undermine the Alamanni position by crossing the river. However, despite having the ships prepared to build river crossings, Barbatio failed to send them, leading Ammianus to claim that the *magister* was purposefully not aiding the *Caesar*.[56] His lack of waterborne help did not stop Julian from forging ahead with his part of the pincer attack on the Alamannic positions. Acting on intelligence gathered from captured German scouts, the *Caesar* sent the tribune of his *Cornuti*, Bainobaudes, to test the defences and the resolve of the Alamanni.[57] Using some improvised canoes, the tribune and his men snuck across to one of the Rhine islands and killed those guarding it. In so doing, they captured several Alamannic boats, which allowed them to launch further amphibious raids against the Germanic river camps. Upon hearing that their island defences had not prevented Roman attacks, large numbers of Alamanni began evacuating Roman territory.[58]

In their wake, Julian moved to re-establish the Roman presence in what is now Alsace through the rebuilding of the fortress at Tres Tabernae, modern Saverne, along the road between Metz and Strasbourg. While his men carried out these repairs, Julian ordered up to a year's worth of supplies and rations for a further twenty days, indicating that his campaigning was far from over. As these supplies were being distributed to Julian's men, Barbatio appropriated a large proportion of them and then destroyed the surplus. The *magister peditum* may have been in great need of resupply due to his march from Italy through Augst but such actions led to further rumours that Julian was being targeted for embarrassment or destruction by Constantius or members of his court.

However, it was Barbatio who was to face embarrassment; and it was all of his own making. In the course of setting up his camp somewhat closer to the Rhine than Julian at Tres Tabernae, the *magister peditum* neglected to post sufficient pickets. This allowed a large column of Alamanni to fall upon Barbatio's camp and put his forces to flight;[59] a flight that did not end until Augst with the Alamanni claiming the fleeing army's baggage and pack-animals. To make matters worse, rather than regrouping, Barbatio "as if he had ended the campaign successfully, distributed his soldiers in winter quarters and returned to the emperor's court, to frame some charge against the *Caesar*, as was his custom".[60] Despite Ammianus claiming that it was unknown whether Constantius was behind actions throughout his deployment in 357, the *magister* would not have withdrawn from a strategy that the emperor had a hand in planning without being confident of gaining Constantius' acceptance.

Whether with the emperor's tacit approval or not, Barbatio's retreat undermined the Roman position in Alsace. Learning through another deserter that Julian had only 13,000 men at his disposal,[61] the Alamannic chief responsible for the defeat of Barbatio and also of Decentius prior to Mons Seleucus, Chnodomarius called together a meeting of his fellow tribal leaders: Westralp, Urius, Ursicinus, Suomarius, Hortarius and his nephew Serapio. He impressed upon them the opportunity to re-establish themselves on the west bank of the Rhine, land which they regarded as their own through right of conquest and even claimed to have been ceded it by Constantius.[62] Convinced by Chnodomarius' rhetoric, the Alamanni sent a delegation to Julian, demanding that he withdraw from their territory,[63] expecting perhaps that the *Caesar* would acquiesce due to his paucity in numbers following the retreat of Barbatio.

Julian was now faced with a big decision. Agreeing to the Alamanni demands was unacceptable not just due to the inevitable accusations of cowardice but also the potential for the barbarians to attack anyway. The safest option would have been to stay put. However, the unlikelihood of relief meant that the walls of Tres Tabernae would only postpone a confrontation and with the depletion of his supplies, Julian will have been in the best shape to fight immediately. Florentius argued that it was rare for the barbarians to offer battle and if the *Caesar* could win just one victory he could win the war in a single stroke. Therefore, in spite of the risks, Julian accepted battle and marched towards the barbarian force near Argentoratum, modern Strasbourg.

To Glory or Ignominy: The Battle of Strasbourg, 357

The timing of the Roman march to Strasbourg is somewhat confused with no specific date recorded. Having spent considerable time restoring Tres Tabernae, Julian set off with the campaigning season well advanced, probably some time in August as it is reported as being hot with the wheat ripe in the fields. With some twenty miles to cover to the Alamanni force, Julian and his men likely set out from Tres Tabernae at dawn to reach the battlefield by midday, although there is a contrary comment from Julian that his men faced a night march to square up to Chnodomarius' host.[64] Alert to the Roman approach, Chnodomarius had wasted little time taking up the gauntlet thrown down by Julian and marched his men from under the ruined walls of Strasbourg to intercept him. His chosen battlefield was on the slope of a hill along the main road between Strasbourg and Tres Tabernae, perhaps near the modern village of Oberhausbergen, two miles northwest of Strasbourg and in Julian's path of advance. The battlefield was also punctuated with wheat fields and perched atop the hill was a wooded area.[65]

Arriving before the Alamanni positions, Julian addressed his men, proposing to let them rest until the next day after the quick march in the heat of high summer; however, Florentius, other officers and the rank and file shouted that they should fight now.[66] This may be evidence of the weakness of Julian's position with his entire army disobeying his command or it may instead show the cleverness of the young *Caesar* in gauging the mood of his troops and in manipulating the situation to demonstrate that despite his imperial rank he listened to the opinions of his men. Even with that, it is unlikely that battle was joined immediately upon the Roman arrival at Strasbourg. The battle and its aftermath ended after the setting of the sun and there is not six hours of action recorded in the surviving accounts. Therefore, despite the picture painted by Ammianus of an army demanding immediate attack at midday, the Battle of Strasbourg probably began in mid to late afternoon, with the intervening time taken up with scouting, strategising, organising, preparation, setting up camp and even resting.[67]

While the sources do not explain the make up of the 13,000–15,000 they attribute for Julian's forces,[68] it is possible to rebuild it from the record of the battle and inferences about the troops assigned to either Julian's *comitatus* or the Gallic field army. From Ammianus' record of the battle itself, Julian's infantry included the *Primani* legion, the *Cornuti, Bracchiati, Batavi* and *Reges* of the *auxilia*, while his cavalry included the *equites Scutarii*, the horse-archers of the *equites sagitarii* and the two units of heavy cataphracts given to him by Constantius.[69] Other units that appear in Julian's forces after Strasbourg may have been present at the battle, such as the twin *Moesiaci* legions, the *Celtae, Heruli* and *Petulantes auxilia* and the *equites gentiles*, while Julian inherited units such as the *Ioviani* and *Herculiani* legions and the *equites Dalmatae* recorded as part of the Gallic field army of Magnentius.[70]

However, even with something approaching a complete roster of units, the exact size of force that they provided is hampered by the lack of consensus on what the full strength of fourth century *comitatenses* units would have been. The legions were probably around 1,000 strong, the *auxilia* around 500 and the cavalry *vexillationes* around 500–800 but it is an almost certainty that none of these units were anywhere near that paper strength.[71] It should also be noted that Roman sources had a tendency to leave out certain types of military unit in their calculation of army sizes, particularly barbarian allies and *limitanei*. It should come as no surprise that the units Ammianus records were all elite.

It is possible then that Julian had the support of some unrecorded men on top of his core force of 13,000 men. The *Caesar* had ordered a major recruitment drive upon his arrival in Gaul[72] so it might be expected to see some of them in the ranks alongside his *comitatus* when he was taking a gamble in confronting such numbers of Alamanni.

Conspicuous by their absence in the record of Strasbourg are foot archers or indeed any skirmishers of any note beyond horse archers as missiles could blunt a fearsome barbarian battle charge. This seems like a glaring omission by Ammianus, perhaps even an intentional one to make the throwing back of the Alamanni charge all the more heroic. It could even be that so obvious was the presence of archers and skirmishers that there was no need to highlight them. Therefore, without being able to identify any numbers, Julian probably deployed archers and light armed troops either in front of his main infantry lines or to the rear to blunt the initial barbarian attack.

It has also been suggested that Severus commanded a division that is to be counted as separate from Julian's *comitatus*. The *magister equitum* and his men do seem to have been separated enough from Julian's force to get caught up in the defeat and flight of Barbatio and could perhaps be seen as an additional reinforcement of the *Caesar's* small force.[73] While an attractive proposition in filling the gap between the figures of Ammianus and Libanius, it seems a somewhat arbitrary conclusion to draw. Instead, Severus likely commanded the left wing of the Roman force at Strasbourg rather than a separate force.

Of the recorded 13,000 under Julian's direct command, it contained a core of around 10,000 legionary and *auxilia* infantry, supported by missile and *limitanei* and a mixed force of around 3,000 cavalry, with the striking power of the heavy cataphracts, the *Scutarii* and the *Gentiles* and the skirmishing of *equites Dalmatae* and *sagitarii*. Even given the possibility of other uncounted troops in his ranks, Julian was still leading a small force into the teeth of a reportedly vast Alamannic host, which held the high ground. Much of Julian's deficiency in numbers will have been made up by the quality of the *palatini* units, "toughened by long experience in fighting".[74] Still, this small Roman force faced an unenviable task.

The reason for this was that the force awaiting the Romans at Strasbourg may have been up to 35,000 strong.[75] With the addition of Vadomarius,[76] there were now seven Alamannic kings plus Serapio and various other chiefs complete with their tribal forces and retinues waiting along the road to Oberhausbergen. Ammianus preserves an eye witness account "that the Germans had been crossing the river for three days and three nights",[77] suggesting that this force was of large proportions. His victories over Decentius and Barbatio will have enhanced the stature of Chnodomarius and his ability to draw men to his banner. Serendipitous timing might also have helped such large Alamanni numbers to congregate. Just months prior, the tribes had been faced with not just Julian and Barbatio but also Constantius' campaign in Raetia on top of strife with their neighbours and amongst themselves.[78] Now in mid-357, Constantius was looking to the Lower Danube, Barbatio had been defeated and pressure had forced the Alamanni of Raetia to renounce the treaty they had signed with Constantius in 355. This was not the only time that Ammianus was to attribute tens of thousands to the Alamanni so in the very least he was consistent in his estimations and some convincing work has been done in demonstrating the socio-political, military and mercantile advances made by the Alamannic confederation by the mid fourth century.[79]

However, the idea that such structural development was enough to enable the bringing together of a force of 35,000 has drawn criticism.[80] Perhaps the most important way in which such numbers have been attacked is in the demographic capacity of the Alamannic tribes to provide them. In particular, the idea that the fourth century Alamanni commanded a vast confederation of immense populace has been rejected as "a reflection of imperial propaganda".[81] The core of the Alamanni force at Strasbourg were the tribal followings of the seven kings, each referred to as a *pagus*. As Alamanni society developed, such *reges* came to command followings of increasing size; therefore, while a *pagus* of the third century could be 600 strong, by the mid-fifth century some were approaching 1,000.[82] Allowing for the more powerful *reges* like Chnodomarius, Westralp and Vadomarius to have larger than average followings, a *pagi* core of 10,000 might not be out of the question.

In choosing to make a stand against the Romans, the Alamanni kings will have looked further afield than their own retinues for manpower. Ammianus suggests that the barbarian army contained men "levied from various nations, partly for pay and partly under agreement",[83] with such a list including other lesser chiefs and their retinues, itinerant warbands, neighbouring tribes such as the Burgundians, Franks and Iuthungi and even some of the rebel *laeti* from Roman territory. It is not beyond the realms of possibility that such recruiting could have produced a similar number as the Alamannic *pagi* but it would seem to be something of a stretch and trebling the number to come close to Ammianus' 35,000 would be out of the question. Therefore, while Chnodomarius could have forged a series of short-term alliances and agreements to bring together a force larger than that of Julian and perhaps even in the order of around 20,000, the Romans were probably not as outnumbered at Ammianus would suggest.[84]

The Roman reaction to Alamanni activity has also been used to estimate the manpower available to Chnodomarius. If Constantius was planning a campaign of terror against the Alamanni then it might be expected that the 38,000 men he placed in the hands of Julian and Barbatio would reflect an overwhelming superiority in numbers over anything Chnodomarius could bring together, perhaps in a magnitude of two or three times greater, leaving the Alamanni figures to be in the same ball park as Julian's force.[85] Of course, such calculations work on averages and given the string of successes of the Alamanni and the presence of so many tribal leaders, Chnodomarius' force was extraordinary rather than average. Indeed, just to demonstrate the lack of a definitive answer about Chnodomarius' force, it should not be overlooked that there has been a suggestion that it was in fact the Alamanni who were outnumbered at Strasbourg,[86] calling into question the numbers recorded by Ammianus and overlooking why the Alamanni would risk battle on an open field if they were outnumbered.

This last point is important when it comes to looking at the make up and quality of the Alamanni force when compared with the elite, well-equipped professionals that made up Julian's force. Chnodomarius and his fellow *reges* will have had some experienced men in their *pagi*, used as the spearhead of the massed charge due to their ferocious appearance and speed afforded to them by their lack of heavy armour. Given that they had been settled along the Roman frontier for centuries and mounting serious raids and even conquests of Roman territory, Chnodomarius' men had access to some higher quality Roman arms, but for the most part Alamanni equipment was of a much poorer standard than that of the Romans, both in terms of weaponry and armour. Alamanni economics might have advanced but it is unlikely that they had progressed far enough to maintain professional retinues ranging into the thousands.

Therefore, the majority of the Alamannic army will have been closer in quality to an armed militia or even peasants pressed into service, armed with spears and hunting axes. Such a lack of training, experience and equipment is perhaps best presented in the tactics of barbarian tribal armies: an initial charge akin to a human wave attack. However, this should not colour the Alamannic force as a disorganised rabble as some of these men will have served with the Roman army and at Strasbourg there is evidence that they were capable of more than a simple charge. It is possible that the *globus* mass that Ammianus records forming amongst the *pagi* to punch through Julian's front ranks was something akin to the Roman *cuneus* wedge formation – also known as the *caput porcinum* or 'hog's head' – where the most well-armoured men formed the outer ranks to provide the striking power. Whilst effective in washing away even the most disciplined Roman forces by sheer weight of numbers, momentum and shock, should such mass charges be resisted and halted by disciplined troops in formation, they would be cut to pieces.[87]

Supporting this core of infantry was the Alamanni cavalry, commanded by Chnodomarius himself but of unknown size and of a quality inflated by the Romans due to its impact at Strasbourg. Ammianus and Aurelius Victor played up Alamannic horsemanship so well that it became something of an accepted fact that they had a more than proficient cavalry arm; this is contrary to the evidence. Hailing from a forested area of Germania, the Alamanni were poor horsemen. This and the price involved in keeping a horse would suggest that the Alamanni cavalry contingent at Strasbourg was small; at most, a similar size to that of the Romans but likely smaller.[88]

As with the Romans, Ammianus does not mention archers in Chnodomarius' army but it is almost certain that there were some present and the historian does record the Alamanni firing arrows at later battles.[89] Even if the Alamannic longbow was not as flexible or powerful as the composite Roman bow, it still produced enough strength to pierce armour. On top of arrows, the sky at Strasbourg was to be filled with copious missiles of all shapes and sizes fired by both sides with the Romans having to shelter under their shields due to hail of javelins, spears, darts, stones and possibly mighty *francisca* throwing axes.[90]

While the two armies were somewhat similar in composition and perhaps even in size, although not quality, there could not be a greater difference between the two commanders who were to clash at Strasbourg. On the Alamannic side, there was a man of vast military experience and success, having defeated Roman armies, conquered Roman territory and seen his primacy recognised amongst the Alamannic confederation. Chnodomarius was a successful battle commander and a superior warrior. This is perhaps borne out in the reports of his enormous physical stature, having received the nickname of *Gigas* or the 'Giant' from the Romans. To present himself as an even more formidable sight, the Alamannic chief donned decorative armour and a tall helmet. From atop his horse, he must have seemed to be some kind of monster.[91] However, it has been warned that this portrayal of Chnodomarius as an arch-troublemaker and formidable Germanic champion may be more "a literary construct... magnified through his conflict with Julian, who needed a redoubtable foe".[92]

While Chnodomarius was in overall command and had his nephew, Serapio, as second in command, it is worth noting that the six other Alamannic *reges* – Westralp, Suomarius, Urius, Ursicinus, Hortarius and Vadomarius – would not have been used to playing such a subordinate role. The chance to defeat a Roman army could be a powerful unifying force and while there is little hint of a clash of regal personalities undermining the German effort at Strasbourg, the *reges* may have rankled having to take orders. The relationship between Chnodomarius and his commanders might be demonstrated by his willingness to dismount and join the infantry on the demand of the ranks. He must have known that once he was in the mire of battle, his ability to lead the army would be compromised, so Chnodomarius must have had some trust in Serapio and the other *reges* to carry out his orders.[93]

Staring across at the magnificent giant from amongst his personal escort, Julian may have been bedecked in similarly ornate imperial armour but there was no hiding that he was a young, inexperienced man of letters plucked from the benches of the Athenian Academy. While he had shown glimpses of military skill and no little daring, Julian had also been reckless and committed almost fatal errors. At best, his military record had been patchy and now he had been shorn of significant reinforcements in the prelude to facing superior numbers. Julian did have the benefit of the experience of Severus, along with the high quality of his men, but marching to Strasbourg was a considerable military gamble regardless of how evenly matched or not the armies were.

Given that a complete roster for either army has not been recorded, only a partial picture of the dispositions at the beginning of the battle is possible, although the overall battle plans for both seem to be straightforward. Having chosen the battlefield, Chnodomarius could place his forces in the most advantageous position. The main body of infantry, under five *reges* and ten petty kings,[94] was therefore placed on the crest of the hill to give momentum to their charge and to force the Romans to attack uphill. The Alamannic right wing, under the command of Serapio,[95] rested across the road to Strasbourg close to the wooded area, which provided protection from the superior Roman cavalry. This saw the barbarian left hanging with the limited natural protection of the slope making it necessary for Chnodomarius to deploy his cavalry on its flank.

Recognising the weakness of his cavalry in the face of Julian's varied mounts, the barbarian commander set a trap. Taking advantage of the unharvested fields, Chnodomarius concealed pockets of infantry amongst his cavalry; the plan being that these men could first help blunt the charge of the cataphracts and then attack the unprotected underside of the Roman horses.[96] This was not the only sector of the battlefield where the Alamanni to set a trap. In the wooded hilltop, a force of infantry was hidden in the hope of ambushing any attempt to seize the hill or outflank Serapio's position. However, despite these defensive measures being designed to secure his flanks and neutralise the Roman cavalry, Chnodomarius' main battle plan remained to break the Roman lines with a downhill charge.

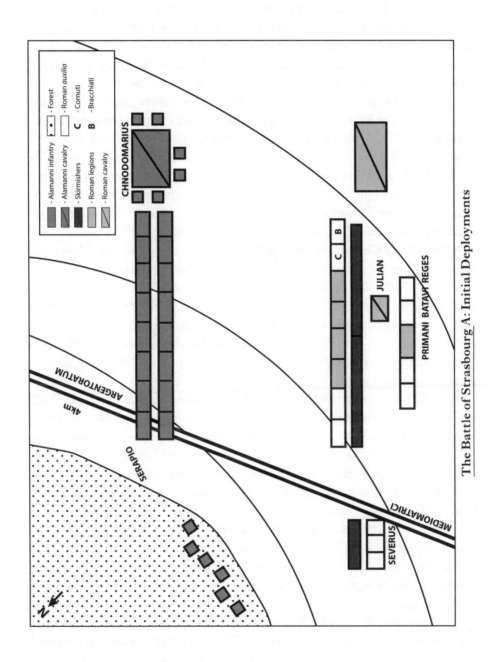

The Battle of Strasbourg A: Initial Deployments

That this massed charge and the expectation of it was central to the Alamanni plan was reflected in the Roman dispositions, even if a complete picture cannot be garnered. The Roman infantry was split into two lines, with the units well spaced and in deep ranks to absorb the barbarian attack. The units of the front line whose position is known are the *Cornuti* and *Bracchiati* on the right flank; *Ioviani*, *Herculiani* or the two *Moesiaci* were likely were deployed in the centre. The second line was anchored on the *Primani* with two *auxilia* units, the *Batavi* and *Reges* on its right. This reserve would prove vitally important for the Romans. Any other *auxilia* units present at Strasbourg such as the *Celtae*, *Petulantes* and *Heruli* were on the left flanks of the front or reserve lines. While not recorded, a line of archers and skirmishers was probably deployed between these two lines or perhaps in front to get unobstructed firing solutions on the opposition before retreating through the gaps as the enemy closed in. On the Roman left, Severus commanded about 2,000 men: perhaps three experience *auxilia* units and some missile infantry.

Upon seeing Chnodomarius and his cavalry deployed on the Alamannic right, Julian massed together all of his cavalry, aside from his personal escort of 200,[97] and placed it opposite the barbarian commander. From this, it seem to make Julian's battle plan rather apparent: while his infantry held the tribal charge, his cavalry would sweep Chnodomarius' horse from the field in a hail of missiles and shock charges before attacking the flanks and rear of the *pagi*. Almost fatally for the Romans, this plan was too predictable and as already seen Chnodomarius had taken steps to counteract it.

With all the pieces in place and Julian riding along his lines to give his men one last burst of inspiration, going as far as to encourage them to decapitate any barbarians they killed in return for a reward,[98] battle was joined with the expected cavalry engagement. After a mutual exchange of missiles, the cataphracts crashed into the Alamannic horse, which cannot have moved too far from their original position for fear of revealing their nasty surprise before time. Thinking they were going to sweep all before them, the Roman heavy horse found themselves beset by the pockets of concealed infantry and soon panicked and broke. That the cream of the Roman cavalry routed in such short order "was a great embarrassment to Julian",[99] which he would punish them for later, but in the heat of battle the flight of the cataphracts was doubly calamitous for the Romans. Not only did their removal leave the Roman formation vulnerable to the Alamanni cavalry, in their headlong flight the cataphracts smashed into the *Cornuti* and *Bracchiati*. These *auxilia* maintained some semblance of order but with the imminent threat of a barbarian charge any disruption could have been disastrous. The cataphracts were rallied by the personal intervention of Julian but he may have succeeded in rallying just

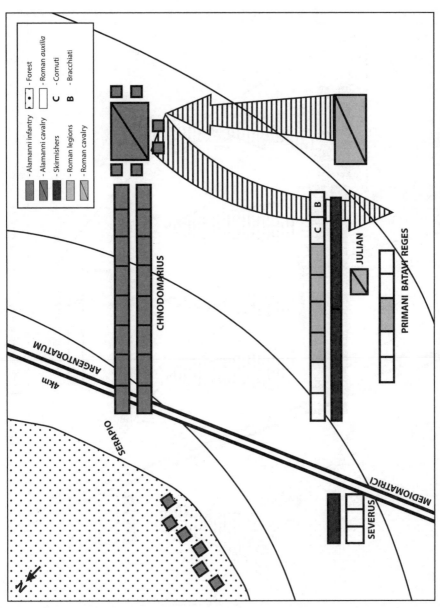

The Battle of Strasbourg B: Repulse and Rout of the Roman Cavalry

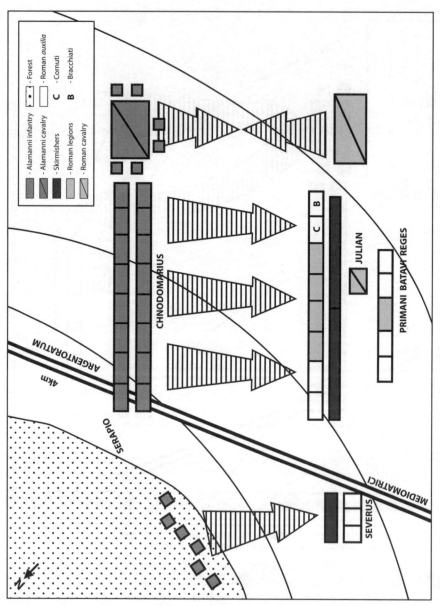

The Battle of Strasbourg C: Alamanni Advance

one of the two units.[100] While the heavy cavalry had disgraced themselves, the actions of the rest of the Roman cavalry are not recorded; however, while Chnodomarius' trap had succeeded in removing the Romans' most potent striking arm, the Alamannic cavalry failed to make any impression on the Roman right flank, suggesting that the likes of the *Scutarii* and *sagitarii*, later to be rejoined by the rallied cataphracts, held the Alamanni at bay.

On the Roman left, Severus was wary of an attack from the wooded hilltop as he advanced on Serapio's position slowly and refused to over-commit. There is some suggestion that the *magister* had his division charge into the woods to flush out the ambush and defeat it, but this would seem counter-intuitive for why, having discovered a trap, would Severus then risk charging straight into it? Similar to the Roman right, there is no further action recorded for this side of the battlefield but the suspicion is that the forces of Severus and Serapio did engage each other, with the superior quality of the Romans telling regardless of the slope and the ambushing forces in the woods.[101]

The neutralising of both wings left the battle to be decided in the centre, where the inevitable barbarian charge smashed into the Roman lines as the Alamanni looked to capitalise on the disruption caused by the routing cataphracts. Through a combination of missiles, a spear-bristling *testudo*, iron discipline and support from the *Batavi* and *Reges* from the reserve, the front line *auxilia* withstood the initial bone-shuddering impact and then several more charges after that, inflicting heavy casualties on the reckless Germans. Recognising the futility of such continued unorganised attacks, the Alamanni formed and launched their aforementioned *globus* at the Roman centre. This 'hog's head' succeeded in punching through the legions, cutting the Roman front line in half, although the *Primani* proved a tougher nut to crack. The *globus* was first fought to a standstill and then thrown back.

What had seemed like a battle-winning breakthrough was now turning into a disaster for the barbarians. The *Primani*-led counterattack re-established the Roman line, where the legions had retained their coherence and with the advancing reserve, the *auxilia* wings and perhaps Severus' division, the *pagi* were soon enveloped. As the noose tightened, the already exhausted and disheartened Alamanni took even heavier casualties before breaking. Any continued fighting on the wings was soon swept away by a ruthless Roman pursuit. Those barbarians not captured or cut down in the chase were forced all the way to the Rhine, which many attempted to swim across and were washed away or struck by Roman missiles.[102]

Alamannic casualties are recorded as being immense: Ammianus suggests 6,000, while Libanius says 8,000, with thousands more drowning in the river, although these should be treated with as much suspicion as the reports of the

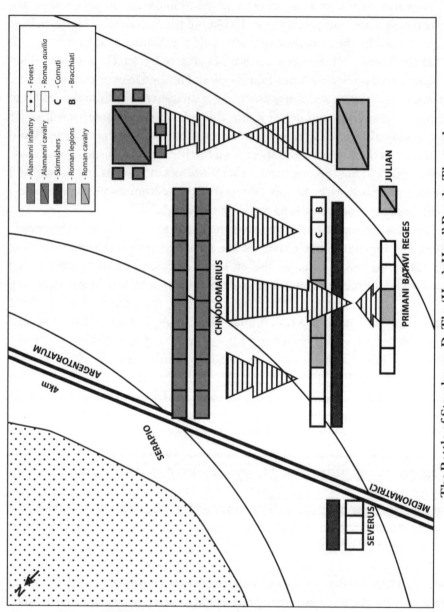

The Battle of Strasbourg D: The 'Hog's Head' Breaks Through

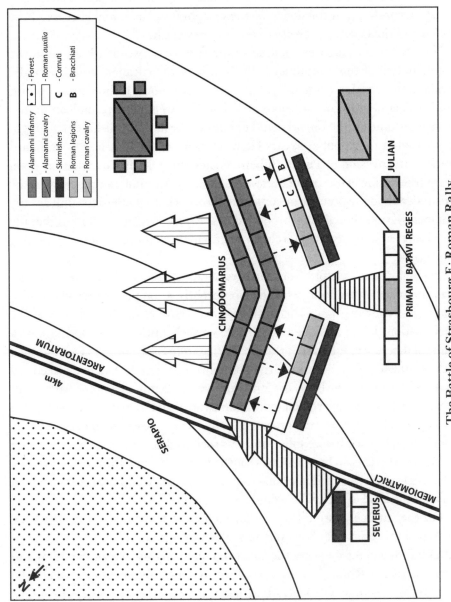

The Battle of Strasbourg E: Roman Rally

size of the Alamanni army. That Chnodomarius, Serapio and the other *reges* survived, despite being in the thick of the fighting might suggest that the Alamanni defeat was not quite as deadly as it is reported. Similarly suspicious are the losses attributed to the Romans: just 243 men. This seems small and overly accurate given the defeat of the cataphracts, the initial success of the *globus* and the general intensity of the infantry clashes.[103]

The Roman casualties included four tribunes, two of which were the commanders of the cataphracts. The death of their leaders could partially explain the cavalry rout but Julian was in no mood to be forgiving but, considering he was low on troops and that they were perhaps on loan to him from Constantius, the *Caesar* could not inflict the harsh punishment he might have wanted to. About six years later, when a cavalry unit lost its standard during his invasion of Persia, Julian considered inflicting decimation upon them (the killing of one out of every ten soldiers in the unit), although either he misunderstood the practice or could not afford to kill a tenth of the unit as only ten men were executed. On this occasion at Strasbourg, it is reported that the surviving cataphracts were forced to wear female clothing as an embarrassing alternative.[104]

Having rescued victory from the jaws of defeat against a larger army, Julian was the toast of his men, who then reportedly attempted to proclaim him *Augustus*. Knowing how Constantius viewed those claiming authority above their station, Julian was quick to turn down such a title.[105] Furthermore, as a show of deference, Julian sent the great prize from Strasbourg to Constantius. Attempting to escape across the river on some boats that he had had placed at a makeshift camp on the ruins of Concordia, about 25 miles from the battlefield, Chnodomarius was overtaken by Roman cavalry and forced to surrender in a nearby wood. Before the congregated Gallic army, the defeated barbarian *rex* supplicated himself before Julian and was then packed off to the imperial court at Milan, where it can be imagined that the *Gigas* was something of a spectacle. The mighty warrior died not longer after at a prison camp near Rome, which was not the kind of mercy he would have wanted.[106]

On the surface, it would seem that victory at Strasbourg broke the back of Alamanni resistance; however, Julian's campaign for 357 was not yet over. After burying of the bodies of the fallen and removing any remaining Alamanni back across the Rhine,[107] Julian returned to Tres Tabernae, from where the spoils of war were sent to Metz. The plan was to use these resources to build a bridge over the Rhine at Mainz in order to invade Alamanni territory but the Gallic army had other ideas. Having fought for much of the year already, with some who had fought with Julian all throughout the winter at Senones too, the soldiers demanded a rest. "By his eloquence and the charm of his language"[108] and no doubt employing a mixture of shame and cajoling, Julian persuaded his men to take advantage of the opportunity that their great victory had afforded them.

This continuation was well timed for the Alamanni too had thought that the Romans would enter winter quarters after Strasbourg and were taken aback by the structure thrown over the Rhine at Mainz and even more so by the subsequent crossing of the river by Julian and his men. However, they had not lost the will to fight. Despite claims of capitulating and then changing their mind,[109] the Alamanni managed to slow Julian's approach by sending envoys to plead for peace, giving them time to lay traps and gather men. Upon hearing of these defences and perhaps realising that he had been duped by listening to these envoys, Julian dispatched 800 men in boats to sneak past the approaching Alamannic force and threaten their homes; it is not recorded whether these men were sent up the Rhine or the Main river, the confluence of which is near Mainz. Given that the Rhine turns west just north of Mainz, this Roman detachment could have been sent up either river to get behind the Alamanni. That the barbarians had set up their camp on high ground opposite Julian does not provide any real evidence of where this confrontation took place, although a later mention of the Alamanni retreating across the Main might make it the river in question.[110]

Regardless of the geography, this ploy by Julian achieved complete success. The next morning, when the Romans advanced up the hill to confront the Alamanni, they found the camp abandoned. After some initial worry that they were walking into a trap, the Romans found that their raid had worked better than perhaps even the *Caesar* himself had hoped for with the Alamanni fleeing upon seeing smoke coming from the direction of their homes. Julian then sent fast moving cavalry after the retreating Germans while his main column set about plundering the Alamanni farms and homesteads. Arriving at a dense forest, Julian was discouraged from driving onward and allowed his men to rest. This caution, which just two years previously the *Caesar* would not have shown, was well placed as a deserter reported that a large German force was concealed in tunnels and trenches amongst the trees. Julian again demonstrated his new-found restraint by refusing to attack or to take the substantial detour required to circumvent such a dug-in position. Wary that winter was coming, the *Caesar* shunned driving deeper into German territory along the Main, although he did not retreat back to Gaul.

Instead, he moved south along the east bank of the Rhine arriving at a fort built and named for the emperor Trajan over 250 years previously and considered to be modern Ladenburg on the banks of the Neckar, which had been recently attacked.[111] The re-establishing of a Roman garrison at this fort in Alamanni territory, coupled with Strasbourg and Julian's punitive strike across the Rhine, did much to restore Roman prestige and broke the resolve of several of the Alamannic leaders as they approached Julian asking for peace. After some deliberation and enough time for the Trajanic fortress to be repaired, garrisoned and supplied, Julian granted the Alamanni a ten month truce in return for providing his new outpost with further supplies.[112]

With this truce agreed, Julian regarded his campaigning for 357 as complete and began to withdraw to winter quarters. However, on his way back to Rheims through Cologne, Severus encountered several columns of Franks engaged in plundering raids on Roman territory. Faced with the return of the Gallic field army, up to 1,000 Franks took possession of two abandoned forts along the Meuse. Despite the onset of winter, Julian and Severus felt it necessary to besiege these footholds but the Franks proved to be far stouter than expected. It took some fifty-four days and careful patrolling of the river to break up any forming ice and prevent any easy escape for the Roman stranglehold to force the capitulation of the defenders.[113] This seems to have been a timely outcome for it was reported that a large Frankish warband was marching to relieve their besieged colleagues only to turn back when word of their capitulation reached them. Rather than chase after this barbarian force, wary of the exertions his men had already faced, Julian led them to winter quarters, taking up residence in Paris.[114] The *Caesar* had been remarkably successful, almost certainly more so than Constantius, his court and probably Julian himself could have predicted, although not as much as Ammianus would have it believed. The historian looked back to the mid-Republic to compare Julian's success with wars in which Rome's very existence was threatened: "In this memorable war, which in fact deserves to be compared with those against Carthaginians and the Teutons, but was achieved with very slight losses."[115]

Despite such prizes as Chnodomarius, other prisoners and spoils and the re-establishment of much of the Gallic frontier, if Ammianus is to be believed, Constantius and his courtiers treated reports of the successes at Strasbourg and along the Rhine, Main and Meuse with disdain and ridicule, facetiously calling Julian *Victorinus* as he often mentioned his victories in dispatches and claiming the defeat of the Alamanni as Constantius' own victory. It cannot be helped but felt that the historian is allowing his personal feelings to cloud his reporting and he may even be misrepresenting Constantius' retelling of his role at Strasbourg, all of which can be explained. Despite Ammianus' indignation, this had been imperial procedure since the earliest days of the Principate almost four centuries before. As ruling *Augustus* and therefore "ultimately responsible for all military activities in the Empire",[116] Constantius was well within his rights to claim credit for Julian's victory and anyone else fighting under his auspices. Indeed, Constantius did not go out of his way to celebrate the victory as his own. He did not take a victory title such as *Germanicus* or *Alamannicus Maximus* and there were no victory issues from the imperial mint at Sirmium, although it could be argued that this lack of propagandising in itself was downplaying Julian's victory.[117]

It is also worth asking as to why Constantius would lavish attention and *kudos* on his *Caesar* for having done the job he had allotted to him, especially when as of 357, the job was not yet completed. Chnodomarius might be in captivity but several Alamanni *reges* remained in open conflict with the Romans, while Frankish and Saxon tribes seemed more than willing to cross the Rhine and interfere in Roman affairs. Maybe Constantius would be willing to congratulate Julian more publicly when these threats were dealt with and the Rhine frontier was re-established as a bastion against *barbaricum*...

Maybe.

Chapter VIII

Adversus Barbaros: Constantius and Julian Across the Rivers

...join your fellow-soldiers and entrust yourselves to me, so that we can move against the barbarians and liberate ourselves...

– Alexander the Great (Pseudo-Kallisthenes, *Historia Alexandri Magni* I.15)

Finishing the Job: Julian's Campaigns of 358 and 359

Instead of a time of celebration for a job well done against the Alamanni and the planning of further campaigns, the Roman winter quarters at Paris were the scene of a political struggle, which was to have important effects on the portrayal of Julian at the imperial court. Late 357/early 358 saw the destruction of the relationship between Julian and the Gallic praetorian prefect, Florentius. The initial subject of this confrontation was taxation, a sphere of influence that the reforms of Diocletian and Constantine had reserved for the civilian praetorian prefect for the reason that "it made good sense to keep the man who held the purse strings and the man who commanded the soldiers separate."[1]

However, Julian found inefficient and antiquarian practices undermining the manpower and funds available to him. Faced with another large deficit, as the man responsible for tax collecting in Gaul, Florentius had simply ordered an additional tax on those who had already paid.[2] Despite some accusations of corruption,[3] such a supplementary levy was standard practice and given the importance of Gaul, Florentius was a respected and capable bureaucrat who was acting in good faith. After conducting a thorough research of the books and in the field, the young *Caesar* felt that this civilian official was not armed with all the facts, specifically the extent of the damage done to the Gallic countryside by war, raids, bad harvest, corruption and just how completely the practice of tax write offs had failed.[4] Florentius did not take kindly to this meddling in his affairs and the concomitant but unspoken accusation that he was unreliable or incompetent. Even when the *Caesar* provided ample evidence that if the normal taxes were collected correctly they were "in excess of the inevitable requirements for government provisions",[5] Florentius ignored his advice and again proposed a supplementary tax. Julian's response was to throw the proposal to the ground unread and unsigned. This caused Florentius to go over the *Caesar's* head, appealing to Constantius over the interference of Julian in civilian affairs.

Despite being accused of not caring about the oppressive nature of supplementary levies and listening to any accusation against Julian, Constantius was aware of the problem of such levies as he legislated against them on two occasions in 356.[6] Therefore, while rebuking him for overstepping his authority, once Julian highlighted the oppressive, unnecessary and counter-productive nature of such supplementary taxes, much to the dismay of Florentius and much of his court, Constantius sided with his *Caesar*. Under orders from the emperor, although Ammianus suggests that Julian persuaded the prefect to do so,[7] Florentius ceded financial control of Gallia Belgica Secunda to Julian to apply his approach to taxation. Instead of raising new taxes, Julian had existing taxes collected, refusing to issue write offs and forcing the larger taxpayers to pay their share. This lessened the burden on the poor, who, not having to worry about oppressive supplementary taxes paid what they owed in far larger numbers, proving that if taxes were collected fairly "there would be no arrears and the yield would be sufficient".[8] Indeed, it was calculated that over the course of his term as *Caesar* in Gaul, Julian reduced the *caput* tax, which corrupt practices had inflated to twenty-five *solidi*, to just seven without undermining the treasury or recruitment.[9] However, that the *Caesar* had been proven correct in his assertion that good government would trump increased taxation did nothing to placate Florentius. If anything, it will have made him even more recalcitrant. One of Julian's letters, without ever naming his target, provides thinly-veiled vitriol against his praetorian prefect, railing against "him" as a thief and a bandit, guilty of scandalous and shameful behaviour.[10]

And Julian and Florentius were soon at loggerheads again, this time over another administrative problem: the grain supply. The main source of grain in Gaul was Aquitania in the south-west but for it to get to the depots of the Rhine frontier meant a long, slow transfer overland. Indeed, it was the slowness of this grain route, along with Julian allowing his men an extended rest after a prolonged campaign, that meant that the Gallic field army was not expected to take the field again until July 358.[11] However, there was a large surplus of grain available to the Romans if they could once again harness it: the wide open fields of Britain. Such a source would have given a timely boost not just to the resources of the Gallic field army but also to northern Gaul itself; a steady food supply, together with renewed military security, would go a long way to re-establishing the population, infrastructure, tax and manpower resources of the region. That the Romans recognised this potentiality is shown by Julian's building of a substantial grain fleet of up to 600 large vessels for the English Channel.[12]

Before that could be achieved, the Romans needed full control of the Channel itself. The campaigns of Constantius Chlorus, Constantine I and Constans had fixed some of the damage done to the connections with Britain during the third century but by the 350s the area of the Rhine–Meuse–Scheldt delta had become infiltrated by Frankish settlers,[13] who began raiding Channel shipping lanes, disrupting the reintroduction of British grain into Gaul. How to deal with these Franks was where *Caesar* and praetorian prefect butted heads. As a civilian bureaucrat, Florentius favoured paying off the pirates and again had precedent on his side. But much like with taxation, Constantius proved open to the more long term solutions of his *Caesar*, particularly when the barbarians demanded two thousand pounds of silver for safe passage across the Rhine. Julian hints that Constantius found the arrangement negotiated by Florentius to be disgraceful and gave his *Caesar* a free hand in dealing with the situation.[14]

Despite having occasionally adopted a cautious approach, Julian proved in his dealings with these Frankish pirates that he was still a dynamic risk taker. If the raids on Roman shipping would not cease when ordered, they would be made to stop at the point of a sword. Hoping to catch the barbarians unaware by marching before the main harvest, Julian set out for Toxandria[15] with just twenty days rations. By the time the Gallic field army had reached Tongres, the Salii had gotten word of his intentions and sent a deputation, asking to be recognised in their lands in return for not raiding Roman territory. Julian appeared to agree to this arrangement but once the Frankish envoys went home, he sent Severus in a sneak attack along the river. Trapped between the two Roman forces, the Salii were so overwhelmed that any thoughts of negotiation changed to surrender with Julian settling them as defeated subjects. This might seem more than a little ungallant but while it was a long established policy to allow the settlement of non-Romans within the empire, it was not policy to allow barbarians in undefeated. It is also possible that with his lack of supplies, Julian required a military victory to provide him with the leverage to requisition food from the Salii, only to be disappointed by the lateness of the northern harvest.[16]

This strike against the Salian Franks then revealed to Julian that there was a reason behind their interloping on Roman territory beyond greed: the aggression of another Germanic tribe beyond the Rhine, the Chamavi.[17] Demonstrating the same ruthlessness that had cowed the Salii, Julian struck at those Chamavi who had crossed the Rhine, killing a large number and taking hostages while those who got away later returned to plead for a similar settlement to the Salii.[18] However, the recording of the subjugation of Frankish tribes suggests a more decisive outcome on the Lower Rhine than was the case. It is probably more correct to speak of Julian coercing these Salian and Chamavian Franks to become part of the Roman systems of defence and supply through military action. It might be even more correct to say that Julian was merely confirming these Franks in a position that they had occupied since the late third century and would retain until the collapse of Roman central authority in the fifth century.[19]

Having secured Roman access to the Rhine–Meuse–Scheldt delta, Julian set about repairing those fortresses along the Meuse that had fallen into disrepair in the previous decades.[20] However, when he moved to the Rhine, the extent of the risk of setting out before the harvest was revealed. When Frankish food stores failed to provide a sufficient yield, the *Caesar* found himself the target of a torrent of abuse from hungry soldiers.[21] It might seem surprising to see how quickly the soldiers turned on their adored commander but one such way to change an army's opinion is through their stomachs. Another is through their pockets and even Ammianus suggests that the soldiers "had good reason for their complaints"[22] as they were not only faced with a shortage of food but for all of their success in the field they had seemingly not been paid since Julian's arrived in Gaul. However, he passes the blame on to Constantius and his officials for not providing Julian with sufficient funds to pay his soldiers their wage or the *donativum* that should have accompanied Julian's appointment.

As Ammianus will have seen it, the emperor was using his ultimate control of finances to keep Julian's popularity and resources in check. The role of the *notarius* Gaudentius, who appears to have been posted to Gaul to spy on and defame the young *Caesar* was just another part of the anti-Julian conspiracy that Ammianus saw unfolding. It should be noted that Julian would have Gaudentius executed when he came to power, so it is possible that there is some truth to what otherwise seems like Ammianus taking his hero's side.[23] However, while the paying of the troops might not have been under Julian's control, their lack of food had been caused by his own impetuousness and miscalculation so he cannot be absolved of blame.

How Julian averted a mutiny and got his men to continue on beyond the Rhine is not recorded with anything other than a cursory claim from Ammianus that Julian sweet-talked them into doing so.[24] Even a suggestion of bribery leads to a further question of 'with what'? Did supplies arrive from southern Gaul or Britain? Did civilian officials like Florentius come through with pay? Perhaps Julian convinced his men that winning booty across the Rhine was the only way to ensure their payment or maybe Ammianus played up the unrest to something more dangerous than it was. The real events along the Meuse following the defeat of the Chamavi will remain hidden.

Whatever the root causes, the outcome was that the Romans forged onward. Having crossed the river into Frankish territory via a pontoon bridge, Julian came up against an unexpected obstacle: the uncharacteristic timidity of his *magister equitum*. After two years of following Julian on his aggressive campaigning, Severus hesitated to move deeper into enemy territory; so much so that Ammianus calls the aged general a coward and suggests that he feared his approaching death.[25] That Severus did indeed die not long after could suggest that his behaviour was born of ill-health; modern diagnoses might include a nervous breakdown or even Post Traumatic Stress Disorder. It could just be that Severus was an old man. However, such focus on Severus' age and health can overlook the fact that the *magister* had valid reasons for urging caution as Julian was attempting to lead an under-supplied, under-paid, restless army away from the safety of Roman fortifications. Presented in this light, this hesitance from Severus appears more like an appropriate streak of caution, which would seem to have been confirmed by the sudden appearance of an Alamanni force under Suomarius.[26] However, rather than continued belligerence, this Alamannic *rex* was eager for a settlement, suggesting instead that Julian's aggression had been correct. Much like the Salii and Chamavi, Suomarius agreed to surrender his Roman prisoners and supply the Gallic field army with food.

Buoyed by this success, Julian now struck into the territory of another survivor of Strasbourg, Hortarius. Lacking guides, the *Caesar* sent out a Nestica tribune of his *Scutarii*, and Charietto, who at this time was little more than a headhunter enrolled in an irregular unit but is described as "a man of extraordinary bravery",[27] to capture a local with knowledge of the surrounding area. When the initial route was found to be blocked by felled trees, the guide led Julian along an alternative track into the farmlands of Hortarius. Roman forces pillaging his lands was enough to bring another *rex* to the negotiating table, where he was intimidated into not just releasing his Roman prisoners but also contributing to the rebuilding of the Rhine frontier. With that, Julian chose to end his campaigning for 358 and sent his men into their winter quarters. This seems to have been a premature end as it was perhaps still early autumn but having cowed two Frankish tribes and two Alamannic chieftains and reopened the Rhine to British grain traffic with limited loss in the face of the disgruntlement of his men and the ill-health of his *magister equitum*, Julian chose to not take any further risks in 358.

CONSTANTIUS II
Bust from Museum of Archaeology,
University of Pennsylvania.
(Mary Harrsch © 2005)

CONSTANTIUS II
In the porch of St John
Lateran, Rome, this was once
thought to be Constantine I
but is instead Constantius II.
(© TcfkaPanairjdde)

MISSORIUM OF KERCH
Depicting Constantius II on horseback with a spear, accompanied by a guardsman and preceded by Victory. (Public domain)

CONSTANTIUS II
Depicted dispensing largesse in a Renaissance copy of a Carolingian copy of the *Chronograph of 354*, Barberini Museum, Rome. (Public domain)

CONSTANTINE I
Head of colossal marble statue, Musei Capitolini, Rome. (Jean-Pol Grandmont © 2011)

CONSTANTIUS GALLUS
Bust in Archaelogical Museum,
Aquileia. (Wolfgang Sauber © 2011)

GALLUS
Constantius Gallus holding
Victory in a Renaissance
copy of a Carolingian copy
of the *Chronograph of
354*, Barberini Museum,
Rome. (Public domain)

THE TETRARCHS IN PORPHYRY
Plundered from Constantinople during the Fourth Crusade,
it now stands on a corner of St Mark's in Venice. (Nino Barbieri © 2004)

CONSTANS
Marble bust in the Louvre.
(Jastrow 2005, public domain)

CONSTANTINE II
Statue on the Cordonata, Rome, Italy.
(TcfkaPanairjdde © 2009)

'GRIGOR ILLUMINATOR
BAPTISES TIRIDATES III
OF ARMENIA'
Francesco Zugno (1708–1787).
(Public domain)

AMIDA
(Gerry Lynch © 2003)

WALLS OF AMIDA
(Brian Dell, 2010, public domain)

THE WESTERN WALL OF AMIDA
(Bjorn Christian Torrisen © 2009)

PALACE OF SIRMIUM
(Marko235 © Mediaportal 2012)

SIRMIUM

A scale model of Sirmium in the Visitor Centre in Srmeska Mitrovica. (Marko235 © Mediaportal 2012)

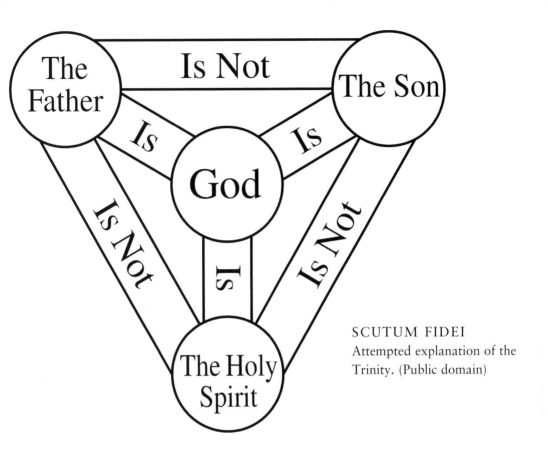

SCUTUM FIDEI
Attempted explanation of the
Trinity. (Public domain)

BRIDGE OVER THE PYRAMUS NEAR MOBSUCRENAE
(© (CC BY 3.0) Klaus-Peter Simon 1996)

PRIEST OF SERAPIS
Formerly thought to be Julian.

SHAPUR II ON THE HUNT
Arthur M. Sackler Gallery,
Washington D.C. (Public domain)

CONSTANTIUS II
Gold solidus, issued 347–350, Antioch

OBV: diademed, draped and cuirassed bust, FL IVL CONSTAN TIVS PERP AVG

REV: GLORIA REI PVBLICAE, enthroned Roma and Constantinopolis holding shield with VOT XX MULT XXX, in exergue SMANS

CONSTANTIUS II
Gold solidus, issued 340–351, Nicomedia

OBV: diademed, draped and cuirassed bust, FL IVL CONSTAN TIVS PERP AVG

REV: GLORIA REI PVBLICAE, enthroned Roma and Constantinopolis holding shield with VOT XX MULT XXX, in exergue SMNS

CONSTANTIUS II
Silver siliqua, issued 340–351, Sirmium

OBV: diademed bust, DN CONSTAN TIVS PF AVG

REV: VOT XXX MVLTIS XXXX within wreath, in exergue PCON

CONSTANTINE II
AE follis, issued 326, Trier

OBV: laureate cuirassed bust, CONSTANTINVS IVN NOB C

REV: turreted camp gate with star, PROVIDEN TIAE CAESS, in exergue STR dotted crescent

CONSTANS
Silver siliqua, issued 337–340, Constantinople

OBV: large plain diademed head to right of Constans, looking upwards

REV: Victory holding wreath and palm branch, CONSTANS AVGVSTVS, in exergue C I

All coins courtesy of Noble Numismatics: www.noble.com.au

CONSTANTINE I
AE centenionalis, issued c.320, Aquileia

OBV: helmeted and cuirassed bust, Medusa on breastplate, CONST ANTINVS AVG

REV: two captives seated at base of VOT X X vexillum, flanked by S-F, VIRTVS EXERCIT, in exergue AQP

CONSTANTINE I
Forgery AE follies in gold, Antioch

OBV: pearl rosette draped bust, CONSTANTI NVS MAX AVG

REV: two soldiers holding standards, GLOR IA EXERC ITVS, in exergue SMAND

CRISPUS
AE follis, issued 324–325, London

OBV: laureate draped and cuirassed bust, FL IVL CRISPVS NOB CAES

REV: turreted camp gate with star, PROVIDEN TIAE CAESS, in exergue PLON

FAUSTA
AE follis, c.300–326, Nicomedia

OBV: diademed draped bust, FLAV MAX FAVSTA AVG

REV: Fausta holding Constantine II and Constantius II, SPES REI PVBLICAE, in exergue MNA

CONSTANTIUS I
AE follis, issued 307–310 (posthumous), Rome

OBV: veiled and laureate draped bust, DIVO CONSTANTIO PIO PRINCIP

REV: Constantius seated on curule chair, REQVIES OPTIMOR MERIT, in exergue RQ

All coins courtesy of Noble Numismatics: www.noble.com.au

CONSTANTIUS I
Silver argentius, issued c.295–297, Rome

OBV: laureate bust, CONSTAN TIVS CAES

REV: tetrarchs sacrifice before turreted open camp gate, VIRTVS MILITVM, in exergue A

HELENA
AE follis, issued 324–325, Arles

OBV: draped bust, FL HELENA AVGVSTA

REV: SECVRITAS REIPVBLICE, Helena standing to left, lowering branch, in exergue T*AR

DIOCLETIAN
Gold aureus, issued 290–292, Antioch and Cyzicus

OBV: laureate bust, DIOCLETIANVS AVGVSTVS

REV: Diocletian holding globe, CONSVL IIII P P PRO COS

MAGNENTIUS
AE double centenionalis, issued 353, Amiens

OBV: draped and cuirassed bust, DN MAGNETIUS PF AVG

REV: large Chi-Rho, between alpha and omega, SALVS DD NN AUG ET CAES, in exergue AMB

VETRANIO
AE centenionalis, issued at Thessalonica

OBV: bearded, diademed, draped and cuirassed, D N VERTAN IO (sic) P F AVG

REV: emperor in military dress holding Chi-Rho banner and shield, VIRTVS EXERCITVM, in exergue TSA

JULIAN
Gold solidus, issued 355–361, Antioch

OBV: draped and cuirassed bust,
D N IVLIANV S NOB CAES

REV: Roma and Constantinopolis
enthroned holding shield inscribed
with star, GLORIA REI PVBLICAE,
in exergue SMANZ

JULIAN
AE 3, 361–363, Sirmium

OBV: helmeted, diademed bust
holding spear and shield DN FL
CL IVLI-ANVS PF AVG

REV: VOT X / MVLT XX in wreath,
in exergue ASIRM

CONSTANTIUS GALLUS
AE centenionalis, 351–354,
Constantinople

OBV: draped and cuirassed bust, D N
FL C L CONSTANTIVS NOB CAES

REV: soldier spearing fallen horseman,
FEL TEMP RE PARATIO, **G* and
dot above, in exergue CONSI

SHAPUR II
Silver drachm

OBV: bust to right with crown,
name in outer margin

REV: fire altar with attendants

SHAPUR II
Gold dinar, Kabul

OBV: bust to right with crown,
flowing hair type

REV: fire altar, text around

All coins courtesy of Noble Numismatics: www.noble.com.au

As with the previous year, Julian again spent part of the winter months seeing to the financial and legal well-being of his provinces, "diligently providing that no one should be overloaded with a burden of tribute... and that no official should with impunity swerve from equity",[28] even going as far as to sit in judgement of numerous cases. However, Julian's main focus remained on the military tasks at hand. His victory at Strasbourg, rebuilding of fortresses and audacious strikes across the Rhine had done much to re-establish the frontiers of Gaul but the job was not yet done. Therefore, Julian and his council determined to once again strike into enemy territory, hoping to repeat the capitulations of the Salii, Chamavi, Suomarius and Hortarius. A tribune, Hariobaudes, was dispatched to Hortarius ostensibly to confer with the allied *rex* about aspects of their treaty, but in reality to discover the preparedness of those neighbouring Alamanni who remained unsubdued. Meanwhile, Julian called together his army and moved north to the Lower Rhine, where he continued the rebuilding of military bases and granaries for the British grain fleet, using barbarian manpower and resources, as per the agreements of 358.[29] With this building complete and Hariobaudes returning to suggest that the Alamanni did not expect another Roman offensive, Julian moved to Mainz. Here, Florentius and Severus' successor, Lupicinus, urged the *Caesar* to build a bridge across the Rhine, although Julian refused on account of the tribes opposite Mainz having already surrendered and building such a bridge and then marching his forces through their territory would only provoke them.

While this was the right decision at the time, it was soon to be proven that the Romans could have done with another lesson in their military might for since Hariobaudes had returned the Alamanni tribes had gotten wind of Julian's plans. They then bullied Suomarius and Hortarius into disavowing their treaties with Rome and contesting any attempted Roman crossing at Mainz. When Suomarius responded that he could not resist the Gallic field army alone, a large Alamanni force converged on the riverbank opposite Mainz. It might be expected that without a bridge to cross and a hostile force in play that Julian will have stepped away from any confrontation, but having gotten to this position, he refused to back down.

The Romans marched up the Rhine in search of a good crossing point, with the Alamanni force keeping pace. Finding a fordable site, Julian and Lupicinus armed 300 light troops with stakes and sent them back downriver under cover of night to sneak across to the east bank. Having negotiated the Rhine, these Roman marines found themselves in the middle of a large drunken feast, hosted by Hortarius, an unwilling participant in the move against Julian. The small size of this Roman force meant that there were few Alamannic casualties but the sheer presence of enemy troops in their camp spread panic amongst the drunken revellers and large numbers of warriors fled on horseback. Within a short time, the large host that had come together to challenge the Roman crossing of the Rhine had dispersed.

This left Julian free to cross into the lands of Hortarius before then driving into the territory of those Alamanni who still offered resistance. The failure to stop Julian at the Rhine coupled with the tactics of terror, burning and looting brought the remaining Alamannic leaders to the negotiating table. Peace was granted to both Macrianus and Hariobaudus but the third chieftain to appear before Julian provided a different challenge. It was Vadomarius. The *Caesar* will have no doubt been of a mood to treat him in a similar manner to any other Alamannic chief who had disavowed his treaties with Rome, but Vadomarius came armed with a letter of commendation from Constantius, likely provided during the emperor's campaign into the Neckar valley in 356. It is worth noting though that regardless of how Ammianus would like to present the emperor, it would be unlikely that Constantius will have continued with such a recommendation after Vadomarius had taken up arms against Rome at Strasbourg. The real problem for Julian was that Vadomarius had been sent as a representative of three other survivors of Strasbourg: Urius, Ursicinus and Westralp. This meant that he could give no definitive acceptance of Julian's terms, which must have frustrated the Romans. However, once their lands were subjected to the same pillaging as those of Macrianus and Hariobaudus, these three kings bent the knee to Julian and were granted peace on similar terms to the other supplicants.[30]

With this capitulation of the Alamannic *reges*, the record of Julian's campaigning in 359 comes to an end with little elaboration as to how much time has elapsed with the rebuilding works and the operations across the Rhine. It would appear that the acceptance of Julian's terms by Urius, Ursicinus and Westralp brought an end to the task that Constantius had allotted to him. The Alamanni who had raided Gaul with impunity for years had been forced back into alliance with Rome as had those Franks who had encroached into northern Gaul and sacked Cologne, with numerous fortresses rebuilt and the tax base being nursed back to health. In the process of doing so, Julian recorded that he crossed the Rhine three times, secured the release of 1,000 Romans, took 10,000 prisoners and recovered all the towns along the Rhine that had been lost.[31] However, despite the praise given to Julian by Ammianus, it could be suggested that his campaigns did little to prevent further warfare and may instead have stirred up the barbarian nest. The power of the Alamanni had not been broken for within five years, they were again on the warpath, forcing Julian's long-term successors in Gaul, Valentinian I and his son

Gratian, into extended campaigns along the Rhine throughout the 360s and 370s.[32]

The next recorded military operation undertaken by the forces of Julian was in another part of the empire, which came under the purview of the *Caesar*: Britain. In the midst of winter 359/360, news reached Paris of renewed raids by the Picts and Scoti across northern Britain in contravention of a past treaty, probably with Constans in 343.[33] Julian was not prepared to travel across the English Channel to deal with them himself but he did send a detachment from his field army. While the size of this force was somewhat limited, at most 3,000, and is described by Ammianus as "light-armed auxiliaries",[34] that should not hide that the units chosen were elite forces – the *Batavi* and *Heruli auxilia* and the twin *Moesiaci* legions – and led by Lupicinus. When supported by the garrisons of Britain, this was not an inconsequential force.

Reflecting the urgency and extent of the reports from Britain, Julian had Lupicinus travel to Bononia, modern Boulogne, to cross the Channel in the height of winter. Gathering together as many ships as he could, the *magister* received a favourable wind and took to the waters, landing at Rutufiae, modern Richborough, near Ramsgate. From there, he marched to London, to receive intelligence about the movements of the invaders and then formulate a strategy to deal with them before he took the field. Little else is known of this British campaign although Pictish, Scoti and Atacotti raids continued in the 360s, which would suggest that Lupicinus had only dealt with the raiders in Roman territory through diplomacy or force rather than affecting their origins beyond Hadrian's Wall or across the Irish Sea. However, as will be seen, it is possible that developments in imperial politics interrupted any campaigning planned by the *magister equitum*.

Imperial Trials and Tribulations

While Julian was fulfilling his imperial mission along the Rhine, the imperial court continued to be a dangerous place full of "abominable acts".[35] Opportunities for advancement by destroying your opponents with any range of accusations, true or false, still remained. Therefore, the rantings of Marcellus and their unravelling by Eutherius was far from the only trial to take place. Demonstrating that no one was safe from such intrigue, one of the main instigators of this atmosphere of backstabbing, Arbitio found himself having to answer accusations of aiming at the imperial throne from the *comes* Verissimus. Ammianus questions the veracity of these claims by highlighting the involvement of a certain Dorus, ex-surgeon of the *Scutarii*, who had a history of accusing others of having such imperial pretensions.[36] That said,

Ammianus does not cover himself in glory by suggesting that when Arbitio's name was cleared, it was not due to his innocence, lack of evidence or the lies of Dorus and Verissimus but the machinations of the imperial chamberlains corrupting the legal system.

Another to find himself hoisted by his own political petard was Rufinus, staff officer of the praetorian prefect of Illyricum. His spies had already brought about the ruin of the governor of Pannonia but now he involved himself in one too many plots. In attempting to lay the foundations of a large case of high treason, complete with the accusation of the robbing of Diocletian's tomb, Rufinus found his female accomplice could not stand up to the scrutiny of the praetorian prefect, Mavortius, and the *comes sacrarum largitionum*, Ursulus, leading to his execution for slander and adultery.[37] Upon hearing of this, Constantius flew into a rage and demanded that Ursulus appear to explain himself. When he arrived at Milan, some tried to prevent Uruslus from speaking with Constantius in the hope that the emperor's anger would go unabated. However, Uruslus, unafraid of such threats, burst into the emperor's presence and explained the extent of the exactions of Rufinus, in all likelihood saving both his and Mavortius' lives.[38]

In the midst of such trials, Constantius visited Rome, where his celebration of a triumph for his defeat of Magnentius drew ridicule as it had been won through the spilling of Roman blood. To Ammianus, this was just an excuse for an undeserved, lavish ceremony designed to inflate the emperor's already swollen pride. He aimed particular vitriol at this triumphal celebration and the military success it implied

> He had not overcome in person any race that made war on him; no news had arrived that any had been defeated by the valour of his generals; he had added nothing to the empire; he had never been seen fighting at the head of his men or even in the front rank in moments of crisis.[39]

But is this the whole truth? Constantius will have known that victories in civil war were not to be celebrated with a triumph so this should perhaps be seen as just the latest step in the besmirching of Magnentius' reputation. And given the prevalence of the fallen usurper's non-Roman parentage in the sources, Constantius' propaganda worked wonders in portraying Magnentius as a non-Roman barbarian invader rather than a Roman emperor, even in the face of Ammianus' vitriol.

While this celebratory triumph was marred in controversy, the visit to Rome was a triumph all on its own. Arriving on 28 April 357 and staying just over a month, Constantius ingratiated himself to the Senate and People of

Rome, unlike Diocletian and his younger brother Constans. He addressed the Senate, attended the races at the Circus Maximus and took in the sites with his respect for the history and traditions of the great city earning him respect in return. Constantius' visit also had important religious results for the city as his even handed approach to paganism, appointing numerous priests and not challenging the still predominantly pagan senators gave Rome something of a special status to continue some of its pagan sacrifices. So enamoured with Rome was Constantius that he looked for a suitable gift to mark his visit and found it in an obelisk from the Egyptian city of Heliopolis, which was transported to Rome and placed in the Circus Maximus, a task conceived by his father but had been slow to progress due to the sheer size of the obelisk: a boat of 300 oarsmen was needed to transport it across the Mediterranean.[40]

The holiday could not last though, and Constantius soon received reports of numerous barbarian raids along the Danube: the Suebi in Raetia, the Quadi in Pannonia Valeria and the Sarmatians in Upper Moesia and Lower Pannonia. He therefore left Rome on 29 May 357 and made for Illyricum through Tridentum, modern Trento in northern Italy, sending word for Ursicinus to join him. It is uncertain if Constantius meant for the experienced general to take command of an army against one of the invading barbarian tribes but Ursicinus had been restored to imperial favour, for when word arrived at Sirmium of the efforts of Musonianus and Cassianus to achieve a more lasting peace with the Persians, Constantius dispatched Ursicinus, together with Ammianus, to the east with his old command of *magister*.

It should be noted that in his attempts to paint a poor picture of the emperor and his court, Ammianus overlooks that Constantius had been active along the upper reaches of the Rhine and Danube prior to his great hero Julian squaring up to Chnodomarius. In what might be an intentional attempt to disparage the emperor in the face of the young, energetic Julian, "tucked away in Ammianus' account of the battle of Strasbourg in 357 is the information that during the previous year Constantius had invaded Alamannic territory by way of Raetia".[41] This 356 campaign was the third time that Constantius had advanced against members of the Alamanni confederation in three years, having advanced against Gundomadus and Vadomarius in 354 and the Lentienses in 355.

As with the 354 campaign, there appears to have been little fighting in 356, although whether this was the Alamanni again refusing battle out of fear and deference or a more strategic withdrawal is not clear. Despite Ammianus' suggestion that this lack of Alamanni resistance was due to the arrival of winter, perhaps in an attempt to play down Constantius' success or the awe in which he was held by many barbarians: "nature defeated the Alamanni, not the emperor",[42] it is more widely considered that the campaign took place in the autumn for Constantius to be back in Milan for 10 November, having extracted another treaty from Gundomadus and Vadomarius.[43] But even this might be doing Constantius a disservice. Attempts have been made to examine what the emperor might have been doing in Raetia in 356, with it being suggested that "Constantius' principal objective was to ensure that Julian ran into no difficulties."[44] By using his contacts and then marching through Bregenz, Windisch and Zurzach, he ensured that Julian's first campaign in 356 was uneventful, with the only troubles coming from miscreants, rebels or other non-Alamanni. This march will also have helped reinforce Roman control of much of the Neckar valley and secure the approaches into southern Gaul, Raetia and even Italy.[45]

Even Barbatio, target of much Ammian vitriol, was not idle during this period, tasked by Constantius with the removal of Juthungi raiders from Raetia. Originally an independent tribe capable of invading Italy in the 260s, by the 350s these Juthungi had become part of the Alamannic confederation.[46] They had taken it upon themselves to ignore the peace treaty they had with Rome, possibly the same treaty that Constantius had forced upon Gundomadus and Vadomarius. They began raiding Raetia and seeing the lack of immediate Roman response moved on to besieging several settlements. This saw Barbatio lead a substantial force against them, likely the same force that had been chased back to Augst by the Alamanni in the prelude to Strasbourg. Perhaps catching the Juthungi committed to these sieges, Barbatio "utterly defeated a large number of the foe, so that only a small remnant, who for fear of danger had taken to flight, barely escaped and returned to their homes, not without tears and lamentations".[47] Despite the extent of his victory, Ammianus cannot help but describe Barbatio as a coward who relied on his oratory rather than leadership to spur on his men. The historian also diverts some *kudos* from the *magister peditum* by playing up the presence and valiant actions of a cavalry commander and future consul, Nevitta.[48]

Any rehabilitation of Barbatio's reputation was short-lived as he too fell foul of the same kind of plotting that he had used against others and much like with Rufinus it was a woman who brought about his downfall. In the climate of backstabbing and opportunism, the *magister*'s wife, Assyria, sent Barbatio a letter pleading with him not to discard her for the empress when he became emperor on Constantius' death. If this was not foolish enough, she dictated the letter to a maid, who took a copy to Arbitio, who in turn reported it to Constantius. Rather than just the sheer stupidity of his wife, the numerous enemies he had made through his previous actions may have caught up with Barbatio and perhaps Constantius had realised that Barbatio was only out for himself even at the expense of the empire, such as his manoeuvres in

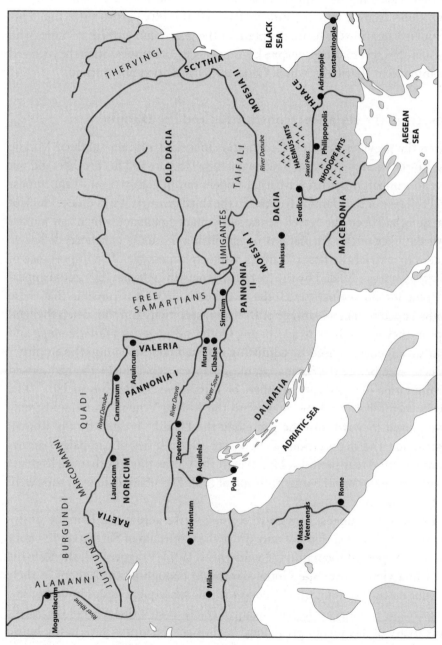

Map 7: The Danube, Italy and the Balkans

the prelude to Strasbourg. Under investigation, Barbatio admitted receiving the letter and both he and his indiscreet wife were beheaded. So followed another wide-ranging inquisition as Barbatio could not have planned such a coup alone, leading to many innocent as well as guilty parties suffering. This included Valentinus, a former captain of the guard and current tribune, who was tortured several times despite his innocence. As compensation, he received a command in Illyricum, where Constantius' attention now turned.

Upsetting the Balance: Constantius and the Danube

Given the previous century, Constantius inherited a rather subdued Middle and Lower Danube frontier. That is not to say that he and his brothers did not have to campaign against barbarian raiders but in comparison to the almost total collapse of the Danube frontier in the third century, it was quiet. Much of that quiet had been due to well-rehearsed Roman diplomacy, which had worked with the likes of the Sarmatians to establish a mutually beneficial defensive system to restrict the flow of raiders as much as possible. The importance of this system was revealed by the fact the Sarmatians felt that they could appeal to Rome for aid against the Goths in the early 330s. It is possible that these Goths hoped to take advantage of Roman distractions and that when they did appear, they would have to accept any Gothic advances as a *fait acccompli* and clear up any mess caused by admitting defeated tribesmen into the empire.[49] Indeed, even before the Sarmatian plea, it appears that the Goths had caused the migration of significant numbers of Taifali into the Balkans in 330.[50] The Goths themselves, perhaps along with the Asding Vandals and Gepids, may have moved forward into the gap along the Danube created by the Roman destruction and deportation of the Carpi after a series of campaigns across an almost fifty-year period.[51] However, if the Goths thought that the Romans were going to ignore the undermining of their Danubian defences, they were sorely mistaken.

The sources suggest a massive Roman strike across the Danube under Constantine II in 332 that not only drove the Goths out of Sarmatian territory but then dispersed them into the wilderness. While exaggerated, the Romans did win a victory over the Goths significant enough to enrol them in their Danube defence system, which, along with his subsequent bridge building, saw Constantine I claim that he had regained Dacia, even if this was not the case.[52] This treaty of 332 was to prove long-lasting as "the Goths gave to the house of Constantine a loyalty that outlasted the dynasty itself,"[53] allowing peace to prevail along the lower reaches of the Danube virtually unbroken between the 330s and the 360s.

However, what Constantine II did after his defeat of the Goths in 332 was to have consequences for the reign of Constantius. Despite coming to their aid, the Romans turned on some of the Sarmatians who had failed in their obligations to the empire. Surrounded by potential enemies – Roman, Gothic and other barbarians – the Sarmatians looked to their own subject peoples for military aid. In arming the superior numbers of this Limigantes coalition, the ruling Sarmatians, recorded as the Agaramantes, assured their own defeat by 334. Constantine largely contained the immediate fall out of this tribal civil war by settling large numbers of the fleeing Sarmatians in Roman territory.[54]

By 357, perhaps through the continued belligerence of the Limigantes and maybe the Goths, Constantius was faced with more barbarian raids as the Sarmatians and Quadi joined together to attack Pannonia and Moesia. Gathering together a large force and having wintered at Sirmium, Constantius crossed the flooded Danube on a bridge of boats early in 358 catching the Sarmatians by surprise and laying waste to their lands. Rather than fight this large imperial army, many Sarmatians fled and despite a well-pressed pursuit, they were able to regroup in their mountain hideaways. It is possible that the Sarmatian retreat was somewhat planned, not wasting their strength in an initial struggle before they could gather together their full strength and allow time for the Quadi to send aid, although it might be somewhat surprising for Ammianus not to record such an action, in an attempt to again downplay what seems to have been a well-planned and coordinated strike by Constantius.

Even if the Sarmatians retreated in the first instance, they still underestimated the strength and resolve of Constantius and his column. The joint Sarmatian-Quadi force was driven out of Sarmatian territory and into that of the Quadi. Not wanting to face similar destruction of their lands, the Quadi petitioned the approaching emperor for peace terms. Despite the inevitable negative slant from Ammianus, who claimed Constantius was too lenient,[55] the emperor's imposition of tolerable terms on the Quadi not only led to their acceptance but soon various other transdanubian tribes were flocking to take advantage of Constantius' clemency, enabling a potential re-establishing of the cooperative defence system. This was not the end to Constantius' dealings with these tribes though as the emperor was soon drawn into conflict with the Limigantes. Uncowed since achieving their independence from the Sarmatians, the Limigantes continued to attack neighbouring tribes and even began raiding Roman territory. Needless to say, Constantius was none too pleased with the flaunting of his settlement along the Danube and was soon marching his army back to the river. Thinking they were protected by the Danube, the Limigantes followed Constantius' summons but had no intention of surrendering to imperial arbitration.

Showing his skills, Constantius predicted such a lack of intent and planned accordingly, dividing his force into several groups and secreting them around the proposed meeting point. The overconfident Limigantes marched straight into the trap and refused to accept the admonishments of the emperor, which perhaps involved a plan to remove them from the immediate vicinity of the Roman frontier due to some fear of overcrowding.[56] When it was clear that the talks were going nowhere, the barbarians had the audacity to form up for battle. However, it was then that the disadvantage of their position was revealed, with the hidden Roman brigades cutting off their line of retreat and then surrounding them. A tense standoff then prevailed before fading light and lack of supplies forced the Limigantes into a massed charge at the emperor's position.

Constantius was ready for them once more; while his bodyguard kept him safe, the main body of the Roman force had been deployed in a large wedge to blunt the Limigantes centre. The Roman right, comprised of infantry, drove back the barbarian left and when the Roman cavalry defeated the Limigantes horse, the outcome was inevitable. The barbarians fought bravely but crumbled under attack from all sides, turning the battle into a major rout that had lasted no more than half an hour.[57] Determined not to give the Danubian barbarians another chance to take advantage of his mercy, Constantius now launched a punitive strike across the river. The territory of the Limigantes was ravaged whilst other Sarmatian tribes who had refused to respect the emperor's peace were also taught a lesson, with the Amicenses and Picenses, constituents of the Limigantes coalition, defeated by a Roman force supported by allied Taifali and Sarmatians.[58]

Happy that he had gotten his message across, Constantius retired to winter quarters at Sirmium, although this proved to be a little premature. Despite being dealt a bloody nose, the Limigantes renewed their raids. That these barbarians would choose to risk the wrath of Constantius again during the winter months demonstrates either supreme confidence, ultimate stupidity or something more primal. Perhaps the Roman invasion of 358 and their removal from the frontier together with all its trading resources had destroyed the ability of the Limigantes coalition to sustain itself. The way they acted in the face of the Roman army suggests the desperation that comes with the threat of starvation.

Worried that they would grow bolder with time, Constantius again called his forces together and through the efficiency of the prefect of Illyricum, Anatolicus, the emperor took the field again before the end of winter. Marching to the Danube through Pannonia Valeria, Constantius confronted a group of Limigantes who were proposing peace talks but were in reality planning to cross the frozen Danube to raid Pannonia. The emperor sent two ambassadors to the barbarian camp to discover why they had disavowed the treaty. Rather than explain themselves, the Limigantes asked permission to cross the river and meet face to face with Constantius to discuss a permanent settlement within the empire. Encouraged by the idea that these tribesmen would be useful in repopulating certain areas and providing military recruits, Constantius agreed to the meeting but wary of their untrustworthiness, he again took precautions. Legionaries were deployed in strategic positions along the river and even in boats to block the barbarians' line of retreat should they again prove troublesome and a large earthwork was built near Acimincum as the meeting place. Despite the clear evidence of mistrust, the Limigantes still marched to Acimincum. That they did so must have encouraged the Romans that these barbarians had learned their lesson and intended to accept a position of subservience within the empire. Either that or they had a death wish. Unfortunately for all involved, it was the latter.

While the Limigantes may have decided to go out in a blaze of glory against the Roman emperor in battle, it is also possible that they acted in good faith and intended to take up a position as subjects of the Roman Empire. Instead, the spark of what was to happen at Aciminicum might have been the anger of Constantius and the traditional Roman response to tribes who asked to enter the empire: to make their integration as straightforward as possible, the tribal structures of the Limigantes had to be destroyed through a crushing military defeat. But even this most Roman of responses might not have been the cause of the incident at Aciminicum. The human tragedy that was to unfold may have just been result of the mistrust and misunderstanding that can occur between two peoples from different cultures and separated by language.[59]

As Constantius prepared to address the Limigantes in mild terms, "intending to speak to them as future obedient subjects",[60] from atop his earthwork tribunal, one of the barbarians threw his shoe at the emperor and issued forth a savage war cry. At this, the Limigantes surged forward in an attempt to get to Constantius but through a combination of the earthwork and the bravery of his attendants, he escaped unharmed. Washing his hands of the Limigantes, the emperor then put his contingency plan into action and the rampaging barbarians were soon surrounded once more. The Romans smashed into the barbarian column with such fury that they "butchered everything in their way, trampling under foot without mercy the living, as well as those dying or dead; and before their hands were sated with slaughter of the savages, the dead lay piled in heaps".[61] Even those who managed to survive the initial onslaught were hunted down in droves. These two successive massacres made sure that the Limigantes would not cause any more trouble.

From a prevalent position along the Danube bend in partnership with the Romans, the Sarmatian tribes had been eliminated from any kind of real power through the actions of Constantine II and now Constantius. While they may have asked for it, their removal as a lynchpin of the Danube frontier set in motion a series of events that was to lead to the collapse of much of the Roman northern frontier. While this seems like a big mistake by Constantius, it needs to be remembered that this kind of tribal elimination was not an uncommon event. The Romans had long crossed into *barbaricum* to provide subject lessons to those tribes who overstepped their mark. The result would normally be another tribe moving forward to the Rhine or Danube from central or eastern Europe to take the place of the dispatched, absorbing the remnants of their predecessor or allowing them to seek haven within the empire itself.[62]

However, 358/359 witnessed a different outcome than the norm. With the power of the Sarmatians shattered, it might have been expected that the Limigantes would be promoted as the new partners in defence along the Danube bend. Instead, their intransigence, bred of newly won independence, in the face of an emperor who was willing to negotiate led to a punitive strike of such brutality that it removed them as a candidate. With no tribe ready to move forward and take their place, the balance was upset as the Quadi and the Goths took advantage of this power vacuum to extend their influence along the river. Initially, the Romans had little problem with this and neither Constantius nor Julian campaigned along what was becoming known as the *ripa Gothica*.[63] Indeed, Julian ignored the Goths because he was "looking for a better enemy",[64] while the rapid expansion of market forts like Commercium as a place of Romano-Gothic trade and the service of many Goths in garrisons on the Roman side of the river suggests that rather than ignoring it, the Romans were fostering the growth of the Gothic state.[65] That the Romans were creating a problem for themselves would be revealed throughout the late 360s and 370s,[66] but in 359, Constantius was happy with the imposition of his settlement on the Quadi and the elimination of the Sarmatian coalition. The army declared their emperor *Sarmaticus* for the second time in his career and Constantius repaid them with an address that praised the successes that they had achieved against various enemies.[67] Constantius then returned to Sirmium before setting out for Constantinople. There was troubling news from Mesopotamia. The Persian army was on the move.

Chapter IX

The Return of the King of Kings

It is folly to suppose that the war can be brought to a conclusion by sitting still, or by prayers, the troops must be armed and led down into the plain, that you may engage man to man. The Roman power has grown to its present height by courage and activity, and not by such dilatory measures as these, which the cowardly only designate as cautious.

– Marcus Minucius Rufus on the Fabian Strategy
(Livy, *Ab Urbe Condita* XXII.14)

Paul the Chain and the Harrying of the East

After focusing on his European domains for the best part of a decade, Constantius' eye was now drawn back to the eastern frontier, even if he himself did not yet move back east, given the continued problems along the Danube. But as with how the focus fell on Gaul in 355, this redirecting of attention to the eastern provinces also incorporates the arrival of the unsavoury individual who did much to ensure that Constantius retained a poor reputation in large parts of the empire: Paul the Chain. Constantius had already used this notorious *notarius* and his particular set of skills in torture, false charges and kangaroo courts in order to root out opposition in the aftermath of the deaths of Magnentius and Silvanus. Since those initial employments by the emperor, Paul had obtained another nickname, Paulus 'Tartareus' – Paul the Diabolical – again hinting at his true nature.

Now in 359, whether for military, socio-political or religious reasons, the emperor found the need to unleash the Diabolical Chain's justice on the east. The catalyst was the nature of several petitions to an oracle to the god Besa at Abydum in Egypt and how they pertained to Constantius. These somehow made their way to the imperial court and, convinced of their malicious intent, the emperor dispatched Paul with the power to conduct investigations and court cases as he saw fit. Paul found a willing partner in Modestus, *comes Orientis*, after the praetorian prefect in the east, Hermogenes of Pontus, was declared too mild-tempered for the type of work this commission would involve. That alone would suggest that this was going to be an ugly business.

Paul and Modestus established their tribunal at Scythopolis, modern Beit She'an in Israel, a place that was chosen due to its relative obscurity but also because it lay midway between Alexandria and Antioch, suggesting that despite the original spark coming from Abydum large sections of the Middle East and Egypt were to be targeted by this judiciary. Men were summoned from all across the east to Scythopolis to answer charges, many of them spurious, and to serve whatever punishment was deemed necessary whether it be imprisonment, confiscation of property, exile or death. A certain Simplicius was accused of asking about gaining imperial power and was faced with torture and then banished.[1] That Simplicius was the son of Flavius Philippus, praetorian prefect in the east in 346, consul in 348 and the same man that Constantius had entrusted with gathering information from the camp of Magnentius in 351 might be the reason why Simplicius was not executed for his 'crimes'. However, it also demonstrates that even the family of someone held in high imperial esteem was not safe from the machinations of the Chain.[2] Parnasius, an ex-prefect of Egypt, was sent into exile for talking about a dream he had; Andronicus, a celebrated poet and scholar, was hauled before the tribunal despite being "under no suspicion"[3] other than he was an intellectual, while an old philosopher called Demetrius Cythras was tried for having offered pagan sacrifice. Demetrius' defence was that he had not done so in an attempt to gain higher office, a defence that he maintained even under torture on the rack so he has allowed to return home to Alexandria.

While such men managed to escape the ultimate punishment, the longer Paul and Modestus continued their rooting out of opposition, real or invented, the more the charges became convoluted and difficult to disprove. It got so bad that "one might almost say that the lives of all involved depended on his nod."[4] As time went on, the Chain proved arbitrary in his treatment of any link to black arts, handing out capital punishments to those found wearing an amulet or walking through a graveyard at night as participants in sorcery or even necromancy. This may hint at the influence of Constantius' policy of imposing religious unity through his Homoean Creed.

That such 'sorcery' and 'plots' against the emperor were uncovered by his agents saw Constantian supporters claim "that he would be immune to ordinary ills, loudly exclaiming that his destiny had appeared at all times powerful and effective in destroying those who made attempts against him".[5] However, Ammianus demonstrates that not all portents were favourable to the emperor, recording the birth of a child near Antioch that had two heads and a beard. This was taken to mean that the Roman state was becoming twisted and deformed.[6] That Constantius employed individuals such as Paul the Chain on more than one occasion suggests that he was either oblivious to the extent of their actions or on some level tolerated, even encouraged, such brutal justice. Neither scenario reflects well on Constantius as he seemed to rejoice in the success of these extreme measures rather looking for opportunity to act leniently towards his subjects.[7]

The Drift Back to War: To Prepare or Not to Prepare?

The ability for Paul to be so heavy handed in the east was due to the quiet that had prevailed on the eastern frontier during the 350s. Against expectations and Shapur's orders to Nohodares "to invade Mesopotamia whenever occasion offered",[8] the tentative ceasefire between Constantius and Shapur from late 350 held rather well. That is not to say that the Mesopotamian front had been shutdown. Roman preoccupation with the mess left behind by Gallus likely saw Persian forces raid Roman and Armenian territory largely unopposed.[9] Because of this impotence in securing the frontier, Domitianus' successor as praetorian prefect, Strategius Musonianus, and Cassianus, *dux Mesopotamiae*, attempted to negotiate a more official truce through another Persian commander in Mesopotamia, Tamsapor, based on the same idea as the original breaking off of fighting in 350; both Constantius and Shapur were occupied with wars on other frontiers so peace would be mutually beneficial. Tamsapor agreed to send the proposal on to his king but the distance to the north-eastern frontier of the Persian kingdom meant that nothing was going to change any time soon.[10]

When the letter did reach Shapur, it was too late as the Persian king had come to an arrangement with the steppe tribes. The exact nature of this arrangement is unknown; Shapur may have inflicted a serious enough defeat on these Chionitae to forcibly enrol significant numbers into his army – he had wintered in the lands of the Chionitae and Kushans[11] – or he himself had been forced to allow large numbers of the tribesmen to settle within his kingdom. Regardless of how it happened, the outcome was clear and it was bad news for the Romans: buoyed by victory or looking to direct the acquisitive ferocity of his new 'allies' away from a widespread plundering of Persian territory, Shapur turned his attention back to the Mesopotamian front. Set on offensive action, Shapur responded to the peace offer from Musonianus with the traditional warning of a Persian king about to go to war with Rome. He reminded Constantius that the Persian Empire had once stretched into Macedonia, before demanding the 'return' of all of Armenia and Mesopotamia. What Shapur was asking for was a rescinding of the Peace of Nisibis, going as far to say that returning these lands, long the source of bloodshed between the neighbours, would aid the Roman Empire.[12]

Constantius sent back to Shapur with a reply that whilst somewhat admitting that his empire had been through some tough times, Rome remained a sound, strong and undefeated nation with no reason to capitulate to demands for several of its eastern provinces that had been won in battle. However, wary of Shapur's warpath, Constantius dispatched an extensive Roman embassy consisting of the *comes* Prosper, the *tribune et notarius*, Spectatus and the philosopher, Eustathius, who were to not only present the emperor's reply and gifts but to also undermine arrangements Shapur had made with the steppe tribes and whatever preparations had been made for an attack on the Roman eastern provinces.[13]

When this embassy reached Ctesiphon to present Constantius' proposal based on the *status quo*, they learned that Shapur was determined to see large parts of Armenia and Mesopotamia ceded to him either at the negotiating table or through force. This should have been a definitive answer for the Romans that war was coming, but in 358, Constantius sent another embassy under the *comes* Lucillianus and the *tribunus et notarius*, Procopius, a maternal cousin of Julian and later imperial usurper in 365/366, perhaps less hopeful of dissuading Shapur and looking more to discover his specific plans.[14] However, while Shapur, "armed with the help of the savage tribes which he had subdued, and burning with superhuman desire of extending his domain, was preparing arms, forces, and supplies, embroiling his plans with infernal powers and consulting all superstitions about the future",[15] the Roman hierarchy did nothing. In fact, they did worse than nothing. Instead of preparing the eastern provinces, it allowed itself to descend into another round of intrigue and backstabbing, with the target this time being the reinstated *magister*, Ursicinus.

Newly arrived in the east with Ammianus in tow, Ursicinus recognised the poor state that the eastern provinces were in to defend against Shapur but rather than listen to his warnings, Ammianus portrays the eunuchs of Constantius' court as being far more interested in undermining Ursicinus. They preyed on Constantius' suspicion of men in powerful positions, suggesting that the *magister* sought promotion and was only in his current position due to the revolt and death of Silvanus rather than through his actual skills. The enmity of the head chamberlain, Eusebius, was particularly damaging to Ursicinus' case for war preparations. Seemingly the eunuch chamberlain took up against him because the *magister* had turned down help from Eusebius and refused to give him a house in Antioch that he desired. He sent several of his fellow eunuchs east to undermine Ursicinus and maintained that the *magister* was on the point of rebelling.

Therefore, at a time when Ursicinus should have been given free rein to prepare the eastern frontier for Shapur's attack, he spent much of 359 having to look over his shoulder for the inevitable eunuch-influenced dagger. When this dagger came, it took a peculiar form – a promotion to the position of *magister peditum in praesentalis* (the master of infantry of Constantius' personal field army) that had just been vacated through the execution of Barbatio. Ammianus suggests that Eusebius manufactured this transfer to take Ursicinus away from the eastern field army and place him at the imperial court where they could contain him. Moving west from his base at Samosata, Ursicinus met his replacement as *magister equitum per Orientem*, a well-read, wealthy man of little or no military ability called Sabinianus, who presented the general with his letter of recall.[16]

The ill-timing of Ursicinus' removal was compounded by news that reached the *magister* before he left Samosata: the defection of Antoninus. A former merchant, accountant and then bodyguard of the *dux Mesopotamiae*, the lack of Roman preparation for the coming war encouraged Antoninus to flee to Persian territory and sell whatever information he had to Shapur, although he was also indebted to several powerful men and the imperial treasury. To facilitate his escape, Antoninus purchased property in the town of Hiaspis near the Tigris so that his presence near the frontier would not raise suspicion. He then employed swimmers to cross the river and deliver secret communications to Tamsapor, who jumped at the chance to gain such a valuable source of information and sent aid in ferrying Antoninus and his household across the Tigris.

Given his knowledge of the Roman dispositions in Mesopotamia and their lack of preparation, Antoninus was taken to Shapur's winter quarters, where he could best advise the Persian king. The defector is said to have spoken in depth about how Shapur needed to use any battle he might win to its fullest as it is suggested that the Persian king had failed in building upon his previous successes at Hileia and Singara. Ammianus goes as far as to equate Antoninus' working upon the king as being like the famous story of Maharbal telling the great Carthaginian general Hannibal that he did not know how to use the victories he had won.[17] In less hyperbolic terms, armed with his information about Roman military lethargy and the preoccupation of Constantius along the Danube, Antoninus persuaded Shapur that he should "take the field as soon as the winter was over".[18]

The news that Ursicinus had been removed from his eastern command will have only bolstered the defector's arguments and after a long debate, Shapur and his council decided to act at the first sign of spring. What Shapur's exact plan was is not quite clear. From Ammianus, it would appear that on the advice of Antoninus, the Persian king aimed to cross the Tigris north of Singara, bypass the major Mesopotamian cities and drive west across the Euphrates to attack Syria, only to be diverted further north by the discovery of the Euphrates being in flood. However, this would suggest that the Persians could not predict a flood of the Euphrates at the end of winter or that they did not have the technological skills to bridge a flooded river, which they did. Instead, Shapur likely planned to head northwest to draw the Roman field army into a decisive battle with his vast host from the start.[19]

Convinced of the inevitability of a Persian invasion, Ursicinus lingered in the Taurus Mountains but eventually had to begin his trip to court. However, when he had reached Thrace, he received a second imperial missive ordering him to return to the eastern frontier but not to resume the position of *magister equitum per Orientem*. Of course, Ammianus viewed this as another eunuch ploy to place Ursicinus in a no win situation for any victory he would achieve would be attributed to Sabinianus, whilst he would be the scapegoat for any defeat. The timing of this letter was more to do with the slowness of communication between Antioch and Sirmium than any real plot to destroy Ammianus' patron. As a loyal servant of the empire, Ursicinus followed the orders of his emperor and returned to Mesopotamia to offer aid to his successor. What he found was Sabinianus in a state of inaction even in the face of the initial stages of a Persian invasion. Ammianus could not withhold his disgust: "we returned, to find Sabinianus a man full of haughtiness, but of insignificant stature and small and narrow mind, barely able to endure the slight noise of a banquet without shameful apprehension, to say nothing of din of battle"[20] and would later accuse the *magister* of resorting to luxury and entertainment in Edessa rather than defending Roman territory.[21]

With this vicious testimony from Ammianus it is easy to judge Sabinianus. However, the new *magister*'s decision to remain at Edessa with the eastern field army was sound even though it appeared to be born of inaction. It put the largest Roman force in the region in a position to react to whatever move Shapur made, while at the same time prevented it from being dragged too far into Mesopotamia where it could have been trapped between the hills and rivers. As things played out, this caution was proven somewhat correct for had Sabinianus followed Ursicinus' race to Nisibis, the Roman force would be caught up in defending that city from Persian raiders and then found itself outflanked when Shapur bypassed Nisibis and continued further north. It was also in keeping with the burgeoning Roman eastern strategy of reliance on the strong defences of the cities in Mesopotamia and not risking the large casualties of battle.[22]

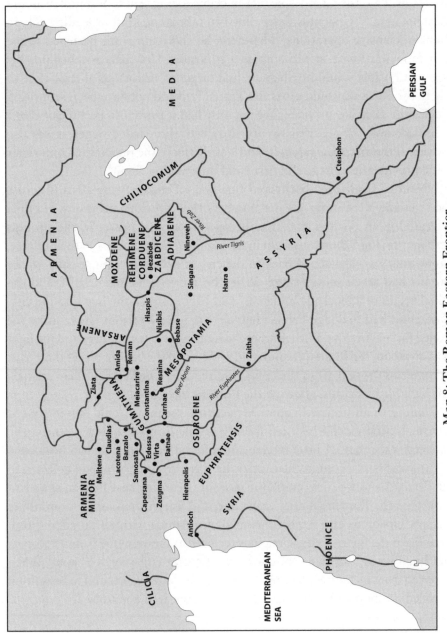

Map 8: The Roman Eastern Frontier

The Road to Amida

With Sabinianus and the eastern field army remaining at Edessa and despite Modestus, Paul the Chain's partner in crime, being sent to Euphratensis and Mesopotamia,[23] Ursicinus determined to take some kind of leading role in Roman defensive operations. Therefore, he and Ammianus hastened to the Roman forward base in Mesopotamia at Nisibis. Ursicinus was hedging his bets that Nisibis would be Shapur's first target or that it was at least close to where the Persians would cross the Tigris. It would not have been surprising for Shapur to strike at Nisibis for not only had it proven to be a major thorn in his side over the previous twenty years with three failed sieges, it was also the seat of the *dux Mesopotamiae* and was therefore the region that Antoninus could provide the most useful first hand information about.

However, Ursicinus discovered that some Persians were already across the river and were in far greater numbers than previous invasions. He then retreated from Nisibis in fear of being surrounded there, in the process perhaps proving Sabinianus right in having not followed him. On their retreat, Ammianus was dispatched back to the city to deliver a missing child whose parents had taken refuge there. When he arrived, the historian found the initial stages of a blockade underway and having snuck the boy into the city, Ammianus had to dodge Persian outriders in order to rejoin Ursicinus at the ruined fort of Amudis. With nowhere to hide in the open country and the light of a full moon, the Roman column tied a lantern to the back of one of their pack animals and drove it off in the opposite direction. The Persian riders mistook this light for Ursicinus, allowing the Romans to escape.

Coming to an orchard called Meiacarire, meaning "cold water" in old Syrian, Ursicinus and his men found a single Roman soldier amongst the deserted settlement. A brief interrogation found that while he had been born in Paris and had served in the cavalry, he was a deserter, who had defected to the Persians and was now employed as a spy. Learning that Persian spies had infiltrated the Roman frontier zones and still wary of pursuers, after killing the spy, Ursicinus and Ammianus made for Amida with all possible speed. Arriving at the fortress city, Ursicinus received a communiqué from Procopius and Lucillianus, the men sent on the most recent embassy to Shapur. When removed from its hiding place in a scabbard, the letter was found to be written in coded symbols and even when decoded it appeared nonsensical.

> Now that the envoys of the Greeks have been sent far away and perhaps are to be killed, that aged king, not content with Hellespontus, will bridge the Granicus and the Rhyndacus and come to invade Asia with many nations.

He is naturally passionate and very cruel, and he has as an instigator and abetter the successor of the former Roman emperor Hadrian; unless Greece takes heed, it is all over with her and her dirge chanted.[24]

The coded nature of the letter, both in terms of symbols and allusion, and the inference of the first line suggest that the envoys had been imprisoned by Shapur or were at least under surveillance. The mention of an "aged king" bridging the Granicus and Rhyndacus rivers, both in Asia Minor, was considered an inference to the outbreak of the Third Mithridatic War in 74/73BCE, with the "aged king" being Mithridates VI. This was deciphered as a reference to Shapur's planned crossing of the Greater Zab and the Tigris for an invasion of Roman territory whilst the naming of Hadrian's successor, the emperor Antoninus Pius, as an "instigator and abetter" was an allusion to the defector, Antoninus, and his role as an adviser to the Persian king.[25]

It might seem that this letter gave Ursicinus valuable insight into the planned movements of Shapur but it still left him with very little idea of where the Persian king intended to attack. Was he going to cross the Zab and the Tigris close together, perhaps at their confluence and then drive at Singara? Or was he going to cross the Zab and then follow the Tigris upriver to the northwest before crossing? And even then where would he cross? Near Nineveh? Bezabde? Amida? Or somewhere in between or beyond? Ammianus had confirmed that raiding parties had reached Nisibis but that also revealed little about Shapur's main thrust.

Desperate to get more firsthand knowledge, Ursicinus sent Ammianus to contact Jovinianus, the Persian satrap of Corduene, a man known to the Romans and perhaps to Ammianus through time spent as a hostage in Syria.[26] The satrap sent Ammianus off with a guide to a cliff that overlooked the area into which Shapur was thought to be marching and after two days of waiting, the historian was confronted by a host that covered the horizon. Shapur led the way with his Persians in the centre, while Grumbates, leader of the Chionitae, and his men held the left flank and the king of the Albani and his contingent the right. While Ammianus did not attempt to give a number to the size of this approaching army, with dramatic flair, he recalls the counting of the great invasion force of the Achaemenid Persian king Xerxes at Doriscus in Thrace, which found the Persian army in 480BCE to be 1,700,000 strong.[27] While Shapur's force was nothing like such an astronomical figure, the presence of the Chionitae, Albani and other tribes alongside the royal army made sure that it was of significant size. And its presence close to Nineveh will have caused significant alarm, although this did not prevent Ammianus enjoying the hospitality of Jovinianus before reporting back to Ursicinus. Ammianus' excuse will have been that he thought it would take at least three days for the entire Persian army to make it across the Tigris.[28]

After hearing of Shapur's crossing, Ursicinus sent out riders to the *dux Mesopotamiae*, Cassanius, and the provincial governor, Euphronius, encouraging them to evacuate the surrounding countryside to the major cities. It was even suggested to evacuate the city of Carrhae itself as it was too weakly defended to resist any attack. Ursicinus also suggested that the grasslands of Mesopotamia be set ablaze to deprive the Persians of fodder. Unlike at court, the *magister*'s suggestions were acted upon so that "from the very banks of the Tigris all the way to the Euphrates not a green thing was to be seen".[29] Several tribunes and *protectores* then set about fortifying the west bank of the Euphrates, placing forts, stakes and catapults at the narrow, shallow sections of the river to slow or contest any attempted Persian crossing into Syria.

Safely across the Tigris, Shapur marched past the Roman garrison at Nisibis and kept close to the foothills of the Tur Abdin in order to avoid the worst of the scorched earth. Arriving at the town of Bebase, Ammianus suggests that word of the swollen waters of the Euphrates left Shapur in a quandary as it had been his intention to drive straight for the river. At least that is what the Romans had planned for as they had only extended their scorched earth policy to the expected Persian line of advance to the Euphrates.[30] The Persian army then turned northwest and headed through territory untouched by the Romans. The seeming intention was a considerable detour past Edessa, heading for the stretch of the Euphrates between Barzalo and Claudias, where it was still shallow and narrow. This was not just a long detour but also a great risk considering the position of the Roman field army at Edessa.

In response, Ursicinus planned to return to Samosata to see the bridges at Zeugma and Capersena pulled down before Shapur could make use of them. It is clear from Ursicinus' focus on delaying tactics that he was suffering not just the lack of real authority but also the lack of preparation and even confidence in the Roman forces of the east. There was no real suggestion of intercepting the Persian force on beneficial ground or challenging his proposed river crossings. If the Persians now planned a long march to the upper reaches of the Euphrates, this provided a good opportunity for Roman raiders to harass the enemy, reducing their numbers and morale. Had the Roman hierarchy been on the same page, Ursicinus and Sabinianus could have trapped Shapur against the Euphrates with the combined forces of the eastern field and garrison forces.

However, setting out from Amida for Samosata, Ursicinus and Ammianus were caught in an ambush. The blame for this was placed on 700 "spiritless and cowardly"[31] Illyrian horsemen who failed to guard a road, allowing Tamsapor and Nohodares to slip past and take up a position within the hills around Amida. This attaching of blame to the Illyrians and the very idea of an ambush might mask a substantial risk by Ursicinus. The Persian commanders supposedly had 20,000 men between them so it must be asked what Ammianus expected 700 horsemen do against such a force aside from raise the alarm. Such an alarm may have prevented Ursicinus from leaving Amida but given the size of the Persian force, Ursicinus would have seen some evidence of its approach from the city itself. The peculiar meeting between the *magister* and Antoninus in the midst of the resulting melee further suggests at least part of this scenario has been embellished, but it appears that in an attempt to repeat their flight from Nisibis, Ursicinus and Ammianus had blundered into the path of the main Persian army.

Caught out in the open by superior forces, Ursicinus' column established enough of a defensive position to hold off the initial attack. In the midst of what would have been a frantic fight for survival, the meeting between Ursicinus and Antoninus seems out of place. The defector treated the general with great respect, telling him that he fled Roman territory not through choice but because of the "exactions of wicked men, as you know, which have ruined me".[32] Even if he did not agree, Ursicinus will have understood given his own personal experiences with the imperial court undermining him at every turn. Perhaps Antoninus was playing for time to enable Persian reinforcements to reach their position as news soon came of another Persian cavalry force approaching. Whether the order was given or the weight of numbers and fear told, the Roman column broke up and scattered in all directions. Some were driven to the waters of the Tigris where they drowned, some stood and fought and others attempted to flee up the slopes of the mountains. Ursicinus was amongst the latter and was saved by the speed of his horse in the company of only a tribune, Aiadalthes, and a groom.

Ammianus fled in the direction of Amida accompanied by Verinianus, an old comrade who had also been part of Ursicinus' entourage when he had been sent against Silvanus. Verinianus had received an arrow in the leg and Ammianus was forced to leave his friend as Persian riders were soon on their tail. Outside Amida, Ammianus joined the crush of people attempting to enter the city through its single approach, an uphill slope covered with defensive obstructions and the bodies of the dead and the living.[33] Such was the crush that Ammianus reports that he was stuck behind the gruesome sight of the body of a soldier who had had his head split from top to bottom but could not fall to the ground. These refugees also had to deal with the constant fire from the city's defences and the approaching Persians. It must have been a horrifying sight, although what awaited Ammianus inside Amida when he finally managed to squeeze through a postern gate cannot have been much better; the city was already crammed "since a throng of both sexes had flocked to it from the neighbouring countryside",[34] exacerbated by the Persian attack coinciding with an annual festival.

That Amida was the target for such an influx of people and could deal with it to a large degree was due to the extension of its walls and defences by Constantius during his time as *Caesar*. The position of Amida had encouraged Constantius to choose it as the hub for the region as it boasted the natural defence of the Tigris to the east while the foothills of the Taurus Mountains provided further protection to the north. To the south and west were the Mesopotamian plains, which provided ample provisions. The hilltop site of the city allowed control of access as Ammianus found out whilst trying to re-enter the city, while near the citadel there was a natural spring to provide fresh water. As well as extending the walls and defences, Constantius also had a substantial armoury built in the city, as well as a formidable battery of artillery.[35]

The permanent garrison of Amida consisted of *Legio V Parthica* and a significant unit of native cavalry. However, the years of intermittent Persian warfare during Constantius' reign and the promotion of Amida to a more prominent position in the Roman east saw the garrison expand. On top of that, garrisons from smaller cities that had retreated in the face of the Persian advance also found themselves in Amida. Therefore, by the time Ammianus re-entered the city, there were six other legions present: *XXX Ulpia*, *X Fretensis*, the *Magnentiaci* and *Decentiaci* raised by Magnentius and transferred east by Constantius, the *Superventores* and the *Praeventores*;[36] the latter, under the command of the *comes*, Aelianus, had made a name for themselves during the siege of Singara in sallying forth whilst still raw recruits and killing a large number of Persians. There was also a large number of *comites sagitarii*, mounted archers of Constantius' guard recruited from non-Romans.

In the days of the classic Roman legion, the presence of seven such units plus auxiliary and artillery support would have seen the Roman forces at Amida approach 50,000. However, the reduction in size of the legion by the fourth century is demonstrated by how an annual fair, pre-existing population, seven legions, auxiliaries, and civilians who had fled from the approaching Persian army reached just 20,000 people. Such paucity in numbers could suggest that Constantius was having some trouble finding sufficient men to defend all of his frontiers, especially when he himself was absent with his personal field army.[37]

Command of the Amida garrison fell to Aelianus, although he does not feature at all in Ammianus' recounting of the siege except for the description of the garrison and his execution at the fall of the city. Ammianus' account sees more junior officers like the tribunes and *protectores* being part of the decision-making processes at Amida, which would not be surprising as Aelianus could not marshal the city by himself and the faith put in such skilled lower ranks had long been one of the strengths of the Roman army. Ammianus and other *protectores* may have had been charged with the deployment of the significant artillery forces arrayed at Amida and the historian does demonstrate some familiarity in siege weaponry. However, it has been suggested that much of Ammianus' knowledge came more from having read other works such as those of Vitruvius and Josephus rather than actual hands-on experience, although that does not discount him having a prominent position amongst the command of the artillery at Amida, something that may be highlighted by his use of pronouns when describing events.[38]

Whilst Ammianus and the Amida garrison were preparing themselves for what would turn out to be a desperate struggle for survival, it is important to ascertain why Shapur ended up before the walls of such a fortress city when he had seemingly planned to drive on to northern Syria. From Bebase, again under the guidance of Antoninus, the Persian king led his army through Horren and Meiacarire and seemed set to strike across Gumathena towards the crossing points of the Upper Euphrates. However, upon passing Charcha, intelligence garnered from deserters suggested that there were large amounts of riches and resources stored in two nearby fortresses, Reman and Busan. Keen to strike a blow to the Romans and to perhaps reward his men, Shapur attacked both forts. Taken by surprise and unnerved by the size of the forces arrayed against them, the Reman and Busan garrisons surrendered without much of a fight, leaving the Persians to take control of not just the fortresses and their accumulated wealth but also those who had taken refuge within the fortresses. Shapur treated these prisoners of war with respect and kindliness, hoping to encourage others to surrender. Buoyed by the rapidity and ease of this success, Shapur likely decided to take a chance at making a show against the walls of Amida in the hope that the same fear would encourage a quick capitulation, removing a significant Roman force and fortress from the fighting.[39]

Seventy-three Days of Hell: The Siege of Amida 359

It is not hard to see why the Persians would have thought the Romans might capitulate given the sight that unfurled before the defenders of Amida as the Persian army approached: "at the first gleam of dawn, the landscape as far as the eye could reach was a-glitter with arms, and fill and plain covered with cavalry in coats of mail".[40] The Persian king himself presented an awe-inspiring sight, mounted on his horse at the head of the army, bedecked in his finest garments and surrounded by a retinue of kings and princes from the far-flung corners of his empire. Eager to make his show against Amida, Shapur and his retinue rode right up to the walls thinking that his mere presence would induce surrender.[41] However, even in all the splendour of his finery, it did not stop the Amida garrison from unleashing a volley of missiles from which the king barely escaped with his life when a lance punctured his ornate garments. Shapur did not take kindly to such insolence and decided that Amida had to pay. However, Antoninus and the king's council assuaged the royal ire by reminding him that their aim was the Euphrates and beyond and that attacking Amida would present an unnecessary distraction. Therefore, Shapur decided to offer the city one more chance to surrender and the next morning, the Chionite leader Grumbates went forward with a group of attendants to present those terms.

It was then that the event that caused the siege of Amida took place. As with Shapur's approach, Grumbates and his followers were scattered by a shower of missiles. However, not everyone escaped unharmed as a *ballista* bolt tore through the breastplate of Grumbates' son. A fierce exchange of fire ensued for the rest of the day as the Chionitae attempted to reclaim his body. After a funeral ceremony and cremation, over the course of a week, the Persian generals debated what to do next. Many will have wished to follow the original plan of continuing on to the Euphrates but Grumbates could not abide leaving Amida before his son had been avenged. It is a testament to the important position that Grumbates and his Chionitae held within Shapur's army that the Persian king felt compelled to overrule his generals in acceding to his ally's demand that Amida share the same fiery fate as his cremated son.

After two days of rest, a large foraging party was sent out to secure fodder from the surrounding plains to provide the Persian army with sustenance for the upcoming siege. Shapur then ordered the complete surrounding of Amida with up to five lines of shields. Grumbates and his Chionitae were stationed on the eastern approaches; the Kushans to the south; the Albani guarded the north and the Segestani, who are recorded as "the bravest warriors of all"[42] and Shapur's elephant corps took up a position opposite the western gate. Watching this vast horde of enemies surround them, the horrified garrison gave little hope to their survival, but instead of capitulating, they determined to sell their lives at the highest cost to the enemy.[43]

After a full day of organisation and what must have been a terrifying night of calm, the Persian forces were at their stations ready and eager for battle. Grumbates stepped forward and, in the custom of many cultures of antiquity, threw a blood-soaked spear in the direction of Amida, signifying a declaration of war on the city. The Persian forces then rushed forward with their siege engines, many of which had been captured from the Romans at Singara over a decade previously.[44] It was a considerable ordeal just to get these machines to the walls, given how the lay out of the approaches to Amida had caused the lone and unburdened Ammianus so much trouble. Pushing large, unstable engines uphill over various obstacles under a constant mutual barrage of stones, bolts, arrows, spears and javelins will have been slow, arduous and deadly. The Roman defenders worked in relays to keep up the barrage and repel any attackers that managed to make it to the walls, but they remained heavily outnumbered and spread thinly to defend the full circuit of Amida's walls. The fighting continued even after light began to fail as the night watches were passed "under the burden of arms as the hills re-echoed from the shouts rising from both sides".[45] The Persians followed a similar plan of attack on the next day, with the trumpets blasting again before dawn and the artillery, archers, slingers and throwers dealing out death on both sides, while the Romans again repelled Persian assaults throughout the day and night.

However, it was not without a price. These earliest days of the siege saw vicious and protracted fighting along the walls, which caused significant casualties to both sides. While the Persians had the wide open spaces to deal with their dead in whatever fashion their constituent peoples demanded,[46] inside Amida there was no room to dispose of the bodies that were piling up. The heat of the summer sun ensured that these corpses decomposed at an accelerated rate, which added to the already unsanitary conditions of the cramped environment of Amida. In such conditions and with the reduced resistance of the populace through their limited diet, physical tiredness, lack of sleep and general stress, the inevitable occurred – disease.[47]

Despite recalling the great historian Thucydides and his description of the plague that rocked Athens in 430–429BCE,[48] beyond mentioning what he thinks contributed to its outbreak, Ammianus did not attempt to match Thucydides' "famous and detailed clinical description".[49] Ammianus' use of the term *pestilentia* has led to suggestions of the disease at Amida being bubonic plague but he would have recorded any tell-tale swollen lymph glands on the groin, neck and armpits of its victims. The lack of defined symptoms, the seeming ten-day period of the outbreak and Ammianus' suggestion that a light rain managed to wash away much of the disease could lend credence to the idea of a contamination such as botulism rather than infection.[50] Whatever its cause, the pestilence at Amida further undermined the numbers and willpower of the defenders in the face of the mammoth Persian army and with no relief in the pipeline.

While Ammianus was witnessing first hand the almost apocalyptic carnage of war, famine, pestilence and death at Amida, Ursicinus was frustrated by the inaction of the Roman military hierarchy. Ammianus again derides Sabinianus for relying on prayer and the protection of his ancestors in the graveyards of

Edessa. This may be an indication that Sabinianus was attempting to keep his army fighting fit with military exercises in the open areas around Edessa while following Constantius' orders to not risk the main field army in battle.[51] The siege of Amida was likely viewed in pragmatic terms for it had led to Shapur's detour from his planned drive across the Euphrates and given more time for Constantius to arrive. Again though, Ammianus sees the personal undermining of Ursicinus and the plan to prevent the general gaining any further renown in the eyes of the public and the army, even if it was to the detriment of the state.[52] Sabinianus' refusal to deviate from orders and the overall strategic plan left Ursicinus helpless to do anything to save Amida apart from sending scouts and attempting to get messages through the Persian siege lines.

Even if they did not launch any further assaults on the city walls during the days that the pestilence raged, the Persians were not idle. Through their artillery barrage, night sallies and defensive measures, the Romans had managed to destroy or disable many of Shapur's siege engines. Despite having brought captured Roman siege engines from Singara, Shapur may not have had the heaviest of his siege equipment present at Amida as his plan had been for a rapid advance to the Euphrates. It should perhaps therefore be no surprise that once the sheer terror of the siege and initial assaults failed to overcome the Amidan garrison, Shapur found his army unable to threaten a fortified and naturally strong position. Therefore, while skirmishing continued, Shapur took advantage of any lull caused by the disease to strengthen his siege train. This led to the Persians setting up various wicker screens and mounds around Amida and building more siege towers.[53] This use of screens to protect these building projects and the men working on them suggests that they were set up within the range of the Roman artillery. The threat of the Roman missile defences also impacted on the design of these new towers for not only were they tall and clad in iron, they housed a *ballista* to clear the walls.

The construction of these mammoth towers unnerved the Roman garrison, in particular the *Magnentiaci* and *Decentiaci* legions, who led various sallies against the Persian lines. These may have disrupted Persian construction somewhat but Ammianus viewed these men as a hindrance to the defence. Unaccustomed to such siege warfare, having been raised to fight pitched battles against the Germanic tribes along the Rhine, their lack of experience with building fortifications or manning artillery saw their frustration boil over into reckless forays.[54] These attacks not only reduced the Gallic ranks without dealing any appreciable damage to the Sassanid army and their preparations, they exposed Amida to potential catastrophe through the frequent opening of gates. Indeed, Ammianus sums up how ineffectual these attacks were by suggesting that they accomplished as much as throwing a cup of water on a large fire. It even appears that their officers had to take stern measures to prevent them from continuing in their forays, including locking them within the city.[55]

The Persians did not pin all of their hopes on overcoming the walls by sheer strength. Taking advantage of the Roman distraction with the rising siege towers and their thin spread along the walls, a group of Shapur's finest archers – *sagitarii ex agmine regio* – were led by a deserter to the south of Amida. There, under cover of darkness, they climbed a staircase carved from the rock that gave the fortress access to the Tigris and secretly took control of a defensive tower. Then in the morning, they raised a red cloak to signal that they were in position and at that another assault commenced. The shock of seeing Persian soldiers within Amida led to indecision amongst many of the Roman defenders; however, one quick-thinking artillery unit manoeuvred its battery of five light *ballistae* to level concentrated fire on the Persian archers emerging from the tower. The viciousness of these bolts, able to puncture two men at once, and the accuracy of the *ballistarii* overwhelmed these elite Persian interlopers and their bridgehead. These *ballistae* were then returned to their original position to help repel the hordes of Sassanid soldiers attempting to scale the walls with ladders. Encouraged by this rapid success and enraged by the thought of almost being undone by a deserter, the Roman defenders redoubled their efforts and before midday they had broken the Persian assault. Such a victory buoyed spirits in the Roman camp and may even have raised hopes of outlasting Shapur.

As the Roman defenders rested from their exertions, dawn brought a wretched sight and another form of attack prevalent in siege warfare: psychological terror. Despite their deployment at Amida, Sassanid forces did not confine themselves to attempting to break into that one fortification. Columns fanned out across northern Mesopotamia between the banks of the Tigris and Euphrates. In the face of these raiders, the Roman population swarmed towards other towns and fortresses in search of refuge. One such fortress was Ziatha, which was situated further upriver from Amida. Confronted by one of these Persian columns, this fortress capitulated and now in full view of the Amidan garrison, the prisoners were paraded on their way to the slave markets of Persia, a terrible demonstration of their ultimate fate. Worse still was that those who refused or were unable to make the forced march, such as the elderly or infirm, were hamstrung and left by the side of the road, no doubt with their pained groans filling the air.[56]

The sight and sound of this wretched parade sparked powerful but varied emotions within Amida. Seeing their own potential future produced fear in many while raising the ire of others, including the already frustrated Gallic legions. These men now demanded offensive action, going as far as to threaten their tribunes with death should they keep them cooped up within the city and forced to die in the destruction of the city without winning glory. Such was their ferocity that Ammianus equated them to caged beasts, "roused to greater fierceness by the odour of carrion".[57] Fuelled by desperation and perhaps fearing that they could not contain these ravenous Gauls, the garrison commanders allowed them to sally forth and attack enemy outposts near the walls but at appropriate times. In agreeing to act as part of an overall plan, the Gauls extracted a proviso that if their next foray was successful they would be allowed to continue to deal out slaughter and sell their lives as highly as possible.

Once the Romans had gathered sufficient munitions at the right places to follow up their possible success and cover any retreat, the Gallic legionaries stole out of a postern gate against the backdrop of a gloomy, moonless night. Their attack on the Persian outposts was so well timed and unexpected that the Gauls were able to kill many as they slept. They moved on to the main Persian camp, killing guards as they went and even threatened to reach Shapur's quarters. Despite having enjoyed good fortune in going undiscovered until then, their luck did not hold out long enough for them to initiate such a strike. Through the commotion of the killing and the groans of the dying, the Persians became aware of an enemy in their midst. Despite the growing throng of enemies and taking casualties from archer fire, the Gauls stood their ground and cut down the startled Persians in droves. At length, the weight of numbers began to tell and the legionaries were forced to withdraw, executing a fighting retreat back to Amida.[58]

This sally had succeeded in killing a large number of Persians, including several high ranking officials and satraps, which in itself suggests how close the Gauls came to the Persian king's tent. With this action, the Gallic legions gained the fame that they had wanted as Constantius would later erect a statue of those who lead the operation in full armour at a prominent spot in Edessa. Ammianus again breaks out the literary comparisons, invoking Homer to state that not even the death of Rhesus and the Thracians at Troy was worthy of the success of the *Magnentiaci* and *Decentiaci* that night. But despite this notoriety, the boost in morale to the Roman garrison and the Persian casualties, the Gallic night attack was a failure. Whether it was a planned objective or not, it had failed to kill Shapur, a feat that would have seen the lifting of the siege and the break up of the Sassanid force. On top of that, the Persians were numerous enough –Ammianus now declares them to be 100,000 strong[59] – to absorb the casualties, while the 400 dead Gauls were felt far more acutely. Therefore, while the Persians asked for a three-day truce after this night attack, giving the

Romans further breathing space, there was no indication of a Persian retreat. The siege would continue.

The Gallic sally perhaps hastened Amida's destruction as having Roman soldiers fight their way to his doorstep awakened Shapur to the idea that the garrison was not just going to wait for capitulation. During this three-day truce, after dealing with their dead, the Persians redoubled their efforts in completing their siege towers. Then when the truce ended, Shapur almost threw everything he had at Amida: missiles of all shapes and sizes, siege towers, mailed infantry and cavalry. To the remaining defenders, it must have been an awe-inspiring but terrifying sight. Tens of thousands approaching from almost every direction at a slow metronomic march at the sound of trumpets must have seemed as if the whole world had taken up against them. But it did not deter the Romans and as soon as the Persian forces came into range, they were met with the now obligatory cloud of missiles. The sheer mass of attackers, mixed with the continued accuracy of the Roman archers and artillery, saw to it that "almost no kind of dart failed to find its mark".[60] Even the most heavily armoured of Persian cataphracts were driven back. The tide turned somewhat when the siege towers, which were much taller than the walls, were able to bring their own firepower to bear on the Roman defenders, causing "terrible carnage".[61]

Therefore, when the fighting died down at the end of the day, while they had survived the initial stages of another assault, the Romans had failed to repel the Persians and were left in a quandary about what to do about these heavily armed and armoured towers. The plan they came to involved the placing of their scorpion onagers, torsion-sprung *ballistae*, in a position to target the towers and when daybreak brought another Persian assault, the high quality of the Roman artillery was again proven as well aimed missiles shattered the joints of the ironclad siege towers, which collapsed under their own weight with fire arrows making sure that they would not be rebuilt. Fire also played a role in the rebuffing of the one Persian weapon that had not yet been thrown at the Amida walls: the elephant corps. The Romans peppered these rampant beasts with various missiles including more fire arrows. At length, the heat, burns and wounds saw the mahouts lose control of their mounts, wreaking havoc amongst their own lines. But even with the blunting of their elephants and the destruction of their ironclad siege engines, the Persians continued to fight until nightfall, with Shapur himself perhaps taking part in the melee, something that had never happened before.[62]

Having failed to conquer Amida through secret passages, demoralising terror, heavily armed infantry and cavalry, marauding elephants and mighty siege towers topped with weapons platforms, the Persians now turned to something far more primitive. During the build up to the Gallic night attack, Ammianus reports a troop of Sassanid infantry being tasked with constructing two siege mounds against the walls of Amida with the Romans building their own counter-mounds.[63] What followed as Shapur launched another attack using these mounds must have been a muddy, bloodstained melee for the city walls with neither side giving an inch. At the height of the fighting, the Roman counter-mound collapsed under the weight. Not only did it throw off its Roman defenders, it fell against the city walls and helped bridge the gap between the Persian mound and the walls.[64] In that one instance of misfortune the Roman defensive effort was irretrievably undermined. Persian soldiers streamed onto the walls and unlike with the previous limited breach of elite archers, the Romans were unable to stem the tide. The weight of Sassanid numbers and the disorganisation caused by the collapse of the earthwork on top of the defenders' emotional and physical tiredness told as the siege of Amida descended into the carnage of a sack. Roman losses are not recorded but a large percentage of the 20,000 occupants will not have escaped as "the unremitting courage of the besieged set death at defiance".[65]

Given that "since all hope of defence or of flight was cut off [and] armed and unarmed alike without distinction of sex were slaughtered like so many cattle",[66] the question must be asked as to how the author of the account managed to survive the gruesome and bloody aftermath. As the Persians swept through the city rounding up remnants of the Amidan garrison, Ammianus hid in a secluded part of the fallen city with two compatriots until nightfall when they made their escape through an unguarded postern gate. Led by the future historian's knowledge of the local terrain, this trio of escapees fled across the desert to the post-house at the tenth milestone. After resting, Ammianus and his companions were confronted by a gruesome sight. Near the post-house, they found a horse that was dragging the shattered remains of its former rider. The body was that of a groom who had tied the reins of the horse around his hand in order not to fall off. However, having been thrown, the groom could not undo the knot and was "torn limb from limb dragged over rough ground and through woods, until the weight of his body brought the tired beast to a stop".[67] Having corralled the horse, the three escapees continued their journey to safety, although it is not mentioned if the beast was shared between them. Ammianus was glad of the much needed relief the horse provided as he went out of his way to complain about his own lack of fitness to deal with such an arduous march, being accustomed to riding on horseback due to his free birth and military rank.

The troop then reached a hot water spring that was tinged with sulphur but so parched were they that they were not put off. The well was deep and there was no rope or bucket to retrieve the water. Improvising, they tore their garments into strips – there is some suggestion that they had taken the clothes of the dismembered groom – to fashion a rope, to which they attached one of their caps to act as a sponge. Their thirst somewhat quenched, the trio made for the Euphrates, hoping to cross it by boat. When they came within sight of its waters, they noticed a small troop of Roman cavalry approaching from their rear. Any relief was quickly dispelled by the revelation that a larger Persian force was pursuing them. Taking flight once more, Ammianus and his companions made it across the river and headed for the mountains through thickets and woodlands, arriving at Melitene, after a 200km journey. Ammianus attached himself to a unit of soldiers about to leave for Antioch under the command of Ursicinus, allowing the *protector* to arrive without further recorded incident in the capital of the Roman east, his own hometown.[68]

After the fall of Amida, Ursicinus returned west, rejoining the imperial court at Constantinople to take up the position of *magister peditum*. However, his 'failure' in the east followed him and his opponents were soon spreading malicious rumours and perhaps even bringing false charges against him. Constantius listened to some of these accusations and together with a pre-existing mistrust of Ursicinus, led to him establishing a commission to find the causes of the fall of Amida. Ammianus took this as a direct attack on Ursicinus but it was hardly biased to seek the underlying causes of such a heavy loss. However, that those who were chosen to carry out the commission's purview, Arbitio and the *magister officiorum*, Florentius, appear to have been too scared to present the full truth, at least as far as Ammianus saw it, suggests that there was at least some question about its judicial standing. Rather than suggest that it was Sabinianus' inaction and Constantius' orders that had led to the destruction of Amida, fearful of both the emperor and the head chamberlain, Eusebius, they dodged the big issues and focused on unimportant details and misfortune.

Exasperated by the intentional ignorance of the imperial court and worried for the future of the Roman east, Ursicinus lost his temper and railed against the establishment. He claimed that if Constantius did not seek out the real truth behind the fall of Amida, then even the emperor himself at the head of his best army would not be able to fix the mess in Mesopotamia.[69] Despite these truths, Ursicinus might as well have presented his letter of resignation to the emperor as those eunuchs who the general was railing against were quick to report this outburst to Constantius and portray it in a negative light. Without stopping to check the facts, the emperor had Ursicinus cashiered and forced to retire from public life. The vacancy of *magister peditum* was filled by Agilo, a former tribune of the imperial guard and the *Scutarii*, a promotion that was viewed as a major step up, suggesting that either Agilo was well regarded by the right people or there were few who wanted to take up a position that seemed a poisoned chalice.

The Persians were not the only military problem facing the Romans in the east in 359. The Isaurians had been quiet after being driven back to their mountain holdfasts by Nebridius in 354, but by 359, through their skill as mountaineers, they avoided the local forces keeping an eye on them and recommenced raiding the surrounding provinces. This led to the appointment of Bassidius Lauricius as *comes Isauriae* in order to deal with them. He proved his worth by using a combination of military threat and action to repulse the raids and even recover a fortified position along the upper reaches of the Calycadnus river north of Germanicopolis, now the Göksu river near modern Ermenek in Karaman province of southern Turkey, that had suffered a "long occupation by bandits".[70] That the Isaurians had held such a position for an extended period may suggest that they posed an even greater threat and exerted even more control over the region than Ammianus records. This would make the actions and achievements of Castricius, Nebridius and now Lauricius all the more understandable and impressive.[71]

Chronology and the Siege of Amida

The importance to the study of the mid fourth century of Ammianus' good fortune in escaping Amida has already been mentioned but despite being one of the centrepieces of his history, there are large gaps in the narrative of the seventy-three days that Ammianus attributes to the siege.[72] After the initial stages and assaults, which are largely recounted day by day in limited detail, Ammianus focuses more on important events such as the pestilence, the Persian infiltration of the walls and the eventual end of the siege without giving much inference of how much time has passed between these events. Even the timeline for the first two weeks of the siege is not beyond reproach for Ammianus occasionally fails to elaborate on the timing of certain events compared to others. An example is his mentioning of an assault on the "fifth day",[73] which one would consider the fifth day since the start of the siege. However, because Ammianus does not indicate when he considered the siege to have started, this has led to discussion over whether this is the fifth day since Shapur initiated the blockade of Amida or the fifth day since the end of the truce that accompanied the funeral games for Grumbates' son.[74] The former would add a potential third Persian assault at the beginning of the siege along with a further two unreported days, which may have been taken up with rest and recuperation after two days of non-stop fighting. Such an interpretation would stretch Ammianus' initial description of the siege from fourteen to seventeen days.

Another event that is difficult to place is the ten day pestilence that ravaged Amida. Considering the rapid decomposition taking place in the humid heat, the outbreak probably occurred not long after the initial Persian assaults,[75] although placing it directly after the "fifth day"[76] is applying a more linear progression to Ammianus' narrative than is acceptable, especially when it jumps from the description of the carnage of that fifth day to Ursicinus' many pleas to Sabinianus rather than straight into the outbreak of disease. It must also be noted that due to Ammianus' failure to say otherwise, it is possible that events such as the ten-day pestilence included an overlap with days where other events are recorded. There are other indications of the passage of time such as the unrecorded forays of the Gallic legions before they were eventually locked within the city and the potential lack of a gap between the wretched parade from Ziatha and the successful Gallic night attack but these give inferences rather than a solid timeframe.

Even tentative acceptance of two extra rest days before a third Persian assault on the "fifth day" taking place during the fifteenth, sixteenth and seventeenth days after Shapur's arrival at Amida and adding in days from before the official start of the siege such as the time it took Shapur to reach the city from Bebase and a couple of days at the end for the sack still leaves the chronology well short of seventy-three days. Indeed, a period of at least a month remains unaccounted for in the narrative,[77] which seems careless but is unsurprising in a work called *Res Gestae* and therefore concerned with "great deeds, heroic and ingenious exploits, violent emotions and suffering".[78] These gaps should perhaps be viewed as Ammianus refusing to litter his text with repetitive, uninteresting reports. After the initial assaults, skirmishing and a mutual exchange of fire, which continued through these unrecorded periods, had become everyday, mundane and beyond the scope of Ammianus' choice of historical writing.[79]

There should also be room for the notion that these gaps reflected the reality of the siege of Amida. Aside from continued skirmishing and missile fire and the day-to-day business of the respective camps, it is possible that nothing of note occurred between the major events. Perhaps the Persians were confident that they could starve the Amidan garrison into submission, although the vengeful wrath of Grumbates would seem to make a forceful capture and bloody sack more their aim. It would also not be surprising to see some drop off in action if the Persians learned of the disease within Amida for fear of bringing it back to their own camp. Preparations for siege warfare were time-consuming, especially if Shapur had not come prepared for such an eventuality. After the initial stages when it became obvious that the Romans were not going to capitulate, the Persians may have had to scramble together resources from increasingly far away having used up the most available supplies in the initial fortnight of the siege.

Day	Action(s)
1 (1)	Shapur arrives at Amida and is shot at when he approaches the walls
2 (2)	Grumbates' son is killed; mutual exchange of fire
3 (3)	Truce and funeral games
4 (4)	Truce and funeral games
5 (5)	Truce and funeral games
6 (6)	Truce and funeral games
7 (7)	Truce and funeral games
8 (8)	Truce and funeral games
9 (9)	Truce and funeral games
10 (10)	Rest, deliberation and preparation
11 (11)	Rest, deliberation and preparation
12 (12)	Persian blockade of Amida initiated
13 (13)	First Persian assault; Grumbates' ceremonial declaration of hostilities
14 (14)	Second Persian assault
15 (15)	Rest
16 (16)	Rest
17 (17)	Third Persian assault
(18)	70 Persian archers sneak into Amida
(19)	Fourth Persian assault repelled by midday
(20)	Parade of the captives of Ziatha
(21)	Gallic night attack
(22)	Truce
(23)	Truce
(24)	Truce
(25)	Fourth Persian assault
(26)	Fifth Persian assault; destruction of the Persian siege towers
(27)	Sixth Persian assault; Roman counter-mound collapses; the city falls

With their victory at Amida achieved and there still being very little in the way of a Roman military response to their presence, it might be expected that the Persians would resume their march to the Euphrates. However, given the seventy-three days it had taken to subdue Amida, Shapur had lost a significant portion of the campaigning season. It may even have been well into the autumn before he could look beyond Amida, a season that brought stormy weather to the region. Therefore, rather than drive further into Roman territory and risk being cut off from home, Shapur made preparations to return to his own lands. Time was not the only thing that the Persians had lost at Amida. The stubborn resistance of the garrison, the forays of the Gauls, and the sharp-shooting of the artillery and missile defences reportedly saw Shapur leave an enormous 30,000 dead behind.[80] Even to an army in the region of 100,000 strong, such losses will have been a huge blow to Shapur's future plans, denting morale and limiting strategic options should they not be replenished, although the invasion the following year would suggest that the casualties suffered at Amida had not decisively undermined Shapur's army.

As angry as the Persian king was at the undermining of his plan for 359 and the casualties, he was not going home empty-handed. Aside from the smoking ruin that was now Amida and the strategic and morale loss that that was to the Romans, Shapur had captured significant numbers of civilian and military personnel to go with the material spoils he had taken. Amongst the newly enslaved were paymasters of the *magister equitum*, Jacobus and Caesius and several other *protectores*. It is not certain if Ammianus is referring to Sabinianus or Ursicinus although the suggestion from his language and his ability to name these men suggests that he knew them personally at the very least through having shared the experience of the siege with them but perhaps even from having served with them on Ursicinus' staff.[81]

Shapur also received another prominent Roman deserter into his camp. During the capture of Reman and Busan, the wife, daughter and property of a certain Craugasius, *curialis* of Nisibis, fell into Persian hands. Shapur planned to take the woman for himself but upon hearing "that her husband ardently loved her, he thought that at this price he might purchase the betrayal of Nisibis".[82] This plan fell by the wayside, perhaps with the prolonged siege of Amida; however, when the Persians withdrew, worried that she was to be separated from her husband and forced to remarry in Persia, Craugasius' wife sent a slave to Nisibis to plead with her husband to join her. Craugasius agreed but suspicions were raised, including those of the *dux Mesopotamiae*, Cassianus, who questioned Craugasius. Worried that his planned flight was about to be discovered, the *curalis* devised a plot to avert these suspicions. Playing on the assumption that his wife was dead, Craugasius pretended to be engaged to a young, high-born maiden and retired to his country house under the pretence of preparing for the wedding. Free from the prying eyes in the city, he met up with a group of Persian raiders, who brought him to Tamsapor and then on to Shapur's court where he took up an advisory position alongside Antoninus.[83]

However, there was one group of men who fell into the hands of Shapur who could not be treated with such a welcoming or be led off into slavery. Someone had to pay for the disruption of Persian plans, the 30,000 men expended against the walls of Amida and the death of Grumbates' son. Those chosen to bear that burden of guilt were Aelianus and his tribunes, "by whose efficient service the walls had been so long defended and the losses of the Persians increased".[84] There was to be no respect or admiration for the military feats of the *comes* and his faithful *tribuni*. And there was to be no quick, painless death either. As a reward for their defiance, Aelianus and his men were crucified. While it is not mentioned by Ammianus or any other source, it is hard to shake the sorry vision of a cadre of brave men left to die on crosses on the approach to what was Amida; a stark warning to those who would dare stand against the King of Kings.

Cutting through the Spin: Constantius, Ursicinus and the Fall of Amida

The fall of Amida raised a lot of questions and as with any major military defeat, the usual complaints of a lack of manpower to man the defences and limited resources to pay for them were carted out.[85] While such complaints are to be expected, they perhaps ring truer with the Roman Empire in 359 than on many other occasions. Even the mightiest of superpowers throughout history have struggled with war on more than one front and in 359 Constantius was faced with at least three fronts: the Rhine, Danube and Mesopotamia. Whilst Constantius, Julian and Barbatio defeated the barbarians of Europe, the sheer number of tribes and flashpoints severely tested the field armies and their frontier support. And in the east, even if Shapur's force was not the extent of 100,000 strong, it was a significant enough force to overwhelm a Roman garrison of several thousand and cause a Roman field army of anything up to 20,000 to refuse to even take the field.

On this backdrop of strained manpower, Constantius' later order to Julian to send him so many Gallic soldiers who lacked experience in eastern warfare,[86] which was viewed as weakening a potential usurper, may be more an indicator of how desperate for men the emperor was. The financial exactions and implications of such a manpower deficit encouraged the *comes sacrarum largitionum*, Ursulus to comment, "What courage our cities are defended by men whom resources of the empire are denuded to supply with pay"[87] upon being confronted with the ruin of Amida; a thoughtless and unfair remark given the heroic defence of Aelianus and his garrison and one that would later cost Ursulus his life but it highlights the problems afflicting the empire.

While it is no surprise that the Roman Empire had problems dealing with so many simultaneous threats, the complaints and questions rising from the fall of Amida focused on the formulating and carrying out of Constantius' strategy.

To Ammianus, it was a disaster that could have been avoided had Constantius, Sabinianus and the imperial court listened to Ursicinus. However, the historian was too close to the events and his opinion is heavily coloured by his allegiance to his *magister* and his own experiences at Amida. He would have it that the actions of the imperial court were aimed more at removing Ursicinus and then placing him in a no win situation than in actually attempting to stave off defeat.

Given this negative portrayal by Ammianus, it takes some care in extracting the reasons behind Constantius' actions during Shapur's invasion of 359. The removal of Ursicinus from the eastern frontier at a time when the Persian king was mustering for another attack seems odd. Ammianus sees the negative meddling of the eunuchs, with them using the usurpations of Magnentius and Silvanus to pique Constantius' wariness and orchestrate the removal of a skilled general from the field due to their fear of his popularity. There is likely a grain of truth in this as Ursicinus was well respected and maybe even loved by the populace, something which Constantius had some justification in being wary of, having already faced three usurpers and harbouring latent suspicions over Julian.[88]

However, given his previous experiences against Shapur, Constantius will not have recalled Ursicinus if he thought it would undermine the defences of Mesopotamia, Armenia and Syria. The emperor had fought hard to retain the Roman position in the east throughout the first two decades of his reign and it is doubtful that he would risk it over the circulating rumours about a general who had shown him nothing but loyalty. In fact, what Ammianus took as the messing around of Ursicinus with his recall and then sending back east could be taken as evidence of Constantius' high regard for the *magister*. Ursicinus being ordered to join Constantius in the Balkans was not a recall in the negative sense. He was not being punished for having done a bad job. Much to the contrary, he was called to the imperial court to assume the position of *magister peditum* in the emperor's personal field army vacated by Barbatio, one of Constantius' most senior and trusted commanders. This was a promotion and Ammianus claiming that this was a eunuch ploy to put Ursicinus under closer scrutiny and remove him from a position of more independent authority seems somewhat like paranoid clutching at straws. If it was the case that Constantius was removing Ursicinus from a position of power, then why did he send Ursicinus back east when reports of the Persian military build up reached him?

That this promotion came at a time when the Romans could ill afford the removal of a skilled general was just unfortunate timing, exacerbated by the slowness of the communication system. Despite the Romans being more connected than many of their contemporaries through their imperial postage services, communication was still slow. Constantius was already in the process of replacing Barbatio with Ursicinus before concrete evidence of Shapur's intentions was revealed and once the gravity of the situation was made known, he sent orders for Ursicinus to return east. Therefore, Ursicinus' removal from and then return to the east should be seen as a combination of reward for his endeavours and the distances between frontiers rather than an orchestrated plot to undermine him.

The lack of preparation in the east for Shapur's invasion is another major issue that Ammianus raises. He suggests that in attempting to get Ursicinus removed, men like Arbitio and Eusebius sowed disbelief in Ursicinus' reports about Persian military build up for their own political ends even if it meant leaving the east more open to attack. Again part of this might be true but perhaps not in the way that Ammianus would have it. Constantius was not leaving the east open to attack through some grudge against one of his generals. He was doing so because it fitted in with his overall strategic plan of defence for the east, which was attuned to the abilities and resources of his empire in 359. This strategy of relying on cities and garrisons rather than pitched battles may have been stumbled upon during his early conflicts with Shapur but Constantius did put some thought into this plan of hard nodal defences, best seen in his expansion of Amida's fortifications and the placing of a high quality armoury within the city.

As sole *Augustus*, it might be expected that Constantius had the manpower and resources to meet Shapur head on. But as mentioned above, in 359, Shapur's attack came when the emperor was engaged with the political and military fall out of the collapse of the dominant Sarmatian position along the Danube. He could not uproot his field army and abandon a frontier in favour of another and Julian was still dealing with the Rhine. Therefore, despite having the resources of the entire empire at his command, posed with war on three fronts and the limitations it placed on manpower and logistics, Constantius chose to rely on the defensive strategy that had already proven successful, even if it was unpopular.[89]

Constantius may have calculated that he had some time to finish off the Limigantes before travelling east to confront Shapur, who would be delayed by the Mesopotamian garrisons. Even when this line of thinking was proven incorrect as Shapur followed the advice of Antoninus and invaded early and headed straight for the Euphrates, Constantius' strategic choices were still proven correct. Many, including Ursicinus and Ammianus, saw the destruction of Amida and its garrison as too heavy a price but Constantius could point to the overall picture. By the end of 359, the Danubian front had been had closed down and Shapur's extended deployment against Amida had reduced the potential damage to the east. The emperor had benefitted from a set of fortunate circumstances with the interception of Ursicinus' column drawing the Persians to Amida and then the death of Grumbates' son forcing them to stay for the duration. However, when Ammianus had been confronted with a Persian army so large that he refused to speculate on its size from the cliffs of Corduene,[90] the idea that all it would accomplish over the next three months would be the destruction of a frontier city and some minor towns and forts would have seemed unlikely.

The question of why Constantius, having sent Ursicinus back east, did he not re-establish him as *magister equitum per Orientem* could be linked to the emperor's need to follow this hard point, low intensity, defensive strategy. He simply may not have trusted Ursicinus to follow that strategy and therefore appointed someone less adept and more pliable in Sabinianus to command the eastern field forces, while sending the more energetic and popular Ursicinus to encourage resistance on a more local scale. If Ursicinus' actions during the siege of Amida are anything to go by – repeatedly petitioning Sabinianus to intervene against imperial orders – then Constantius was vindicated in not trusting Ursicinus to carry out his overall strategic plan. Had Ursicinus been in command of the field army at Edessa, he may well have marched it into battle against overwhelming odds in an attempt to save Amida, which would have led to the loss of not just the city but perhaps the entire eastern field army as well.

Ursicinus' dismissal in the aftermath of the fall of Amida would seem to go some way to justifying the negative picture of the imperial court painted by Ammianus and how it was setting Ursicinus up to fail. But even this may mask part of the truth. Blame for Amida was not immediately placed at the feet of Ursicinus as he was allowed to assume his position of *magister peditum* at Constantinople.[91] It was only when he felt that the enquiry set up to investigate the fall of Amida was leaning towards placing the blame on him that Ursicinus spoke out against those he perceived as his enemies at court. This would not have irked Constantius as his *magister* had every right to defend himself. However, when Ursicinus "added tactless aspersions against Constantius' advisers"[92] and claimed that not even Constantius himself could save Mesopotamia the following year if the emperor continued to listen to sycophantic eunuchs who knew nothing of war rather than his generals, he crossed the line.[93] Now he was directly questioning the skills and decisions of the emperor and that, along with the clear division within the imperial court and perhaps his own paranoia, was what got Ursicinus cashiered rather than blame for the fall of Amida.

The Persian Invasion of 360

Even if Ammianus was mistaken in his portrayal of imperial politics, it does not mean that Ursicinus was mistaken in his rant. His claim that even Constantius himself and the best units would not save Mesopotamia should the eunuchs remain in favour would be put to the test. After spending the winter mulling over the disappointment of his 359 campaign and regrouping his forces, Shapur invaded once more in 360. Burning "with the desire of gaining possession of Mesopotamia whilst Constantius was busy",[94] Shapur crossed the Tigris, perhaps at a similar position to the previous year, and thrust towards Singara.

It might be queried as to why Shapur would chose to attack a fixed position after putting so much emphasis on driving deeply into Roman territory the previous year, especially one that was well enough defended in one of the most arid parts of Mesopotamia. Buoyed by his success at Amida, Shapur may have relished the opportunity to restore his prestige by removing the blot on his career that was Singara's successful resistance. However, this change of strategy and the choice of Singara may have come about through some idea of pragmatism. The presence of Constantius and his field army in the east, albeit only at Constantinople for the winter and perhaps Cappadocian Caesarea by March 360,[95] may have discouraged Shapur from attempting a repeat of his plan to forge across the Euphrates as he could not risk being confronted with the combined forces of Sabinianus and Constantius. That said, the confidence in the Persian camp will still have been high and Shapur will have wanted to take advantage of that so a strike at an important Roman base distant from the Roman field forces will have been a good alternative to a risky strike further north.

It will also have crossed the mind of Shapur and his advisers that word of their total victory at Amida and the fate of those who fell into their hands after their futile resistance will have reached the inhabitants and garrison of Singara. The Persians may have hoped that the fear of a repeat performance might have seen the city fall to them with limited fighting. Should Singara not fall to terror and Shapur was forced into a siege, he will have had some reason to be confident, despite the remoteness of his target and his previous failure. On that previous occasion, Constantius had been present with the eastern field army and even then had not been able to defeat the Persian king in battle. Now, in 360, Shapur had a larger army, intelligence that suggested that Constantius was not yet in a position to intervene and the precedent that Sabinianus had not moved to save Amida, a city that was much closer to Edessa than Singara.[96] So armed, Shapur may have seen this as a perfect opportunity to conquer one of the easternmost outposts of the Roman Empire, which while a demanding task for his forces would provide perhaps an even bigger task for the Romans to relieve.

For Constantius, regardless of its objective, a Persian invasion in 360 could not have come at a worse time as his relations with Julian had taken a dramatic turn for the worse by March 360.[97] Once again, the emperor was faced with a potential war on two fronts and the decision of whether to shore up eastern defences or to turn west and deal with a challenge to his power. Shapur will not have heard of this internal distraction for his imperial opponent before having chosen his target and it would be speculative to suggest if such knowledge would have altered his strategic approach for 360.

Once Shapur was across the Tigris and it was clear that neither Constantius nor Sabinianus were going to march to its rescue, Singara's fate was sealed. There is little to suggest that the city was as well-armed or strongly garrisoned as Amida had been; however, the Roman forces within, *I Parthica* and *I Flavia* bolstered by what are called *indigenae* by Ammianus and some auxiliary cavalry that had taken refuge there,[98] seem to have been confident in their ability to resist the coming storm. Perhaps they placed too much stock in their previous resistance, the arid conditions faced by the Persians or the possibility of relief but as the Persian army approached, the defenders "distributed themselves on the towers and battlements, eager for the fight, collected stones and engines of war, and when everything was ready stood to arms, prepared to repel the enemy host if it dared approach the walls".[99]

Regardless of its show of defiance, such a small garrison was not going to scare a confident and numerous Persian army.[100] Shapur began his attempt on Singara with peace overtures, hoping to avoid another prolonged and expensive siege in arid, enemy territory. Given the defensive preparations though, it will have come as no surprise that his overtures were rejected. Shapur showed that he had not expected surrender by launching an assault the very next morning with a vast array of ladders and siege towers attacking the walls, while large penthouses and manlets protected large numbers of men working to undermine the Singaran walls. Against this onslaught, the Roman garrison, "standing upon their lofty battlements, from a distance with stones and all kinds of missile weapons tried to repel those who boldly strove to force an entrance".[101]

While not in the detail of his account of Amida, Ammianus depicts the siege of Singara with similar if more short-lived intensity. These Persian assaults and mutual exchange of fire continued for "several days"[102] with neither side able to break the resolve of the other. At length, the Persians brought up an immense battering ram to the same round tower that they had breached during their previous attempt on Singara. As this mighty ram went about its work, it became the focal point of the entire siege as the garrison forces attempted to set the great siege engine on fire with torches and flaming arrows. Perhaps due to the Persians cladding the ram in metal or soaked skins, the Romans were unable to do significant enough damage to prevent the ram smashing against the tower walls. It is possible that the repairs were so recent that the bricks and mortar used were still somewhat weak, leading the tower to give way.[103] With their position undermined by the collapse of the tower, the deaths it caused and the pouring of Persian forces into the breach, the Roman defenders attempted an orderly withdrawal but there was to be no respite as Shapur's men swept into Singara, overwhelming resistance and forcing what was left of the garrison to surrender. As those survivors were led away into captivity in Persia, Singara suffered a heavy sack.

Having achieved the destruction of this Roman outpost, perhaps quicker than he may have planned for, Shapur was free to look for further targets in Mesopotamia. The biggest challenges remained those Roman troop concentrations at Edessa and Nisibis but with the former being too far north and having already failed before the walls of the latter on three separate occasions, Shapur decided to look elsewhere. His royal gaze fell upon another important position in the Roman eastern defences, the fortress at Bezabde. Perhaps 120km north of Singara on the site of what is now Cizre in the Simak province of Turkey, Bezabde sat on the eastern side of the Tigris in Zabdicene. Should it fall into his hands, along with the destruction of Amida, Shapur's grip over a long stretch of the Middle Tigris will have been tightened. Given its strategic location, the fortress at Bezabde boasted a larger garrison than Singara: three legions, *II Flavia, II Armenia* and *II Parthica*, together with a large contingent of skilled Zabdiceni archers, who were perhaps predecessors of the modern day Kurds. The fortress itself presented a formidable obstacle, perched "upon a hill of moderate height which sloped towards the banks of the Tigris and where it was low and therefore exposed to danger, it was fortified by a double wall".[104]

Upon arriving at the fortress, Shapur again made a show of strength by personally leading a large, mounted reconnaissance of Bezabde, in the hope of gaining information about its defences and perhaps even inducing surrender. However, as the king came close to the walls, a repeat of the initial moments of the siege of Amida unfolded as the Roman garrison unleashed a flurry of missiles, hoping to remove the head of the Persian snake. Shapur's bodyguards threw up a screen of interlocked shields and escorted their king to safety. Despite the anger he must have felt at this replay, Shapur stuck to his game plan and sent heralds forward to offer the Bezabde garrison the chance to surrender. That these heralds were not pelted with missiles in a similar manner to Shapur and Grumbates was because the Persian king sent several captives from Singara along with them, betting that the garrison would not risk the deaths of their comrades. The garrison not only held their fire, they held their tongues when it came to the offer of peace.[105]

His magnanimity spurned, Shapur was free to attack the fortress and after a day, the assault began with the Persians once again struggling to get their ladders and siege engines to the walls under an intense barrage from the Roman defenders. The fighting continued throughout the day, only ceasing with the setting of the sun but even before it rose again, battle was rejoined with even more ferocity so that "on either side equally great heaps of dead were to be seen."[106] Such was the intensity of the fighting that having again separated in the failing light, mutual consent gave the following day over to rest, treatment of the wounded and reformation. Indeed, so great was the slaughter that the head of Bezabde's Christian community was given permission to journey to the Persian camp, where he pleaded with Shapur to withdraw, claiming that all that could be gained from continued fighting was mutual slaughter. Such pleas fell on deaf ears with Shapur swearing that he would not retreat until the fortress was in his power. This bishop would later come under suspicion of having given Shapur intelligence of where the walls of Bezabde were weak, but despite being no friend to Christians, Ammianus claims that these accusations were unfounded.[107] The only evidence against the bishop would appear to be that, not long after his meeting with Shapur, the Persians turned their attention to the weaker section of the Bezabde walls.

The Roman garrison continued to fight ferociously, showering the attackers with missiles, fire and pitch but through this hail of death, the Sassanids manoeuvred a huge ram to the walls. Much like at Singara – it could even have been the same ram – this mighty machine breached the walls of a tower, and its subsequent collapse saw many defenders and attackers "dashed to pieces or buried".[108] The Persians charged into the gap and amidst vicious hand to hand fighting superior numbers told. Roman resistance crumbled into a battle for survival as "the swords of the infuriated enemy cut down all that they could find, children were torn from their mother's breasts, and the mother themselves were butchered."[109] This Persian bloodlust was quickly overtaken by a want of plunder and soon "laden with spoils of every sort, and leading off a great throng of captives, they returned to their tents."[110]

There may have been another reason from the staying of a bloody Persian sack in favour of pragmatic plunder. Rather than see Bezabde left in a smoking ruin, Shapur wanted to occupy the fortress and installed a garrison force of his own there to reinforce his control of the Middle Tigris and the Zabdiceni tribes, who had sided with the Romans. He then spent time repairing the fortress he had just destroyed and collecting together large amounts of supplies for the men he had chosen to establish there. Bezabde would also have allowed Shapur easy access across the Tigris and a staging point for further operations into Roman territory in the future.

Having completed this occupation of Bezabde, Shapur began to withdraw south towards his own territory. While the king's thoughts may have been turned towards winter, that did not stop him from continuing to undermine the Roman defensive positions along the Tigris by attacking several smaller strongholds before approaching the ancient fortress at Birtha, usually recognised as modern Tikrit in Iraq, thought to have been built by Alexander the Great.[111] This identification of the fortress called Virta by Ammianus has not been universally accepted as being the Birtha built by Alexander and can have a significant impact on the direction of Shapur's campaign in 360 post-Bezabde. The suggestion is that instead of retiring south, Shapur drove west to another fortress called Birtha on the west bank of the Euphrates, modern Birecik in the Sanliurfa province of Turkey.[112] Such a move would have been almost suicidal. Not only was it marching a considerable distance from safe territory, it would have put the Persian column within the reach of Constantius' forces near Antioch, whilst putting the Roman garrisons at Edessa and Nisibis in a position to cut any line of retreat, a line already hindered by the Euphrates. However, that such a move cannot be discounted demonstrates the lack of clear information, even from Ammianus, about the direction and timing of Shapur's actions following his capture of Bezabde.

Whichever Birtha the Persian army approached, Ammianus gives the impression of a formidable fortress that sounds almost modern with its use of "walls built zigzag with salients and re-entrants"[113] and other devices to make the approach to the city difficult. Despite the size and strength of this obstacle, buoyed by his successes at Amida, Singara and Bezabde, Shapur settled in for another siege. However, this time the combination of promises, threats, manpower, siege engines, embankments and a hail of missiles failed to make sufficient inroads against the fortifications and whatever garrison forces were protecting them. After suffering significant losses, Shapur raised the siege and returned back to his own territory.

While he might have failed to reduce Birtha, Shapur could look on his latest invasion of Roman Mesopotamia with satisfaction. He had captured several Roman fortresses, including one that had eluded him in the past and another that allowed him to solidify his control of the Middle Tigris; all without exposing his forces to the kind of extended deployment that had unfolded at Amida or a dangerous battle against the combined Roman forces at Antioch, Edessa and Nisibis. However, the time of the Persian king having such free rein to march across Roman Mesopotamia would seem to be at an end for by September 360, Constantius and his long-absent field army had arrived at Edessa. The stage looked set for another showdown between the Roman *Augustus* and the Sassanid *shahanshah* in Mesopotamia, but this was not to be. Constantius had arrived in the east with news ringing in his ears of yet another challenge to his authority: Julian had been proclaimed *Augustus* by his troops.

Chapter X

The Usurpation of Julian: Ungrateful Brat or Left No Choice?

Poverty is the parent of revolution and crime.

– Aristotle, *Politics* II.6

The Cracks Appear

While Constantius met the news of Julian's revolt with "an immoderate blaze of anger",[1] it can hardly be said to have been a bolt from the blue. Ammianus' presentation of an organised plot by Constantius and his court to undermine Julian through spies, slander and a lack of cooperation might be going a little too far, but there was a gradual deterioration in relations between *Augustus* and *Caesar* throughout the latter's time in Gaul. Julian must have rankled under the dual nature of his position and the east/west split in his treatment. Constantius had made it clear that he was to be regarded as a figurehead imperial presence but in the intervening years, Julian had so established himself with his army that he was now treated with the deference that a *Caesar* should command in the west. However, when dealing with appointees from Constantius or anyone who thought that they could achieve a reward from the emperor or his cronies, Julian was treated as being far below that imperial station. Barbatio and Florentius acted like they had imperial authorisation to dictate to or even ignore the *Caesar*. They may even have had it.[2]

The record of service to Julian by several of these officials does little to dispel such rumours. While Severus had been an able ally, Marcellus had proven himself a liability; Barbatio had proven to be less than useful despite having 25,000 men under his command; Florentius had been obstructive in Julian's attempts to lessen the Gallic tax burden and pay the troops; and the *Caesar* harboured suspicions about the loyalties of Lupicinus. Meanwhile, at court, the military and eunuch cabals of Arbitio and Eusebius sullied Julian's reputation at every opportunity downplaying his successes and mocking the frequency of his reports, suggesting that they approached the point of exaggerated boastfulness despite the lack of noteworthy victories, which Strasbourg was not counted as.

This lack of recognition and reward will have irked not just Julian but also his soldiers. Lest it be forgotten, Julian's men had tried to proclaim him *Augustus* at Strasbourg. While this may just be ecstatic soldiers showing their love for the man who had led them to victory against barbarians who had ravaged their homes for years, it could also be evidence that there was continuing mistrust and anger towards the central government of Constantius over lack of pay, over-taxation and general abandonment. After all, Gallic forces had supported two rebels against the Constantinian family during the 350s and the harsh punishment meted out in the form of Paul the Chain further stoked the flames of opposition to Constantius rather than quenching them.[3]

The deterioration in imperial relations was not just due to military and political factors as there is a suggestion of a private and altogether sinister dimension. At some stage, Julian's wife Helena travelled to Rome, probably for the celebration of Constantius' *vicennalia* in 357; however, Ammianus paints this visit as a plot by Eusebia on account of the jealousy she felt for Helena and her current pregnancy given how the empress and Constantius had been unable to conceive. This jealousy reportedly went so deep as to see Eusebia encourage Helena to drink a rare potion that induced a miscarriage. And this was supposedly not the first time that the empress had dealt in such infanticide with the suggestion that Helena had already given birth to a boy during her time in Gaul only for him to not survive for more than a few days because Eusebia had bribed the midwife to cause the infant's demise by cutting the umbilical cord too short. At his most dramatic, Ammianus laments how "such great pains and so much thought were taken that this most valiant man might have no heir."[4]

Much doubt has been cast over such claims. Julian's son probably died due to being born prematurely and Helena could have miscarried naturally or perhaps through the rocky journey to Rome.[5] Also, while such plotting from Eusebia cannot be ruled out,[6] it would be contrary to her previous dealings with Julian where she defended him and even encouraged his promotion to *Caesar*. Indeed, Julian does not seem to have harboured any suspicions about the role of Eusebia in the repeated miscarriages of Helena and if he did, he did not record them in his writings. Why then, if there is little or no evidence of such infanticidal plotting, did Ammianus conjure up such accusations? The historian may be defending his Julianic hero from the same charges of divine ill-favour that had been levied at Constantius and Eusebia for their lack of an heir. Without the plotting of an evil emperor and his wife, Helena's miscarriages and infant deaths look like the judgement of the gods. Where Ammianus portrayed the hand of a jealous empress, it was likely the cruel hand of Fate.

In this air of rumour, mistrust and mockery, the real catalyst for the final falling out between the imperial cousins was another instance of Constantius flexing his imperial prerogative. While his celebrating of Julian's victories as his own had little direct effect on those in the Gallic field army, despite how Ammianus would have it, Constantius' next move, while again within his rights, was to cause disquiet amongst the soldiery. As the emperor was gathering up his forces for the march east and receiving word about the loss of the Amida garrison and the size of Shapur's forces, it became obvious that he would require more men. As he was being assailed by reports regarding the successful exploits of Julian, reducing Franks and Alamanni to "tributaries and tax-payers",[7] it will have occurred to the emperor that he could requisition some of Julian's men seeing as how the Rhine frontier had been shut down. Therefore, Constantius sent a *tribunus et notarius* called Decentius with orders for Julian to send his *Heruli, Batavi, Celtae* and *Petulantes auxilia* units along with 300 picked men from every other unit of the Gallic field army under the command of Lupicinus. Taking his army at Strasbourg as something of a template, Constantius was demanding the transfer of a minimum of 7,500 men.[8]

To the biased eye of Ammianus, this removal of forces from the command of Julian was the cynical act of a jealous emperor stung by the growing popularity of his *Caesar* and therefore weakening his military position as prelude to removing him as he had done with Gallus.[9] However, looking at this transfer from a more measured point of view, not only was the emperor well within his rights to demand the transfer of what were his troops, if Julian had been as successful as he presented himself as being then his need of the troops was far less than that of Constantius. It is possible that the emperor did have an additional motive to just bolstering his forces. Part of the idea may have been to lure Julian into exposing himself either as an exaggerator of the extent of his victories or as planning to improve his position through force. Simply put, Constantius may have been trying to ascertain how far he could trust his *Caesar.*

Oblivious Bystander, Ultimate Opportunist or Master Manipulator?

Acting out of loyalty or self-preservation, Julian acquiesced to Constantius' order,[10] although he could not fulfil it immediately as Lupicinus was still in Britain, along with the *Heruli, Batavi* and the *Moesiaci* legions. The commander of the imperial stables, Sintula, was tasked with picking the best men from the *Scutarii* and the *Gentiles* and leading them east.[11] Julian was irked by having to give up such a substantial part of his already small field army. Not only would it leave him undermanned in defending his Gallic and British territories, forcing these men to go east went against one of the main tenets of Julian's agreement with many of them when they enlisted: that they would not have to serve beyond the Alps.[12] The *Caesar* contended that forcing these men east would make Rome look dishonest, could incite anger and undermine future recruiting prospects among the Gauls and Germans. Such pleas fell on deaf ears and Sintula was soon underway with the first batch of picked forces.

Julian felt that fulfilling the rest of the imperial transfer order risked undermining the military position he and his men had worked so hard to rebuild in the previous four years. But on the other hand, not sending the troops was liable to incur the wrath of Constantius, and while Julian claimed that he would rather lay down his imperial title and face that wrath than allow Gaul to fall into ruin once more, it was still an unenviable position to be in.[13] Worried that whatever choice he made would be wrong, Julian turned to his praetorian prefect. Given the already poor relations between the two, it would seem unlikely that the *Caesar* wanted the advice of Florentius but instead, perhaps similarly to Constantius, he was testing his loyalty. If so, it was a test that Florentius failed. The prefect left winter quarters at Paris for Vienne, ostensibly to oversee the gathering of supplies but really he had removed himself from Julian's camp out for fear of personal attack as it had been Florentius who had suggested to Constantius that he remove the elite units from Gaul.[14] When Julian sent word for him to return to Paris, Florentius ignored the summons.[15]

Left with few options and recognising that he could not trust those around him and perhaps under pressure from Constantius' agents,[16] Julian made preparations for the transfer of *Celtae* and *Petulantes*, calling them from their winter quarters. When word of the reason for this call circulated, one of the *Petulantes* displayed a letter that contained the thoughts of those afflicted by this imperial transfer:

> We are to be driven to the ends of the earth like condemned criminals while our nearest and dearest, whom we have set free from their previous captivity after desperate fighting, again became the slaves of the Alamanni.[17]

Upon hearing of these complaints, Julian displayed understanding of their plight but in the end still ordered them to start out for the east, although he did put the wagons of the Roman public transport service, the *clavularis cursus*, at their disposal so they could bring their families.[18]

These men then travelled past Paris, where Julian encouraged them to do their duty and earn great rewards from Constantius with their continued good service. The *Caesar* went as far as to invite several of the leading men from the force to join him for dinner. Wined and dined, and likely well into their cups, these leaders returned to their camp and discussed matters with their fellow soldiers. Then, in the middle of the night, these men rose in revolt, saluting Julian as *Augustus*. The *Caesar* waited until morning to face them, possibly hoping that sobriety would breed calm, but when he appeared, the soldiers reiterated their proclamation. Julian made a show of resisting this clamour, demonstrating displeasure that these men seemed eager to tarnish their good military record by sparking a civil war but promising to put their case to Constantius if they should desist from this revolt.[19]

Despite this overt display of resistance to the idea of his elevation to *Augustus*, Julian's role in the whole affair appears suspicious. Constantius, his court and perhaps even an impartial observer may view the progression and timing of events that overtook Gaul in 359–360 as involving a few too many coincidences. The absences of Lupicinus and Florentius could draw accusations of opportunism or design. It is difficult to justify any suspicion that might fall on Julian for the absence of the latter due to the souring of their relationship over the previous two years and the prefect removing himself from the vicinity rather than being removed. However, Julian does seem to have been wary of the reaction of his *magister equitum*. While Lupicinus worked well with the *Caesar* during the 359 campaign and was "a warlike man… skilled in military affairs",[20] his character was not beyond reproach as he is recorded as being unsavoury and greedy. Coupled with the fact that he had been appointed by Constantius and had troops under his command, Lupicinus' character made Julian suspicious of how he would react to any such planned usurpation. At a stretch, the dispatch of Lupicinus to Britain could be seen as removing a potential opponent from the scene, although more likely Julian was reacting to the raids of the Scoti and Picts. That said, Julian did orchestrate the neutralisation of Lupicinus. A *notarius* was sent to Bononia to control traffic across the English Channel, preventing word reaching the *magister* of Julian's elevation and when this failed, Lupicinus was arrested when he set foot back in Gaul.[21]

However, it is Julian's involvement with the troops who were to elevate him and their movements that draws the most criticism and even accusations of orchestration. While it was not improper for Julian to meet his troops as they passed by or to even entertain its officers before they set off,[22] the question must be asked as to who the choice for these soldiers to march past the quarters of their beloved *Caesar* at Paris was made by. Both Ammianus and Julian record that it was the choice of Decentius against the advice of the *Caesar*,[23] but from such partial sources, this suggestion must be treated carefully. Even if he had nothing to do with the route these men took and was well within his rights to meet them, in demonstrating to these already disgruntled men that they were not only leaving their homes but also the service of a benevolent ruler for that of an unpopular emperor, who many of these soldiers will have waged war against alongside Magnentius, Julian was either naïve of the potential circumstances or intentionally manipulative.

Julian's failure to front up to the rebels in the dead of night is usually seen as an attempt to dull their enthusiasm and give them a chance to recant; however, it could be the opposite. By failing to address and dispel them as soon as possible, Julian may have helped encourage the soldiers by giving the impression that their act of high treason was not going to be punished. Even when he did face the soldiers, his promise to put their case to Constantius could be seen as disingenuous; an overt show of passing the blame onto the emperor and placing himself on the side of the disgruntled soldiers. Of course, it could just be that Julian underestimated the scale of the situation unfolding outside his palace window. Or he understood it all too well and was perhaps scared of the potential ramifications of his acceptance or rejection of the soldier's acclamation.

That there is such room for questioning the role of Julian in the events leading up to his elevation suggests that if the *Caesar* was in any way behind this elevation, he had played his cards in a masterful way. He had provided himself with plausible deniability; it appeared just as likely that he was taking advantage of the situation unfolding before him rather than guiding it or was an innocent bystander caught up in events he had nothing to do with rather than the master manipulator. Julian may even have viewed his rise to power as the will of the gods and therefore did not fight against it. Regardless of his involvement, Julian could be forgiven for allowing fear to get the better of him that night in the imperial palace as he had several examples of how Constantius dealt with those who aspired to his power, proven or otherwise, and as a learned man, he will have read of how disgruntled soldiers could treat even an emperor who stood in their way.

Even if he had nothing to do with the events of 359–360, the *Caesar* will have recognised that plausible deniability was not going to appease the imperial court. In the hands of individuals like Arbitio and Eusebius, Julian's orchestration of proceedings will have been all too easy to present: the absences of Lupicinus and Florentius; the lack of cooperation with Decentius and Sintula; the march past Paris; 'conspiring' with the officers over dinner; and his failure to punish the rebels were all cogs on the wheel of revolution, a traceable line of development in a "premeditated conspiracy".[24] Much like with Silvanus, whether Julian had orchestrated his elevation or not did not matter. What mattered was that prevalent members of the imperial court could make it seem like he had, playing on Constantius' wariness of usurpers. This spectre of imperial intervention may have forced Julian to see usurpation as the only alternative, even if he had not planned to do so.

Whether he meant it or not, Julian's plea for calm amongst the rebellious soldiers fell on deaf ears and perhaps just to keep the peace and save his own skin, he accepted his acclamation. The soldiers then proclaimed Julian as *Augustus* one more, placing him on an infantry shield, an action that demonstrates the origins of many of these men as it was "in the manner of proclamation of a Germanic chieftain".[25] Julian was then encouraged to produce his imperial diadem so he could be given an 'official' coronation; however, when Julian responded that he had not been given a diadem upon his investiture as *Caesar*, an alternative was sought. A necklace or head ornament belonging to Helena was rejected as being inauspicious, as was a horse-trapping. Becoming frustrated by this seeming reluctance, a standard bearer of the *Petulantes* called Maurus removed his own chain collar and placed it on Julian's head. Realising that he could not avoid the spectacle any longer or deciding that he had given enough of a deferential show of reluctance, Julian acquiesced and promised the soldiers an accession donative of five gold *aurei* and a pound of silver per man.[26]

It would be remiss to ignore the possibility of another cause behind the impatience of these soldiers: money. As mentioned earlier, with the failure of Diocletian's reforms to arrest the collapse of the silver coinage through price fixing, military pay had come to rely on the donatives that accompanied imperial accessions, birthdays and anniversaries. Financial need would add an extra level of understanding to the frustrations and impatience of the *Petulantes* in the face of Julian's stalling and their willingness to elevate him to *Augustus*, knowing that he would be obliged to pay them more money.

Despite having accepted his elevation, Julian appeared far from happy with the situation or at least that is how Ammianus presents it. The newly acclaimed *Augustus* withdrew from public view and neglected even the most pressing of matters, out of fear for his future. Maybe Julian was only now realising the burden that had fallen upon him and the potential danger to him from the agents and armies of Constantius, that great victor over rebels. Maybe he was trying to figure out where he would get the cash for the donative? Or maybe he was just collecting himself and planning his next moves. Whatever the reason, this self-imposed seclusion almost saw the situation devolve into further chaos.

Concerned about the lack of an appearance from Julian, a *decurion* from the imperial palace ran to the camp of the *Celtae* and *Petulantes* crying out that the newly crowned emperor had been slain. It is perhaps a testament to the reputation of Constantius that this *decurion* would jump to the conclusion of assassination without proof. This roused the soldiers into a tumult and with their weapons drawn, they charged the imperial palace, forced their way in and scared off many of Julian's bodyguard and retinue, who would have received blame for the supposed assassination. They then refused to leave until they were given direct access to Julian.[27]

The throng of agitated soldiers and palpable tension was increased by the return of those *Scutarii* and *Gentiles* who had departed east under Sintula. News of Julian's elevation had reached them and they returned to Paris to make common cause with their beloved commander. In the midst of the tense setting, a proclamation was issued that all should congregate in an open plain of the city the following morning. At the allotted time, Julian appeared, bedecked in all the imperial finery, surrounded by military standards and banners and looking every bit the *Augustus* that the soldiers had demanded of him. However, Julian had not dropped his guard as cohorts of armed men separated him from those arrayed before him, in case the situation turned ugly.

Julian again praised the bravery of his men for protecting him and the Roman state, invoking their great victory at Strasbourg, and urged them to continue on with such valour in the coming months and years. In return for such continued protection and good service, the emperor promised them reward on the basis of merit rather than the self-perpetrating, self-interested bureaucracy that had been allowed to fester in the imperial court.[28] Unsurprisingly, the thought of being rewarded for their deeds rather than their position appealed to the congregated soldiery and they responded with rapturous cheers. After the dithering and hand-wringing of the previous few days, this was a complete change of tact from Julian. In drawing such a distinction between what was perceived as the corruption of the imperial court and how he claimed he would rule, Julian was laying the foundations for a complete break with Constantius and civil war.

Julian also told his close friends of a dream he had had before his proclamation as *Augustus*, which featured the guardian spirit of the state telling him that it was behind his elevation. This might hint at Julian beginning to acknowledge his paganism but it could also demonstrate that he knew the potential power of such oneiromancy, shown by Constantine on the eve of Milvian Bridge in 312. As a member of the imperial family and having had a consummate education, Julian will have been in a position to recognise the impact that this dream had had not just on the battle but also on the religious direction of the empire. Perhaps Julian was hoping for a similar impact in any fighting that was to follow.

Imperial Correspondence

Despite knowing that Constantius would never accept his proclamation as *Augustus*, Julian sent envoys to the imperial court to inform the emperor of what had happened at Paris,[29] although he suspected that Constantius' spies will have already made sure that his proclamation was known about. In his letter, Julian recalled how he had remained loyal throughout his time as *Caesar*, reporting to Constantius on a regular basis and refusing to seek personal glory for the good of the empire. He remarked on how the failure to pay and reward the soldiers had sparked discontent, his horror at how this turned to rebellion when they were forced to leave home and his own failure at preventing it. He then claimed that he accepted his proclamation to prevent a bloody civil war as the soldiers had threatened to acclaim someone else in his place. Julian then demonstrated his willingness to remain the junior partner by agreeing to send troops east and to accept Constantius' appointment as praetorian prefect as was his right as senior *Augustus*. However, Julian also showed his intention to retain his elevated rank as he claimed the right to appoint his own officials and refused to raise any more troops to send against the Persians "since the onsets of the barbarians are not yet checked and... these provinces which have been vexed with constant calamities need aid themselves from without".[30]

As well as this letter for public consumption, it is reported that Julian sent a second more personal letter for Constantius alone. Its exact contents are not recorded but as Ammianus suggests it was "written in a more reproachful and bitter tone",[31] it is easy to imagine Julian pointing out how he had been given a job to do in Gaul and despite the lack of support and even overt opposition from members of Constantius' court and military hierarchy, he had succeeded. Alamannic and Frankish tribes had been cleared from Gaul and forced back into a pro-Roman alliance, the Gallic tax base was being nursed back to health and Britain had been saved from raiders, yet he was still viewed with a mix of suspicion and ridicule. Julian may also have written with an air of "I told you so" when it came to the transfer of the Gallic forces to the east. He had warned the emperor about how poorly these men would receive the overturning of a major part of their agreement to enlist when combined with the failure to pay them and the lack of recognition for their achievements.

To deliver these letters, Julian chose Pendatius and Eutherius, the former his *magister officiorum* and the latter his head chamberlain. Along with the written reports, these two were to reiterate verbally the events in Gaul leading up to Julian's proclamation. The need for such respected envoys was made all the more imperative by the flight of Florentius to the court of Constantius, where he would be expected to portray Julian as a traitor. It was therefore vital for Pendatius and Eutherius to arrive before Constantius was whipped up into a rage by a mixture of reports, rumour and exaggeration. However, they were delayed as they advanced across Italy and Illyricum so that by the time they reached Constantinople, Constantius had already departed for the eastern provinces. They did not catch up to the emperor until Cappadocian Caesarea, modern Kayseri in central Turkey. Upon reading the letters, Constantius erupted into a rage and dismissed the envoys without questioning them.

In a move that might seem somewhat surprising for an emperor who was renowned for his success in and even pathological hatred of civil conflict, Constantius chose not to march against Julian immediately. Of course, such a suggestion would be buying into all the negative propaganda recorded about the emperor. First and foremost, Constantius was a pragmatic commander and he was not going to make such an important military decision based on his own fury at the betrayal of a family member. Instead, he will have reviewed all the evidence before him, weighing up the threat of Shapur against the threat of Julian. Constantius had the clear evidence of what the Persian king was capable of with the recurrent warfare on the eastern frontier since the death of Constantine, the Persian capture and sack of major Roman settlements and even his own personal experiences of battle against the King of Kings, while the threat from Julian was a lot less clear cut. On the surface, it seems rather straightforward: the emperor was faced with a general who had taken a battered and demoralised Gallic field army and turned it into a loyal fighting force that had defeated those barbarians who had been sweeping across Gaul throughout the last two decades with the bare minimum of resources and time. However, repeated ridicule from the imperial court may have seen Constantius question just how much stock he could put in Julian's success as a military commander. The emperor also needed to judge how far he could trust Julian's word that he remained a faithful servant of Constantius despite his assumption of the title of *Augustus*.

On weighing up these two threats, Constantius followed the same instinct that had led him not to confront Vetranio and Magnentius before he had secured the eastern frontier a decade previously; the frontier security of the Empire took precedence. The threat of the Sassanid king was more immediate and more potentially damaging than that of a claimant to the imperial title. Constantius therefore continued his advance towards Syria and Mesopotamia where he planned to at least take the sting out of Shapur's invasions or even reverse Persian conquests before returning west to deal with any conflict that was to break out with the latest usurper. That is not to say that he was going to ignore Julian and his transgressions. In response to Pendatius and Eutherius, the emperor dispatched a *quaestor* called Leonas to Gaul to deliver a letter of his own to Julian, in which Constantius rejected his assumption of the title of *Augustus* and threatened Julian with execution should he fail to return to the rank of *Caesar*. To further demonstrate his continued superiority, Constantius then ordered the promotion of Julian's *quaestor*, Nebridius, to succeed Florentius as praetorian prefect and that of the *notarius* Felix to *magister officiorum*, a position that Julian had given to Pendatius.

When Leonas arrived in Paris, he was treated with honour, as he should being a messenger bearing the word of the emperor. However, Julian then displayed some of the skills in stage management that taint his earlier claims to have had nothing to do with his elevation. Instead of meeting Leonas immediately and in private, Julian waited until the following day when Constantius' letter could be presented to him and read before a public congregation of his supporters. Constantius' rebuke and demand that Julian return to the rank of *Caesar* was met with a vicious roar of disapproval and "on all sides terrifying shouts arose: *Julianus Augustus!*"[32] With this sight and sound reverberating in his mind, Leonas returned east with another letter from Julian: he would accept the appointment of Nebridius as praetorian prefect as that was Constantius' prerogative, but he refused to accept Felix as *magister officiorum* as he had already appointed his own man to that position.[33]

After the departure of Leonas, Julian was careful not to remain idle. The support of the soldiery and people of Gaul could ebb away to be replaced by increasing restlessness through inaction in the face of a civil conflict against a feared and hated emperor. To that end, Julian called his army together and marched it towards the city of Tricensima along the Lower Rhine.[34] From there, Julian then crossed the river into the territory of the Atthuarian Franks, a people not dissuaded from raiding Roman territory by Julian's victories, so confident were they that the surrounding terrain kept them safe from reprisals. It must have come as quite a shock when they found an elite Roman army headed by a young, confident emperor storming through their lands; so shocking that resistance was easily brushed aside. The remaining Atthuarians flocked to throw themselves on the mercy of the victorious Julian, begging to be allowed to live in peace. This he granted, likely on similar terms to those that he had given to the other surrendering tribes: return prisoners of war and contribute manpower and resources to the rebuilding of the Rhine defences.[35]

And it was to these Rhine defences that Julian then turned his attention, travelling upriver towards Augst and then on to Vienne via Vescontio to establish his quarters for the winter of 360–361. That there is little mention of further fighting during what was a long trek from Tricensima to Augst – over 600km – could be a testament to the degree to which Julian had temporarily subdued the tribes on the east bank of the river. However, that he would choose now to march the length of the Rhine inspecting and refortifying that frontier and serving up a subject lesson to troublemakers before moving south to Vienne shows that he was preparing it for the absence of himself and the Gallic field army. It would seem that for all of his professions of continued subservience to Constantius, Julian already had some idea of where fate would take him and his army in 361.

Chapter XI

War Within and Without: Constantius' Final Year

Deep are the wounds that civil strife inflicts

– Lucan, *Belli Civilis* I.32

Constantius in the East: The Second Siege of Bezabde

While Julian was settling into his usurped role as *Augustus* and Shapur was reducing the Roman strongholds along the Tigris, Constantius had arrived in the eastern theatre and was quick to involve himself in military affairs. Even before moving on from Caesarea, a second embassy arrived from Arsaces, king of Armenia, summoned by the emperor so he could garner assurances that he would remain Rome's ally against the Sassanids. Arsaces admitted that Shapur had tried to threaten, cajole and bribe him away from his pro-Roman alliance; reports of such Persian overtures may have encouraged Constantius to call this meeting in the first place. Should Shapur gain a foothold in Armenia, it would put the Roman positions in Syria and Mesopotamia under greater pressure, open Anatolia to Persian raids and deprive the Romans of vital Armenian manpower.

Wary of the emperor's reputation, Arsaces was quick to offer oaths that he would rather die than go back on his Roman allegiance. In practical terms, the Armenian king recognised that switching sides would have seen him caught between two opposing armies with no help coming from either. With more than a century of enmity between the Arsacid and Sassanid dynasties, he could not rely on reasonable treatment from Shapur, whilst turning his back on Constantius would incur the wrath of an emperor. Therefore, by remaining a Roman ally, Arsaces was not only following over one hundred years of Armenian policy, he was taking a pragmatic approach to what was a difficult position.[1] Reassured of the Armenian king's support, Constantius resumed his advance through Melitene, Lacotena and Samosata before crossing the Euphrates and entering Edessa.[2]

While he brought a significant force with him from Sirmium, Constantius will not have denuded the Danube garrisons due to the continued upheavals and rumblings from Julian about the requisition of Gallic forces. Therefore, the emperor ordered large amounts of equipment and supplies to be prepared for the upcoming campaign and undertook a large recruitment drive to bolster his army and to replace the losses already suffered in Mesopotamia. Not only did the emperor recruit vigorous young men from within the empire and transfer men from other sections of its army, he also demanded auxiliaries from the Danubian tribes "either for pay or as a favour".[3] These new recruits and reinforcements were likely directed to join the emperor at Edessa where he remained throughout the summer of 360.

Why Constantius was so inactive during the height of the campaigning season can only be hinted at. The combination of his personal forces and those under Sabinianus presented him with an army capable of making a demonstration of its presence not just to Shapur but also to the Roman and allied populaces of the east. The size of Shapur's army will have discouraged Constantius from open battle until he felt he could bring his full might to bear against the Persians: but this saw Singara, Bezabde and several other towns and forts left to the same fate as Amida. Regardless of its strategic and tactical benefits, it is easy to see how such military passivity would be badly received as Roman civilians and soldiers resisted the Persians. If whispers of dismay were in the air during the summer of 360, they did nothing to sway the emperor from his preparations and it was not until after the autumnal equinox that Constantius set out from Edessa for the ruins of Amida. When he set eyes on the sorry wreck of what had been one of Rome's foremost eastern garrisons, hand picked and developed by the emperor himself, Constantius is said to have wept at the suffering of its defenders during those seventy-three days. This was where Ursulus gave his tactless opinion on what the ruins of Amida represented;[4] Constantius did not punish this sarcastic rebuke but some of those present to hear or heard of it did not forget.

Having surveyed the destruction, perhaps setting in motion the rebuilding of Amida and stirred to take the fight to the destroyers of the city, Constantius led his army towards the nearest concentration of Persian troops: the garrison at Bezabde. The Romans surrounded the fortress with a palisade and trenches before, demonstrating a similar attention to detail as Shapur, the emperor rode around the fort to discover first hand the condition of the walls. What he found cannot have filled him with much confidence as those sections that had proven vulnerable to the Persian battering rams due to "age and neglect had been restored to greater strength than ever".[5] This in itself was not an insurmountable obstacle as the Romans had sufficient skill in siege warfare but the time and manpower required to reduce such a well-defended position were against Constantius. Therefore, the emperor turned to diplomacy, sending an embassy to offer terms to the garrison, including safe passage back to their homelands if they surrendered and even offering them "honours and rewards"[6] if they were to defect. However, as Shapur had garrisoned Bezabde with some of his best and most loyal troops, such offers fell on deaf ears, leaving Constantius no option but to settle in for a siege.

The blasting of trumpets saw the legions march forward arrayed in *testudo* formation. Upon reaching the walls, the men within the formations attempted to undermine the fortifications but the shower of missiles from the defenders was so ferocious that it broke through the interconnected shields of the *testudo* and forced the legions to retreat. After a day spent recuperating, which in itself seems to highlight how brutal that first day of fighting had been, the Romans attacked with scaling ladders. The Sassanid garrison again attempted to repel this attack with a missile barrage but the Romans were better protected with wicker screens, allowing them to reach the walls unharmed. However, the Persians were prepared for this as they bombarded the attackers with increasingly large missiles, including millstones and sections of stone column. Against such heavy fire, wicker proved ineffectual and the Romans were again forced to retreat before they made any impression on the walls.

Either this kind of fighting prevailed for the best part of a week and goes unrecorded by Ammianus or there was a lull in the action for it was not until the tenth day that the story resumes. By then, the lack of progress was causing consternation within the Roman ranks and it led Constantius to order the bringing up of a huge battering ram. This was not just some normal oversized ram though; it was over a century old, of Persian construction and had been used by the Sassanids to capture Antioch during the 250s. It had been left at Carrhae where the Romans took possession of it when they reclaimed the city.[7] The importance of the ram lay not just in its size but also in the ingenuity of its design as it could be easily dismantled for transport and quickly rebuilt.[8] The sight of this infernal machine unnerved the Persian defenders, perhaps because some of them remembered how Bezabde had fallen to Shapur. However, they were quick to pull themselves together and set about devising counter-measures. As the Romans were constructing the behemoth and building earthworks, the mutual missile exchange continued to cause a steady drip of casualties to both sides.[9]

Once the great ram was ready, with several smaller rams in support, it was moved up to the walls. The Persians put in a mammoth effort to set it alight with a hail of fire arrows and darts but the Romans had been careful to fireproof their rams with damp hides and rags and flame retardant alum. Thus thwarted, the Sassanid defenders turned to other ways of disabling the great ram. Perhaps using some inside knowledge of the Persian-built ram, they targeted its mechanisms throwing a "subtle device",[10] which may have been as simple as a large net suspended from ropes, over the ram's head. There it got tangled and prevented the ram from being drawn back far enough to build the necessary momentum to damage the walls. This neutralising of the great ram allowed the defenders to focus on the smaller rams and those Romans trying to untangle the great ram, with the missile barrage supplemented by boiling pitch poured down from the battlements. With the attack stalled but not halted, the Persian garrison resorted to a sally against the Roman vanguard, only to be beaten back.[11]

The focus of the siege now switched to the Roman earthworks and the mounds that the Persians had piled up in reply. While the defenders prevented the firing of the wooden supports of their mounds, their position became desperate as the earthworks would soon allow the Romans to bring their numerical superiority to bear. To that end, they resorted to another sally, aimed at firing not just the Roman siege engines and earthworks but also the packed ranks of infantry and their wicker screens. Such was the smoke produced by these numerous fires that the Romans had to rely on their trumpets to know where the enemy was coming from. In the process of this struggle, the Romans finally extricated the giant ram by cutting the ropes holding it in place before the Persian fire-starters could destroy it, although this Persian sally did destroy many of the other Roman machines.

Darkness brought an end to the fighting, although neither side got much rest as the Romans redeployed their forces. Their few remaining siege engines were removed from the range of the Persian archers and artillery while two *ballistae* were placed on top of the earthworks, which having now been completed, overlooked the walls of Bezabde. The plan for the next Roman assault assumed that these towering artillery positions would force the Persians to take cover, allowing for an unhindered attack on the walls. While the presence of the *ballistae* did see the Romans move their scaling ladders and the great ram towards the walls largely unmolested, the defenders did not hide and await the inevitable. Instead, they launched yet another sally through a postern gate to distract the Roman infantry while an incendiary force again went after the remaining siege engines. These fire-starters, "stooping low and creeping along, pushed live coals into the joints of one of the mounds [which]... burst into flames".[12] While not dealing major casualties to the attackers, this combination of postern feint and fiery onslaught forced many of the Romans to focus on saving their remaining siege engines rather than scaling the walls.

With the failure of his forces to capture Bezabde, Constantius contemplated a withdrawal from the siege, perhaps in order to drive further into Mesopotamia and re-establish a Roman presence. However, the lateness of the season and the prestige that was now tied up in the siege, as well as the strategic position of Bezabde itself, caused the emperor to stay the course. The stubbornness and ingenuity of the garrison encouraged Constantius to change tact and focus more on a blockade than a renewed assault, relying on his superior numbers and supply lines to starve the Persians into submission. Unfortunately for the Romans, the weather intervened. Heavy rain turned the ground around Bezabde into a quagmire, while lightning provided further potential danger. Such terrible weather caused awful living conditions in the Roman camp and on top of the failure to take Bezabde led Constantius to lift the siege out of fear of mutiny and disease. Leaving the Bezabde garrison bruised but unbroken, the Romans marched back to Syria through Hierapolis to winter in Antioch, resting up for a more concerted effort in the campaigning season in 361. However, various circumstances would ensure that those plans would not come to fruition. In particular, events in the west were escalating.[13]

Preparations and Outbreak

While his move to Vienne for the winter of 360/361 suggests that Julian had an inkling of where his continued claim of the title of *Augustus* would lead him, the question could still be asked as to what his next move was going to be. Despite his successes, Julian must have wanted to avoid a military confrontation for, cutting through all of the Ammian propaganda, Constantius' military record was impressive and his ruthless cunning made him even more dangerous. On top of that, Constantius commanded the lion's share of the Roman army. Julian will also have known that continued attempts to persuade Constantius to accept his elevation were to fall on deaf ears. The example of Vetranio may have highlighted that Constantius was not beyond negotiation, but there were far more, less encouraging examples of how the emperor dealt with those who threatened his position: Magnentius, Decentius, Silvanus, Gallus and an entire branch of his family tree had all met with oblivion by getting in Constantius' way and if history was anything to go by, he would soon be coming to add Julian to that list.

This left Julian in an unenviable position. Direct confrontation was unlikely to go in his favour and neither was sitting waiting in Gaul. There was, however, one other option. The distraction of the Persian king provided Julian with a military opportunity – a rapid strike into Constantius' western territories. Such a risky strategy was likely the reason behind Julian moving from his more established base at Paris to Vienne. His celebration of his fifth anniversary of imperial authority with quinquennial games bedecked in "a magnificent diadem, set with gleaming gems"[14] would also suggest that he was making some preparations for war by playing up to his role as *Augustus* and giving the troops a boost in morale due to the donative that would have accompanied such a celebration.

Julian's religious beliefs may also have emboldened him as his skills in divining the future through dreams and other signs told him that Constantius would soon be dead, although this smacks of reporting with the benefit of hindsight with Ammianus using it to elevate Julian further in the eyes of his readers.[15] Despite his resorting to such pagan practices, Julian was still careful to give an outward showing of Christianity so as not to lose the support of the growing Christian community, which again could suggest that he was planning for a military strike of some kind.[16] Even Ammianus, who might be excused for trying to hide any warmongering on the part of his hero, suggests that whilst pleading continued allegiance to Constantius and a hopefulness of avoiding civil conflict, it had become obvious that as "Gaul was quieted, his desire of first attacking Constantius was sharpened and fired."[17] A collision course had been set.

Meanwhile, almost 2000 miles away, Constantius was making preparations of his own, although his target remained Shapur II. Much as he had done before going to war with Magnentius in 350, Constantius took the dynastic precaution of marrying, "having long since lost Eusebia",[18] possibly through complications from fertility treatments in her desperation to give Constantius an heir.[19] Despite rumours of her involvement in Helena's miscarriages, Eusebia's death may represent the loss of an important connection between Julian and Constantius as the empress was an ameliorating influence on the emperor and had been instrumental in protecting Julian in the aftermath of Gallus' downfall and in getting him appointed *Caesar*.[20] Of Eusebia's successor as *Augusta*, a woman called Faustina, very little is known before or after this loftiest of elevations. The most important thing about Faustina is that she was to give Constantius that which he had yearned for almost three decades: an heir. However, Fate was to be doubly cruel for not only would his heir be female, she, named Constantia, would be born posthumously.[21]

As well as this matrimonial arrangement, Constantius also made political arrangements. Florentius was appointed praetorian prefect of Illyricum and along with Taurus, the praetorian prefect of Italy, he was elevated to the consulship of 361. This might seem like Constantius was rewarding him for his loyalty in the face of what will now have been seen as the initial steps in Julian's usurpation, but it was also an orchestrated military move by the emperor as both these consular prefects were now the front line of defence against Julian. Constantius was putting men he could trust and who owed him their position in these prominent roles. The combination of a praefecture and a consulship will have gone a long way to ensuring that allegiance, plus having achieved the enmity of Julian, Florentius was unlikely to capitulate to the usurper.

Constantius also sent the *notarius* Gaudentius, who had already proven his worth in opposition to Julian, to Africa to secure the province. This was a prudent move as Africa provided much of the grain supply for the western provinces as well as a sizeable tax contribution from its large population. In moving to exert his authority over Africa, Constantius was demonstrating to his western supporters that he had not forgotten them and improving his strategic position whilst undermining that of Julian. Arriving in Africa Province, Gaudentius presented the *comes Africae*, Cretio, with a letter from Constantius. This imperial missive and the presence of Gaudentius secured the loyalty of not just the *comes* and the African garrison but also the Mauretanian provinces, which provided light-armed troops.[22] These African units formed a force that Cretio was to use to fend off any attempt by Julian to conquer this vital source of revenue and grain. It is suggested that a pro-Julian force later gathered along the southern coast of Sicily, ostensibly to defend the island and the Italian mainland from invasion but was also prepared to cross to Africa should the opportunity arise.[23] Constantius also made Helpidius of Paphlagonia his new eastern praetorian prefect in place of the recently deceased Hermogenes, although much like his predecessor, Helpidius proved to be ill-suited to the bloody business of high office under Constantius as he later offered his resignation rather than torture an innocent man.[24]

As with Julian, Constantius' preparations also involved some claims to divine backing. Whilst in Antioch, the emperor was confronted with a former tribune, Amphilochus of Paphlagonia, who was accused of sowing discord between Constantine II and Constans. Despite believing Amphilochus to be guilty, the emperor ordered that he be left unharmed as no court had yet found him guilty of any crime. However, supposedly the following day, at the games taking place in the Circus, a railing that Amphilochus was leaning against broke and he and several others fell some distance to the ground. Several sustained minor injuries but the former tribune was found to have died through severe internal injuries. Constantius rejoiced in what he declared to be a display of God's favour towards him in the punishing of someone who had wronged the imperial family. The cynic might suggest that agents of Constantius were either responsible for that 'accident' or in at least making sure that Amphilochus did not survive it rather than a mere coincidence or a divine punishment.[25]

On top of this political, spiritual and dynastic planning, Constantius continued to marshal large amounts of military equipment and reinforcements of various types: cavalry units, legionary reinforcements and provincial levies were all raised to supplement his existing forces. Clothing, weaponry, artillery pieces, siege engines, provisions and beasts of burden were also gathered in vast quantities. Fortunately for Constantius and the empire, the severity of the Mesopotamian winter that had hindered the recapturing of Bezabde had also seen Shapur retreat deep into his own territory, slowing his preparations for a return to Mesopotamia. This left Constantius with more time, which he used to send out numerous envoys to the petty kings and governors on both sides of the frontier to entice them with gifts to either remain loyal to Rome or to draw them away from their neutrality or allegiance to Shapur. The most important of these envoys were to Arsaces of Armenia and Meribanes, king of Iberia, as should either relinquish their Roman allegiance, the Roman defensive position in Mesopotamia could have been catastrophically undermined.[26]

With the pieces all in place in two separate theatres, it would seem a straightforward next step to open conflict, but the outbreak of war in 361 is clouded in some mystery. Depending on the point of view taken, the first shot in the civil war between Constantius and Julian was either the developments along the Upper Danube early in the year or in the propaganda manipulation that followed them. The root of this confusion was that Alamnnic troublemaker, Vadomarius, who chose now to raid Raetia. Julian dispatched the *Celtae* and *Petulantes* from their winter quarters under the *comes* Libino to intercept these raiders. Catching them near Sanctio, modern Bad Sackingen in the Baden–Württemburg state in Germany, Libino launched a reckless attack on the Alamanni, who had seemingly predicted the Roman response as they made some defensive preparations in the surrounding valleys. His rashness cost Libino his life at the very outset of the confrontation and the superior numbers of the Alamanni told in forcing the Romans to retreat.[27]

The difference in opinion comes in regard to who was the instigator of this renewed Alamanni raiding. Ammianus records the rumour that Vadomarius had been encouraged by Constantius, much like how the emperor had done to Magnentius, with the suggestion that Vadomarius would keep Julian occupied in Gaul to prevent him from taking advantage of Constantius' deployment in the east. Julian reportedly uncovered this imperial connivance through the capture of a secretary sent by Vadomarius to Constantius with intelligence on Julian, despite the Alaman professing continued loyalty to Julian.[28] The contrary opinion is that Julian or Ammianus used another Alamanni raid to construct a narrative, complete with secret messages and a barbarian leader with connections to Constantius, "to blacken the reputation of his absent colleague".[29]

Whatever the backdrop, the defeat of Libino demanded retaliation and further encouraged by their previous dealings, Julian targeted Vadomarius in the hope of preventing further raiding. To that end, he sent a trusted *notarius* called Philagrius, later *comes Orientis* under Theodosius, to conduct business in the area but furnished him with a letter that he was to open should he encounter Vadomarius in Roman territory. With no knowledge of Julian's plan and likely feeling safe if he had the backing of Constantius, Vadomarius crossed the river to converse with a local military commander, who invited the Alamanni chieftain to a banquet, at which Philagrius just so happened to be present. Upon coming face to face with Vadomarius, the *notarius* retrieved the letter and upon reading its contents had Vadomarius arrested by the local commander at the conclusion of the feast.

The barbarian leader was taken to Julian's camp, where he was confronted by his secretary and his letter to Constantius. He was therefore left with little choice but to accept his fate, although Vadomarius may have been surprised by the leniency extended to him. Instead of execution, the Alaman was exiled to Spain. If Julian still saw Vadomarius as a potential nuisance, why did he not execute him as a traitor? Julian might have seen him as the valuable military asset he would later become, although the real reasoning probably lies in using the threat of his execution or return to help keep Vadomarius' son and successor, Vithicabius, in line once the majority of the Gallic field army went east.[30] Julian was surprised by how quickly his plan with Philagrius achieved success but those Alamanni raiders responsible for the death of Libino still required a lesson to deter further raiding. Therefore, Julian mobilised a unit of his *auxilia* and stole across the Rhine in the dead of night. They then located and surrounded the killers of Libino and after a few were dispatched in their sleep, the remainder surrendered.

These successes against the Alamanni further emboldened Julian and highlighted to him the benefits of rapidity of action. Because it cannot be ruled out, it is also possible that Julian was angered by Constantius' use of Vadomarius to distract him. If it happened at all, such Constantian use of barbarians, both now and against Magnentius, will also have brought into sharp focus for Julian what kind of ruthless and resourceful opponent he faced; one who could affect things in Gaul despite being on the far side of the empire. He would have to take war to Constantius rather than await the inevitable.

Having gone through a series of pagan rites to gain good omens from the goddess of war, Julian called together his forces. Addressing them in flattering terms, he announced that they would march east and capture large parts of the Balkans in order to save the Roman state from a protracted and destructive internecine conflict.[31] Such a plea to the soldiers' loyalty and bravado had the desired effect as they took solemn oaths to follow Julian. Amongst this cacophony of support, there was but one detractor: the praetorian prefect, Nebridius. Professing before Julian that he could not enter into an oath to make war on the emperor who had been responsible for his promotion and had shown him kindness in the past, Nebridius risked the ire of the troops. However, when several rushed forward to slay the prefect, Julian covered Nebridius in a cloak in a demonstration that he was not to be harmed. During a later meeting in the imperial palace, Julian allowed Nebridius to depart without fear of reprisal as he respected the perfect's loyalty to the man responsible for his lofty position.[32]

This defection of Nebridius allowed Julian to appoint his own praetorian prefect for Gaul, although it is not quite clear who he appointed as two names are mentioned. Sallustius is recorded as being promoted to prefect and sent back to Gaul while a certain Germanianus was ordered to take the place of Nebridius. It is possible that the latter was made prefect in the interim before the former took up the role. The waters are further muddied by Germanianus succeeding Sallustius as prefect in 363.[33] Julian then "took his time to reorganise his economic and military high command",[34] promoting Nevitta to *magister equitum* in place of Gomoarius, who Julian suspected of disloyalty due to the persistent rumour that he had betrayed Vetranio. Another German, Dagalaif, was promoted to command Julian's *domestici* with Jovius becoming *quaestor* and Mamertinus *comes sacrarum largitionum*. While the latter two appear to be Roman, this promotion of non-Romans to high office by Julian – he would later allow Nevitta to assume the consulship of 363 – flies in the face of the scathing attacks he launched on both Constantine and Constantius for their recruiting, subsidising and promoting of non-Romans.[35]

Lightning Advance

With the forces of Gaul behind him and his affairs in order, Julian advanced east to a potentially messy civil war.[36] The willingness of these soldiers, who had refused to go east away from their families to serve at the behest of Constantius, to now march east under Julian so readily raises a few questions regarding the nature of Constantius' unpopularity in Gaul and whether or not Julian had taken advantage of it. However, even if they arouse suspicion, it is speculative to give these questions any real standing. These soldiers gave their loyalty to Julian, the man who had led them in battle for the past five years, rather than to Constantius, whose dealings with Gaul had been negative, and marching in support of their emperor in a civil war was far more financially beneficial than going to fight on the eastern frontier against a dangerous Persian king.

Wary of the attention his force would garner and hoping to outrun news of his advance while not putting pressure on local populations, Julian divided his army into three separate groups; Jovinus and Jovius went along the normal routes across Italy, Nevitta was to travel through Raetia, while Julian followed the Danube with a smaller force under his direct command. The plan was for these three groups to meet up at Sirmium,[37] which was not just an important military position in the Balkans; its capture would represent a propaganda coup with it being the birth place of Constantius.

Little information survives about the advances of Jovinus and Nevitta. While this might suggest that they were uneventful, such an argument from silence is dangerous. Constantian forces will have occupied some of the major cities in northern Italy, while Nevitta could have come across some barbarian raiders in Raetia. Julian did warn his men to be wary of Constantian loyalists, barbarian raiders and disgruntled locals, a warning that must have been extended to his commanders. Julian himself attempted to travel as quickly and as quietly as possible but despite traversing the Black Forest and the navigable section of the Danube, it was not a straightforward march. The column had to make do with the meagre rations they could carry with them as foraging was limited in order to restrict interaction with towns where word of Julian's march could spread.

Despite these attempts at covert movement, news of the advance leaking out was inevitable. While Taurus and Florentius withdrew at word of what appeared to be vast forces – a benefit of sending his forces along three separate routes – the *comes* Lucillianus, father-in-law of the future *Augustus*, Jovian,[38] collected together a force of two legions and a cohort of archers at Sirmium. Landing at Bononia, modern Banošter in northern Serbia, about nineteen miles from Sirmium, Julian received word of Lucillianus' preparations and "like a meteor or a blazing dart"[39] hastened towards his target. Once within striking distance, Julian dispatched Dagalaif with a small force to parley with Lucillianus. Rather than resorting to diplomacy and trust that the *comes* would come quietly to Julian, Dagalaif and his men stole into Lucillianus' abode while he slept and surrounded him. Faced with such an intrusion, the *comes* wisely accompanied them to Julian's camp, although not without protest. Brought before the usurper, Lucillianus refused to kowtow, displaying a bravado perhaps born of the belief that Julian would not execute him. He ridiculed Julian for the small number of men with which he had invaded another's territory, advice that the usurper cast aside with the sardonic retort that it was Constantius that would require such counsel.[40]

The neutralising of Lucillianus allowed Julian to move to Sirmium. Expecting to face some armed resistance from the *comes'* forces, Julian was surprised to find that no sooner had he reached the suburbs that he was welcomed warmly by the inhabitants and the soldiers, who delivered Sirmium to him without any resistance. After a brief celebration complete with chariot

races, Julian sent the Sirmium garrison to serve in Gaul and then retook
the field to join up with Nevitta. Together, they moved against another city
with Constantinian links, Naissus, although its importance lay beyond its
position as the birthplace of Constantine. Much as modern Nis does today,
Naissus controlled the main routes from central Europe to the Aegean and
Constantinople along the Nisava, Morava and Vardar rivers.[41] Perhaps even
more importantly, due to its proximity to the Danube frontier, Naissus was
the site of a large number of state arms factories, control of which would allow
Julian to re-arm his own men whilst depriving his enemies.

For a city of such importance, Julian and Nevitta occupied Naissus without
any resistance. Perhaps Constantius had removed a proportion of its troops
when he went east and Lucillianus had stripped it of its garrison to defend
Sirmium. Whatever the reason, after his rapid advance, Julian was now
within a few weeks' ride of his ultimate goal, Constantinople. However, it
was not a straightforward march for not only were there two considerable
mountain ranges – the Haemus and Rhodope – between him and the eastern
capital, there were also garrisoned fortresses at Philippopolis and Adrianople,
modern Plovdiv in Bulgaria and Edirne in European Turkey along the
route. Julian was in no way equipped to take on the fortified, mountainous
road to Constantinople even with the corps of Jovinus due to rejoin him at
Naissus.

Julian refused to be overawed, understanding that while the Haemus–
Rhodope chain provided a great barrier for him to overcome, it worked the same
for any Constantian forces marching against him. Therefore, demonstrating
his grasp of the strategic situation, Julian sent Nevitta to occupy the only
navigable route between the mountains: the pass of Succi, now the Ihtiman
Pass in Bulgaria. Controlling Succi gave Julian a strong defensive position
should he be faced with an attack from the east. By not advancing any further,
Julian was also playing a psychological game with Constantius, for Succi had
marked the boundary between the territory of Constans and Constantius
agreed at Sirmium in 337. Therefore, in the most technical of terms, albeit
superseded by Constantius' unification of the empire in 353, Julian could claim
that he had not invaded Constantius' territory, preserving his propagandist aim
of ruling alongside Constantius rather than in place of him.

Having seen to the occupation of Succi, Julian returned to Naissus for the
winter and set about applying the same financial and administrative reforms
that had been so successful in Gaul. Taxes were reduced and attempts were
made to make up the grain deficiency caused by Constantian control of
Africa and its grain fleet. To aid these reforms, a further raft of promotions
came, including the historian Sextus Aurelius Victor being made governor of

Pannonia Secunda and the elevation of his finance minister Mamertinus to prefect of Italy, Africa and Illyricum as well as consul designate.[42] A senator called Maximus was chosen as prefect of Rome over Symmachus, father of the celebrated writer of letters and promoter of paganism of same name, a choice that appears to be a favour to Maximus' uncle, Rufinus Vulcatius, who would later succeed Mamertinus as praetorian prefect.

As he settled into winter quarters at the end of 361, Julian could be forgiven for thinking that his decision to move against Constantius had been proven correct. He had claimed several major strongholds in Illyricum and had been well received by sections of the civilian population, while any potential opposition had melted away. However, such a positive appraisal obscures major missteps, in which he failed to comprehend some sensibilities or certain loyalties. From Naissus, he distributed a series of letters to Rome, Athens, Sparta, and Corinth, attempting to justify his revolt. The invective he aimed at Constantius and other members of the imperial family was poorly received. Instead of a justification for revolt, these criticisms were viewed as a massive, clumsy step away from the idea of co-operative rule that Julian had espoused up until now. Such blatant opportunism did not sit well with many, especially considering that the target of the vitriol was not only not present to defend himself but was busy fending off a foreign invader. In Rome, a city still glowing from the visit of Constantius in 357, the letters went a step beyond blatant opportunism. By attacking Constantine for being "the very first to advance barbarians even to the rods and robes of consuls",[43] Julian was painting himself as a complete hypocrite having himself made extensive use of barbarians and elevated Nevitta to the consulship. Outraged, the Roman Senate demanded that the usurper show reverence for his ancestors and for the man who had promoted him to imperial rank. In this one series of letters Julian squandered much of his political and propaganda capital.[44]

Julian also overestimated his ability to inspire loyalty in Lucillianus' men. Much like with how Julian's own men had rebelled at being ordered to serve on the far side of the empire, these soldiers were unhappy about being forced from their Balkan homelands to Gaul. Whipped into hysteria by Nigrinus, a Mesopotamian cavalry commander, the soldiers seized the formidable defences of the strategic and wealthy city of Aquileia and shut the gates. They were joined by the city populace, out of fear for Constantius and any retribution he might seek following his 'inevitable' victory. This revolt by the former garrison of Sirmium and the population of Aquileia encouraged other Italians, many of whom already held pro-Constantian views and were rankling under the shortage of grain, to side with the emperor against his ungrateful and rebellious cousin.

Upon hearing of Aquileia's revolt, Julian looked to prevent opposition spreading and to cajole the city and its garrison back into compliance. Aquileia presented Julian with something of a propaganda opportunity for despite having been besieged on many occasions, the city had never been stormed or forced to surrender. Should Julian succeed where so many others had failed, including a previous emperor during a civil war,[45] his military cause would be given a tremendous boost. Therefore, Julian sent word to Jovinus, who was crossing northern Italy, to take his corps to the walls of Aquileia. He also gave orders that any troops passing through Naissus be enrolled in his forces for the time being. As Jovinus approached Aquileia, he sized up the situation; his corps may have been up to 10,000 strong and outnumbered Nigrinus' 2,500 legionaries and archers but the vast Aquilean defences and a supportive civilian populace saw that disparity count for very little. This ruled out a direct assault, leaving Jovinus to begin the job of investing Aquileia in a blockade, hoping to starve the defenders out.

Despite its initial military successes, by the end of the campaigning season of 361, it appeared that Julian's usurpation had a limited shelf life. Fear of Constantius and his military record, epistolic faux pas and the Constantian blockade of Italy all combined to make the usurper unpopular. Militarily, the siege of Aquileia forced him to divide his already under-strength forces at a time when Constantius was expected to arrive at the head of Illyrian and eastern field forces. Indeed, news reached Julian that the Thracian army had been called from their winter quarters by the *comes* Martianus with the aim of challenging Nevitta at Succi, forcing Julian to call many of his own units and some of the Illyrian forces that had defected to him back into action. It appeared that the first bloodshed of the civil war between Constantius and Julian was about to take place. However, just when things were about to heat up, further news reached him from the eastern frontier that was to change everything.

The Death of Constantius and the Imperial Succession

Emerging from his winter quarters at Antioch, Constantius may have received some word of Julian's advance into Italy in spring 361 but he remained focused on the east, hoping to shut down that frontier so he could move against his rebellious cousin without having to look over his shoulder. This seemed like the right move as news arrived from Mesopotamia that the disparate units of the Persian army had amassed once more under Shapur. Another attack on Roman Mesopotamia was imminent but Constantius' commanders, scouts and spies in the field could not discern where the Sassanid column was going to cross the Tigris. This roused the emperor and he was soon in the field with his elite cavalry and infantry to get a better, firsthand appraisal of the military situation. Passing through Gephyra and Doliche before crossing the Euphrates at Capersana, Constantius made for Edessa, where he awaited further news of Shapur's movements.[46]

The emperor's immediate aim for the summer of 361 seems to have been to launch another attempt to retake Bezabde; however, he was prevented from making such a move by the indecision of Shapur. Camped east of the Tigris, the Persian king was awaiting good omens and perhaps word from his own spies about Constantius' intentions before crossing into Mesopotamia. Should the Romans move against Bezabde, Shapur may have been left with an uncontested crossing of the Tigris and even a chance to surround the Romans at Bezabde. Constantius will also have been wary of having the strength and morale of his soldiers sapped away by another protracted siege with the potential for battle with both Shapur and Julian on the horizon.[47]

Despite this prevailing military indecision, the emperor refused to remain inactive and so ordered his *magister peditum* and *magister equitum*, Arbitio and Agilo, to drive towards the Tigris with a significant force, not to provoke Shapur but to provide first hand intelligence of the Persian king's movements, composition of his forces and to perturb Shapur from crossing the river. Constantius made sure to give both *magistri* explicit orders that if Shapur and his army were to begin crossing the Tigris, they were to retreat. While this scouting mission was taking place, Constantius continued to prepare his forces at Edessa and in the surrounding countryside by making several limited forays towards neighbouring towns to see to their defences and to spur on morale.

The reports that arrived from the Tigris proved of little use as they could not give any definitive idea of what the Persians planned to do. The root of this uncertainty was the tightening of security around Shapur, with the Persian king only sharing his plans with a very select few. It might also be argued that the lack of intelligence might have stemmed from Shapur having not yet made up his mind. However, Arbitio and Agilo were far more decisive in their assessment of the situation. Both were in no doubt that should the Persians move to cross the Tigris, they would be in no position to affect a successful withdrawal due to the rapidity of Shapur's cavalry, sending repeated missives to Constantius advising him to mobilise his field army and march to the Tigris. With this combination of a lack of intelligence about Persian moves and fear, verging on terror, from his subordinates, it is easy to see why Constantius was undecided his next move.

It was through these clouds of uncertainty hanging over the eastern frontier that news arrived from Europe. Julian had lifted Italy and almost all of Illyricum from Constantian loyalists, claimed the pass of Succi and now seemed poised to strike at Constantinople. The immediacy, decisiveness and success of this eastward thrust shocked Constantius. While still "sustained by the one comforting thought, that in civil strife he had always come off the victor",[48] Julian's advance forced Constantius to be more proactive towards Shapur. First he sent reinforcements to Arbitio and Agilo, perhaps with a change in orders regarding contesting any Persian crossing, before setting off at the head of the rest of his field forces. One of the largest Romano–Persian battles of the fourth century seemed to be in the offing. But it was not to be. Supposedly, the very next day after Constantius departed Edessa, word came that Shapur had taken his entire army home as the auspices had failed to give a positive reading for any invasion of Mesopotamia.

Whether it was the flight of birds, the entrails of slaughtered beasts or most likely the flames of ritual fire, these poor auspices had in a stroke removed Constantius' most immediate threat. And the emperor was determined to take advantage of Fortune's smile. Arbitio, Agilo and their field forces were recalled from the Tigris and once they had all congregated at Hierapolis, Constantius appeared before his men to explain what was ahead of them.[49] The emperor confessed to not learning from his past mistakes, claiming that

Julian, to whom we entrusted the defence of Gaul, while you were fighting the foreign nations that raged around Illyricum, presuming upon some trivial battles which he fought with the half-armed Germans, exulting like a madman, has involved in his ambitions a cabal of a few auxiliaries, whom their savagery and hopeless condition made ready for a destructive act of recklessness and he has conspired for the hurt of the state...[50]

While there is some exaggeration and half truths incorporated, Constantius likely held some belief in what he was saying. He was surely disappointed not just in Julian for succumbing to ambition but perhaps also in himself for either not dealing with the situation sooner or for allowing it to happen again. Having said that, whether or not Constantius believed what he was spouting about Julian is a moot point for all he needed was for his army to believe that their emperor had been stabbed in the back by an ungrateful usurper puffed up by a few minor victories. Whatever the emperor's thoughts about Julian and the circumstances surrounding his usurpation, the imperial army gathered at Hierapolis were forthright in "brandishing their spears in anger... [replying] with many expressions of goodwill and then [asking] to be led at once against the rebel".[51] Buoyed by the full support of his army, Constantius sent forces on ahead of his main column under Arbitio and Gomoarius, perhaps hoping they could discourage Julian's expected advance from the pass of Succi towards Constantinople.

With the confrontation between the *Augusti* looking a matter of time and with the benefit of hindsight, Ammianus goes into an excursus on the omens of Constantius' impending death. On top of Julian's oneiromancy, the emperor was complaining of nightmares in which Constantine handed him a child who would dislodge Constantius' orb, the emblem of an emperor's power and authority depicted in statues and on coins. He also spoke of seeing an apparition, perhaps a guardian spirit deserting him, which was taken as a sign of his impending doom.[52] Despite this seeming preponderance of ill-omens, Constantius remained eager "to encounter civil disturbances at their outset".[53] He force-marched his army from Hierapolis to Antioch and having completed his remaining preparations and despite murmurings of dissent about the lateness of the year, set out through the Taurus Mountains.

Less than three miles from Antioch at a suburban estate called Hippocephalus, the emperor was confronted by another bad omen. Discarded by the side of the road was a decapitated corpse "lying stretched out towards the west",[54] foretelling that the Roman Empire was about to lose its imperial head, although this omen was hardly unambiguous as it could be interpreted that the headless man represented Julian instead of Constantius. Perhaps troubled but not deterred by his prophesised end, Constantius continued on at a rapid pace towards Tarsus. While there, Constantius contracted a slight fever but "in the expectation of being able to throw off the danger of his illness by the motion the journey",[55] he continued on towards Mount Taurus. However, by the time the emperor had reached Mobsucrenae, modern Yakapinar in the Adana province of Turkey, where Constantius had had built an excellent bridge over the Pyramus river, his fever had gotten worse. By the next morning, it was so severe that it prevented the emperor from moving and his temperature had become so high that "his body could not be touched, since it burned like a furnace".[56] It was clear to Constantius that his end was fast approaching. The omens had been right. He was dying.[57]

While he bemoaned his fate, Constantius kept enough of his wits about him to think about the future of the empire. Despite his new wife being pregnant, Constantius had no designated successor. The cynic would say that much of that was the emperor's own fault given the massacre of his extended family in 337 while the religiously and philosophically minded, such as Julian, would claim that his failure to produce an heir with any of his three wives during his lifetime was divine or karmic retribution for his actions during his life and reign. Of course, Constantius could not shoulder all of the blame for the sorry state of the succession. He had had nothing to do with the deaths of any of his brothers and when he had entrusted his surviving cousins with imperial authority, they had proven unruly, seemingly disqualifying them from consideration. However, even if Constantius did harbour grudges towards what remained of his family, now in his dying hours, he demonstrated the foresight and pragmatism he had been capable of throughout his life and did not allow those grudges to cloud his judgement. Rather than nominate a non-Constantinian or leave his generals to choose, ensuring a destructive civil war that could have seen the end of his family line, Constantius named Julian as his successor to the imperial throne. The usurper was to be sole *Augustus*.

Without full testimony from Constantius, it is difficult to gauge his thinking as to why he performed such an about-face in choosing a usurper as his successor. Even if his collaboration in the 337 massacre suggests otherwise, he had pride in the imperial power of his family and thought its continuation and the peace of the empire to be more important than any posthumous revenge that might be meted out by his generals. It could also be that Constantius was far more impressed with Julian's military and civil accomplishments in Gaul than is depicted by both Ammianus and Julian himself. His opportunistic drive into Illyricum may have further impressed the emperor even if it was at his own expense.

As to his only other surviving family, it is unknown if Constantius made any provision for his unborn child as part of his final arrangements. He may have been unwilling to tempt Fate given that it was likely early in the pregnancy and his previous wives had been blighted by miscarriages; although perhaps needs must in this situation so it would be surprising had he not attempted to secure his offspring's future. Of course, specific plans were difficult to make without knowing the gender of the unborn child, but it is intriguing to speculate on what any plans could have entailed. Julian would be into his early forties by the time a female child of Constantius was eligible for marriage, although such a disparity in age and close blood relation had not stopped Roman emperors in the past. Whether or not Julian will have been willing to forsake the "inviolate chastity"[58] he followed since the death of Helena to prevent a dynastic dead end is another matter. Such chastity would have been a bonus had Constantius' child been male for then he would have been the only viable imperial option for Julian's eventual successor whilst saving the empire from any potential confrontation between the offspring of Constantius and Julian in the future. However, Constantius could only hope that Julian might adopt his child as his heir: a son as his direct successor, a daughter to marry or marry off to continue the family line. A lot of this wrangling over the succession was rendered moot – or perhaps even more important – when Julian died within two years of Constantius without a successor.

And while the events of 363 would undermine any succession plan Constantius attempted to make on his deathbed, even in 361, these pragmatic arrangements relied on one rather important proviso: the acceptance of Constantius' generals and courtiers. Many of them had spent much of their time manoeuvring themselves into positions of increasing importance and denigrating the reputation of Julian, so would they now accept such an unexpected turnaround? That remained to be seen. Constantius and his brothers had refused to accept the succession plan of their father, someone who they held in far greater esteem than many of the Constantian court held Julian.

With the future of the empire and the continuation of his family dynasty addressed, Constantius, much like his father, had himself baptised by Euzoius, the bishop of Antioch. That Euzoius was a supporter of the Homoean Creed is not surprising but this choice helped solidify the poor reception that contemporary and later Christians would give Constantius as an 'Arian'. In the eyes of his detractors, on his deathbed, Constantius had the chance to repent for his attempts to force unity on the Church but instead stuck to his heresy, damning him forever. His immortal soul tended to, Constantius slipped away, dying on what Ammianus records as the *tertium nonarum Octobrium* (the equivalent of 5 October 361). This date is now considered to be a mistake and has been reworked as *tertium nonarum Novembrium* (3 November).[59]

He had exercised imperial authority in various forms for thirty-eight years but at the time of his death, Constantius was still only forty-four years old. In antiquity, this was not necessarily young but it by no means made Constantius an old man. He appeared to be in rude health through his sharing of the military burdens of his men and having lived a "prudent and temperate manner of life and by moderation in eating and drinking".[60] Throughout the last two years of his life he continued to show a healthy vigour, campaigning along the Danube before travelling to the east to match wits with Shapur once more, all the while dealing with the machinations of Julian and then showing remarkable speed in striking out from Edessa to square up to the usurper after Shapur's retreat. Perhaps had Ammianus been less disposed against Constantius, there might have been some suggestion of foul play in the sudden and unexpected nature of the emperor's passing given his portrayal of how robust and austere he was.

This vigour could have played a part in undermining Constantius' health. Even a young man would have had trouble keeping up with such a schedule and the mental and physical exertions involved. In a short period of time, Constantius was caught up in two Limigantes sneak attacks, faced the Persian conquests of Amida, Singara and Bezabde, his own failure to recapture the latter despite an immense effort, frustration over the continued problems within the Christian church, anger and disappointment over the rebellion of Julian and upset by the death of his beloved Eusebia. On top of the inherent pressures and travel involved in what was a long military and imperial career, even with the joy of a pregnant wife, these "various disasters both political and personal, had taken their toll".[61] It had been an unexpected and in many ways anti-climatic end for an emperor who had spent so much of his reign on a war footing. Constantius himself, even if he accepted the inevitability of his death, will likely have been frustrated and saddened at not being able to finish the job against Shapur, teach his rebellious cousin a lesson and see his line perpetuated through the birth of Constantia.

After being cleaned and placed in a coffin, a *protector domesticus*, Jovian, escorted the emperor's body to Constantinople, a city that owed almost as much to Constantius for its growing position as it did to his father. During the procession, as the man accompanying the body, Jovian was presented with soldier's rations and was shown horses of the courier service as a tribute to the dead emperor. With the benefit of hindsight, Ammianus records these as omens of Jovian's later accession to imperial power.[62] With their emperor now dead, his generals and courtiers were left in a quandary: should they follow Constantius' wishes and accept Julian or should they elect another in opposition? Elements within the Constantian court, led by Eusebius, a man who had everything to lose due to his overt opposition to Julian, did investigate the idea of promoting another.[63] However, either not finding anyone to accept a nomination, wary of Julian's approach or just out of respect for the dead emperor's wishes, the majority dispatched two German *comites*, Theolaifus and Aligildus, to inform Julian of Constantius' passing, and to urge him to hasten east to claim what was now his by right of inheritance: sole ownership of the imperial throne.

Chalcedon and Aquileia: The End of Constantius' Court

At Naissus, despite his rapid advance through Italy and Illyricum, Julian was nervous. There had been little movement from his enemies, which could suggest the calm before a massive military storm. Such nervousness will have heightened had word of Shapur's failure to cross the Tigris reached him. Determined to get any indication of what the future held, Julian consulted every kind of divination he could – dreams, entrails, flight patterns – but they refused to give him anything beyond "ambiguous and obscure predictions".[64] Eventually, one *haruspex*, Aprunculus of Gaul, brought positive news from the liver he had been inspecting: Julian would soon be sole *Augustus*. And then supposedly on the very day that Constantius expired, the soldier helping Julian up onto his horse slipped and fell, causing Julian to announce that "the man has fallen who has raised me to my high estate."[65]

Despite these positive omens, Julian remained on guard until the arrival of Theolaifus and Aligildus brought word of the emperor's passing at Mobsucrenae and his nominating of Julian as emperor. Overcome with elation and no little relief, the new sole *Augustus* broke camp and marching through the pass of Succi, past Philippopolis, and made for Constantinople to claim his inheritance. That Julian could travel past those fortresses at Philippopolis and Adrianople, which had caused him such consternation, suggests that the news of Constantius' death and nomination of Julian had preceded him, probably from Theolaifus and Aligildus.[66] Perhaps inspired as much by the prevention of another civil war and for self-preservation rather than love for Julian, the Senate and people of Constantinople came out to meet and applaud him on his approach to the city on 11 December 361. It had been a spectacular change in fortune for not just Julian but for the Roman Empire.[67]

One of Julian's first actions was to give his predecessor an appropriate burial. He met the funerary cortege led by Jovian, who was to be Julian's successor, in the harbour of Constantinople and then took the lead himself of the procession to the Church of the Holy Apostles, which Constantius had overseen the construction of and was now interred in a porphyry sarcophagus beside his father.[68] In treating Constantius with such respect Julian was attempting to smooth over the transition of power. A large section of the military forces present in the east were as loyal to Constantius as those in Gaul were to Julian, while drawing on the respect for Constantius meant respect for his decisions, most importantly his choice of successor.

After a period of respectful mourning, Julian moved to secure his new regime and "if convention and a desire for unity meant that Constantius could not be attacked, he had no such compunctions about his predecessor's lackeys."[69] His own supporters received high office with Salutius Secundus becoming praetorian perfect of the East and Jovinus praetorian prefect of Illyricum but this was just the beginning of Julian's clear out of Constantian officials. At Chalcedon, the city opposite Constantinople over the Bosphorus, the new emperor set up a tribunal consisting of himself, Mamertinus, Nevitta, Jovinus, Arbitio and Agilo to sit in judgement of those felt to have committed offences. It was a significant list.

Constantius' former *magister officiorum*, Palladius, was exiled to Britain for having spied on Gallus; Pendatius was threatened with a similar exile for abetting the destruction of Gallus but was able to justify his actions and was acquitted; Constantius' last *magister officiorum*, Florentius, son of Nigrinianus, was exiled to the Dalmatian Island of Boae, modern Ciovo in Croatia, while the other Florentius, Julian's former praetorian prefect in Gaul, was condemned to death but escaped into hiding with his wife and did not reappear until after Julian's death. Others such as the *comes rei privitae*, Evagrius, the former *cura palatii*, Saturninus, and Cyrinus, a former *notarius*, were also exiled.

The most infamous accused to appear before the tribunal of Chalcedon were dealt with in a much more harsh way. While Constantius may have been blind to the extent of his actions, those actions caught up with the diabolical Paul the Chain and in a reflection of his barbaric treatment of others, he was burned to death. Joining the Chain on the roasting spit was Apodemius, the *agent in rebus* involved in the downfalls of Silvanus and Gallus. Eusebius too, despite some tacit acceptance of Julian's accession as Constantius' heir, was condemned to death by the judges, although it is not recorded if he met with a similar fiery fate. Indeed, Julian made sure to remove eunuchs from the imperial court for their perceived greediness and corruption. He also made great strides in reducing the size of the imperial retinue due to the expenditure and corruption involved.[70]

However, the justice meted out at Chalcedon was far from just. Even Ammianus was far from happy. He thought Taurus, praetorian prefect of Italy, worthy of a pardon, asking "for what sin did he commit, if in fear of a storm that had arisen he fled to the protection of the emperor?"[71] although it should be noted that the Vercellum that Taurus was exiled to may well be Vercellae in northern Italy, his hometown, making it far from a vicious punishment. The real origin of Ammian outrage came from the treatment of Ursulus. Despite having aided Julian during his time in Gaul by making funds available to the army, the *comes sacrorum largitionum* was put to death on the insistence of those soldiers who remembered his tactless comment made before the ruins of Amida. In another display of dramatic hyperbole, Ammianus wailed that "justice herself seems to have wept."[72] The historian concedes that these instances of overstepping the mark were partly Julian's fault with his timidity and inexperience seeing him appoint Arbitio to oversee the hearings, despite him being one of the prime culprits in the intrigue that poisoned Constantius' court, and then fail to show mercy towards Ursulus in the face of the army's baying for blood.[73]

The tribunal at Chalcedon was not the only dealings with Constantian supporters left to complete for Julian. The appointment of Jovinus as praetorian prefect of Illyricum and then to the tribunal saw his removal from the command of the ongoing siege of Aquileia. The low intensity of the blockade encouraged Julian to remove Jovinus to more important affairs in the east. This left the *comes* Immo in charge of the Julian forces at Aquileia, who attempted to induce the defenders to surrender, highlighting the lack of aid coming to the city's inhabitants and garrison. Nigrinus and his men remained obstinate. The size and history of Aquileia's walls gave them great belief that they could hold out long enough for what was still considered to be Constantius' inevitable victory. After having his peace overtures rebuffed and perhaps looking to make a name for himself, Immo abandoned the blockade and launched an assault, but this was repulsed.

This complete failure to make any real impression against the walls discouraged Immo's men. Their attempts to find advantageous avenues for attack were also revealing why the city had withstood so many sieges in the past: the course of the Natisone river snaked so close to walls that it was nearly impossible to bring rams, siege towers or sapping equipment to bear on the city. The presence of the river did present Immo and his men with an alternative avenue of attack as they built several siege towers higher than the walls and placed them on three ships, which were lashed together to form one large floating platform. From atop these floating towers, infantry could attempt to wrestle control of the walls from the defenders, while from lower sections light-armed troops would emerge on bridges to discharge missiles and undermine the walls.

Despite the ingenuity and daring of these plans, they were quickly undone. As this platform neared the walls, the defenders met it with a barrage of various flammable materials and kindling followed by pitch-covered fire arrows, setting the platform ablaze. The combination of fire and the weight of men caused the towers to collapse into the Natisone, killing many of their occupants. The rest of the men were left exposed to the same hail of missiles and while they fought on, it was ultimately futile. When the signal for retreat came, the attackers were left with nothing to show for their efforts aside from a no longer floating platform and a long casualty list. Despite this failure, after a night's rest and some food, the besiegers renewed their attack the following morning with scaling ladders and attempts to break the city's iron gate, only to again be forced back by fire arrows and stones. This was perhaps a diversionary attack as another group crossed the city's moat and made some progress against the walls, only to be beaten back by a sally from a postern gate.

These failures to make any real headway against the walls saw the siege degenerate back into the attempted blockade that Jovinus envisaged at the outset. Immo cut the city's water supply but when even the destruction of Aquileia's aqueducts did little to undermine the determination of the garrison, the besiegers turned their attention to the Nastione and "with a mighty effort the river was turned from its course."[74] Even this epic achievement of a small force proved to be in vain as the garrison and inhabitants of Aquileia showed their self-restraint and fortitude in surviving on the water provided by the wells within the walls.

Hearing of the struggles of Immo's force, Julian dispatched Agilo to the city. Upon his arrival, the *magister peditum* was escorted towards the city by a shield wall and called to the defenders with news of Constantius' demise and his willing of power to Julian. Even a general of Agilo's stature was "overwhelmed with endless abuse as a liar".[75] It was not until the *magister* agreed to enter the city and swore an oath to the events of November 361 that the Aquileian garrison began to accept the truth. At length, the city gates were opened and the siege was brought to an end. In an attempt to deflect blame, the Aquileians and the soldiers offered up Nigrinus and a handful of his co-conspirators as the instigators of this entire incident. Once the praetorian prefect, Mamertinus, had carried out an investigation, Nigrinus was burned alive while two Aquileian senators, Romulus and Sabostius, were beheaded for "having sown the seeds of discord without regard to its dangerous consequences".[76]

With the Chalcedonian purge of the imperial court and the capitulation of Aquileia, any overt opposition to Julian from the supporters of Constantius was extinguished. Any remaining doubters within the military hierarchy were won over or at least distracted by Julian's almost immediate determination to take the fight to Shapur with a grand Persian expedition in 363. The deceased emperor would have been spinning in his sarcophagus as the benefits of his hard point strategy and balancing of the empire's resources were squandered in a fruitless quest for the Alexandrian dream less than two years after his death. Any grim satisfaction at being proven right would have been overridden by the tragic outcome of Julian's Persian expedition both for the Roman Empire and the Constantinian dynasty.

Epilogue

Constantius II: A Good Emperor Lacking a Publicist?

Conceal a flaw, and the world will imagine the worst
— Martial, *Epigrams* III.42

lavius Julius Constantius is a difficult emperor to judge. He was not a
great military conqueror like Julius Caesar or Trajan. He was not a great
reformer like Diocletian. Nor was he a philosopher king like Marcus
Aurelius or Julian. But just because he did not set the ancient world alight
and there is a shortage of dependable information does not mean that a reign
of twenty-four years should be passed over as being a stopgap between that
of Constantine the Great and Julian the Apostate. The reign of Constantius
not only encompasses a quarter of the fourth century, it also highlights the
troubles of civil conflict, barbarian invasion, Persian war and the new problem
of religious conflict, all faced while attempting to consolidate the extensive
reforms of Diocletian and Constantine.

Any portrayal of Constantius is greatly coloured by the records of Ammianus,
Julian and the Christian sources, making it difficult to see anything more
than "a conscientious emperor but a vain and stupid man, an easy prey to
flatterers... timid and suspicious, and interested persons who could play on
his fears for their own advantage".[1] And such a summation of Ammianus'
depiction is perhaps more measured than the depiction given by the former
protector may warrant. Ammianus' Constantius was not just manipulative
and paranoid; he was a kin-slaying child-killer. Such a negative portrayal of
Constantius prevailed until the dawning of more modern academic scrutiny
and the investigation into why these sources may have said what they did. This
allows for the lid to be lifted somewhat on who this emperor was and what he
achieved; but only somewhat. Even attempting to extrapolate the 'truth' behind
the panegyric and over-criticism does not see a seismic shift in the perception
of Constantius II. From a paranoid monster, at best he can be seen instead as
something of an enigma, capable of the good, the bad and even ugly sides of
imperial rule.

The door remains open to Ammianus being largely right in his portrayal, at least on a personal level. Constantius may well have been a bitterly paranoid, child-killing, kin-slayer, who could put his imperial office and family history above justice and the welfare of the empire. Even accounting for some Ammian exaggeration by toning down the vitriol still leaves a picture of a potentially unpleasant man. Constantius may not have been Caligula, Domitian or Commodus, but on various occasions, he proved himself to be ruthless and unscrupulous, whether it was the purge of 337, the encouraging of the Alamanni to raid Roman territory, the removal of Gallus or the employment of men like Paul the Chain.

Even attempts to defend Constantius against these excesses do not reflect favourably on the emperor: either he was ignorant or he ignored, even encouraged, them. And even when it is pointed out that the actions of Paul were only recorded in the aftermath of the removal of a threat: Magnentius, Silvanus and Gallus, neither scenario of incompetence or complicity paints a positive picture. A similar ambiguity can be found in Constantius' choice of underlings and courtiers.[2] Even with room for exaggeration and perhaps the masking of Constantius' willingness to listen to the advice of others, the excuses offered by Libanius suggest at the very least the emperor was blind to the atmosphere that he had allowed to permeate the imperial court and the upper echelons of the civilian and military hierarchies through the appointment of unscrupulous politicians, eunuchs and military men; at worst, he fostered such poisonous competition amongst his closest subordinates out of sheer paranoia.

In the religious sphere, Constantius' dire reputation stemmed from his 'Arianism', his interfering in the workings of the church and his poor fortune of running into the immovable object that was Athanasius of Alexandria. This negativity of the sources glosses over the original arguments between Constantius and the ultra-Nicene party. The emperor was by no means championing Arianism as his opponents were suggesting; if anything, he was backing the viewpoint of Eusebius of Nicomedia, which encouraged ecclesiastical discourse on the doctrinal issues raised by the philosophical approach of men like Arius, without agreeing with their tenets. In doing so, Constantius was backing a more progressive and open approach to Christian doctrine than those who castigated him during and after his reign.

However, Constantius does deserve criticism for his religious policies, even if focusing on his 'Arianism' is to look in the wrong place. Instead, it was his reaction to the continued opposition of Athanasius, Julius and Liberius that should be criticised. Despite his father's failure with the Donatists of Africa, Constantius assumed that his position as *Augustus* gave him the right to dictate doctrine to the Church. Achieving the acceptance of the Homoean

Creed through a series of partisan councils, threats and physical coercion was never going to be well received. However well intentioned it was donned, to Constantius' opponents, the cloak of a reformer and unifier was the perfect disguise for an Antichrist.

Outside of doctrinal disputes, Constantius' reign represents the continued consolidation of his father's adoption and promotion of the church. The foundations for the spread of Christianity to non-Roman tribes were laid through the acceptance of men such as Ulfila into the empire, even if it was to be seen as heretical Arianism. Numerous churches were established or expanded including the Church of the Holy Apostles, not to mention Constantinople as a whole, including its Senate, as not just an imperial capital but also a Christian city. Perhaps without such a stubborn opponent as Athanasius, Constantius may have enjoyed a reputation more akin to that of his father, having nurtured the growth of Christianity and even been responsible for new orthodoxy. Instead, he was labelled a heretic and even an Antichrist.

While there is some room to reassess Constantius' religious legacy, it is perhaps in the realm of the military that his reputation can be best rehabilitated. While the complaint of Ammianus that he "never defeated any foreign people that made war on him, nor did he ever stand in the first line of battle, nor add to the territory of the empire"[3] echoed the sentiments of many contemporary Romans, a more detached appraisal of Constantius' military record suggests that he deserves more credit than he typically receives. Given the number of threats he faced, portraying the lack of foreign conquests as a failure seems unfair, even intentionally misleading. Various great emperors including Constantine had not conquered any new territory and even if it was "scarcely an impressive tally for twenty-three years of campaigning",[4] Constantius advanced into foreign lands on each of the three major fronts of the empire: the rivers Rhine, Danube and Tigris.

Even with his bias against him and repeated attempts to quantify it, Ammianus is unable to hide the strong reputation Constantius had as a military commander. The poor treatment of Ursicinus recorded by Ammianus did not undermine the *magister*'s holding of Constantius in high regard as a commander in the field,[5] while some of Shapur's movements belie a healthy respect for his imperial opponent's skill, the suggestion being that the presence of Constantius and his battle-hardened army played a major role in that decision to shy away from a possible confrontation in 361. The assumption of many contemporaries that his victory over Julian was inevitable also highlights Constantius' command reputation.

On top of those contemporary opinions, the insult that he was only victorious in civil wars still shows some skill in leadership as these battles had to be fought.

Contests between two Roman forces were usually won by the larger army or the more skilled commander so at the very least Mursa suggests that Constantius was extremely capable of marshalling large numbers of men under his banner through the strength of his character, his willingness to share the military burden and perhaps even a natural charisma when speaking to soldiers, much like his father. Julian was likely encouraged to pose as a similar inspiration to his men in Gaul through the advice and example of Constantius.

While there may be more examples lost in the source black hole of the 340s and the mass slaughter at Mursa was not something to be proud of, Constantius' record on the battlefield was almost impeccable. Losing control of his army at Singara is the only real blemish when he led men in person. He defeated armies of Persians, Sarmatians, Quadi, Limigantes, Alamanni and probably other tribes on top of the two large Roman armies of Magnentius; all of this achieved with an army that was in a transitional phase of its development not just from the reforms of Constantine but also the increasing regionalisation sparked by the divisions of the central field army between his sons.

On several occasions, Constantius showed a strong understanding of his enemy, planning ahead for the treachery of the Limigantes, recognising the Persian trap at Singara and launching a spoiling attack against the Alamanni around the Neckar valley in Julian's early months in Gaul. And while he does not have the best reputation for judging the actions and ambitions of his political underlings, when it came to his military men, he demonstrated a good grasp of who would follow his overall strategies. This is best seen with his decision to sideline Ursicinus in favour of Sabinianus, which might have doomed Amida but saved the eastern field army from destruction by Shapur's vast host as Ursicinus may have led a rash attempt to relieve the besieged city.

It was the potential strategic considerations behind the promotion of Sabinianus that represents the least popular aspect of Constantius' military approach with his lack of offensive strikes and major battles against foreign enemies seen as un-Roman and cowardly. However, it is in this realm of military strategy that Constantius demonstrated a far greater insight into the abilities of the fourth century empire, its army, its officers and its opponents than many of his contemporaries, even if it was to the detriment of his own reputation. Far from meeting "loss and disaster"[6] in his dealings with Shapur II, Constantius' attritional strategy of relying on the walls of cities and forts, even if they occasionally failed, should be seen as making the best out of a bad situation and a demonstration that Constantius understood the kind of prioritising that was necessary to defend the Roman Empire.

Throughout his reign, Constantius held a massive Persian army headed by perhaps the greatest Sassanid king at bay at a time of Roman military transition, imperial division, usurpation and barbarian invasion. During the 340s, he had even managed that with just a third of the empire's resources at his disposal. Constantius had not been the first to incorporate such hard point defences into his eastern strategy but his successful resistance to the territorial ambitions of Shapur, even if there was some good fortune involved such as the death of Grumbates' son stopping the planned strike across the Euphrates, meant that he would not be the last; although as the fifth century was a time of extended peace between Rome and Persia, there is little evidence for this more defensive posture until the building of the fortress of Dara in 505 by Anastasius I.

Perhaps the best promoting tool for Constantius' eastern strategy was not his blunting of Shapur but the disaster that was to befall the empire when his more defensive strategy was abandoned as Julian succumbed to "Alexander the Great syndrome" in 363.[7] At least 65,000 men were mobilised from the *comitatenses* of the east, Illyricum and Gaul, supported by frontier troops and marched headlong into Persia.[8] The campaign quickly became a fiasco as Shapur resorted to scorched earth, feigned flight and hit and run attacks. As Julian struggled to extricate his army from enemy territory, the Persians bled the Roman army through constant harassment. The final straw came when Julian himself was killed in pursuit of a fleeing band of Arab auxiliaries in Persian service, less than five hundred days after the passing of Constantius II.[9] To save the expedition from complete collapse, the newly elected Jovian signed a "shameful"[10] treaty that erased 150 years of Roman eastern expansion. Roman interests in Armenia and beyond the Tigris were surrendered but more disastrously, the defensive position in Mesopotamia was eviscerated with the surrender of fifteen fortresses including Singara and Nisibis.[11] Given the courage shown by the latter on three separate occasions, it is unsurprising that its ceding to Shapur in 363 was considered one of the great humiliations suffered by Rome in her long history.[12]

Julian's Persian expedition also contributed to the ultimate failure of his restoration of the Rhine frontier, where his aggressive approach was not overly successful in bringing about prolonged peace, as the Alamanni began raiding again once Julian removed east with the Gallic field army.[13] It would require significant fighting from Valentinian and his generals to curb the Alamannic confederation, which showed that it would not be cowed by a comprehensive defeat such as Strasbourg.[14] And while to suggest that a more Constantian approach, treating these tribes more like a state such as Persia, something that Constantius himself is unlikely to have done, might have been more successful in becalming the Rhenan tribes is mere speculation, it is perhaps worth noting that it took Valentinian's extensive building of defensible camps, forts and watch-towers along and beyond the rivers to check trouble.[15] The appearance of Saxons on the Rhine[16] might demonstrate another example of how Julian's campaigns were ultimately a failure. In cowing large numbers of Franks and Alamanni, Julian may have made it possible for the Saxons to move forward to challenge Valentinian. However, Constantius also committed a similar "better the devil you know than the devil you don't" error along the Danube, where his elimination of the Sarmatians encouraged Limigantes, Quadi and Goths to take advantage of the vacuum. So it would be incorrect to suggest that Constantius had all the strategic answers to the problems of the empire, particularly in Europe.

That said, despite that lapse along the Danube, the military rehabilitation of Constantius should continue. Rather than the Ammian failure who could not defeat any opponent who was not Roman and did not add anything to the empire, Constantius was closer to the commander who appears in the panegyrics: strategically astute, conscientious, respected by the troops who served under him and well-regarded and even feared by enemies and allies alike. He used those traits to preserve the frontiers, restore the unity of the empire and to continue the development of the imperial field armies.

However well his military leadership can be rehabilitated, a reader of the history of Constantius' reign still cannot help be feel a little disappointed. While Ammianus' masterpieces of Strasbourg and Amida, supplemented by the sieges at Singara, Bezabde and Aquileia and the various campaigns along and beyond the Rhine and Danube, provide a rich military story, there are numerous other events lacking clarity and detail due to the inadequacy of the sources, such as the ambush at Aquileia, the three sieges of Nisibis and the battles of Narasara, Singara, Mursa and Mons Seleucus to name but a few. The military story of Constantius suffers from other circumstances beyond his control with climactic battles with Shapur and Julian thwarted by poor weather, poor omens and poor health. And those are only the events that are known about. Who knows what else might be missing from the 340s? Perhaps there were European campaigns launched by Constans. Perhaps there was more on the manoeuvres on the eastern frontier. Perhaps Constantius and Shapur squared up to each other on more than one occasion. Of course, that is a lot of 'perhapses' and such speculation (and hope) can only be answered by the uncovering of some delicate papyrus from the deserts of Egypt or the rediscovery of a book within a book from the darkened corners of a late antique/early medieval monastic library. Wishful thinking, but not impossible.

What is known about Constantius is that for someone so willing to fight to uphold the imperial grandeur of his father's dynasty, he was responsible for the destruction for a large part of it. While any court machinations in favour of the descendants of Theodora gave Constantius cause for concern, regardless of how understandable his motives were or what level of coordination there was with his brothers, that does not excuse Constantius' perpetrating of the murder of Dalmatius Censor, Dalmatius *Caesar*, Julius Constantius, Hannibalianus and others in the summer of 337. And he did not stop there, adding the blood of Gallus to his already stained hands in 354 and he would likely have killed Julian too had he lived to see his expected victory in their showdown.

The purge contributed greatly to the endangerment of what it was supposed to protect – the imperial succession and the future of the Constantinian family – although that was only revealed in the fullness of time. Constantius could not have foreseen that not one of five Constantinians he shared imperial power with in some guise between 337 and 361 would have the good fortune or the good sense to perpetuate the dynasty either through siring children or adopting heirs. Constantius could not have done anything about the heirless early deaths of Constantine II, Constans, Nepotianus and Julian through their own recklessness, misfortune, lifestyle choices or orientation. Nor could he have done more to secure his own succession, marrying three times and nominating two successors in Gallus and Julian, only for both of them to act above their station.

Even then, Constantius still managed to leave a daughter and designate his rebellious half-cousin as *Augustus* on his death bed, a move that saved the empire from another destructive civil war and perhaps should have seen the purge of 337 overlooked. That it was not was due to Julian, who failed in his duty to put the needs of his family above his own personal glory. In 363, Julian *did* know the poor state of the imperial dynasty and yet still chose to continue a life of chastity and not leave any clear instructions, regardless of the claims of Procopius, for the succession as he set off on his Alexandrian adventure. So when that spear plunged into his side during the skirmish at Samara, the fate of the Constantinian dynasty rested in the infantile hands of Constantia, who at little more than a year old was to spend her life as a legitimising pawn for emperors and usurpers. Constantius might have pruned a major branch of the family tree but it was Julian who ensured that it died.

It seems clear then that, while he was deserving of the criticism he received for some of his actions, Constantius was not the militarily incompetent, paranoid Antichrist that most of the sources might have it believed. And yet, through their negativity, Constantius is relegated almost to the position of placeholder between his father and cousin, despite reigning for a quarter of a century. That is to do him a disservice. While he might not have been a great conqueror, in facing a rampant enemy at the head of a vast army, Constantius was the right man at the right time: a fourth century CE Fabius Maximus

Cunctator, shielding Rome from disaster by delaying his Hannibal through an unpopular strategy, the abandonment of which led to calamity.

Constantius may not have been a great reformer but he was the first to have to deal with the fall out of a raft of political, military and religious reforms much like Tiberius had to in the wake of Augustus over three centuries previously. Indeed, a comparison between Constantius and Tiberius might also stretch not just to their following of great men and their poor treatment by the sources but also to their treatment of the political bodies around them and potential rivals. Both may have been oblivious to how their standoffish approach was causing trouble (Constantius with the ill-behaviour of his courtiers and Tiberius with the feisty yet spineless agitation of the Senate) and both dispatched political opponents with ruthless cunning (Constantius' disarming Gallus and purging his family while Tiberius eventually dispatched Sejanus).

It is perhaps only with his cultural side that the sources are the most accurate with Constantius. Despite the attempts of his panegyrists to say otherwise, there is no real hint that Constantius was anything approaching a philosopher king. Perhaps 'intelligent but uncreative' would be a reasonable summation. And while that lack of philosophical leanings may make Constantius a far less romantically appealing character than Julian, it may also have made him far more pragmatic, a difference in character best borne out by their approaches to the Persians: Constantius followed a Fabian strategy whilst Julian allowed his philosophical romanticism to lead him off in search of the Alexandrian dream, only to find a nightmare.

While it is easy to draw pleasing if somewhat superficial comparisons between Constantius and men he was drastically detached from such as Fabius Maximus or Tiberius, it is necessary to compare Constantius to his contemporaries in order to gain a more accurate view of his actions in terms of their context. Mention has already been made of Julian and how Constantius stacked up against him as a ruler – only one of them brought military disaster down upon the empire – but Julian was only on the imperial stage for eight years. Constantius with his twenty-four year reign needs to be judged alongside those of similar longevity and in the fourth century, there are only two such men: Constantius' father, Constantine (306–337) and the last ruler of a united Roman Empire, Theodosius (379–395), both of whom are remembered with the sobriquet of 'great'. It would seem that Constantius pales in comparison to two such men, but was he all that different to these two 'great' emperors?

In military terms, both of these emperors lacked external conquests[17] and built their reputations in civil wars and fighting barbarians; achievements that are used as examples of failure for Constantius. Could either of them have gotten more out of war with Shapur with the same lack of resources and split attention than Constantius managed? In religious terms, as both Constantine and Theodosius were as forthright in their pressing of religious orthodoxy through legislation and councils as Constantius had been, would either of them have done anything different when faced with the likes of Athanasius and his stubborn cronies? And neither Constantine nor Theodosius were immune from accusations of massacring the innocent as Constantius had done, with the former killing Licinius and his son, his own son Crispus and his wife while the latter saw to it that thousands of Goths were killed in battle and perpetrated a massacre of citizens of Thessalonica, leading to his famous penance in the face of St. Ambrose.

It seems that Constantius II was much more like his father and Theodosius than his detractors would have it believed. The main difference between Constantius and these 'great' emperors of the fourth century was one of spin rather than achievement. Through the recalcitrantness of Athanasius and his own heavy-handedness, Constantius was successfully depicted as anti-Nicene and with the almost total victory of the Nicene party under Theodosius, along with the opposition of Ammianus, Constantius' fate was sealed; his successes in restoring the unity of the empire and protecting its frontiers for two decades passed over due to his 'Arianism' and hostility towards Julian and Ursicinus.

Perhaps then the difference between being remembered as great or average, saint or an 'Antichrist', was not action or deed but being on the right side of religious history and having a good publicist?

Appendix I

Consuls During the Life of Constantius II

317	Ovinius Gallicanus	Caesonius Bassus (from February)
318	Licinius I (fifth)	Crispus
319	Constantine I (fifth)	Licinius II
320	Constantine I (six)	Constantine II
321		
(West)	Crispus (second)	Constantine II (second)
(East)	Licinius I (sixth)	Licinius II (second)
322		
(West)	Petronius Probianus	Amnius Anicius Iulianus
(East)	*Post consulatum Licinii Augusti VI et Licinii Caesaris II*	
323		
(West)	Acilius Severus	Vettius Rufinus
(East)	*II post consulatum Licinii Augusti VI et Licinii Caesaris II (East)*	
324	Crispus (third)	Constantine II (third)
325	Valerius Proculus (until May) suff. Julius Julianus	Sex. Anicius Paulinus
326	Constantine I (seventh)	Constantius II
327	Flavius Constantius	Valerius Maximus
328	Flavius Ianuarinus	Vettius Iustus
329	Constantine I (eighth)	Constantine II (fourth)
330	Flavius Gallicanus	Aurelius Valerius Tullianus Symmachus
331	Junius Annius Bassus	Ablabius

332	Lucius Papius Pacatianus	Maecilius Hilarianus
333	Flavius Dalmatius	Domitius Zenophilus
334	Flavius Optatus	Amnius Manius Caesonius Nicomachus Anicius Paulinus Honorius
335	Iulius Constantius	Caeionius Rufius Albinus
336	Virius Nepotianus	Tettius Facundus
337	Flavius Felicianus	Fabius Titianus
338	Flavius Ursus	Flavius Polemius
339	Constantius II (second)	Constans
340	Septimius Acindynus	L. Aradius Valerius Proculus Populonius
341	Antonius Marcellinus	Petronius Probinus
342	Constantius II (third)	Constans (second)
343	M. Maecius Memmius Furius Baburius Caecilianus Placidus	Flavius Romulus
344 (West)	Domitius Leontius	Flavius Bonosus (until April/May) suff. Iulius Sallustius
(East)	Domitius Leontius	Iulius Sallustius
345	Flavius Amantius	M. Nummius Albinus
346	Constantius II (fourth)	Constans (third)
347	Vulcacius Rufinus	Flavius Eusebius
348	Flavius Philippus	Flavius Salia
349	Ulpius Limenius	Fabius Aconius Catullinus Philomathius
350	Flavius Sergius	Flavius Nigrinianus
351		
(West)	Magnentius	Gaiso
(East)	Sergius	Nigrinianus
352		
(West)	Decentius	Paulus
(East)	Constantius II (fifth)	Constantius Gallus
353	Constantius II (sixth)	Constantius Gallus (second)

354	Constantius II (seventh)	Constantius Gallus (third)
355	Flavius Arbitio	Q. Flavius Maesius Egnatius Lollianus Mavortius
356	Constantius II (eighth)	Julian
357	Constantius II (ninth)	Julian (second)
358	Censorius Datianus	Neratius Cerealis
359	Flavius Eusebius	Flavius Hypatius
360	Constantius II (tenth)	Julian (third)
361	Flavius Taurus	Flavius Florentius

Laws Under Constantius II

Some of these laws are those of Constans, which have been incorrectly attributed to Constantius, while several post-350 laws seem to have been recorded with the name of Constans, when it should be that of Constantius Gallus or even Julian.

CTh I.2 Various kinds of rescripts

CTh I II.7 [=brev I II.5]
Milan, 5 July 356, with Julian

CTh I.5 The office of Praetorian Prefect

CTh I.5.4
30 July 342

CTh I.5.6
Haerbillo/Helvillum, 7 June 358

CTh I.5.5
Milan, 18 July 355

CTh I V.7
Milan, 10 June 357/358

CTh I.6 The office of the Prefect of the City

CTh I VI.1
[Gephyra], 3 May 361

CTh I.7 The office of the Master of Soldiers

CTh I.7.1
Sirmium, 28 May 359

CTh I.9 The office of the Master of Offices

CTh I.9.1
1 November 359, with Julian

CTh I.15 The office of vicar

CTh I.15.2
28 September 348

CTh I.15.3
Sirmium, 3 December 352/353

CTh I.28 The defenders of the Senate

CTh I.28.1
[Gephyra], 3 May 361

CTh II.1 Jursidiction and where a person must be sued

CTh II.1.1 [=brev II.1.1]
8 March 349

CTh.2.1.3 [=brev.2.1.3]
25 September 357, with Julian

CTh.2 I.2 [=brev.2.1.2]
Milan, 25 July 355

CTh II.6 The statutory time limits and the renewal of notification

CTh II VI.4 [=brev II VI.4]
27 December 338, with Constantine II
and Constans

CTh II VI.5 [=brev II VI.5]
Aquileia, 9 April 340, with Constans

CTh II.19 Inofficious testaments

CTh II.19.4 [=brev II.19.4]
18 June 361, with Julian

CTh II.20 Inofficious gifts

CTh II.20.1 [=brev II.20.1]
18 June 361, with Julian

CTh II.21 Inofficious dowries

CTh II.21.1 [=brev II.21.1]
Sirmium, 19 December 358

CTh II.21.2 [=brev II.21.2]
Sirmium, 19 December 360, with
Julian

CTh III.5 Betrothal and antenuptial gifts

CTh III V.7
Cologne, 9 June/11 July 345, with Constans

CTh III.12 Incestuous marriage

CTh III.12.1
Antioch, 31 March 342, with Constans

CTh III.12.2 [=brev III.12.1]
Rome, 30 April 355, with Julian

CTh III.13 Dowries

CTh III.13.1 [=brev III.13.1]
20 September 349, with Constans

CTh III.18 Those persons who shall petition

CTh III.18.1 [=brev III.18.1]   *CTh* III.18.2
15 July 357, with Julian   31 March

CTh IV.11 Prescription of long time

CTh IV.11.2 [= 13,2 h.]
22 June 349, with Constans

CTh IV.13 Imposts and forfeitures

CTh IV.13.4 [= 12,4 h.]   *CTh* IV.13.5 [= 12,5 h.]
Constantinople, 19 January 356, with Julian   14 July 358, with Julian

CTh V.6 The estates of soldiers

CTh V VI.1 [=brev.5 IV.1]
Hierapolis, 11 May 347

CTh V.13 Farms of the privy purse and woodland pastures of the divine imperial household

CTh V.13.1 [= 5,14,1 h.]   *CTh* V.13.2 [= 5,14,2 h.]
Antioch, 12 February 341, with   Antioch, 12 February 341, with
Constans   Constans

CTh VI.4 Praetors and quaestors

CTh VI.4.3   *CTh* VI.4.11
25 March/6 April 339   12 August 357

CTh VI.4.4   *CTh* VI.4.12
28 June 339   Gephyra, 3 May 361

CTh VI.4.5   *CTh* VI.4.13pr.
Antioch, 9 September 340   Gephyra, 3 May 361

CTh VI.4.6   *CTh* VI.4.13.1
Antioch, 9 September 340   Gephyra, 3 May 361

CTh VI.4.7   *CTh* VI.4.13.2
14 March 353   Gephyra, 3 May 361

CTh VI.4.8   *CTh* VI.4.13.3
Milan, 11 April 356   Gephyra, 3 May 361

CTh VI.4.9   *CTh* VI.4.13.4
Milan, 11 April 356   Gephyra, 3 May 361

CTh VI.4.10pr.
9 May 356

CTh VI.4.10.1
9 May 356

CTh VI.4.10.2
9 May 356

CTh VI.4.14
Sirmium, 22 May 359

CTh VI.4.15
Sirmium, 22 May 359

CTh VI.4.16
[Constantinople], 30 December 359

CTh VI.22 Honorary imperial leeters patent

CTh VI.22.2[?]
Thamugadi, 27 November 338

CTh VI.22.3
28 June 340

CTh VI.27 The secret service

CTh VI.27.1
8 March 352/353/354

CTh VI.29 Confidential agents

CTh VI.29.1
Milan, 22 July 355

CTh VI.29.2pr.
Milan, 17 April 357, with Julian

CTh VI.29 II.1
Milan, 17 April 357, with Julian

CTh VI.29 II.2
Milan, 17 April 357, with Julian

CTh VI.29 II.3
Milan, 17 April 357, with Julian

CTh VI.29 II.4
Milan, 17 April 357, with Julian

CTh VI.29.3
30 November 359, with Julian

CTh VI.29.4
30 November 359, with Julian

CTh VI.29.5pr.
31 October 359

CTh VI.29 V.1
31 October 359

CTh VII.1 On military affairs

CTh VII.1.2
Sirmum, 27 May 349

CTh.7 I.3
30 May 349

CTh.7 I.4
27 June 350

CTh VII.4 The issue of military subsistence allowances

CTh VII.4.2
6 April 355

CTh VII.4.5
Constantinople, 14 March 359

CTh VII.4.3
Sirmium, 18 December 357, with
Julian

CTh VII.4.6
Hierapolis, 17 May 360, with
Julian

CTh VII.4.4
29 December 358

CTh **VII.8 Quarters**

CTh VII.8.1
[Gephyra], 3 May 361

CTh **VII.9 Extras shall not be furnished to quartered persons**

CTh VII.9.1
Capua, 12 August 340, with Constans

CTh VII.9.2
11 October 340–344?

CTh **VII.13 Recruits**

CTh VII.13.1
6 July 353

CTh **VII.20 Veterans**

CTh VII.20.6
Sirmium, 24 June 352[?]

CTh VII.20.7
11 August 353[?]

CTh **VII.21 Honorary tribunes and imperial bodyguards in consequence of testimonial letters**

CTh VII.21.2
1 May 353

CTh **VII.22 Sons of military men, apparitors and veterans**

CTh VII.22.6
2 February 349

CTh **VIII.1 Civil accountants, military accountants, bureau clerks and secretaries**

CTh VIII I.5
Rome, 6 May 357

CTh **VIII.2 Registrars, tax accountants and tax assessors**

CTh VIII.2.1
24 June 341 [probably a law of Constans]

CTh VIII.4 Gubernatorial apparitors, chiefs and secretaries of office staffs and commissary officers

CTh VIII.4.4
2 February 349

CTh VIII.4.5
6 May 353/354

CTh VIII.4.6
Milan, 22 May 358

CTh VIII.4.7
29 August 361

CTh VIII.5 The public post, postwagons and supplementary postwagons

CTh VIII.5.7
Antioch, 3 August 352/353/354

CTh VIII.5.8pr.
Milan, 24 June 357

CTh VIII.5.8.1
Milan, 24 June 357

CTh VIII.5.8.2
Milan, 24 June 357

CTh VIII.5.9pr.
Milan, 6[?] December 357

CTh VIII.5.9.1
Milan, 6[?] December 357

CTh VIII.5.10
Sirmium, 27 October 357

CTh VIII.5.11
16 November 360

CTh VIII.7 The various offices, their apparitors and the imperial certificates of approval

CTh VIII.7.3
Sirmium, 27 May 349 [a law of
Constans]

CTh VIII.7.4
14 May 353/354

CTh VIII.7.5
18 May 353/354

CTh VIII.7.6
6 October 353/354

CTh VIII.7.7
Milan, 27 May 358

CTh VIII.10 Extortion by advocates and apparitors

CTh VIII.10.2
29 June 344

CTh VIII.12 Gifts

CTh VIII.12.6
24 December 341, with Constans

CTh VIII.12.7
24 April 355

CTh VIII.13 Revocation of gifts

CTh VIII.13.1pr.
20 Setember 349, with Constans

CTh VIII.13 I.1
20 Setember 349, with Constans

CTh VIII.13.2 [=brev.VIII.6.1]
20 September 349, with Constans

CTh VIII.13.3 [=brev. VIII.6.2]
28 March 355

CTh VIII.13.4 [=brev. VIII.6.3]
23 June 358

CTh VIII.18 Property of mothers and from the maternal side; the abrogation of cretion

CTh VIII.18.4
Heliopolis, 14 March 339, with Constans

CTh VIII.18.5
6 April 349

CTh IX.1 Accusations and inscriptions

CTh IX.1.7
18 October 338

CTh IX.7 On the Julian law on adultery

CTh IX.7.3
Milan, 4 December 342, with Constans

CTh IX.16 Magicians, astrologers and all other like criminals

CTh IX.16.4 [=brev.IX.13.2]
Milan, 25 January 357, with Julian

CTh IX.16.5
Milan, 4 December 357

CTh IX.16.6
5 July 358

CTh IX.17 The violation of tombs

CTh IX.17.1
Milan, 25 June 340

CTh IX.17.2pr.
28 March 349

CTh IX.17.1.1
28 March 349

CTh IX.17.1.2
28 March 349

CTh IX.17.3
356, with Julian

CTh IX.17.4
Milan, 13 June 357

CTh IX.21 Counterfeit money

CTh IX.21.5 [=brev.IX.17.1]
Antioch, 18 February 343

CTh IX.21.6
12 February 349

CTh IX.23 If any person should melt down money or should transport money for the purpose of trade or should handle forbidden money

CTh IX.23.1pr.
Constantina, 8 March 356, with Julian

CTh IX.23.1.1
Constantina, 8 March 356, with Julian

CTh IX.23.1.2
Constantina, 8 March 356, with Julian

CTh IX.23.1.3
Constantina, 8 March 356, with Julian

CTh IX.24 The rape of virgins and widows

CTh IX.24.2
12 November 349

CTh IX.25 The rape or marriage of holy maidens and widows

CTh IX.25.1 [=brev.IX.20.1]
22 September 352/353/354

CTh IX.34 Defamatory writings

CTh IX.34.5
18 June 338

CTh IX.34.6
Milan, 31 October 355

CTh IX.38 Pardons of crimes

CTh IX.38.2
Lugdunum, 6 September 353

CTh IX.40 Penalties

CTh IX.40.4
15 October 346[?]

CTh IX.42 The goods of proscribed and condemned persons

CTh IX.42.2
Milan, 8 March 356, with Julian

CTh IX.42.3
28 August 357

CTh IX.42.4
Sirmium, 4 January 358

CTh X.1 Fiscal law

CTh X.1.6
24 April 348

CTh X.1.7
Vallis, 26 June 357, with Julian

CTh X.8 Ownerless property

CTh X.8.3 [=brev.X.6.1]
3 August 352/353/354

CTh X.8.4
9 June 346

CTh X.10 Petitions, property granted voluntarily, and informers

CTh X.10.4
Viminacium, 12 June 338

CTh X.10.7
Trier, 15 May 345 [a law of Constans]

CTh X.10.5
Naissus, 2 February 340

CTh X.10.8
Sirmium, 5 March 352/353

CTh X.10.6
Savaria, 6 April 342 [a law of
Constans]

CTh X.14 If an associate in a petition should die without an heir

CTh X.14.2
Milan, 17 June 348 [a law of Constans]

CTh X.15 Advocates of the fisc

CTh X.15.3
Aquileia, 9 April 340 [a law of Constans]

CTh X.20 Collectors of purple dye fish, imperial weavers, imperial minters and packanimal drivers

CTh X.20.2
Milan, 19 March 358

CTh XI.Taxes in kind and tribute

CTh XI.1.4
Thessalonica, 6 December 337
[a law of Constans]

CTh XI.1.6
Milan, 22 May 354, with Constans

CTh XI.1.5
3 February 339

CTh XI.1.7
[Gephyra], 3 May 361

CTh XI.7 Tax collections

CTh XI.7.5
Nisibis, 12 May 345

CTh XI.7.7
Thessalonica, 6 December 346/353,
with Constans

CTh XI.7.6
8 March, 349

CTh XI.7.8
Dinummae/Carthage, 2 September 355

CTh **XI.9 The sales of pledges which are held for the payment of tribute**

CTh XI.9.2
12 December 337

CTh **XI.12 Grants of tax exemptions**

CTh XI.12.1
29 April 340

CTh **XI.15 State purchases**

CTh XI.15.1
[Gephyra], 3 May 361

CTh **XI.16 Extraordinary and menial compulsory public services**

CTh XI.16.5
Bononia, 25 January 343 [a law of
Constans]

CTh XI.16.6
Constantinople, 7 May 346, with
Constans

CTh **XI.22 Transfer of tax payments shall not be requested**

CTh XI.22.1
28 July 346, Constans

CTh **XI.23 The chief tax collectorship for recruiting taxes**

CTh XI.23.1
[Gephyra], 3 May 361

CTh **XI.24 The patronage of villages**

CTh XI.24.1
Constantinople, 4 February 360, with Julian

CTh **XI.30 Appeals and the penalties thereof; references of cases to the emperor**

CTh XI.30.18
Serdica, 19 June 339/329

CTh XI.30.24
8 November 348, with Constans

CTh XI.30.19
26 November 339

CTh XI.30.25
Messadensi/Capua, 25 July 355

CTh XI.30.20 [=brev.XI.8.3]
9 June ?, with Constans

CTh XI.30.26
30 July 355

CTh XI.30.21
28 November 340, with Constans

CTh XI.30.22
Cyzicus, 24 February 343, with Constans

CTh XI.30.23
Rome, 2 July 345, with Constans

CTh XI.30.27
Sirmium, 357, with Julian

CTh XI.30.28
Singidunum/Rome, 18 June 359, with Julian

CTh XI.34 Those persons who have not appealed through fear of the judge

CTh XI.34.2
Milan, 1 January 355

CTh XI.36 Whose appeals shall not be accepted

CTh XI.36.4
29 August 339, with Constans

CTh XI.36.5
7 April 341, with Constans

CTh XI.36.6
Antioch, 11 May 342, with Constans

CTh XI.36.7
9 December 344, with Constans

CTh XI.36.8 [=brev.XI.11.2]
Ancyra, 8 March 347, with Constans

CTh XI.36.9
23 July 353

CTh XI.36.10
Constantinople/Carthage, 18 January 354[?]

CTh XI.36.11
25 July 355

CTh XI.36.12
29 July 355

CTh XI.36.13
Sirmium, 23 June 358

CTh XI.36.14
3 August 361

CTh XI.39 The trustworthiness of witnesses and instruments

CTh XI.39.4
Constantinople, 27 August 346, with Constans

CTh XII.1 Decurions

CTh XII.1.23
Antioch, 11 October 338

CTh XII.1.24
Carthage, 12 December 338

CTh XII.1.39
Antioch, 1 April 349

CTh XII.1.40
Ravenna, 21 July 353

CTh XII.1.25
Emesa, 28 October 338

CTh XII.1.26
1 November 338, with Constans

CTh XII.1.27
Trier, 8 January 339 [a law of Constans]

CTh XII.1.28
26 November 339, with Constans

CTh XII.1.29
Naissus, 19 January 340 [a law of Constans]

CTh XII.1.30
Bessae, 12 August 340, with Constans

CTh XII.1.31
Lauriacum, 24 June 341 [a law of Constans]

CTh XII.1.32
17 August 341

CTh XII.1.33
Antioch, 5 April 342

CTh XII.1.34
Antioch, 8 April 342

CTh XII.1.35
Hierapolis, 27 June 343

CTh XII.1.36
Trier, 30 June 343 [a law of Constans]

CTh XII.1.37
28 May 344

CTh XII.1.38
Caesenae, 23 May 346

CTh XII.1.41
23 July 353

CTh XII.1.42pr.
Milan, 22 May 354

CTh XII.1.42.1
Milan, 22 May 354

CTh XII.1.42.2
Milan, 22 May 354

CTh XII.1.43
Milan, 17 July 355

CTh XII.1.44
Sirmium, 22 May 358

CTh XII.1.45
Sirmium, 22 June 358

CTh XII.1.46
Mursa, 27 June 358

CTh XII.1.47 [=brev. XII.1.5]
14 June 359

CTh XII.1.48
[Gephyra], 3 May 361

CTh XII.1.49pr.
29 August 361

CTh XII.1.49.1
29 August 361

CTh XII.1.49.2
29 August 361

CTh XII.2 The payment of salaries

CTh XII.2.1
Constantinple, 3 October 349

CTh XII.6 Tax receivers, provosts and treasurers

CTh XII.6.3
1 August 349, with Constans

CTh XII.12 Delegates and the decrees of instructions to delegations

CTh XII.12.1
Milan, 1 August 355, with Constans

CTh XII.12.2
Milan, 15 January 356, with Julian

CTh XIII.1 The lustral tax payment

CTh XIII.1.1
Rome, 2 December 356, with Julian

CTh XIII.1.3
[Gephyra], 3 May 361

CTh XIII.1.2
Carthage, 10 July 360, with Julian

CTh XIII.4 The exemptions of artisans

CTh XIII.4.3
6 July 344, with Constans

CTh XIII.5 Shipmasters

CTh XIII.5.9
Rome, 1 June 357, with Julian

CTh XIII.10 Taxation and tax assessment

CTh XIII.10.3
Milan, 30 May 357

CTh XIV.1 The decuries of the City of Rome

CTh XIV.1.1
Constantinople/Rome, 24 February 360, with Julian

CTh XIV.3 Breadmakers and packanimal drivers

CTh XIV.3.2
Milan, 6 July 355

CTh XIV.6 The limeburners of the Cities of Rome and Constantinople

CTh XIV.6.1
25 March 359

CTh XV.1 Public works

CTh XV.1.5
Sirmium, 27 July 338, with Constans

CTh XV.1.7
[Gephyra], 3 May 361

CTh XV.1.6
Constantinople, 3 October 349, with
Constans

CTh XV.8 Procurers

CTh XV.8.1
Hierapolis, 4 July 343

CTh XV.12 Gladiators

CTh XV.12.2
17 October 357, with Julian

CTh XV.14 The invalidation of those acts that were affected under the tyrants and the barbarians

CTh XV.14.5
Milan, 3 November 352, with Constantius Gallus

CTh XVI.2 Bishops, churches and clerics

CTh XVI.2.8
27 August 343

CTh XVI.2.9
11 April 349

CTh XVI.2.10
Constantinople, 26 May 352/353/354

CTh XVI.2.11
26 February 342/354

CTh XVI.2.12 [=brev. XVI.1.2]
23 September 355

CTh XVI.2.13
Milan, 10 November 357, with Julian

CTh XVI.2.14pr.
Milan, 28 December 357, with Julian

CTh XVI.2.14.1
Milan, 28 December 357, with Julian

CTh XVI.2.14.2
Milan, 28 December 357, with Julian

CTh XVI.2.14.3
Milan, 28 December 357, with Julian

CTh XVI.2.14.4
Milan, 28 December 357, with Julian

CTh XVI.2.15pr.
Milan, 30 June 360, with Julian

CTh XVI.2.15.1
Milan, 30 June 360, with Julian

CTh XVI.2.15.2
Milan, 30 June 360, with Julian

CTh XVI.2.16
Antioch, 14 February 361

CTh XVI.8 Jews, Caelicolists and Samaritans

CTh XVI.8.6
13 August 339

CTh XVI.8.7 [=brev.XVI.3.2]
Milan, 3 July 357, with Julian

CTh XVI.9 No Jew should have a Christian slave

CTh XVI.9.2
13 August 339

CTh XVI.10 Pagans, sacrifices and temples

CTh XVI.10.2
341

CTh XVI.10.3
1 November 346, with Constans

CTh XVI.10.4
1 December 346, with Constans

CTh XVI.10.5
23 November 353

CTh XVI.10.6
Milan, 19 February 356, with Julian

Footnotes

Introduction

1. Jones (1964), 116.
2. Whitby in Drijvers and Hunt (1999), 77.
3. Tougher in Drijvers and Hunt (1999), 71.
4. Harries (2012), 185.
5. Goffart (1971) offers insight into his motives and influences while Ridley (1982) provides a good translation but only a brief commentary and bibliography; the best modern commentary on Zosimus is the French work of Paschoud (1971–1989); Blockley (1981) provides invaluable insight in Zosimus' sources such as Eunapius.
6. Harries (2012), 185.
7. Julian, Or. I.4c.
8. Whitby in Drijvers and Hunt (1999), 79.
9. cf. Tacitus, *Annals* IV.33.4.
10. Libanius, *Ep*, 369; Vanderspoel (1995), 77–29.
11. Whitby in Drijvers and Hunt (1999), 77–88.
12. Matthews (2000) warns that these laws need to be taken in their historical context. Robinson (1997) provides a good overview of the problems facing the study of Roman law; Harries (1999) demonstrates the interaction of late Roman law with socio-political life while Honoré (1998) attempts to identify those who constructed much of the legal documents.
13. The exhaustive study of the *Notitia* by Jones (1964) has yet to be replaced. Kelly (1998) presents a good overview while Goodburn and Bartholomew (1976) collected articles looking at its various aspects. The works of Brennan in Nicolet (1996) and Brennan (1998) provide analysis of its nature, history, date, purpose and evolution while Kulikowski (2000) argues that while the eastern half of the *Notitia* offers some useful information on the mid 390s, constant amendments to the western half undermine its usefulness.
14. The *Approaching the Ancient World* series provides general overviews on the various types of physical evidence: Bagnall (1995) on papyri, Bodel (2001) on epigrahy, Howgego (1995) on numismatics and Biers (1992) on archaeology.
15. Harries (2012), 186

Chapter I: Crisis and Renewal: The Third Century and the Tetrarchy

1. Campbell (1994), 234.
2. Herodian IV.4.7; to pay for this and to fuel his luxurious lifestyle, Caracalla issued his famous *Constitutio Antoniniana* in 212, extending Roman citizenship to all freeborn men

in the Empire and therefore increasing the number of men liable for taxation as well as military service.

3. Maximinus Thrax, Gordian I, Gordian II, Pupienus and Balbinus, Gordian III, Philip the Arab, Decius, Trebonianus Gallus, Aemilius Aemilianus, Valerian, Gallienus, Claudius II, Quintillus, Aurelian, Tacitus, Florianus, Probus, Carus, Numerian and Carinus.

4. *SHA Claudius* XII.1–2; Aurelius Victor, *de Caes.* XXXIV.5; Zosimus I.46.1; Zonaras XII.26; McNeil (1977), 130–132; Stathakopoulos (2007), 95.

5. *SHA Carus, Carinus and Numerian* VIII.2; Zonaras XII.30; Aurelius Victor, *de Caes.* XXXVIII.2–4; Festus, *Brev.* 24; Eutropius IX.18; Jerome, *Chron.* 284.

6. Barnes (1981), 11–12; Williams (2000), 58–59.

7. Lactantius, *DMP.* 9.5–8; Eutropius IX.24–25; Ammianus XIV.11.10; XXII.4.8; Peter Patricius frag. 14.

8. Barnes (1982); Williams (2000).

9. Williams (2000), 108.

10. Lactantius, *DMP* 7.4; Jones (1964), 43; Ferrill (1986), 41.

11. Williams (2000), 96.

12. Eumenius 18.4; Zosimus II.34; Jones (1964), 55.

13. Whittaker (2004), 28–49; Williams (2000), 93, 96; Luttwak (1976), ch.3; Lactantius, *DMP* 7.9 on there being numerous arms factories at key strategic points suggesting that the army was active along the frontiers; the pragmatic Diocletian found alternative sources of manpower, with Frankish tribes employed to help defend northern Gaul while the Nobades operated as a deterrent to the Blemmyes on the Nile.

14. Jones (1964), 56.

15. Mann (1983), 66 on the peaceful conditions that had prevailed in the early second century being responsible for having "produced a surplus of population that found an outlet in military service" amongst the Danubians

16. Williams (2000), 97 suggests 14 new legions as a bare minimum while Nischer (1923), 8 has 34 new legions from 235 to 305. Jones (1964), 59–60 goes further to suggest that there were at least 35 new Diocletianic legions stating that this "figure is more likely to err on the low."

17. *ND Or.* XXVIII.

18. Jones (1964), 680; Coello (1996), 15; Duncan-Jones (1978), 553; [Hyginus], *De Munitionbus Castrorum* 5; John Lydus, *De Mag.* I.46; *ILS* 2726; 531; Casey (1991), 14; Cameron (1993), 34; Treadgold (1995), 89; Williams (1985), 247, n.6; Crawford (2011), 3–4.

19. MacMullen (1980), 459.

20. Williams (2000), 97; Ferrill (1986), 42 on the distribution of detachments of III *Diocletiana* to five different parts of the Empire in the *Notitia Dignitatum*.

21. Lactantius, *DMP* 7.4; Rostovtzeff (1960), 282 suggests that the second century army of 500,000 "at least doubled" by the fourth century.

22. Agathias V.13.7–8; John Lydus, *De Mensibus* I.27; Jones (1964), 680 suggests that Agathias' figure must have been from a period before the division of the Empire in 395; Treadgold (1995), 44; Coello (1996), 14 n.6.

23. MacMullen (1980), 451–460; Lactantius *DMP* 7.5; Jones (1964), 60.

24. Rees (2004), 17; Cameron (1993), 33.

25. Williams (2000), 97; Cameron (1993), 34.

26. Southern and Dixon (1996), 11.
27. De Blois (1976), 27; while conservative in his employing of foreigners, Diocletian did use non-Romans along the frontiers, "whose names read like a list of Rome's enemies: Saxons, Vandals, Goths, Alamanni, Franks, Sarmatians, Quadi, Juthungi, Sugambri" (Williams (2000), 98) as well as "Atecotti from Ireland or Scotland... Lazi, Tzani, Iberians, Armenians and other Caucasian peoples [and] Persians." (Jones (1964), 619).
28. Zosimus I.52; Jones (1964), 54–55, 608; Ferrill (1986), 42; Treadgold (1995), 9; Southern and Dixon (1996), 15, 17.
29. The term *comitatus* evolved over time and it is anachronistic to apply what it became under Constantine to an earlier period. Under the Republic and early Empire, it was a magistrate's entourage. The more official *sacer comitatus*, a body of men who accompanied the emperor on campaign appeared in the third century, with men serving in it before the reign of Diocletian: Optatus Milevitanus, *Against Parmenian*; Jones (1964), 53.
30. Southern and Dixon (1996), 14.
31. *SHA Gallienus* 14–15; *Passion of St. Sergius and Bacchus* 1–2; Lactantius, *DMP* 19.6; Aurelius Victor, *de Caes.* XXXIX.1; *ILS* 2779, 2781; Zosimus I.40–41, Zonaras XII.25, 31; Jones (1964), 52–54; Speidel (1975), 212, 225; De Blois (1976), 25, 85, 106; Casey (1991), 10–12; Cameron (1993), 33; Southern and Dixon (1996), 14–16; Rees (2004), 17.
32. Southern and Dixon (1996), 16, 17; despite not yet being treated differently in law (*CJ* VII.64.9; X.55.3), that it comprised the best units of the army meant that a transfer to the *comitatus* was a promotion.
33. Nicasie (1998), 83; Elton (1996a), 128 suggests that a replacement rate of 5 per cent was needed just to cover discharges. Boak (1955), 91–94 suggests that if full strength were to be maintained then up to 96,000 recruits were needed per year, assuming a 19.2 per cent replacement rate; the modern British army usually has a recruiting target of 25,000 per year for an army of 150,000: a 17 per cent replacement rate, showing that in a time of poor medical knowledge and perpetual warfare, the Roman army compares well to that of modern times; Crawford (2011) on late Roman recruiting.
34. Zosimus IV.12.1, 23.1–4, V.0.2; Vegetius I.9–18; *NTh* XXIV.1.1[443]; Ammianus XIV.11.3; Claudian, *BGet.* 250–51; *De IV Cons. Hon.* 320–23; Libanius, *Or.* XII.44; Mauricius, *Strat.* III.5, 6; XII.8.24; Lee (2007), 51–66 on maintaining a soldier's loyalty; Elton (1996a), 140 on non-Roman recruits forgetting their barbarian past.
35. Duncan-Jones (1990), 115, 106 on it reaching 1,800 *denarii* a year; Watson (1969), 91; officers received substantially more with a *praepositus* of the *equites promoti* of II *Traiana* recorded receiving 18,000 *denarii* in *stipendium*, probably only for a period of four months giving a total of 54,000 *denarii* per year. (*P. Beatty Panopolis* 2; Jones (1964), 1257–1258 n.31).
36. Ammianus XX.8.8; Elton (1996a), 121 on the *stipendium* probably being discontinued by the fifth century and the lack of any recorded protest may give credence to its lack of value.
37. There are other types of payment recorded for the army. Julian promised his men a reward for any barbarians they killed at Strasbourg (Libanius, *Or.* XVIII.45) while later he promised a reward of 100 silver pieces for bravery against the Persians (Ammianus XXIV.3.3). There were exemptions from poll tax (*CTh* VII.13.6[370]) and the *praemia militiae* discharge bounty, which increasingly came as land allotments and the tools needed to farm it (*CTh* VII.20.3[320/326]); the exact rate of the *annona* has been the

subject of some discussion, although whether it was $66^2/_3$ *denarii* every four months or 200 *denarii* every four months (Jones (1964), 623 *cf.* Duncan-Jones (1990), 108), it was largely insignificant. However, the regularity of commutation of the annona for such a limited amount of cash demonstrates how desperate the soldiery was becoming (Jones (1964), 676).

38. Suetonius, *Augustus* 101 on Augustus bequeathing 1,000 *sesterces* to each Praetorian, 500 each to the urban cohorts and 300 to each legionary; Suetonius, *Claudius* 10 on Claudius bribing each Praetorian with 15,000 *sesterces*; Dio LXXIV.11.5 on Didius Julianus paying each Praetorian 25,000 *sesterces* to become *Augustus*.

39. Duncan-Jones (1990), 109, 116; other special occasions such as imperial consulships and anniversaries every five years provided opportunities for further donatives.

40. Jones (1964), 360, 624, 670.

41. Elton (1996a), 140.

42. Southern and Dixon (1996), 79; Duncan-Jones (1990), 106, 116 suggests that the combination of *stipendium, annona* and *donativum* might provide 12,400 *denarii* a year plus 30 *modii* of wheat; Jones (1964), 623.

43. *ILS* 642.

44. *ILS* 642; Lactantius, DMP 7.6–7.

45. Cameron (1993), 36; Jones (1964), 396.

46. Treadgold (1995), 154; postings and accommodation could also affect zeal. The billeting of field troops in cities forced householders and innkeepers to provide one-third of their home for a guest. This was an onerous burden that opened citizens to the practices of *salgamum* (provisions of food, oil, wood, and so on), *cenaticum* (paying for the soldier's supper), demanding baths or being carried back to their lodgings on the shoulders of passers-by (Ammianus XXII.12.6). These abuses were outlawed but were not rigorously enforced (*CTh* VII.4.12; 9.1–4; VII.11.1, 2). Such was the weight of this burden that exemption from it was considered a privilege (*CTh* VII.8.2, 5, 8; XIII.3.3, 10, 16, 18, 4.4; XVI.2.8). Resorting to abuses might suggest that this system of billeting and inadequate pay exposed soldiers to poor conditions and spread dislike for military service. This may have been a reason why a recruit asked to be sent to the *limitanei* instead of the *comitatenses* (*P. Abinn.* 19). Service in frontier units was far more relaxed as a soldier lived a sedentary existence in a fort or camp with his family nearby, although it also opened the soldier to the depredations of a barbarian raid.

47. Jones (1964), 60.

48. *CTh* VII.22.1[313].

49. Jones (1964), 615.

50. *CTh* VII.18.10[400]; 17[412]; 22.1[313/319]; not just sons of veterans: *CTh* VII.13.4[367]; 10[381]; Suetonius, *Augustus* 24.

51. Ammianus XXXI.4.4; the attributing of conscription by taxation to Diocletian is not universally accepted. Mommsen (1889), 244–248 suggests that the traditional system of the *dilectus* was retained until 375; Brunt (1974a), 113–115 suggested that while Diocletian associated conscription with the *capitus* tax, his system was by no means new, perhaps merely reactivating the long standing military duties of the cities, which had lapsed during the third century (Zuckerman (1998), 120). The word '*dilectus*' itself was still used in official government laws (*CTh* VII.18.10[400]). Whitby in Cameron (1995), 61–124 maintains that a system similar to the *dilectus* was maintained in the east up until the reign of Heraclius.

52. This relief undermined the system as landowners preferred to spend money or resources than lose a worker. The offering of vagrants, fugitives or sons of veterans as payment of this tax became widespread enough for Valentinian and Valens to legislate against it: *CTh* VII.13.6[370]; Williams (2000), 97, 98 suggests that Diocletian imposed direct conscription on the *vagi* and idle mobs of Rome, Alexandria and other cities with a grain dole. That this proved so unpopular that it led to the widespread amputation of thumbs suggest that this was not the best source of recruits. However, the only real evidence of this comes from the beginning of the fifth century rather than the time of Diocletian (*CTh* VII.18.10[400]; 17[412]).

53. *CTh* VII.13.1[353]; 22.2[326].

54. *CTh* VII.22.4[332]; this suggests that a recruit is no longer liable for military service if he has evaded call up for sixteen years after he became eligible, which when coupled with eligibility from "their nineteenth year" gives an age of between 34 and 35.

55. Vegetius I.5; the Roman foot was about a third of an inch less than the modern measurement so 5 feet 10 inches Roman equates to about 5 feet 8 inches; *CTh* VII.13.3[367].

56. Jones (1964), 619; Speidel (1975), 229 on elite barbarian units being paid the same as legionaries in 293.

57. Williams (2000), 98; Zosimus V.26; Ammianus XVII.13.3; XX.7.13; XXVIII.V.4.

58. Liebeschetz (1990a), 12; Southern (2001), 264; Grosse (1920), 208–209.

59. Jones (1964), 620.

60. Augustus settled 50,000 Getae in Moesia (Strabo VII.3.10); Tiberius allowed 40,000 Germans to take up residence in Gaul (Suetonius, *Augustus* 21; *Tiberius* 9; Eutropius, *Brev.* VII.9; Augustus, *Res Gestae* 32; Orosius VI.21.24); Claudius allowed Quadi to settle in Pannonia (Tacitus, *Ann.* XII.29–30); under Nero, some 100,000 *Transdanuviani* were transferred to Moesia (*CIL* XIV.3608 = *ILS* 986), while a similar feat might have taken place in Pannonia under Vespasian (*CIL* X.6225 = *ILS* 985); various barbarian settlements are recorded under Marcus Aurelius: Vandals (Dio LXXI.21.1), Cotini in Pannonia (*CIL* VI.32542), 5,500 Iazyges in Britain (Dio LXXI16.2), 3,000 Naristae (Dio LXXI.21) and Marcomanni in Italy (*SHA Marcus* XXII.2) to name a few; Commodus settled 12,000 Dacians (Dio LXXII.3.3); Severus Alexander settled 400 Persians in Phyrgia (Herodian VI.4.6; Zonaras XII.15); Gallienus gave part of Pannonia to the Marcomanni ([Aur. Vic.], *Epit.* XXXIII.1; Aurelius Victor, *Caes.* XXXIII.6); Claudius II settled Goths (*SHA Claudius* IX.4; Zosimus I.46.2); Aurelian settled defeated Carpi in Thrace (Aur. Vic., *de Caes.* XXXIX.43; *SHA Aurelianus* XXX.4; Lactantius, *DMP* 9.2); Probus settled Burgundians and Vandals in Britain (Zosimus I.68.3) and Bastarnae in Thrace (Zosimus I.71.2; *SHA Probus* XVIII.1); de Ste Croix (1981), Appendix III 509–518.

61. *Pan. Lat.* IX 21.§1; *CTh* XIII.11.10[399].

62. Williams (2000), 98.

63. Barnes (1976), 176 notes that Diocletian's imperial title suggests that between 284 and 301 there were six victories over Germans, four over Sarmatians, two over the Persians and one each over the Carpi, Armenians, Medes, Adiabenes and Britons.

64. Lactantius, *DMP* 12.3–5; Eusebius, *HE* VIII.11 on Adauctus as *magister rei privitae* and *rationalis samarium*.

65. There is some suggestion that Diocletian had marked the outset of his reign with a persecution given the martyrdoms of Maximilian and Marcellus (*Acta Maximiliani*;

Musurillo (1972), 250–259), but these instances are individual rebellion against some of the practices that service in the Roman army involved rather than against governmental persecution. Such martyrs represent a minority opinion amongst Christians but their actions "headstrong and rash, too eager to die... [may have brought] trouble on the bearers of the name" (Tertullian, *De Corona Militis* 1.4–5) of Christian by bringing them to imperial attention as shirkers.

66. Lactantius, *DMP* 10; *Divine Institutes* IV.27.4; there is little consensus for the date of this event with between 297 and 302 being championed: Woods (1992), 128–131 for 297; Helgeland (1974), 159 for 301 while Barnes (1976), 245 argued for 302 or "not long before" but in (1981), 18–19 accepted 299.

67. Lactantius, *DMP* 11, 14; Eusebius, *HE* VIII.4.3 on Galerius employing a *magister* to force Christian officers to sacrifice or be dismissed or even executed; *contra* Williams (2000), 173.

68. Lactantius, *DMP* 15 on Diocletian's persecutory tendencies being tempered by his wife and daughter, Prisca and Valeria, who were both secretly Christians.

69. *CAH* XII.665.

70. Lactantius, *DMP* 12–13; Eusebius, *HE* VIII.2.

71. Lactantius, *DMP* 14.

72. Lactantius, *DMP* 14–15; Eusebius, *HE* VIII.6.

73. Lactantius, *DMP* 18.1–7; *Pan. Lat.* VII(VI)15.16; Lactantius, *DMP* 20.4

74. Lactantius, *DMP* 18 concocts a conversation between Diocletian and Galerius over the new *Caesares*, with the latter arguing for men who would follow him over the independently minded Maxentius and Constantine.

75. Eusebius, *Mart. Pal.* 3 §1.

76. Jones (1964), 74.

77. Lactantius, *DMP* 15.7; Eusebius, *HE* VIII.13; *VC* I.16

78. Optatus Milevitanus, *Against Parmenian* I.2.

79. Stephenson (2009), 116.

80. Constantine was proclaimed *Augustus* by his overzealous troops, leading to Galerius having to rein him in with recognition of his position of *Caesar*, which was confirmed at Carnuntum in 308.

81. Lactantius, *DMP* 29–30; Stephenson (2009), 123.

82. Eusebius, *HE* VIII.16; Lactantius, *DMP* 33.

83. Lactantius, *DMP* 23–25; Eusebius, *HE* VIII.7; IX.1.

84. *Pan. Lat.* VI (VII).2.1–3, 2.5–4.6; *RIC* VII.180; Julian, *Or.* I.6d–7a, III.51c; Syme (1971), 204, 334; (1974), 240–242; *contra* Lippold (1992a); Eutropius X.2 impugns this pseudo-genealogy; Grant (1993), 26–27 on Licinius attaching himself to Philip the Arab; *ILS* 730, 732 demonstrate the sons of Constantine reaffirming not just their descent from their father, their grandfathers Maximian and Constantius Chlorus but also Claudius II.

85. Lactantius, *DMP* 44.4.

86. Lactantius *DMP* 44.4–6 records a dream the night before the battle where Constantine is told to mark the *ChiRho* on the shields of his men. Eusebius *VC* I.27–29 claims that while on the march, Constantine saw a cross over the sun and the words *In Hoc Signo Vinces* – 'by this sign, you will conquer' – although Eusebius also mentions a dream where Constantine is visited by Christ, who encourages Constantine to take the *labarum* (a *ChiRho* mounted on a military standard) as his standard; it may not have been a *ChiRho*

Christogram but a slightly different staurogram made of the slanted Latin X and P; Frakes in Lenski (2012), 113–116.

87. Barnes (1981), 41–43; Curran (2000), 66–68 provide good overviews of Constantine's Italian campaign.

88. Eusebius, *Mart. Pal.* 4 §8; 9 §2.

89. Jones (1964), 72.

90. There were in fact three separate works from three separate periods that went by the name *Acts of Pilate*: an early Christian document known to Justin Martyr in c.150, the pagan construct of Maximinus Daia and a later fourth century pro-Christian version.

91. Lactantius, *DMP* 45–46; Lactantius claims that Licinius had just 30,000 men to Daia's 70,000, although this is likely an exaggeration of Licinius' peril to play up the 'miracle' of his victory over the hated persecutor.

92. Lactantius, *DMP* 47.

93. Lactantius, *DMP* 49.

94. Harries (2012), 100.

Chapter II: Preparation for the Purple: Constantius' Upbringing and Accession

1. The date of Cibalae is disputed with MacMullen (1987), 67; Jones (1948), 127; (1964), 82 suggesting 314, while Treadgold (1997), 34; Potter (2004), 378; Odahl (2004), 164 suggest 316.

2. Given the timings of the births of both Constantine II and Constantius II in 316 and 317, Constantine was shoring up his dynasty in the face of conflict with Licinius.

3. Julian, *Or.* I.9a.

4. *CIL* III.352=7000; *ILS* 6091; Drinkwater (2007), 69.

5. [Aur. Vic.], *Epit.* XLI.11–12.

6. Woods (1998), 70–86; Stephenson (2009), 219–223.

7. Ammianus XXI.16.8; Szidat (1977–1996), 208–212; Matthews (1989), 241.

8. Ammianus XXI.16.1.

9. Julian, *Or.* I.9d – how would Julian know? He was only about six or seven when Constantine died.

10. Sozomen IV.19.1; Theodoret, *HE* II.27.

11. Ammianus XXI.16.11.

12. Athanasius, *Apol. c. Ar.* 51.2 records Constantius calling himself philanthropic, Cyril of Jerusalem and Athanasius picked up on the emperor's wish to be portrayed that way, with the latter referring to Constantius as such on seven occasions in the *Apol. c. Cons.* alone; Bihain (1973), 264–296; Libanius, *Or.* LIX.85, 97, 122; Julian, *Or.* I.17a–20b, 38b, 45d, II.58b, 88b–89b 99a–b, 101b–d, III.114c; Themistius, *Or.* I.4d, 6a, 13c, 14b–15a, 16a; Vanderspoel (1995), 78–93; Dagron (1968), 129–132; Daly (1972), 355–360 on Themistius.

13. Julian, *Or.* I.31c–d; II.77c; Themistius, *Or.* III.45b–46a.

14. Whitby in Drijvers and Hunt (1999), 79; Julian, *Ep. Ad Ath.* 270c–d, 281b challenges Constantius' reputation for *philanthropia* and highlights his anger.

15. Ammianus XXI.16.1–7; Matthews (1989), 238–242 on Ammian obituaries.

16. Aur. Vic., *de Caes.* XLII.18.

17. Ammianus XXI.16.7.

18. Rohrbacher (2005).
19. Ammianus XXI.16.7.
20. Ammianus XXI.16.8.
21. Ammianus XXI.16.15.
22. Aur. Vic., *de Caes.* XLII.19; Ammianus XXI.16.16, cf. XIV.5.4; XVI.12.67; Julian, *Ep. ad Ath.* 272d, 283c; Matthews (1989), 274
23. Libanius, *Or.* LIX.22; *cf.* Themistius, *Or.* I.17b–18a; Julian, *Or.*91b–d.
24. Ammianus XXI.16.18.
25. The Church of the Holy Apostles began as the church attached to Constantine's mausoleum and its development into the great edifice it became may have been Constantine's plan; however, Constantine was perhaps more interested in his own final resting place than venerating the Apostles, leaving the construction of the Church of the Holy Apostles as more the responsibility of Constantius (Mango (1990), 51–61; Downey (1951), 51–80; Dark and Özgümü (2002), 393–413).
26. Whitby in Drijvers and Hunt (1999), 79.
27. Theodoret, *HE* II.16; any such pronouncement would have been seen as hypocritical by his opponents as he was going against the decrees of Nicaea by not condemning Arians.
28. Ammianus XXI.16.4; Aur. Vic., *de Caes.* XLII.18.
29. Libanius, *Or.* LIX. 8–9, 12–14, 33–34; *cf.* Aur. Vic., *de Caes.* XLII.18; Julian, *Or.* I.31c–d.
30. Julian, *Or.* I.11c–d, 47a.
31. Libanius, *Or.* LIX.36; Julian, *Or.* I.14a on Constantius being taught to govern through nature and law.
32. Libanius, *Or.* XLII.23; Eunapius, *V. Soph.* VI.3.1–7; Athanasius, *Festal Letter.* 4; Ablabius' mother told a tale of how a prophecy at his birth claimed that she had almost bore an emperor.
33. There are various laws addressed to him in the *Codex Theodosianus* as well as numerous mentions of his lofty position in the surviving sources: *PLRE* I.3–4 'Ablabius 4'.
34. Aur. Vic., *de Caes.* XLII.18.
35. Julian, *Or.* I.12a, 13b; *RIC* VII.73 on Constantine at Siscia; Aur. Vic., *de Caes.* XLI.13; Barnes (1976), 154 on Constantius not having the title *Sarmaticus* in early 337 using *AE* (1934), 158 but had added it sometime before the Pannonian conference in September the same year (*CIL* III.12483 = *ILS* 724); Ammianus XVII.13.25 states that Constantius took the title for a second time in 358; this question over Constantius' victory titles prompted a back and forth between Arce (1982); (1984) and Barnes (1983).
36. It had previously been called Drepanum and is now Altinova in north-western Turkey.
37. Aur. Vic., *de Caes.* XLI.16; Eutropius X.8.2.
38. Eusebius, *VC* IV.62.
39. Stephenson (2009), 280; Hippolytus of Rome, *Apostolic Tradition* XVII.1 on a catechumen requiring three years preparation, although XVII.2 includes a clause allowing baptism sooner with good conduct.
40. Hippolytus of Rome, *Apostolic Tradition* XVI.2–16 says that pimps, prostitutes, painters and sculptors of idols, actors, charioteers, game attendees, gladiators, officials at gladiator shows, military officials, takers of the military oath, military governors, prospective recruits, eunuchs, enchanters, magi, astrologers, diviners, oneiromancers and men with concubines should be refused baptism.
41. Eusebius, *VC* IV.63.

42. Zonaras XIII.5 records his principal residence as Naissus between 337 and 340 but as his realm included Italy, Moesia and Pannonia, he could easily have been at Milan, Aquileia, Sirmium or other major cities.

43. Burgess (2008) provides a tremendous examination of the succession and the massacre in 337.

44. Harries (2012), 187.

45. *Anon. Val.* 6.35; [Aur. Vic.], *Epit.* XLI.20; Ammianus XIV.1.2; Philostorgius III.22; *Chron. Pasch.* 335.

46. Burgess (2008), 7–10, 43–45 on Constantine planning to reinstate a tetrarchic system with Constantine II and Constantius II as the *Augusti* and Constans and Dalmatius as the *Caesares*; DiMaio (1988), 336.

47. Eusebius, *VC* IV.51, 58; Gregory of Nazianus, *Or.* IV.21; Zosimus II.40.2; Philostorgius II.16; Eutropius, *Brev.* X.9.1; [Aur. Vic.], *Epit.* XLI.18.

48. Ammianus XXI.16.8; Julian, *Ep. ad Ath.* 270c; Zosimus II.40; Libanius, *Or.* LIX.48.

49. Julian, *Or.* I.17a; *Ep. ad Ath.* 270c, 271b.

50. Burgess (2008), 26.

51. Burgess (2008), 22; Dalmatius *Caesar* appeared on small bronze coins from those mints.

52. This might have been initiated by a unilateral move by Constantine II to distance himself from the massacre. He had the least to gain as he was already the eldest and was not losing any territory to Dalmatius or Hannibalianus. Given his attack on Constans in 340, such a selfish act would not be beyond Constantine II.

53. Burgess (2008), 27.

54. Potter (2004), 461.

55. Burgess (2008), 26.

56. Harries (2012), 187–188.

57. Burgess (2008), 27; *Anon. Val.* V.29 presents a potential precedent for the use of an orchestrated military revolt to remove an imperial opponent when Constantine used it to remove Licinius.

58. Humphries (2008), 99.

59. Burgess (2008), 43.

60. Barnes (1976), 154; Burgess (2008), 33 nn.101–102; Athanasius, *Apol. ad Const.* 5.2; that Constantius likely took command of Dalmatius' forces for this campaign displays some need to control the flow of information regarding the purge; Burgess (2008), 35–40 on the possible itineraries in the run up to the Pannonian conference.

61. In more specific terms, Constantine II received the dioceses of Britannia, Galliae, Septe Provinciae and Hispaniae; Constans got the dioceses of Italia, Suburbicaria (southern Italy, Sicily, Sardinia and Corsica), Africa, Illyricum and Dacia while the dioceses of Aegyptus, Oriens, Pontica and Asiana fell to Constantius.

62. The diocese of Macedonia included the provinces of Epirus Nova, Epirus Vetus, Thessalia, Macedonia, Achaea and Crete while the diocese of Thrace was Scythia, Moesia II, Thracia, Haemimontus and Rhodope.

63. Cameron (1993), 32.

64. Southern and Dixon (1996), 18.

65. Southern (2001), 276; Blockley (1992), 9; while facets of the *comitatenses* field army can be traced to Constantine's campaign against Maxentius in 312, most had antecedents and it was not until 325 that the new divisions in the army – *comitatenses, ripenses, alares*

and *cohortales* – were recorded (*CTh* VII.20.4[325]). How much thought was put into these changes is debateable. A gradual evolution through a series of independent choices is more likely than sweeping overnight changes (Ferrill (1986), 45).

66. Jones (1964), 97, 99, 100; Hoffmann (1969), 156–157 suggests that the *auxilia palatina* was formed by Maximian; these units were named sometimes for the provinces they served in such as the *Dacisci*, *Moesiaci* and *Scythici* but most bore the names of tribes: Cornuti, Bracchiati, Petulantes, Batavi, Tungri, Nervii, Celtae, Heruli, Salii, Tubantes (Jones (1964), 100).

67. Roman soldiers were trained to march thirty-two kilometres a day while their pack animals could manage no more than that and uneven ground would reduce this distance (Vegetius I.27; Sallust, *BJ* 29, 90–91; Caesar, *BG* VII.17, 56; *BC* III.47–48; Goldsworthy (1996), 110); Ferrill (1986), 46 suggesting the core of Constantine's field army could take two months to reach the Rhine from Italy; Grant (1993), 74; Williams and Friell (1994), 78.

68. Zosimus II.34; Jones (1964), 97; Southern and Dixon (1996), 20, 34; although some field troops could be transferred to the frontiers.

69. Lee (1993), 70; Eutropius III.10; *ILS* 696, 8942; Wolfram (1988), 61; Kulikowski (2007), 83.

70. *CTh* VII.20.4[325]; the exact meanings of these terms were less straight forward than simply 'river patrol' or 'boundary patrol'. The former applied to all higher stature frontier troops including legions, *equites*, *cunei equitum* and *auxilia*, all of whom received some privileges similar to the *comitatenses* (*CTh* VII.20.4[325]). The latter term had two meanings. Originally, *limitanei* embraced all frontier troops defending the *limes* but came to be identified with those legally bound to serve as a militia, defending and cultivating their land (*CJ* I.27.2 §8[534]). It is anachronistic to impose the latter definition of *limitanei* as peasant-soldiers than full time professionals that Malalas XII.308 would have understood on the reigns of Diocletian and Constantine.

71. Jones (1964), 612; 649–651; *CTh* VII.20.3[320] is addressed "*ad universos veteranos*" while *CTh* VII.20.8[364] granted them "*omnibus benemeritis veteranis*."

72. Southern and Dixon (1996), 37.

73. *Pan. Lat.* XIII.3, 5 on Constantine only using a quarter of his forces, 40,000 men, while invading Italy; Zosimus II.15; Jones (1964), 1084, n.45; Constantine left the majority of his forces behind to protect the frontiers and for speed of movement (Southern and Dixon (1996), 18). Maxentius is recorded as having access to 188,000 men, which is not only suspiciously high, but also surely a total for all of his lands in Africa and northern Italy rather than the army he had available to face Constantine. Perhaps only 80,000 were at his immediate command and many will have been of suspect loyalty given that he had bribed them away from Severus II, Galerius and Licinius.

74. Jones (1964), 98.

75. Zosimus II.2; Ferrill (1986), 43.

76. *Anon. Val.* 16, which also suggests that Licinius had 35,000 at the battle.

77. Wardman (1984), 225; Thrace and its manpower was a much needed boon for Constantius; the promotion of *limitanei* as *pseudocomitatenses*, the transfer of *comitatenses* to the frontiers and the *palatini* and the service of palatine units in regional field armies suggests that the armies were at the limits of their manpower (Ammianus XVIII.9.3; XX.7.1; Crump (1973), 93); the permanent reinforcing of the *limitanei* garrison of Africa

with *comitatenses* saw the *dux Africae* promoted to *comes* (Ammianus XXI.7.4; *CTh* VII.1.4[349]; VIII.7.13[372]).

78. Ammianus XXI.16.15.

79. Ammianus XIV.10.11–14 on Constantius referring to his men as *commilitones*; Zosimus III.9.1; Ammianus XIV.10.11–14, XVII.1.2; Zosimus III.9.1 on Constantius and Julian sharing the burdens of their men, while Constans lost support for distancing himself from the military; the emperor's field army was commanded by a *magister peditum* and *magister equitum*, styled *in praesenti* or *praesentalis* to differentiate them from the other *magistri* (Jones (1964), 124–25, 1089–91 n.26 on Constantius II's *magistri* using Ensslin (1931), 107ff).

80. The Tetrarchy had seen the Praetorian Guard reduced to just another garrison force. By reinstating Rome as an imperial residence and restoring prestige and privileges to the Praetorians, Maxentius made them his staunchest supporters but after many of them died at Milvian Bridge, Constantine disbanded this menace (Eusebius, *HE* IX.9.5; Zosimus II.17.2; Aur. Vic., *de Caes*. XL.25); as Constantine will not have trusted his personal security to a brand new unit and must have had some kind of bodyguard since 306, the *scholae* predated the disbanding of the Praetorians; Southern and Dixon (1996), 18; Hoffmann (1969), 281 on 312; a precursor for this new guard is likely, for it appears that all palatine corps were modelled on the *schola* (Frank (1969), 47–48; *CIL* VI.32965; Baynes (1925), 201–204; Parker (1933), 175–189); Zosimus II.15; Frank (1969), 51 on this personal allegiance shown by many *scholares* adopting the emperor's *nomen*, explaining the number Flavii; by 363, powerful individual German generals elected a *commendabilis*, Jovian, as *Augustus*.

81. Wardman (1984), 221; Ammianus XV.5.16; XXXI.13.14; XXXI.15.8; Jerome, *Vita S. Hilarionis Eremitae* 22; Ammianus XXV.3.6 demonstrates their importance as Julian had become detached from his bodyguard when he was killed in Persia; *CTh* VIII.1.10[365] reveals the elevated position of the *scholae*.

82. Jones (1964), 89; *CTh* VII.20.4[325]; VII.22.2[326]; Goffart (1974), 25 n.13 suggests Constantine aimed "to absolve veterans from all public charges;" 53–60 on the nature of exemptions from *caput* and *capitatio*; Constantine was faced by decurions illegally joining the army : *CTh* XII.1.10[325]; XII.1.11[325]; XII.1.13[326]; and Constantius II legislated against this: *CTh* XII.1.38[357]; Eusebius, *HE* X.7; *CTh* XVI.2.1–2[313]; XVI.2.7[330]; *CTh* XVI.2.6[326]; XVI.2.3[320] on clerical immunity and its abuse.

83. Grant (1993), 68; Ammianus XV.5.33; Eusebius, *VC* IV.7 on Bonitus serving under Constantine; Elton (1996a), 273 tabulates the origins of known *magistri*, suggesting non-Romans were the minority, although Jones (1964), 1084 n.46 and Liebeschuetz (1990a), 8 note barbarians assuming Latin names like the imperial *nomen*.

84. MacMullen (1976), 50–54.

85. Zosimus II.15.1, 17; Eusebius, VC IV.6; Jordanes, *Getica* 112, 145; Jones (1964), 57; Lee (2007), 53; Socrates I.20; Sozomen II.7; on *laeti and dediticii: Anon. Vales*. 32; Eusebius, *VC* IV.6: 30,000; Ammianus XVII.12.17–19; Zosimus II.22.1.

86. Ammianus XIX.11.7; XX.8.13; *Expositio totius* XLIII; Jones (1964), 613–14, 1253 n.12; Thompson (1966) 96–97; Wolfram (1998), 79–80; Agilo the Alaman (Ammianus XIV.10.8); Nevitta (Ammianus XXI.8; XXI.10.8); Gomoarius (Ammianus XXI.8.1); Victor the Sarmatian (Ammianus XXXI.12.6); Hormisdas the Persian (Ammianus

XVI.10.16); Silvanus (Ammianus XV.5.11); Dagalaif (Ammianus XXI.8.1); Theolaif and Abigild (Ammianus XXI.15.4).
87. Ammianus XXI.10.

Chapter III: The Sins of the Father: Constantius' War with Shapur II

1. Colledge (1967), 168.
2. The regal numbers, names and identities of these two warring Parthian kings are greatly muddled. Vologaeses, numbered VI or VII, may not have been the elder brother of Artabanus, numbered IV or V, or even a son of the previous Parthian king, rather a usurper called Walakhash/Balash.
3. As with any origin tale, what of this tradition is true is impossible to say. Frye (1984), 291 suggests that rather than the father of the dynasty, the name Sasan was adopted from a minor deity with links to the Achaemenid family to lend legitimacy; the Romans accepted Sassanid claims to Achaemenid roots (Dio LXXX.3).
4. Dio LXXX.3; Herodian VI.2.6–7; legitimate king or usurper, Vologaeses/Walakhash/Balash was defeated by 228/229.
5. This list included Iberians, Albani, Alans, Armenians and Medians in the Caucasus, Elymaeans, Characenes, Arabs and Persians around the Persian Gulf and Surens, Sakas, Yuezhi, Indians and Chionites in the east. Shapur I's inscription at Ka'ba-i Zardusht mentions petty kingdoms of Armenia, Meshan, Sakastan, Gelan, Adiabene, Kerman, Iberia, Kushanshahr, Choresmia, Pardan, Makran, Gurgan, Balasgan, Albania, Segan, the Lakhmids and Edesssa all subjected to the Sassanid King of Kings.
6. Despite the later suggestion that the Persians did "not know how to wheel about suddenly against their attackers, as do the Scythian nations", (Mauricius, *Strat.* XI.1) Sassanid cavalry retained the ability to discharge arrows backwards while they pretended to flee, known to history as the 'Parthian shot'.
7. Ammianus XXV.1.11–14.
8. Ammianus XXV.1.11–14.
9. Ammianus XXIII.8.83; XXIV.6.8; XXV.1.11–14, 18; Mauricius, *Strat.* XI.1; Wiesehöfer (2001), 191, 197.
10. Ammianus XIX.5; XX.6; Mauricius, *Strat.* XI.1; Wiesehöfer (2001), 198; Sassanid military science reached a sophisticated level with detailed manuals on organisation, horses, riding, archery, tactics and logistics.
11. Dio LXXX.3.2–3, 4.1–2; Herodian VI.2.1–2; Zonaras XII.15, 20–22; Herodian VI.5.1–6 records the Roman response to Ardashir that could be described as hostile; Dodgeon and Lieu (1993), 26–28 highlight other sources which suggest that Alexander Severus' forces were victorious, although these veer towards Severan propaganda.
12. Aur. Vic., *de Caes.* XXVII.7–8; Dodgeon and Lieu (1993), 355 n.9 on the ancient sources of Gordian III's Persian expedition and death; opinion is mixed as to just how badly the Romans were defeated at Misiche. Shapur would claim that Gordian III was killed in the battle, but that seems like Persian propaganda. The real culprit in the young emperor's death was either his successor, Philip the Arab or a frustrated army.
13. Dodgeon and Lieu (1993), 360 n.6 on no Roman source recording the defeat at Barbalissus; Zosimus I.27.2; Lactantius, *DMP* 5.

14. Zonaras XII.23; *SHA Valerian* IV.2–4; *Gallienus* I.1; III.1–5; X.1–8; Festus, *Brev.* 23; Jerome, *Chron.* 266; Eutropius IX.10.
15. There are several excellent works on this third century nadir of Rome and its recovery such as De Blois (1976) on Gallienus; Stoneman (1995) on Palmyra and Watson (1999) on Aurelian.
16. *SHA Probus* 20.1 on Probus supposedly planning a Persian campaign on his death in 282.
17. That Adhur-Narseh managed to get the military nobility and the priesthood, the two factions of Sassanid society who were almost constantly feuding, to join together to remove him could suggest the extent of his cruelty. However, Adhur-Narseh likely attempted to impose his will on the nobles and priests as any new king might have but was not strong enough to back it up, leaving those who should have helped him run the state to eliminate him. They could then paint Abhur-Narseh as a tyrant through their propaganda.
18. Daryaee (2009), 16.
19. Boyce (1979), 29.
20. Boyce (1979), 1.
21. Wiesehöfer (2001), 200.
22. Daryaee (2009), 133–149 on the Sassanid economy.
23. Lieu in Freeman and Kennedy (1986), 476–483.
24. *Chronicle of Arbela* 53.22–24.
25. Wiesehöfer (2001), 199.
26. Daryaee (2009), 15–16; Hormizd II recognised the opportunity of such a split in Armenia in marrying his daughter Hormizddukht to Vahan, a member of the powerful Mamikonian dynasty in Armenia. While they would produce saints of the Armenian church by the fifth century, it is difficult to gather when the Mamikonians converted to Christianity and therefore whether Hormizd was looking to reach out to a newly Christianised family or one that was still Zoroastrian in the first decade of the fourth century. That Vassak Mamikonian would lead Armenian general against Shapur II in the 350s shows that these overtures were unsuccessful.
27. Eusebius, *VC* IV.8–14; Aphrahat, *Dem.* IV–VI.
28. Buoyed by their killing of Hormizd II, Arab tribesmen crossed the Persian Gulf to raid Fars and in around 325, Shapur led a counterattack into the Arabian Peninsula, advancing to al-Yamama in the central Najd, inflicting a defeat on the Arab tribes and deporting many to Persian lands.
29. Movses Khorenantsi, *History of Armenia* II.92; the atmosphere in the east in the early 330s was not helped by famine and plague wreacking the region (Theophanes, *Chron.* AM5824; Jerome, *Chron.* 233).
30. Matthews (1989), 499 n.15.
31. Any attempts to attribute persecution of Christians to Constantine's motives for war with Shapur were largely propagandist in nature as any persecution likely came after war broke out as Shapur attempted to nullify any potential 'fifth column' activities from Persian Christians (Barnes (1985), 126).
32. Julian, *Or.* I.13b.
33. Theophanes, *Chron.* AM5815; Festus, *Brev.* 27; Dodgeon and Lieu (1993), 154 n.25 on Ensslin (1936), 106 n.1 identifies Narasara as being along the road from Amida to Tigranocerta, while Peeters (1931), 44–45 suggests that Narasara and the death of Narses were part of a later battle of Singara.

34. Dodgen and Lieu (1993), 152–153, 380 n.22 on the mess of the sources for Sassanid interference in Armenia.

35. Socrates II.7; Libanius, *Or.* LIX.75, 77.

36. Ammianus XVIII.9.1–2.

37. Constantius was returning to and building upon the strategy that Diocletian had implemented in the aftermath of the Peace of Nisibis (Dodgeon and Lieu (1993), 136–138; Lee in Campbell and Trittle (2013), 715–716; Pollard (2000), 291 on Constantius' fortress at Constantia.

38. Harries (2012), 215.

39. Peter the Patrician fr.14; *Exposito totius mundi* 22.

40. Ammianus XXV.8.14, 9.1 on Nisibis having vast defences by 363, although it not big enough yet to house a field army as those forces that visited Nisibis camped outside the city (Ammianus XX.6.9; XXV.8.17); Dio XXV.3.2, XXXVI.6.2.

41. Ammianus XIV.9.1; XIX.9.6; XX.6.9; Lightfoot (1988), 106–107.

42. Ephraem, *CN* XIII.18 on the Mygdonius outside the city; Zonaras XIII.7 on it through the city; Lightfoot (1988), 111.

43. Theodoret, *HR* 1304, line 22; *HE* II.30.5; Dodgeon and Lieu (1993), 165–168 present the sections of Theodoret's *HR* and *HE* as describing the first siege of Nisibis in 338, while Lightfoot (1988), 112 uses them for the third siege in 350, with inferences to Constantine's death being evidence of Theodoret's muddling of the account; Maroth (1979), 240–241 on Theodoret using Ephraem as a source.

44. Lightfoot (1998), 108; Van Berchem (1952), 27–30; the presence of *Nisibena* in the title of *Legio I Parthica* (*ND Or.* XXXVI.29) had led to suggestions that it may have resided at Nisibis at some stage pre–363 (Hoffmann (1969–1970), 419; Lightfoot (1988), 108–109).

45. Procopius, *BP* I.5.10–15.

46. It is here that Theodoret's account may place a manipulation of the Mygdonius by Shapur's men to undermine the Nisibean walls. Rather than insert that episode here, I have chosen to include it later.

47. Socrates II.7; Zonaras XIII.5.5–6; the year of this first siege of Nisibis has been the subject of some debate. Barnes (1985), 133 excludes 338, although Matthews (1989), 499 n.15 suggests either August of 337 or 338.

48. Julian, *Or.* I.20a–21a; at this time, Constantius also dealt with embassies from Arab tribes, who had become restless follwoing the deaths of their own leader and that of Constantine (Julian, *Or.* I.21b; Lightfoot (1981)).

49. Eunapius, *V. Soph.* VI.3.9–13; Zosimus II.40.3; Jerome, *Chron.* 338; Libanius, *Or.* XLII.23.

50. Barnes (1993a), App. VIII collects together much of this surviving information.

51. Julian, *Or.* I.21b–22a; that Constantius felt the need to train much of his field army in 338 might suggest it contained a significant number of new recruits, perhaps raised in and around Pannonia after the conference.

52. Julian, *Or.* I.37c–38a; Hoffmann (1969–1970), I.265–270.

53. Ammianus XVIII.7.1.

54. Libanius, *Or.* XVIII.206; LIX.76–87; Julian, *Or.* I.22a–d; Athanasius, *Hist. Ar.* 16; *CIL* III.3705= *ILS* 732; *CTh* XII.1.30; Oates (1968), 61–62, 75–76; Dodgeon and Lieu (1993), 179 n.18.

55. Julian, *Or.* I.26b on the battle taking place about six years before January 350; *Consul. Cons.* 236; Jerome, *Chron.* 348; Jacob of Edessa 293 on 348; Festus, *Brev.* 27 records two

battles while Ammianus XVIII.5.7 records battles at Singara and Hileia; Barnes (1980), 163 n.13 on one in late 343 and another in 348; Barnes (1993a), 312 nn.19, 23; Dodgeon and Lieu (1993), 188 n.25 suggests that the sources have conflated several engagements of varying size at or near Singara into one; Stein and Palanque (1959), 138 on Singara.

56. Ammianus XX.6.5; XVIII.9.3.

57. Libanius, *Or.* LIX.107 on 150 stades; Julian, *Or.* I.22d–25b on 100 stades; the length of a στάδιον varies depending on region, although it is likely that Libanius and Julian would be using the Olympic or Italian measurements – about 175metres and 185metres respectively.

58. Julian, *Or.* I.24a–25b.

59. Libanius, *Or.* LIX.99–120; Julian, *Or.* I.22d–25b; Dodgeon and Lieu (1993), 181 n.21; Oates (1968), 97–106; Blockley (1992), 16.

60. Eutropius, *Brev.* X.10.1; Ammianus XXI.16.15; Libanius, Or. XVIII.205–7; expectations were high for Constantius with comparisons made to Alexander the Great by Aphrahat, *Dem.* V, Julian, *Or.* 1.10b, 17c–d, 41c–d, 43c–d, 45d–46a; Flavius Polemius, *Itinerary of Alexander*; Warmington (1977) and Kaegi (1981) on Constantius' eastern strategy.

61. Matthews (1989), 499 n.15; Lee (2007), 30; Isaac (1992), 187, 254–255; the legions stationed in eastern cities had a tendency to fall into ill-discipline (Tacitus, *Ann.* XIII.35).

62. Jerome, *Chron.* 348 on nine major engagements, although only listing Singara, two sieges of Nisibis, and those of Bezabde and Amida. The battle of Narasara, the third siege of Nisibis and the fall of Singara could be added to that list, but it would still be short.

63. Firmicus Maternus, *de err. prof. rel.* 3; Jerome, *Chron.* 346; Theophanes, *Chron.* AM5837; *CTh* XI.7.5 on Constantius in Nisibis on 12 May 345.

64. Libanius, *Or.* LIX.94–97; Socrates II.13.7; Jerome, *Chron.* 235; *Chr. Min.* I.236; Barnes (1993a), ch.IX; 220 n.18 on the redating of two laws issued by Constantius at Constantinople from Oct 349 to Oct 343; *CTh* XI.36.8; Themistius, *Or.* I.

65. Julian, *Or.* 1.21B–22A; Libanius, *Or.* LIX.92–93; Ammianus XVIII.9.

66. Lightfoot (1988), 111; Theodoret, *HE* II.30.5; *HR* 1304–1305; Ephraem, *CN* I–III; XI.14–18; XIII.14–18; *Chron. Pasch.* 216–218, which may quote a letter from Vologaeses, bishop of Nisibis during the 350s; Zonaras XIII.7.2–13; Julian, *Or.* I.27b–28d, 30a; II.62b–66d.

67. *Chron. Pasch* 216, lines 2–5 on Shapur having mercenary princes in his force, which could have been Arabs, Kushans or Chionitae; *PLRE* I.517–518 'Lucillianus 3.'

68. Ephraem, *CN* II.2; Julian, *Or.* II.62b; Philostorgius III.22; *Chron. Pasch.* 215 lines 22–24; Theodoret, *HE* II.30.1–2, 9–10, 31.1; Lightfoot (1988), 113 on Constantius staying at Edessa during similar circumstances in 361 (Ammianus XXI.13.1–8).

69. Lightfoot (1988), 113 n.53 on Julian not hearing of the revolt until the winter of 350, although Julian's exact whereabouts at the time are not conclusively discernible.

70. *Chron. Pasch.* 216 line 2; Julian, *Or.* I.28d, II 28d; that Theodoret, *HE* II.30.4 gives a lower figure of seventy days could be further reason to doubt that he was talking about the siege of 350 rather than that of 338.

71. Ephraem, *Humni contra Iulianum* II.26; Theodoret, *HE* II.30.4; *HR* 1304 lines 13–20; Zonaras XIII.7.

72. Lightfoot (1988), 114.

73. Ephraem, *CN* I.1–8, III.7, XII.7.

74. Zonaras XIII.7; Ephraem, *CN* III.18 on a spring within Nisibis.

75. Lightfoot (1988), 116.
76. Julian, *Or.* I.27b–c; II.62b–63a; Homer, *Iliad.*7–11, 20–21, 300–302, 325; Lightfoot (1988), 117; Szepassy (1972) on Julian's account being inspired by Heliodorus, *Aeth.* IX.3–11; Lightfoot (1988), 118 n.87 on the opposite opinion that Heliodorus was inspired by Julian.
77. Dodgeon and Lieu (1993), 165 n.6.
78. The sources fail to agree on how many breaches were made – *Chron. Pasch.* 216, line 10, 217, lines 1–2 and Theodoret, *HR* 1304 lines 26–28 on one; Theodoret, *HE* II.30.6, again showing his ability to contradict himself, gives two; Ephraem, *CN* II.19; III.10 suggests three.
79. Julian, *Or.* II.65d–66a; *Chron. Pasch.* 216, lines 12–13, 217, lines 4–7; Ephraem, *Hymni contra Iulianum* II.19; see also Ammianus XXV.1.15.
80. Theodoret, *HE* II.30.7; *HR* 1304, lines 31–32; Zonaras XIII.7.
81. Lightfoot (1988), 124; *Chron. Pasch.* 217, lines 9–13; Ephraem, *CN* XIII.19–21; Theodoret, *HE* II.30.2, 11–14; *HR* 1304, lines 20–22, 35–37, 43–49; Baynes (1955), 248–260; Mango (1980), 155–159.
82. Lightfoot (1988), 125.
83. Theodoret, *HE* II.30.1–2, 8–10, 31.1; *HR* 1304, lines 46–53; Ammianus XVIII.75; XIX.9.9; XXIV.8.3; Herodian III.9.5–6 on the defenders of Hatra launching pots filled with poisonous flies at the army of the emperor Severus in 198; Brown (2006), 87–88; Neufeld (1980).
84. *Chron. Pasch.* 218, lines 13–15; Zonaras III.7; *cf.* Theodoret, *HE* II.26; Julian, *Or.* I.30b.
85. Lightfoot (1988), 125.
86. Wardman (1984), 231 on Julian presenting Constantius as a conscientious emperor, who secured the eastern frontier before marching to deal with Magnentius, while the usurper is described as denuding the Gallic frontier (Julian, *Or.* I.29a–30b, 34d–35a).
87. Kazuo (1955), 757–780.
88. Theodoret, *HE* II.30.1, 31.13; Zonaras XIII.7.

Chapter IV: Fraternal Civil War and the Usurpation of Magnentius

1. *CIL* III.12483 = *ILS* 724 records Constantine II as having the victory titles of *Alamannicus Maximus* and *Germanicus Maximus* while a letter from his father to the Senate in spring 337 records merely that of *Alamannicus* (*AE* (1934), 158), suggesting that Constantine II had campaigned against the Alamanni again.
2. [Aur. Vic.], *Epit.* XLI.1; Eutropius X.9; Zosimus II.41.1.
3. *CTh* XII.1.27[339] was issued with the names of both Constantine II and Constans but the former's name was placed first in a province that was part of latter's realm.
4. Barnes (1993a), 311 n.5.
5. Jerome, *Chron.* 235; *Chr. Min.* I.236; [Aur. Vic.], *Epit.* XLI.21; Socrates II.5; Zonaras XIII.5.7–14.
6. *CTh* XI.21.1[340].
7. Cahn (1987) proposes the withdrawal of Constantine II's coinage; *CIL* III.474, 477, 7198 at Smyrna in Asia Minor, *CIL* III.5207 in Noricum, *CIL* V.8030 at Brescia in Italy and

CIL VIII.12272 at Avita Baba in Africa bear witness to the erasure of Constantine's name; Barnes (1993a), 51–52.

8. Harries (2012), 192; *PLRE* I, 'Titianus 6', 918–919; 'Eugenius 5', 292; Libanius, *Or.* XIV.10; *ILS* 1244 on the statue, which was restored during Constantius' 357 visit after being damaged by the supporters of Magnentius.

9. Libanius, *Or.* XIV.10.

10. Harries (2012), 192–193 on Constans' court.

11. Harries (2012), 192; Eunapius, *VS* 492 has the Athenian philosopher, Prohaeresius, visiting Trier in 342.

12. Harries (2012), 194; Vogler (1979), 112–123 on the creation of the praefecture of Illyricum.

13. Septimius Acindynus, consul in 340, would serve Constantius as eastern praetorian prefect while Roman senators, Furius Placidius, consul 343 and Vulcacius Rufinus, consul 347, both held the short-lived position of *comes per Orientem Aegypti et Mesopotamiae.*

14. *ILS* III.1, 309–310; Rüpke (2005); *CTh* XVI.10.1[341]; Firmicus Maternus, *de err. prof. rel.* 28.6.

15. Aur. Vic., *de Caes.* XLI.23.4.

16. Julian, *Or.* I.34ab involves some exaggeration on Magnentius' financial appropriations but there was likely some factual basis; *RIC* VIII 41, 57; Harries (2012), 194–195.

17. [Aur. Vic.], *Epit.* LXI.24; Eutropius X.9.3.

18. Libanius, *Or.* LIX.144–149, although such waxing lyrical should be taken with a pinch of salt, "the habit of making journeys with only a small escort may account for his vulnerability in 350" (Harries (2012), 190 n.23); Ammianus XXX.7.5; Libanius, *Or.* LIX.127–136.

19. Pannonian conference – Julian, *Or.* I.19a; Libanius, *Or.* LXIX.75; Naissus base – Zonaras XIII.5; Thessalonica – *CTh* XI.1.4, 7.7; Viminacium – *CTh* X.10.4; Sirmium – *CTh* XV.1.5; *CJ* X.48.7; Sarmatian campaign – *CIL* III.12483; Savaria – *CTh* X.10.6.

20. Aquileia – *CTh* II.6.5; *CTh* X.15.3; Milan – *CTh* IX.17.1; Lauriacum (Enns in Austria) – *CTh* VIII.2.1; XII.1.31; Rome – Philostorgius III.1; *ILS* 726; *AE* (1988), 217; fighting the Franks – Jerome, *Chron* 235; *Chr. Min.* I.236; Libanius, *Or.* LXIX.127–136; Trier – Socrates II.13.4, 18; Milan – Athanasius, *Apol. ad Const.* 4.3; *CTh* IX.7.3.

21. Bononia – *CTh* XI.16.5; *CJ* III.26.6; British campaign – Firmicus Maternus, *de err. prof. rel.* 28.6; Libanius, *Or.* LXIX.137–140; Ammianus XX.1.1; return to Gaul – Libanius, *Or.* LXIX.139, 141; *CTh* XII.1.36; Athanasius, *Apol. ad Const.* 3.7, 4.4; Scots had not crossed from Ulster to give their name to Scotland.

22. Libanius, *Or.* LXIX.133; Athanasius, *Apol. ad Const.* 3.3, 3.7, 15.4; *Index* 17; Socrates II.22.5.

23. *CTh* X.10.7; III.5.7; Athanasius, *Apol. ad Const.* 4.5, 3.7.

24. Sirmium, Caesena in Italy and Milan – *CTh* VII.1.2; VIII.7.3; X.10.8, 14.2; XII.1.38.

25. Donatus was not the original leader of the Donatists, having been the successor of a certain Majorinus.

26. Tilley (1996), xvi.

27. Frend (1952), 159–162.

28. Optatus, *Against the Donatists* III.3; Frend (1952), 177–178; this *notarius* Paul could conceivably be Paul the Chain, who will be met later.

29. Optatus, *Against the Donatists* III.3.

30. Augustine, *Cont. Litt. Pet.* II.97.224, which suggests that there was a mass exile of Donatists enforced in 347 (*Passion of Maximian and Isaac* §3); Shaw (2011) provides a tremendous study of the violence and hatred in African Christianity in the late fourth/early fifth centuries.

31. Harries (2012), 190, which also mentions similar accusations against the emperor Gratian, who was also overthrown and killed by the Gallic army; similar enough to raise suspicions of the veracity of both accusations.

32. Aur. Vic., *de Caes.* XLI.24; Eutropius X.9; Zosmius II.42; cf. [Aur. Vic.], *Epit.* XLI.24; DiMaio (1977), 279ff; Harries (2012), 190.

33. Zosimus II.42.2–5; Julian, *Or.* II.57d–58a; [Aur. Vic.] *Epit.* XLI.22; *Chr. Min.* I.237; Jerome, *Chron.* 237.

34. That Magnentius was possibly of barbaric origin (Zosimus II.54; Julian, *Or.* 1.34A; Themisitus, *Or.* III.43a; VI.80c; Aur. Vic. *de Caes.* XLI.25; [Aur. Vic.], 4 *Epit.* XLII.7) demonstrates the acceptance of barbarians in imperial service.

35. Julian, *Or.* I.33c–d, 34d, 42a, II.6c, 95c; Whitby in Drijvers and Hunt (1999), 81 suggests that Julian had an ulterior motive in portraying Magnentius as a barbarian for at the time of writing this panegyric, he had just been given responsibility for the Rhine frontier; Drinkwater (2000), 138–145.

36. [Aur. Vic.], *Epit.* XLI.23; Aur. Vic. *de Caes.* XLI.21.23; Zosimus II.41–42; Ammianus XV.5.17; Barnes (1993a), 101–102; Harries (2012), 195–196; Laniogaesus would later appear serving with Silvanus, while Gaiso was reportedly a *magister* under Magnentius and was rewarded for the death of Constans by sharing the western consulship of 351 with the usurper.

37. Harries (2012), 196; Julian, *Or.* I.34ab.

38. Salama (1987), 203–216; *Chr. Min.* I.69; Chastagnol (1962), 107–111; *RIC* VIII.325/6 Aquileia 122 celebrating Magnentius' arrival at Aquileia in early March, 350.

39. *Chr. Min.* I.237; Philostorgius III.22.

40. Harries (2012), 187; Barnes (1982), 108 on not just Julius Nepotianus' father being consul but also his grandfather, another Virius Nepotianus in 301; Eutropius X.11.

41. Tertullian, *de Spectaculis* 22; *CTh* IX.18.1[315]; XV.12.1[325].

42. Aur. Vic., *de Caes.* XLII.6–9; Eutropius X.11; [Aur. Vic.] *Epit.* XLII.3; Zosimus II.43.2–4; Socrates II.25; Sozomen IV.1.

43. Sasel (1971), 205–216.

44. Barnes (1993a), 102.

45. Zonaras XIII.8, this is not a fully accepted dating of Decentius' elevation with his serving of consul only in 352 leading to the suggestion of a promotion to *Caesar* in mid-351 instead of 350 (Barnes (1993a), 102 n.10); *ILS* 742; *RIC* VIII.213–214 Arles 131–132, 158–159; VIII.261 Rome 168, 207–208, 266–267.

46. Zosimus IV.43.1; John of Antioch frag. 187; Rougé (1958); Barnes (1982), 44, 103; this would not be the only time that Justina's supposed imperial heritage would be used to add legitimacy to a new regime as Valentinian I would take her as his second wife and her daughter Galla would marry Theodosius I, providing a link between the Constantinian, Magnentian, Valentinian and Theodosian dynasties.

47. *RIC* VIII.157 Trier 260 depicting Magnentius in military dress on a ship holding Victory on a globe and a labarum with its Christogram; Barnes (1993a), 102.

48. *CTh* XVI.10.5[353]; *CTh* XVI.10.1[341] on Constans' ban; Eusebius, *VC* II.45.1 on

Constantine's ban on pagan sacrifice following his defeat of Licinius; Barnes (1981), 210–211; (1984), 69–72; (1989), 322–325, 330.

49. Barnes (1981), 75, 209.

50. Athanasius, *Apol. c. Ar.* 49.1; *Apol. ad. Const.* 9–11; *Hist. Ar.* 51.4; Barnes (1993a), 94–100.

51. Zonaras XIII.7.

52. Jerome, *Chron.* 238; Chr. Min. I.238; Zosimus II.44.3–4.

53. Ammianus XXI.10.2.

54. Barnes (1993a), 105; Sasel (1971), 210–216; Zosimus II.45–53; Seeck (1911), 435; Baynes (1925), 149–151; Paschoud (1971), XLII, 120–121, 253–261.

55. *RIC* VIII.372 Siscia 318/319.

56. Zosimus II.46.3.

57. Zonaras XIII.8.17.

58. Sulpicius Severus, *Chron.* II.38; RIC VIII.368–369, 386, 416.

59. Ammianus XV.5.33; Bonitus' rank under Constantine is not known; while none of Constantine's *magistri* are known, barbarians serving at virtually all levels and the scathing attacks launched by Julian on Constantine for his promotion of barbarians (Julian, *Caes.* 329b; Ammianus XXI.10), Bonitus being a *magister* is not unlikely.

60. Drinkwater (1997) accepts Constantius encouraging a barbarian invasion but not without reservations; Drinkwater (2000), 142 suggests that some historians were encouraged to formulate Magnentius' barbarian origins in order to paint him as leading the Alamanni into the empire rather than Constantius encouraging them.

61. Faulkner (2000), 241.

62. Ammianus XVIII.9; Julian, *Or.* II.98D; 1.28, 35A.

63. Zonaras XIII.8.17.

64. Eutropius X.12.

65. Sulpicius Severus, *Chron.* II.38.

66. Julian, *Or.* II.58c–59b on Marcellinus' body never being found.

67. *Chr. Min.* I.238; Sulpicius Severus, *Chron.* II.38.5–7; Socrates II.28.33; Zosimus II.45.3, 48.3; Socrates II.28.33, 29.1 on Constantius being present at the Council of Sirmium in October, 351; *CJ* VI.22.5[352] and *CTh* III.5.1[352] have him at Sirmium in February and May of 352.

68. Barnes (1983), 235; Barnes and Vanderspoel (1984), 175–176 using Constantius taking the victory title *Sarmaticus Maximus* before 358; Ammianus XVII.13.25, 33; Julian, *Or.* I.9d on Constantius winning a victory over the Getae, something of a catch all term for the tribes beyond the lower Danube.

69. *AE* (1982), 383 is an epitaph dated by the consulship of Decentius and Paulus rather than Constantius and Gallus Chr. Min. I.69; Camodeca (1978) on the defection of the governor of Aemilia et Picenum.

70. *CTh* XV.14.5[352]; Athanasius, *Hist. ac.* I.7; *Index* 25; *CTh* XI.1.6, XII.1.42, XVI.8.7.

71. Ammianus XVI.12.5; Lorenz (1997), 23–24; Zotz (1998), 391; Drinkwater (2007), 201.

72. *RIC* VIII.164–165 Trier 328–337; Ammianus XV.6.4; Kent (1959), 105–108; Bastien (1983), 187–189.

73. *CTh* XI.1.6 and XII.1.42 have been amended from 22 May, 354, which would place Constantius at Milan on that same date in 353; a similar amendment has been made to *CTh* XVI.8.7 from 3 July, 357, which would see Constantius still in Milan in early July, 353.

74. Eutropius X.12.
75. Eutropius X.12; *Chr. Min.* I.238.
76. *Chr. Min.* I.238; Eutropius X.12.2; Athanasius, *Apol. ad Const.* VII.3 on Magnentius hanging instead of stabbing himself; this Senones is likely modern Sens in Bourgogne, although it could be the commune of Senon.
77. *CTh* VII.13.1[353]; this law provides evidence that recruits would rather serve in the cavalry than infantry (Pharr (1952), 170 n.6); Crawford (2011), 33–40, 44–52, 56–69 on recruiting during the life of Constantius.
78. Ammianus XVII.3.2.
79. *CTh* IX.38.2[353]; Ammianus XVI.5.1.
80. Ammianus XIV.5.4.
81. Matthews (1989), 36.
82. Ammianus XIV.5; XV.5.35; Matthews (1989), 33.
83. Ammianus XIV.5.6, although Ammianus XV.3.4 claims Paul was a Persian by birth.
84. Ammianus XIV.5.8.

Chapter V: Drunk with Power: The Rise and Fall of Constantius Gallus

1. Eusebius, *VC* IV.49 on Constantine celebrating the marriage of his second son in the thirtieth year of his reign, which would tabulate with the removal of Crispus' memory.
2. Barnes (1993a), 105.
3. Whether or not Nepotianus would have been considered a candidate had he not jumped the gun in June 350 and got himself killed as a result will never be known.
4. Ausonius, *Com. pro. Burd.* 17.11; Ammianus XIV.11.17; Julian, *Ep.* 20.
5. Libanius, *Or.* I.434, 524.
6. Julian, *Ep. ad Ath.* 273B; Zosimus II.40.2; Libanius, *Or.* XVIII.31.
7. Libanius *Or.* XVIII.10; Socrates III.1; Sozomen V.2.9; Theophanes, *Chron. AM* 5831; Athanasius, *Hist. Ar.* 69.1 suggests being Constantius' brother-in-law aided Gallus' survival, although it had not helped his older brother.
8. Ammianus XXII.9.4; Vanderspoel (1995), 116 suggests Constantius imposed this move to Macellum when he visited Constantinople to expel Paul of Constantinople in early 342 (Libanius, *Or.* LIX.94–97; Socrates II.13.7); Socrates III.1; Julian, *Ep. ad Ath.* 271B; Gallus had seemingly inherited property near Ephesus, reflected in the bequeathing of land to the Ephesian church by Basilina (Palladius, *Dial.* XIII; Photius, *Bibl. Cod.* 96).
9. Gregory of Nazianzus, *Or.* IV; Sozomen V.2; Julian, *Ep. ad Ath.* 271C–D; they were not completely cut off from society and Constantius visited them in around 347 (Julian *Ep. ad Ath.* 274A; Bidez (1930), 24 n.6).
10. Ammianus XIV.11.28.
11. *Con. Const.* 351; Zonaras XIII.8.4; *Chr. Min.* I.238; Philostorgius III.22, 26, 28; Theophanes *AM* 5842; *Passio Artemii* 11–12; Peter the Patrician fr. 16; Julian *Ep. ad Ath.* 272D; Vanderspoel (1995), 85 n.58.
12. Ammianus XV.2.7; Libanius, *Or.* XVIII.17; Julian, *Misopognon* 351B.
13. Socrates II.28.22; *Chr. Min.* I.238; *Passio Artemii* 11; *Cons. Const.* 351; Barnes (1993a), 316 n.54 on a cross in the sky above Jerusalem recorded by Cyril of Jerusalem with the suggestion that the star on Antiochene coinage commemorates this event (Seeck (1919),

198); Gallus had the relics of St. Babylas moved into the precinct of Apollo at Daphne (John Chrysostom, *Homily on St. Babylas* 101; Sozomen V.19.12–13). Julian saw such a desecration of a temple of Apollo as being the root of Gallus' destruction (Zonaras XIII12), although Christians could have seen the moving of a martyr's remains to a pagan shrine in an equally impious light. Gallus was also dragged into the doctrinal controversies through his interactions with the anomoean Aetius. Originally, the *Caesar* was prompted by Basil and Eustathius to order Aetius' execution, only to be dissuaded by Leontius, bishop of Antioch. Gallus then had Aetius appointed as a tutor to Julian, although Aetius would later be involved in the trials in Antioch (Philostorgius III.27; Barnes (1993a), 102–105).

14. *Passio Artemii* 12; Philostorgius III.26.
15. Philostorgius III.28; *Passio Artemii* 12; Zosimus III.1.
16. Ammianus XIV.1.1.
17. Ammianus XIV.7.5.
18. Ammianus XIV.11.28.
19. Ammianus XIV.3.1.
20. Ammianus XIV.3.2.
21. Ammianus XIV.3.3.
22. Matthews (1989), 406.
23. Ammianus XV.5.19; XVIII.6.2.
24. Ammianus XIV.11.4.
25. Thompson (1947), 56–59; Blockley (1972), 441–443; (1975).
26. Jerome, *Chron.* 238.
27. Socrates II.33; Sozomen IV.7; Jerome, *Chron.* 282; Theophanes, AM 5843; Credenus I.524; Arce (1987); Geiger (1979a); (1979b); Bijovsky (2007) investigates coin hoards from the areas affected by the revolt and looks at the other literary and archaeological evidence as well.
28. Ammianus XIV.4.1.
29. Ammianus XXIII.3.8; XXV.6.9–10; Julian, *Or.* 1.21B; Philostorgius VII.15.
30. Lenski (2002), 197; Lenski (1999b), 431–446.
31. Lenski (2002), 199; Lenski (1999a); (1999b) on Isaurian revolts in Ammianus.
32. Ammianus XIV.2.13.
33. Ammianus XIV.2.20; XIX.13.1–2; XXVII.9.6–7; Zosimus IV.20.1–2; Eunapius fr. 43.4; Basil of Caesarea, *Ep.* 200, 215, 217; the Isaurians would become a valuable source of recruits for the Roman army over the course of the fourth century and in 461, the Roman emperor Leo I would form a 300-strong bodyguard originally made up entirely of Isaurians called the *Excubitores*, and in 474, Leo's Isaurian son-in-law, Tarasicodissa, became *Augustus* under the name Zeno.
34. Ammianus XIV.1.1.
35. Barnes (1993a), 106.
36. Ammianus XIV.9.1.
37. Ammianus XIV.1.1.
38. Ammianus XIV.1.2.
39. Ammianus XIV.1.2.
40. Ammianus XIV.1.8, 2.
41. Ammianus XIV.1.4, 7.4; Zonaras XIII.8.25–31.

42. Ammianus XIV.1.3, 9.

43. Libanius, *Or.* I.91, 96–97, 99–100; *Ep.* 64.

44. Ammianus XIV.7.7–8; that the sack of Celse is recorded in a lost book of Ammianus suggests that it took place before Gallus' elevation.

45. Ammianus XIV.7.2; perhaps Honoratius' intervention here was the reason why he was replaced as *comes Orientis* by Nebridius by the time of the Isaurian siege of Seleucia.

46. Ammianus XIV.7.5–7; Libanius, *Or.* I.103, XIX.47; Julian, *Misopognon* 370C.

47. Ammianus XIV.1.10.

48. It is somewhat surprising not to see Gallus or Constantina accused of some involvement in the timely passing of a prefect who had stood up to them.

49. Ammianus XIV.7.11.

50. Ammianus XIV.7–13–14; Philostorgius III.28 on Constantina attacking Montius.

51. Ammianus XIV.7.18.

52. Ammianus XIV.7.21, 15–20.

53. Ammianus XIV.9.

54. Ammianus XIV.10.5.

55. Ammianus XIV.10.11–15.

56. Ammianus XIV.10.16.

57. Ammianus XIV.11.1–3.

58. Ammianus XIV.11.6 on her body being brought for burial at what would become Santa Costanza, although more recent archaeology has suggested that she may not have been buried there immediately as the mausoleum may not have been finished in time (Webb (2001), 249–252).

59. Ammianus XIV.11.8.

60. The *agentes in rebus* were essentially an imperial secret service, led by the *magister officiorum*; originally, the *frumentarii*, who were in charge of the grain supply, they became a secret police by the early second century CE before being reconstituted as the *agentes in rebus*.

61. Ammianus XIV.11.23; Ammianus took some glee in reporting that those whose lies brought Gallus to his death suffered for their actions – Scudilo died of a liver abscess having "vomited up his lungs" while Barbatio was found guilty of the same kind of aspirations that he had accused Gallus of (Ammianus XIV.11.24).

62. Ammianus XV.1.3.

63. Ammianus XV.4.1 records a second Alamannic tribe joining the Lentienses but the text is corrupted.

64. Ammianus XV.2.3.

65. Ammianus XV.3.4–6.

66. Ammianus XV.3.7–11.

Chapter VI: "This Turbulent Priest": Constantius, Athanasius and Religious Politics

1. Athanasius, *Festal Letters*, Index III records Athanasius answering the charge of being too young to have been appointed Patriarch of Alexandria on 8th June, 328 and canon law stated that a minimum age of thirty for ordination (twenty-nine on inclusive reckoning); that Constantine took no action suggests that Athanasius was close enough to the limit to

ignore it or was over the age limit; his enemies would not have brought it up continually had he not been close to the limit, so it seems likely that Athanasius was born in the last years of the third century CE; *Epistula Ammonis* 13.

2. Barnes (1993a), 1.

3. Barnes (1993a), 13–14; Seeck (1911), 332, 503–504; *contra* Frend (1974), 21 n.1 who, using Sozomen II.17.10, sees Athanasius as a product of the Alexandrian middle class.

4. Barnes (1993a), 13; the term 'Copt' has a long etymology through Latin, Arab, Coptic, Greek and ultimately Ancient Egyptian – before reaching its modern English version. In the simplest terms, it is an adaptation of the Greek word Αἰγύπτιος, meaning 'Egyptian' and during the Roman period was used by the Greek inhabitants of Egypt for the native Egyptian population and did not symbolise any specific religious persuasion. It was only after the Muslim conquest of Egypt in the seventh century that it became increasingly restricted to an ethnoreligious meaning for those Egyptians who followed their own branch of Christianity.

5. Rufinus X.15; Socrates I.8.13, 15; Sozomen II.17.3–31; Gelasius of Cyzicus III.13.10–14; Barnes (1981), 215–219 on the agenda of the Council.

6. Alexander was not the immediate successor of Peter as a certain Achillas served between 312–313.

7. Barnes (1993a), 14; see Barnes (1993a), 14 n.50 on the extent of the modern discussion on Arius' theology.

8. Sozomen I.5, 15.

9. Sozomen I.15.

10. Barnes (1993a), 15 gives the list of prominent men; the importance of Eusebius' support was not just his considerable intellect but also his being the bishop of Nicomedia, the current residence of Licinius.

11. Sozomen I.15.11; Epiphanius, *Pan.* 69.3.2.

12. Sozomen I.15; when Peter retreated from Alexandria during the Great Persecution, Melitius, bishop of Lycopolis, usurped his position. Upon his return, Peter excommunicated Melitius (Athanasius, *Apol. c. Ar.* 59.1), who was then deported to the mines of Palestine, where he founded the schismatic 'Church of the Martyrs'. Upon the cessation of the Persecution, Melitius returned to Egypt to establish his own churches in opposition to the jurisdiction of Alexandria. (Barnes (1981), 201–202; Vivian (1988), 15–50; *EOMIA* I.634–636; Epiphanius, *Pan.* 68.1.4–3.4; Sozomen I.15.2; *P.Lond.*)

13. Barnes (1993a), 15.

14. Barnes (1993a), 16 using Eusebius *VC* II.63–73; Socrates I.7.1 on the identification of Hosius as Constantine's envoy, which is disputed by Warmington (1982), 95–96 who argues for the *notarius*, Marianus.

15. Socrates I.9.1–4; Theodoret, *HE* I.9.2–13; Eusebius, *VC* III.13–14.

16. Athanasius, *Apol. c. Ar.* 45.2; *Fug.* 3.3; *Hist. Ar.* 5.2.

17. Barnes (1993a), 18.

18. Athanasius, *Festal Letter* 4.5; *Apol. c. Ar.* 60.4, 63.4; *Index* 3.

19. Barnes (1993a), 22 – this order was aimed at Athanasius who had refused to attend a council at Caesarea the previous year; Eusebius, *VC* IV.41.3–4; Athanasius, *Apol. c. Ar.* 81.

20. Not without objection from Athanasius about the identity of the commissioners (Athanasius, *Letters to the Bishops of Libya and Egypt* 7; *Apol. c. Ar.* 73.2–81.2).

21. Sozomen II.25.15–19 on Athanasius' deposition stemming from four factors: (i) his fleeing Tyre before learning his fate, an act that was considered an admittance of guilt (ii) his refusal to attend the council at Caesarea in 334 demonstrated contempt for the emperor and the Church (iii) he had attempted to disrupt the Council of Tyre by employing a gang (iv) the destruction of Ischyra's chalice.

22. Constantine had imbued church councils with an authority that no magistrate could overturn; however, he did retain "the right to decide whether a particular gathering of bishops was a properly constituted council whose decisions were to be regarded as divinely inspired. Moreover, he both claimed and exercised the right to summon a council of bishops, to refer matters to it, and to define is agenda" (Barnes (1993a), 24).

23. Athanasius, *Index* 8; *Apol. c. Ar.* 87.4; Epiphanius, *Pan.* 68.9.5/6.

24. Barnes (1993a), 32.

25. Athanasius, *Hist. Ar.* 8.1.

26. Athanasius, *Apol. c. Ar.* 87.4–7; *Hist. Ar.* 8.2; by the time Athanasius had been allowed to return to his see, he no longer had to contend with Arius who had died at Constantinople in 336. The undignified and horrific demise that Arius suffered – "a violent relaxation [which left] his bowels protruded, followed by a copious hemorrhage, and the descent of the smaller intestines; moreover, portions of his spleen and liver were brought off in the effusion of blood" (Socrates I.38) – was considered divine retribution for heresy. Ashrafian (2014) gives the medical explanation of a rectal prolapse and also suggests that an intestinal parasite such as the helminth whipworm (*Trichuris trichiura*) might be the underlying cause of such a devastating physical event.

27. Athanasius, *Apol. ad Const.* 5.2.

28. Barnes (1993a), 36; App. VIII on Paul of Constantinople.

29. Barnes (1993a), 36; Theodoret, *HE* II.3.8.

30. Athanasius, *Apol. c. Ar.* 18.2; *Index* 10; *Vita Antonii* 69–71; the information he gathered for his defence would later become the basis for his *Apologia Contra Arianos* and *Apologia ad Constantium*.

31. Athanasius, *Hist. Ar.* 10.1.

32. Socrates II.10.1; Athanasius, *Index* 11.

33. Athanasius, *Encylical Letter* 1.1–9, 2.2–4.5.

34. Barnes (1993a), 52 on Athanasius, *Apol. ad. Const.* 4.1 using "any others" in place of a specific mention of Constantine II.

35. Barnes (1993a), 53; Athanasius, *Encyclical Letter* 1.6–8, 7.3; it is possible that *Apologia contra Arianos* was composed around this time with its main aim being to highlight the heretical nature of Arius' Christology rather than political manoeuvrings.

36. Barnes (1993a), 53; the cause of Athanasius and Julius was boosted by, or perhaps undermined by, the arrival in Rome of Marcellus of Ancyra. He too had refused to subscribe to the rulings of councils of Jerusalem and Tyre. A council at Constantinople in 336 deposed him, although the same amnesty that saw Athanasius return to Alexandria allowed Marcellus return to Ancyra, amidst rioting. This saw Eusebius of Caesarea taking up against Marcellus for his use of violence and his heretical beliefs. The same Council of Antioch that deposed Athanasius also removed Marcellus once more. He went first to Constans in Illyricum before arriving in Rome in the spring of 340 (Epiphanius, *Pan.* 72.2.3; Barnes (1993a), 57; (1981), 263–265).

37. Athanasius, *Apol. c. Ar.* 21–35 records the back and forth between Julius and the bishops at Antioch.

38. Sozomen III.8.3; Socrates II.15.3.Athanasius, *Apol. c. Ar.*21.2, 20.3 on Julius' 341 synod.
39. Socrates II.12.1.
40. Socrates II.12.2–13.7.
41. Barnes (1993a), 69.
42. Theodoret, *HE* II.16.21.
43. Jerome, *Chron.* 235; *Chr. Min.* I.236; Socrates II.13.4 on Constans being engaged in campaigning against, defeating and settling the Franks in Toxandria; Lucifer of Caralis, *De Athanasio* I.29.28; Athanasius, *Apol. ad Const.* 4.4; Barnes (1993a), 71 n.2 on the arguments over the date of the Council of Serdica.
44. Socrates II.20.6 suggests seventy-six; *CSEL* 65.74–78 gives a surviving list of seventy-three names.
45. Athanasius, *Hist. Ar.* 16.2; Festus, *Brev.* 27; Theophanes, *Chron.* AM 5834–5835; any such Persian victory is not identified – was this the potential first battle near Singara? Or the raid across the Tigris that saw the capture of Nineveh? Or something else?
46. *CSEL* 65.181.13–182.2; this letter along with the synodical polemic and a third letter from Constans commending the exiles reached Constantius at Antioch around Easter 344; Athanasius, *Hist. Ar.* 21.2.
47. Athanasius, *Hist. Ar.* 20.2–5; Theodoret, *HE* II.8.54–10.2.
48. Socrates II.22.5; Athanasius, *Apol. ad Const.* 3.3; Theodoret, *HE* II.16.21.
49. Barnes (1993a), 90; Athanasius, *Apol. c. Ar.* 51.2–4; *Hist. Ar.* 21.1–2; *Index* 18.
50. Athanasius, *Hist. Ar.* 22.2; *Apol. ad Const.* 4.5.
51. One casualty of the Council of Serdica was Marcellus of Ancyra. In shoring up their own position, his western backers recognised the "inherently heretical" (Barnes (1993a), 92) nature of his beliefs. This removal of support makes the recording of his return to Ancyra (Socrates II.23.42; Sozomen III.24.3) in the aftermath of Serdica unlikely. However, Marcellus did make it back to Ancyra before his death in 371 (Epiphanius, *Pan.* 72.11), perhaps under Julian's mass restoration of all exiled eastern bishops in the winter of 361/362. Despite a long career – he was likely over ninety by the time of his death – Marcellus was tarnished by heresy and the Council of Constantinople formerly condemned his ideology in 381.
52. Socrates II.26.6; Athanasius, *Hist. Ar.* 7.1, 3–6.
53. It is possible that the bishop of Alexandria wrote his *Apologia contra Arianos* in order to meet this peril and meant for it to be read before this latest council.
54. Barnes (1993a), 102.
55. Athanasius, *Apol. ad Const.* 23; *Hist. Ar.* 51.4.
56. Barnes (1993a), 114.
57. Sulpicius Severus, *Chron.* II.39.3–6.
58. Ammianus XV.7.6–10.
59. Athanasius, *Apol. ad Const.* 22; *Hist. ac.* 1.9.
60. Athanasius, *Apol. ad Const.* 25; 27.1–28.4; *Hist. Ar.* 54–81; *Fug.* 6.1; *Hist. ac* 1.10; *Index* 28.
61. Athanasius, *Hist. Ar.* 81 records strong resistance in Alexandria, with pro-Athanasians remaining in control of numerous churches until June. They were removed by the new prefect, Cataphronius, and the *comes* Heraclius but even so George did not arrive in Alexandria until 24 February 357 only to be almost lynched on 29 August the following year, forcing him into flight. The *dux* Sebastianus regained control of Alexandria on Christmas Eve 358 but George dared not return. An imperial edict was delivered on

23 June 359 demanding the acceptance of the current bishop but it was not until after Constantius' death that George re-entered Alexandria, only to be lynched four weeks later (Athanasius, *Hist. ac.* 2.2–6; *Index* 29).

62. Athanasius, *Apol. ad Const.* 30–31; Frend (1989); Barnes (1993a), 120 n.65–67 on Constantius' dealings with the peoples of the Nile head waters and beyond.

63. *Letter to the Bishops of Egypt and Libya, Defence of his Flight, History of the Arians* and *On the Councils of Arminium and Seleucia* were all composed during this period, on top of numerous letters to his supporters.

64. Barnes (1993a), 132; Athanasius, *Hist. Ar.* 1.2; *CTh* XVI.2.12 suggests that, despite Athanasius' criticism, Constantius followed his father's guideline that only a council could condemn and depose one of their own.

65. De Clerq (1954), 55 argues against the suggestion that Hosius might have had Egyptian roots.

66. Barnes (1993a), 138, 139.

67. Hilary, *Syn.* 11; Athanasius, *Syn.* 28 – *homoiousios* was also mentioned in later texts of the letter.

68. *Homoousios* is made up of the Greek words *homos* and *ousia* meaning "same essence", which demonstrates that its upholders saw the three parts of the Trinity being the same. *Homoiousios*, made from *homoi* and *ousia*, meant "similar essence", suggesting that the parts of the Trinity were distinguishable and therefore not equal.

69. They attached significance to the term *anomoios*, which comes from *av* and *homoi*, meaning "not similar".

70. Athanasius, *Syn.* 38.4.

71. Hilary, *Syn.* 8; Socrates II.39.1–7; Sozomen IV.16.14–22.

72. Athanasius, *Syn.* 8.7.

73. Socrates II.37.96; Sozomen IV.19.8.

74. Barnes (1993a), 148.

75. Athanasius, *Syn.* 30.8–10; Socrates II.41.8–17; Theodoret, *HE* II.21.3–7.

76. Barnes (1993a), 150; Hilary of Poitiers, *Ad Const.* 8.1.

77. Barnes (1993a), 150–151.

78. Hilary of Poitiers, *In Const.* 1/2, 5–11, 27.

79. *CSEL* 65.198.5–15.

80. Barnes (1993a), 153; Brennecke (1984), 360–367 on indirect evidence of Julian wooing the support of Constantius' ecclesiastical opponents.

81. Barnes (1993a), 153.

82. Brennecke (1984), 87 n.1 suggests that Julian was present, although that would go against Julian's campaigning beyond the Rhine before spending the winter at Vienne.

83. Barnes (1993a), 154.

84. Barnes (1993a), 155; Athanasius, *Hist. ac.* 3.1/2; Greogry of Nazianus, *Or.* IV.84–85; Rufinus VIII.33.

85. Barnes (1993a), 155; (1981), 148–163.

86. Athanasius, *Hist. ac.* 2.8–10, 3.3–4, *Index* 35; Julian, *Ep.* 110.398c–399a, 111.432c–435d; Rufinus X.35; Socrates III.14.1–6; Sozomen V.15.3; Theodoret, III.9.3–4.

87. Athanasius, *Hist. ac.* 4.4, *Index* 35; Rufinus XI.1; Barnes (1989).

88. Eutropius, *Brev* X.18.2; Ammianus XXVI.1.5; Socrates III.36.5, IV.1.1; Ammianus XXVI.1.7, 2.1–2, 4.3; *Chr. Min.* I.240.

89. Socrates IV.16; Sozomen VI.14; RufinusXI.5; Theodoret IV.17.1–4; Lenski (2002), 234–263 on religion under Valens.
90. Barnes (1993a), 164.
91. *CTh* XVI.1.3[381], 2[380]; Liebeschuetz (1990a), 146–153 on Theodosius' religious politics.
92. *CTh* IX.16.2[312].
93. Eusebius, *VC* III.54; Libanius, *Or.* XXX.6, 37, LXII.8; Julian, *Or.* VII.228b.
94. Eusebius, *VC* IV.10.
95. Zosimus II.29.1–4; *CTh* IX.16.1–9; XII.1.21, 5.2; XVI.2.5, 10.1[320].
96. Brown (2003), 74.
97. Firmicus Maternus, *de err. prof. rel.*XVI.4
98. Libanius, *Or.* XXX.7.
99. *CTh* XVI.10.2[341], 4[346], 5[353], 6[356]; IX.16.4[357], 5[356], 6[357].
100. Curran (2000), 193.
101. Curran (2000), 183–188 presents the arguments of Martroye (1930), 672; Noethlichs (1971), 54, n.325; Tomlin (1973), 448; Salzman (1987); Firmicus Maternus, *Mathesis* II.30.10 on nocturnal sacrifice and divination.
102. *CTh* XVI.10.3[342]; Curran (2000), 185–186, 188–190.
103. Ambrose, *Ep.* XVIII.31.
104. *CTh* XVI.10.3; IX.17.2; Ammianus XII.4.3; Sozomen III.18; Libanius, *Or.* XVIII.23.
105. Garnsey (1984), 19.
106. Ambrose, *Ep.*XVIII.32; Symmachus, *Rel.* III.4, 6; Sheridan (1966), 186–187; this altar had been installed by Augustus in 29BCE and would be restored soon after.
107. *CTh* VIII.4.7; XII.1.49; XV.8.1; XVI.2.8, 9, 11, 14, 15.
108. Brown (2003), 74.
109. Eusebius, *VC* III.18–19; Theodoret, *HE* I.9.
110. *CTh* XVI.9.1[335]; XVI.8.2–4.
111. *CTh* XVI.9.2[339].
112. *CTh* XVI.8.7; XVI.9.2.
113. Julian, *Ep.* 25; Bowersock (1978), 79–93 on Julian's religious policies, including allowing the Jews to return to Jerusalem and to rebuild the temple.
114. Barnes (1989), 313–321; Edbrooke (1976), 40–61; *PLRE* I.512–514 'Lollianus 5'.
115. *PLRE* I.3–4 'Ablabius 4'.
116. Optatus, *Against the Donatists* III.3.
117. Barnes (1993a), 169.
118. Barnes (1993a), 107.
119. Barnes (1993a), 106.
120. Schäferdiek (1978); Halsall (2007).

Chapter VII: From Student to Soldier: The Rise of Julian

1. Aur. Vic., *de Caes* III.16.
2. Ammianus XIV.5.3–14.
3. Nutt (1973).
4. Ammianus XV.6.3.
5. Drinkwater (1994); Hunt in Drijvers and Hunt (1999), 46–56; Ammianus XV.5.

6. Ammianus XV.5.29.
7. Ammianus XV.5.31.
8. Ammianus XV.5.35.
9. Ammianus XV.6.
10. Ammianus XV.6.1.
11. Ammianus XV.6.2.
12. Ammianus XV.5.35.
13. Amminaus XV.8.4.
14. Ammianus XV.8.5–9.
15. Ammianus XV.8.12–14.
16. Ammianus XV.8.13.
17. Ammianus XV.8.14.
18. Suetonius, *Tib*. XXV.1.
19. Homer, *Iliad* V.83.
20. As no primary source records her year of birth, it is not possible to state Helena's age with certainty but as she was the daughter of Constantine and Fausta, with the latter dying in 326, she had to be at least twenty-nine when she married Julian in 355, while Julian was twenty-three or twenty-four.
21. *Itin. Burd.* 557.7; Ammianus XV.8.19 records this position as being the spot marked by two columns, lying between Laumellum and Ticinum as well as the suppression of the news of Cologne's fall; Matthews (1989), 88.
22. Ammianus XV.8.19.
23. Ammianus XV.8.21–22 on Julian being a "lawful prince" in contrast to Magnentius and Decentius.
24. Blockley (1972), 446.
25. Julian, *Ep.* 277D–278A; Eunapius fr.14.2; Socrates III.1; Sozomen V.2; Libanius, *Or.* XVIII.42
26. Barnes (1993a), 106; Matthews (1989), 81–93.
27. Julian, *Ep. ad Ath.* 277a–278b.
28. Ammianus XVI.2.5.
29. Matthews (1989), 88.
30. Ammianus XVI.1.3.
31. Ammianus XVI.1.4; Eutropius X.16.5; Julian, *Ep. ad Them.*
32. Ammianus XVI.2.9.
33. Ammianus XVI.2.4 – this woodland area is now the Morvan Regional Natural Park, a protected area of lakes, farmlands and forests in central France.
34. Ammianus XVI.2.5.
35. Ammianus XVI.2.11.
36. Ammianus XVI.2.12.
37. Tacitus, *Germania* 16
38. Murdoch (2003), 49.
39. That Constantine had seen to the refortifying of Divitia on the opposite bank of the Rhine less than fifty years previously might suggest that the reason for the rebuilding needed by Julian was not age but that the Franks had destroyed its walls rather than settle there.
40. Julian, *Ep. ad. Ath.* 279a.
41. Ammianus XVI.4.2.

42. Ammianus XVI.5.3 on Julian frequently "contenting himself with the coarse and ordinary rations of the common soldiery", enhancing his popularity with the Gallic forces.
43. Murdoch (2003), 51.
44. Libanius, *Or.* XVIII.48; Julian, *Ep. ad. Ath.* 279a–b.
45. Ammianus XVI.7.2; this does not assuage accusations of plotting against Julian, even if the emperor was allowing a formerly trusted official to give his side of the story before casting him into exile.
46. Ammianus XVI.7.4–7 speaks very highly of Eutherius despite him being a eunuch, suggesting that even "among brambles roses spring up". Born free in Armenia only to be captured and gelded by a hostile tribe and sold to the Romans, Eutherius had earned a reputation for self-restraint, intelligence and problem solving. Ignored by Constans, he served Julian well and was not afraid to rebuke the *Caesar* for frivolousness.
47. Ammianus XVI.5.9–15.
48. Ammianus XVI.11.1.
49. Ammianus XVI.11.4.
50. Hoffmann (1969), 156–157; Jones (1964), 99–100.
51. Thompson (1966), 96–97; Wolfram (1998), 79–80.
52. Ammianus XIX.11.7.
53. Jones (1964), 120.
54. Ammianus XX.4.2; Constantius also hired Goths and Scythians (Libanius, *Or.* XII.62; Ammianus XX.8.1.
55. Julian, *Caesares* 329B; Ammianus XX.8.13; XXI.10; XXIII.2.2; XXIII.5.1; XXXII.2.1–2; XVII.8.3–4; Simpson (1977b), 519
56. Ammianus XVI.11.8.
57. This was seemingly the same man partly blamed for the *laeti* debacle. His rapid recall has seen doubts raised over the reasoning for Valentinian's exile with Lenski (2002a), 49 highlighting, but not accepting, the claim that he was dismissed for not offering pagan sacrifice due to his Christianity; Woods (1995a), 32–33, (1995b), (1997); Lenski (2002b); there is discrepancy in the destination of Valentinan's exile – Philostorgius VII.7 on Thebes in Egypt; Sozomen VI.6 on Melitene in Armenia; *Chron. Pasch.* XIII.337 on Selymbria in Thrace and Theodoret, *HE* III.12 on "a fortress in the desert".
58. Ammianus XVI.11.8–10.
59. Julian's advance scouts may have failed to see the approach of this Germanic force because they were employed in gathering resources to replace the supplies taken by Barbatio.
60. Ammianus XVI.11.15.
61. Ammianus XVI.12.2–3.
62. Ammianus XVI.12.5 on Chnodomarius' defeat of Decentius.
63. Ammianus XVI.12.3.
64. Ammianus XVI.12.11, 19.
65. Ammianus XVI.12.19; Lorenz (1997), 47–48; Libanius, *Ep.* 140 muddles the topography of the battle by suggesting that there was a swamp crossed by a waterway present.
66. Ammianus XVI.12.14.
67. Ammianus XVI.12.8–13; 62.
68. Ammianus XVI.12.2–3; Libanius, *Or.* XVIII.49, 54.
69. Ammianus XVI.12.2, 7, 43, 45, 49, 63.

70. Ammianus XX.1.3, 4.1, 2; Zosimus II.58.
71. Jones (1964), 680–684; Coello (1996); Elton (1996a), 89–90; Tomlin (2000), 169–173; Lee (2007), 76.
72. Zosimus III.67.
73. Ammianus XVI.11.14.
74. Ammianus XVI.12.43.
75. Ammianus XVI.12.26.
76. The more powerful of the two Alamanni chiefs in Raetia – Gundomadus – had been murdered, perhaps when he refused to aid Chnodomarius; Ammianus XVI.12.17 claims he was killed through treachery but without naming names. It was his brother and fellow chief – Vadomarius – who stood to gain the most from Gundomadus' demise and with Ammianus XXI.3.4 hinting at Constantius later using Vadomarius as a check on Julian, there could be some imperial connection to the murder of Gundomadus; however, it would seem far-fetched to suggest that the emperor would have orchestrated the elevation of Vadomarius only for him to lead his men against Julian at Strasbourg, even with Constantius' previous encouragement of the Alamanni to invade Gaul.
77. Ammianus XVI.12.19.
78. Ammianus XVI.12.16.
79. Ammianus XXVII.2.4, 7 – a three-pronged army in 366 with a division of 10,000; XXXI.10.5 – a force in 378 of 40,000; Heather (2009), 36–72.
80. Rosen (1970), 110–114; Lorenz (1997), 45 n.47 both offer reviews of the arguments.
81. Drinkwater (2007), 141, 142, 169; (1997), 1 and n.2.Wolfram (1990), 28; Aur. Vic., de Caes. XXI.2; Ammianus XVI.12.6 records the Alamanni as "swarming" over Roman territory.
82. Steuer (1997a), 149–150); (1998), 284–285, 314–317); Mueller-Wille (1999), 41–63); cf. Carroll (2001), 137; Drinkwater (2007), 238, 331, 334.
83. Ammianus XVI.12.26; Heather (2009), 61–62 on Alamannic economics having advanced enough to hire mercenaries.
84. Drinkwater (2007), 163–166, 238–239.
85. Drinkwater (2007), 238.
86. Delbrück (1980) II.2.2.
87. Ammianus XVI.12.43, 49–51.
88. Aur. Vic., de Caes. XXI.2; Drinkwater (2007), 141–142, 175–176, 239; Elton (1996a), 58.
89. Ammianus XXVII.1.3; XXXI.10.8.
90. Ammianus XVI.12.44, 46.
91. Libanius, Ep 143; Ammianus XVI.12.24.
92. Drinkwater (2007), 237, which also hints that Chnodomarius' victory over Decentius was exaggerated; cf. Rosen (1970), 120–121.
93. Ammianus XVI.12.34–35.
94. Ammianus XVI.12.26.
95. Ammianus XVI.12.19 on Serapio having experience in battle despite his youth.
96. Ammianus XVI.12.22.
97. Ammianus XVI.12.28.
98. Libanius, Or. XVIII.45; Julian would later promise a reward of 100 silver pieces for bravery against the Persians (Ammianus XXIV.3.3).
99. Drinkwater (2007), 239.
100. Ammianus XVI.12.21, 37–41; Zosimus II.58.

101. Ammianus XVI.12.27; Libanius, *Ep.* 140.
102. Ammianus XVI.12.42–51, 55–56.
103. Ammianus XVI.12.63; Libanius, *Ep.* 141.
104. Ammianus XXIV.3.1–2; Lendon (2005), 295, 309; Zosimus III.68; Ammianus XVI.12.38–41; *cf.* Libanius, *Or.* XVIII.56–59; Rosen (1970), 126); Lorenz (1997), 48–49.
105. Ammianus XVI.12.64.
106. Ammianus XVI.12.58–61, 65–66.
107. Ammianus XVII.11.2; Drinkwater (2007), 239 called this "ethnic cleansing", which in a literal sense is correct but would seem to invoke more vile actions than was likely the case.
108. Ammianus XVII.2.
109. Ammianus XVII.1.3.
110. Ammianus XVII.1.6.
111. Ammianus XVII.1.11; this fort lay in the Rhine–Danube angle known as the *Agri Decumates*, which had been Roman territory from the Flavian dynasty until its abandoning and conquest by Alamannic tribes in the 260s; Julian would recall how impassable these forests of Germany were (Julian, *Shorter Fragments* 2); Pomponius Mela III.29: "the land itself is not easily passable, because of its many rivers it is rugged on account of its numerous mountains; and to a large extent it is impassable with its forests and swamps."
112. Ammianus XVII.1.1–14.
113. Ammianus XVII.2.3 records Julian sending the surviving tribesmen to Constantius, who, given his later demand of recruits from his *Caesar*, probably enrolled them in an auxiliary unit.
114. Ammianus XVII.2.
115. Ammianus XVII.1.4.
116 Drinkwater (2007), 240; Ammianus XVI.12.68–70; cf. Aur. Vic., *de Caes.* XLII.13.
117. Drinkwater (2007), 240, which also suggests that this might have been out of some guilt for the treatment of the Alamanni since they helped Constantius defeat Magnentius; *RIC* VIII.346, 382; Lee (2007), 38.

Chapter VIII: *Adversus Barbaros*: Constantius and Julian Across the Rivers

1. Murdoch (2003), 67.
2. Ammianus XVII.3.2.
3. Libanius, *Or.* XVIII.84: on the one recorded occasion that he was accused, Florentius asked Julian to try his case, a request he refused.
4. Such write offs seemingly benefitted everyone but in reality they benefited the bigger taxpayers who would have had the influence to postpone payment, while the lesser taxpayers had to pay on time. It would be these lesser taxpayers who would be targeted for supplementary taxes, discouraging most from paying tax at all.
5. Ammianus XVII.3.4.
6. Ammianus XXI.16.17; *CTh* XI.16.7[356]; 8[356].
7. Ammianus XVII.3.6.
8. Jones (1964), 119–120.
9. Ammianus XVI.5.14–15; XVII.3.4; Blockley (1972), 449.

10. Julian, *Ep.* 4.
11. Ammianus XVII.8.1 says that July was the normal time for the beginning of the Gallic campaigning season.
12. Julian, *Ep. ad Ath.* 279d; Zosmius III.5.2.
13. *Pan. Lat.* IV.9.1–4, 21.1 on the settlement of Franks in Roman territory by Constantius Chlorus; perhaps more importantly, *Pan. Lat.* VII.6.2 has been read as imperial sanction of the Salian Franks settling in Batavia and some of the islands in the mouth of the Rhine, although there has been discussion about the identity of the emperor involved, Constantius Chlorus in c.297, Constans in 341–342 or Magnentius in 350–353.
14. Julian, *Ep. ad Ath.* 280a–c.
15. A region that covers North Brabant in the Netherlands and large parts of the Belgian provinces of Antwerp and Limburg.
16. Ammianus XVII.8.1–4; 9.2.
17. Ammianus XVII.8.5; Julian, *Ep. ad Ath.* 280a–c; Zosimus III.6.1–3 suggests that the Salii had been forced into Roman territory by the Quadi while the Saxons, the tribe directly east of Frankish territory, have also been mentioned as a possible candidate; the distance to Quadi lands would seem to rule them out and while the Saxons may have entered into the piratical raiding of the English Channel, there is little reason to suspect that Ammianus and Julian are wrong in their identification of the Chamavi as the immediate root of the problem.
18. Ammianus XVII.8.5; Julian, *Ep. ad Ath.* 280a–c.
19. Orosius VII.40.3; Gregory of Tours, *HF* II.2.9; Whittaker (1994), 160–166 on the *Limes Belgicus* and the Lower Rhine in the fourth century; James (1988), 39; Southern and Dixon (1996), 48; that is not to say that Romano-Frankish relations were completely friendly during this period as both Arbogast and Stilicho had to campaign against the Franks (Zosimus IV.47.1; 53.1; Orosius VII.35.12; Philostorgius X.8; Gregory of Tours, *HF* II.9; [Aur. Vic.], *Epit.* XLVIII.6; Prosper Tiro 1191; Hydatius 17; Paul Mil. *Vita Amb* 30; *CIL* XIII.8262 = *ILS* 790; Whittaker (1994), 166).
20. Ammianus XVII.9.1.
21. Ammianus XVII.9.3.
22. Ammianus XVII.9.6.
23. Ammianus XXII.11.1.
24. Ammianus XVII.10.1.
25. Ammianus XVII.10.1–2.
26. That an Alamannic chieftain like Suomarius could be operating so far north as to be in territory suggests how fluid and ill-defined ownership of much of this barbarian territory really was.
27. Ammianus XXVII.10.5; Charietto represents a curious use of barbarian manpower as he began his career as what was essentially a headhunter, attacking and killing barbarian raiders who strayed into Roman territory. So successful was he and his gang that they were brought to the attention of the local Roman commander and later Julian, who had Charietto and his head-hunters enlisted as an irregular army unit. Continued success saw him promoted to *comes per utramque Germaniam* by 365 before he was killed in battle against the Alamanni (Ammianus XXVII.1–2; Zosimus III.7; Whittaker (1994), 163–164, 193).
28. Ammianus XVIII.1.1.

29. Ammianus XVIII.2.4 records the names of seven of these re-established forts – *Castra Herculis* (Arnhem–Meinerswijk in the Netherlands), Quadriburgium (probably Qualburg near Cleves in Germany), Tricensimae (better known as *Colonia Ulpia Traiana*, now modern Xanten), Novaesium (modern Neuss), Bonna (modern Bonn), Antennacum (modern Andernach) and Vingo (modern Bingen); Lendering and Bosman (2013).
30. Ammianus XVIII.2.
31. Julian, *Ep. ad Ath.* 280c–d.
32. Valentinian won a bloody battle against the Alamanni at Solicinium in 368, while Gratian's forces under Naniemus and Mallobaudes defeated the Alamannic Lentienses at Argentovaria in May 378; Ammianus XXVII.1–2, 10, XXVIII.2.1–10, 5; XXIX.4; XXX.3; XXXI.10.
33. Ammianus XX.1.1.
34. Ammianus XX.1.3.
35. Ammianus XVI.8.1; the extension of the death penalty to those found consulting soothsayers or using pagan portents (Ammianus XVI.8.2).
36. When he was commander of the night-patrol of public buildings and monuments of Rome under Magnentius, Dorus accused the urban prefect, Adelphius, of a similar crime (Ammianus XVI.6.2).
37. Ammianus XV.3.7–11; XVI.8.3–6.
38. Ammianus XVI.8.11.
39. Ammianus XVI.10.2.
40. Ammianus XVI.10.13–14; Symmachus, *Rel.* III.7; Julian, *Or.* II.77; Aur. Vic., *de Caes.* XLII.23; [Aur. Vic] *Epit.* XLII.18; Duval (1970); Edbrooke (1976); Klein (1979); MacCormack (1981), 40–43; Vera (1981), 35–36; Matthews (1989), 231–235; Curran (2000), 192–193; these good relations between Rome and Constantius did not guarantee the good behaviour of the city's inhabitants. In 359, Tertullus, prefect of the city, was assailed by the public for the lack of grain as bad weather had prevented the grain ships from putting in at Portus harbour. The prefect supposedly offered his own infant sons to the mob, telling them that his boys were Roman citizens too and affected by the grain shortage just as they were. This appeased the rioters long enough for the weather to turn and allow the ships to make port (Ammianus XIX.10.4).
41. Drinkwater (2007), 220; Ammianus XVII.12.16.
42. Drinkwater (2007), 221.
43. *CTh* XVI.2.13; Barnes (1993a), 222; two laws from the summer and autumn of 356, *CTh* XI.30.25 and XI.7.8 were issued from Messadensis and Dinumma, which have been identified as being in Raetia; however, rather than being proof of the extent of Constantius' third Alamannic campaign, their geographic location should be largely discounted as these two places are otherwise unknown (Barnes (1993a), 314 n.34).
44. Drinkwater (2007), 221.
45. Lorenz (1997), 36–38; Drinkwater (2007), 122, 221–224; Libanius, *Or.* XVIII.104 mentions banditry practised by survivors of Magnentius' army; *cf.* Drinkwater (1984), 369.
46. Heather (2009), 129; Dexippus frg.6–7; Aur. Vic., *de Caes.* XXXV.2; Ammianus XVII.6.1; Drinkwater (2007), 227 n.71 on the Suebi mentioned by Ammianus XVI.10.20 being these Juthungi faced by Barbatio.
47. Ammianus XVII.6.2.

48. Ammianus XVII.6.3.
49. Kulikowski (2007), 84.
50. Zosimus II.31.3.
51. Barnes (1981), 300 n.30 on defeat and settlement of the Carpi in 307 by Galerius; Ammianus XXVIII.1.5; XXVII.5.5; Eutropius IX.25; Heather (2009), 128 on the Romans using defeated barbarians to repopulate devastated frontier lands.
52. *Cons. Const.* s.a. 332; Eusebius, *VC* IV.5–6; Aur. Vic. *de Caes.* XLI.13; Eutropius X.7; Jordanes, *Getica* 112, 145; Blockley (1992), 8.
53. Eutropius X.4; the usurper Procopius based his claim to imperial office on his Constantinian affiliation and gained Gothic backing because of it (Eunapius fr.37).
54. Wolfram (1988), 63.
55. Ammianus XVII.12.9.
56. Heather (2009), 85.
57. Ammianus XVII.13.8–11.
58. Ammianus XVII.13.16–20.
59. Heather (2009), 85.
60. Ammianus XIX.11.10.
61. Ammianus XIX.11.14.
62. Heather (2009), 128.
63. Kulikowski (2007), 106; Julian, Or. 1.9D.
64. Ammianus XXII.7.8.
65. Kulikowski (2007), 106; *CIL* III.3653 = *ILS* 775.
66. Valens found the Gothic army a tough proposition in the aftermath of Procopius' usurpation and it took three years of hard campaigning and economic depredations before he could claim victory (Themistius, *Or.*X.133a, 135c–d; Ammianus XXVII.5.7, 10; Zosimus IV.11). While these campaigns left the Goths prone to the Huns, these decades of growth along the Danube helped them maintain enough coherence to provide Valens with another test in 378 that he was to fail fatally at Adrianople; Lenski (2002a); Barbero (2007); Hughes (2013).
67. Ammianus XVII.13.25, 26–33.

Chapter IX: The Return of the King of Kings

1. Macrianus, *Digest* XLVIII.22.5 on the three different types of exile: exclusion from named places, confinement to a certain area or banishing to an island.
2. Libanius, *Ep.* 1481; Ammianus XIX.12.9.
3. Ammianus XIX.12.11.
4. Ammianus XIX.12.13.
5. Ammianus XIX.12.16.
6. Ammianus XIX.12.19.
7. Ammianus XIX.12.18.
8. Ammianus XIV.3.1.
9. Ammianus XV.13.4; Zosimus III.1.1.
10. Ammianus XVI.9.
11. Ammianus XVI.9.4, XVII.5.1, with the former recording the Kushans as the Cuseni, although poor reproduction or copying saw Ammianus' use of *Cusenos* corrupted to

Eusenos; that Shapur could be wintering simultaneously in the lands of two separate peoples could be explained by the Chionites and Kushans struggling for control of the same regions in Central Asia.

12. Ammianus XVII.5.3–8; Zonaras XII.9.25–27.
13. Ammianus XVII.5.9–15, Zonaras XIII.9.28–29.
14. Ammianus XVII.14, XVIII.6.17–18; on the revolt of Procopius – Ammianus XXVI.6–10; Lenski (2002a), 68–115.
15. Ammianus XVIII.4.1.
16. Ammianus XVIII.5.5, 6.1.
17. Ammianus XVIII.5.6–8; Livy XXII.51; Florus I.22.19.
18. Ammianus XVIII.5.8.
19. Warmington (1977), 515 using Ammianus XVIII.6.3, 7.9–11; *contra* Dodgeon and Lieu (1993), 389 n.16; Lessen in Drijvers and Hunt (1999), 40–50 on unravelling Ammianus' reporting of the developments in the east prior to the Persian invasion of 359.
20. Ammianus XVIII.6.7.
21. Ammianus XVIII.7.7
22. Lightfoot (1981), 143; Matthews (1986), 555–556.
23. Libanius, *Ep.* 46, 367, 383, 388; *PLRE* I.605–608 'Modestus 2'.
24. Ammianus XVIII.6.18; Frontinus, *Strat.* III.13.5 advises such use a hiding place of secret letters.
25. Blockley (1986) on decoding the letter; Appian, *Mithr.* 69–71; Matthews (1989), 42–43; Mayor (2009) on Mithridates VI; respectively, the Granicus and the Rhyndacus are the modern Biga and Mustafakemalpasha/Orhaneli rivers in north-western Turkey. The former is most famous as the site of Alexander the Great's first victory over the Achaemenid Persian Empire in 334BCE, while the latter was the site of two Roman victories over the forces of Mithridates VI, first by Flavius Fimbria in 85BCE (Frontinus, *Strat.* III.17.5) and again by Lucullus in 73/72BCE (Plutarch, *Lucullus* XI.2–3).
26. That Ammianus considered Jovinianus to be a Persian satrap rather than a Roman governor demonstrates the somewhat fluid nature of the eastern frontier at this time. Corduene had been ceded to the Romans by the Peace of Nisibis but at some stage in the intervening years, it had reverted to Persian control. But even this idea of Persian 'control' might still be misleading, with Jovinianus, more a local chieftain than part of either the Roman or Persian systems of government, occupying something of a neutral, buffer territory that both Rome and Persia laid claim to but did little to enforce. In light of this approach, in helping Ammianus, rather than demonstrating his covert allegiance to Rome, Jovinianus was following his own interests, maintaining his balancing act between the two empires and not wanting either to be overwhelmingly victorious. Shapur's execution of any troops from Transtigritane regions, including Corduene, found serving in the Roman army after the siege of Amida and the suggestion that Jovinianus was dead by the time of the Persian attack on Bezabde in 360 might suggest that "something went badly wrong with his calculations". (Matthews (1989), 55–57).
27. Ammianus XIX.6.11 would later declare that Shapur's force was 100,000 strong but this looks a suspiciously round figure and was only ventured in the course of celebrating the bravery of a night attack against it by a Roman force of at most 2,000 and quickly follows up by referencing Homer's Iliad; Herodotus VII.59–60 on Xerxes' force.
28. Ammianus XVIII.7.1.

29. Ammianus XVIII.7.4.
30. Ammianus XVIII.7.10.
31. Ammianus XVIII.8.2.
32. Ammianus XVIII.8.6.
33. Ammianus XV.5.22; Verinianus is not heard about again and while it is an argument of silence, it is hard to shake the feeling that Ammianus does not mention him again due to the guilt he felt for having abandoned a friend to his death; Wilson (2001) on the possibility of the presence of water-mills at Amida.
34. Ammianus XVIII.8.13.
35. Ammianus XVIII.9.1–2; Ammianus got his orientation of Amida slightly wrong. While his recording of a tower on the southeastern side of the city overlooking the Tigris is right, he incorrectly states that the south side of Amida is washed by the river and that the eastern side borders the Mesopotamian plains. The fact that it was the other way around might suggest a typographical error, although the bend in the Tigris might suggest that Ammianus was not quite so wrong as it first suggests; Gabriel (1940) I.85–205; Matthews (1989), 57–66; Lenski in Lewin and Pellegrini (2007), 220; while the walls of Amida were repaired between 367 and 375 (*CIL* III.6730), those that can be seen today were built during the reign of Justinian (Procopius, *De Aed*. II.3.27).
36. Both units would later be listed as light cavalry, although it is possible that there were still infantry in 359.
37. Ammianus XVIII.3.4 on the Amida garrison; XIX.2.14 on the mass of people within Amida; some attempts were made to recalculate this to 120,000 – Clark (1910) – gaining some acceptance (Rolfe translation in Loeb, 1939–1950) but Ammianus' original tally has since been confirmed (de Jonge (1982), 54); Isaac (1992), 169 notes that such limited garrison forces and a reliance on legionary *vexillationes* had been a common theme in the Roman east long before Diocletian so the shrinking of the legion would have had little real impact there.
38. Ammianus XXIII.4 on a digression on siege engines; Den Hengst in Drijvers and Hunt (1999); Matthews (1989), 64–65; Trombley in Drijvers and Hunt (1999), 24–26.
39. Ammianus XIX.1.5.
40. Ammianus XIX.1.2.
41. Bivar (1983), 210–211 suggests that it would have been a Chionite prince who rode up to the walls of Amida and was almost killed rather than Shapur; Matthews (1989), 488 n.25.
42. Ammianus XIX.2.3.
43. Ammianus XIX.2.2–5.
44. Ammianus XIX.2.8.
45. Ammianus XIX.2.11.
46. Choksy (1989); Schmidt (1994), 247–268; Daryaee (2009), 65–67 on Zoroastrian death practices.
47. Ammianus XIX.4.
48. Thucydides II.47–55.
49. McNeill (1998), 120; even with the detail of Thucydides' description, there was little consensus throughout the 20th century on the identity of the disease. Bubonic plague, epidemic typhus, smallpox, toxic shock syndrome, measles, viral haemorrhagic fever were all proposed. The main problem for diagnosing such antique disease is that not only were the likes of Thucydides and Ammianus not trained doctors, the same disease can

present with different symptoms. It is even possible that that ancient disease no longer exists. Modern DNA testing has suggested that the Plague of Athens was typhoid fever (Papagrigorakis, Yapijakis, Synodinos, and Baziotopoulou–Valavani (2006) 206–214), although even this has yet to meet with universal acceptance.

50. Gaudin (1988); Stathakopoulos (2004), 189–190.
51. Ammianus XIX.3.2; XVIII.7.7; Matthews (1989), 44.
52. Amminaus XIX.3.2.
53. Ammianus XIX.5.1.
54. Ammianus XIX.5.2; 6.4.
55. Ammianus XIX.5.2.
56. Ammianus XIX.6.1–2.
57. Ammianus XIX.6.4.
58. Ammianus XIX.6.10 is of uncertain meaning.
59. Ammianus XIX.6.11.
60. Ammianus XIX.7.4.
61. Ammianus XIX.7.5.
62. Ammianus XIX.7.8.
63. Ammianus XIX.6.6, 8.1.
64. Ammianus XIX.8.2–4; Lenski in Lewin and Pellegrini (2007), 223.
65. Ammianus XIX.8.2.
66. Ammianus XIX.8.4.
67. Ammianus XIX.8.7.
68. Ammianus XIX.8.5–12.
69. Ammianus XX.2.4.
70. *ILS* 740; Matthews (1989), 364, 380; Lauricius was also attended the Council of Seleucia (*PLRE* I.497); Syme (1968), 46 suggests that Lauricius was potentially a source of information for Ammianus.
71. Matthews (1989), 355–367 on the Isaurians.
72. Ammianus XIX.9.9.
73. Ammianus XIX.2.12.
74. Lenski in Lewin and Pellegrini (2007), 222; Matthews (1989), 58.
75. Matthews (1989), 59; Ammianus XIX.9.9.
76. Lenski in Lewin and Pellegrini (2007), 222 puts the subsiding of the disease on the twenty-seventh day since Shapur's arrival, which means he is placing the outbreak of this ten day pestilence on the same day as his proposed third Persian assault on Ammianus' "fifth day".
77. Matthews (1989), 58, 60.
78. Matthews (1989), 60, 287; Naudé (1959); Crump (1975).
79. Ammianus XIX.5.1, 6.6.
80. Ammianus XIX.9.9.
81. Ammianus XIX.9.2; Matthews (1989), 65.
82. Ammianus XVIII.10.3.
83. Ammianus XVIII.10; XIX.9.3–8; Kagan in Mathisen and Shanzer (2011), 167–168.
84. Ammianus XIX.9.2.
85. *Pan. Lat.* III.1
86. Ammianus XX.4.2.

87. Ammianus XX.11.5.
88. Ammianus XVIII.6.2; Matthews (1989), 40, 46, 100.
89. Julian, *Or.* 1.18A–20A implies that Constantius had not done well out of his dealings with Shapur, although the consistent use of this defensive system along the frontier with Persia (Jerome, *Chron a.* 2354; Theophanes, *Chron AM* 5829) over the centuries suggests that many of Constantius' successors saw the benefits of it.
90. Ammianus XVIII.6.22.
91. Ammianus XIX.11.17.
92. Matthews (1989), 47.
93. Ammianus XX.2.4.
94. Ammianus XX.6.1.
95. Sozomen IV.23.4–7; Hilary of Poitiers, *Ad Const.* II.2; *CTh* XI.24.1[360]; Ammianus XXX.9.1; Barnes (1993a), 223
96. This is some suggestion from Ammianus XX.6.9 that "the greater part of the army was in camp guarding Nisibis" rather than still at Edessa. This would mean a large reduction in the 300km distance between Edessa and Singara but would still have a potential Roman relief force 100km of rough arid terrain away.
97. Ammianus XX.9.1.
98. Ammianus XX.6.8.
99. Ammianus XX.6.2.
100. Whether Shapur had made up the losses he had suffered before the walls of Amida or not during the winter of 359/360, even though he was not thrusting deeply as deeply into Roman territory as before, he still had a sizeable force under his command.
101. Ammianus XX.6.4.
102. Ammianus XX.6.5.
103. Ammianus XX.6.7.
104. Ammianus XX.7.1.
105. Ammianus XX.7.4.
106. Ammianus XX.7.6.
107. Ammianus XX.7.9.
108. Ammianus XX.7.13; the similarities in the Persian attacks on Amida, Singara and Bezabde may just be Shapur repeating the psychology and tactics that had proven successful or reflecting the similarity of the terrain involved but the similarity between the opening of the sieges of Amida and Bezabde are striking while the reporting of almost the entirety of the sieges of Singara and Bezabde bear more than a passing resemblance – a captured ram being used against its makers, collapse of a round tower and earthworks. It could be suggested that needing to fill in gaps or bulk up his limited knowledge of events, Ammianus was recycling events he had seen in person at Amida or had heard from others.
109. Ammianus XX.7.15.
110. Ammianus XX.7.15.
111. Ammianus XX.7.17; Dodgeon and Lieu (1991) 390 n.20.
112. Cumont (1917)
113. Ammianus XX.7.17.

Chapter X: The Usurpation of Julian: Ungrateful Brat or Left No Choice?

1. Ammianus XX.9.2.
2. Matthews (1989), 96.
3. Even before these rebellions against the House of Constantine, the Gauls had been the centre of resistance to the central authority with a breakaway Gallic Empire seceding from the Roman state in 260 and lasting until its reincorporation in 274.
4. Ammianus XVI.10.19.
5. Barnes (1998), 123.
6. Aujoulat (1983b), 437–438; Tougher in Whitby (1998), 122; although Prioreschi (1995), 658 dismisses the existence of a one use, lingering abortifacient.
7. Ammianus XX.4.1.
8. Ammianus XX.4.2–3; the *Heruli, Batavi, Celtae* and *Petulantes* at 500 each accounted for up to 2,000 infantry; 300 men each from the remaining four *auxilia*, five legions and six cavalry units could account for a further 2,700 infantry and 1,800 cavalry.
9. Jones (1964), 120.
10. Ammianus XX.4.4.
11. Julian, *Ep. ad Ath.* 280c–d claims he sent seven infantry units and two cavalry.
12. Ammianus XX.4.4.
13. Ammianus XX.4.8.
14. Ammianus XX.4.6.
15. Matthews (1989), 94–97 on the relations between Julian and Florentius.
16. Julian, *Ep. ad Ath.* 283b–c.
17. Amminaus XX.4.10; Herodian VI.7.3 demonstrates that this was not a unique complaint.
18. Ammianus XX.4.11; *CTh* VII.1.3[349].
19. Ammianus XX.4.16.
20. Ammianus XX.1.2.
21. Ammianus XX.9.9; Julian, *Ep. ad Ath.* 281a; Matthews (1989), 95–96.
22. Ammianus XX.4.12; Julian, *Ep. ad Ath.* 284a.
23. Ammianus XX.4.11; Julian, *Ep. ad Ath.* 283d–284a.
24. Matthews (1989), 98.
25. Matthews (1989), 98; it could also be the Roman army taking on formulaic barbarian traits as a military fashion in order to appear more barbaric (Halsall (2007), 101–110; Crawford (2011), 209–212).
26. Ammianus XX.4.14–18;
27. Ammianus XX.4.19–22.
28. Ammianus XX.5.3–7.
29. Ammianus XX.8.5–17.
30. Ammianus XX.8.16.
31. Ammianus XX.8.18.
32. Ammianus XX.9.6–7.
33. Ammianus XX.9.8 records a certain Anatolius being given that position by Julian perhaps as a replacement for Pendatius, already mentioned as *magister officiorum* (Ammianus XX.8.19); it was perhaps as a result of Constantius' letter that Julian now moved to neutralise Lupicinus (Ammianus XX.9.5).

34. Now modern Kellen in the region of Kleve in Germany, just across the German–Dutch border from Nijmegen.
35. Ammianus XX.10.

Chapter XI: War Within and Without: Constantius' Final Year

1. It cannot have harmed the Roman cause that Constantius had presented Arsaces with his wife, Olympias, daughter of Ablabius, and the formerly betrothed of Constans.
2. Ammianus XX.11.4; Socrates II.44.7, 46.1 implies that Constantius travelled to Antioch in early 360 but Barnes (1993a), 223 n.40 suggests that this comes from a confusion of the events of the following winter.
3. Ammianus XX.8.1; Kulikowski (2007), 106 sees these 'Scythians' as Goths encouraged to serve under the Peace of 332.
4. Ammianus XX.11.5.
5. Ammianus XX.11.6.
6. Ammianus XX.11.7.
7. Records of that period are sketchy with the interruption of Roman imperial coinage production in 253 the only evidence of a capture of Antioch (Southern (2001), 78); Matthews (1989), 288 n.13 on the suggestion that Ammianus has erred on the history of this ram as it is unlikely that Shapur I attacked both Antioch and Carrhae during the same campaign; although the clever nature of the ram and the fact that it had survived a century intact could have seen it deployed on separate campaigns.
8. Ammianus XX.11.11.
9. Ammianus XX.11.12 suggests that Persian archers targeted those who removed their helmet in the hope of being recognised for their good deeds and rewarded by the emperor.
10. Ammianus XX.11.15.
11. Ammianus XX.11.15.
12. Ammianus XX.11.23.
13. *CTh* VII.4.6[360], XVI.2.16; Ammianus XX.11.32; Socrates II.45.10.
14. Ammianus XXI.1.4.
15. Ammianus XXI.1.6.
16. Ammianus XXI.2.4–5.
17. Ammianus XXI.1.6.
18. Ammianus XXI.6.4; the date or even the year of Eusebia's death is not known and even the suggestion that because he is said to have loved her greatly ([Aur. Vic.], *Epit.* XLII.20), and may therefore have spent a prolonged period in mourning would quite possibly have been overridden by the need to secure the succession.
19. Philostorgius IX.7 on the Arian bishop and renowned healer Theophilus the Indian being recalled from exile to attempt to reverse her barrenness; the potential danger of such fertility drugs in antiquity might lead some to suggest that Eusebia was facing karmic justice for any involvement in the miscarriage of Helena.
20. Ammianus XV.8.3; Julian, *Or.* III. 114b–115a, 121b, 123a–b; *Ep. ad Ath.* 273a, 274b, 275b–c; Zosimus III.1.2–3, 2.3.
21. Both Faustina and her young daughter fell into the hands of the usurper, Procopius, who used the heir of Constantius as a "dynastic talisman" (Lenski (2002a), 102) and to inspire the loyalty of the soldiers against Valens (Ammianus XXVI.7.10). Faustina disappears

after the usurper's defeat in 366 but the imperial heritage of Constantia meant that she remained a useful tool in bestowing legitimacy. In 374, she married Gratian, the eldest son of the emperor Valentinian, and on the way to meeting her betrothed she was almost captured by Quadi raiders near Sirmium (Ammianus XXIX.6.7). With her new husband, Constantia then served as *Augusta* at Trier (Lenski (2002a), 102–103 n.210), although she did not live a long life with for while John Chrysostom (ad vid. iun. 4 = Migne 48, 605) mentions her still being alive in 380, she was dead by the autumn of 383 with her remains arriving in Constantinople for burial (*Chron. Min.* I.244; *PLRE* I.326 'Faustina'; I.221 'Constantia 2').

22. As there were three separate Mauretanian provinces – Tingitana, Caesariensis and Sitifensis – by the fourth century, the fact that Ammianus XXI.7.4 speaks of Cretio calling troops from only two Mauretania provinces might seem like an error. However, as mentioned in the dispute between Constantine II and Constans, Mauretania Tingitana was part of the diocese of Spain and therefore not under the control of Cretio as *comes Africae*. The two Mauretanian provinces Cretio and Gaudentius called for support from were Caesariensis and Sitifensis; the former comprised what is now the Mediterranean coast of Algeria and the latter named for its capital at Sitifis, modern Setif in Algeria. Diocletian also divided Africa Province into three – Zeugitana in the north around Carthage, Byzacena largely around the Sahel region of modern Tunisia centred on Hadrumentum, modern Sousse, and Tripolitana, the Mediterranean coastline of western Libya centred on Tripoli.

23. Ammianus XXI.7.5.

24. Ammianus XXI.6.5, 9.

25. Ammianus XXI.6.1–3.

26. Ammianus XXI.6.6–8.

27. Ammianus XXI.3.3.

28. Ammianus XXI.3.4–5; Julian, *Ep. ad. Ath.* 286a–b.

29. Harries (2012), 302.

30. This was far from the end of Vadomarius' career with him next heard of serving as *dux Phoeniciae* (Ammianus XXI.3.5). There is no information about this appointment although it is likely Julian's doing (Matthews (1989), 318), perhaps taking the Alaman with him when he struck east against Constantius or maybe later once he had become sole *Augustus*. As *dux*, Vadomarius served the emperor Valens, first in an attempt to retrieve the city of Nicaea from the grasp of the usurping Procopius. Vadomarius was unsuccessful in this task (Ammianus XXVI.8.2) but did not fall out of favour for in 371 Valens dispatched him along with the general Traianus to deal with another Persian invasion of Mesopotamia and Armenia by the long-lived Shapur II. This military adventure proved much more successful with victory at the Battle of Bagavan going a long way to retrieving the Roman position in the east (Ammianus XXI.4.1–6; Zosimus III.4.2; III.7.6; Aur. Vic., *de Caes.* XLII.17; Hoffmann (1981); *PLRE* I, 'Vadomarius'; Elton (1996a), 139).

31. Ammianus XXI.5.2–8.

32. In the event, Nebridius travelled to his home in Tuscany, although he would later be appointed praetorian prefect in the east by Valens and imprisoned by the usurper, Procopius (Ammianus XXVI.7.4).

33. *PLRE* I.392 'Decimius Germanianus 4'; I.797–798 'Flavius Sallustius'.

34. Murdoch (2003), 88.
35. Julian, *Caes.* 329B; Ammianus XXI.10; XXIII.2.2; XXIII.5.1; XXXII.2.1–2; Julian also saw *adulescentes laetos* as worthy of service in *palatini* units, an indication of their military prowess (Ammianus XX.8.13; Simpson (1977b), 519) and was also more than willing to allow the Franks to remain on abandoned Roman land as long as they provided soldiers and produce and he valued them highly enough to see it a huge concession to provide Constantius with *laeti* and *dediticii* for his *scholae* (Ammianus XVII.8.3–4; XX.8.13).
36. Matthews (1989), 100–105 on civil war between Julian and Constantius.
37. Murdoch (2003), 88–90.
38. Ammianus XXI.9.7 also records Lucillianus as a *magister equitum*.
39. Ammianus XXI.9.6.
40. Ammianus XXI.9.7–8.
41. In modern times, Nis' importance stems from its position along the railway lines from Belgrade to Thessalonica and Sofia rather than its proximity to waterways.
42. Ammianus XXI.10.8, 12.24.
43. Ammianus XXI.10.8.
44. In a rare divergence from Julian, Ammianus XXI.10.8 disagrees with the promotion of Nevitta to the consulship calling him "a man neither in birth, experience, nor renown comparable with those on whom Constantine had conferred the highest magistracy, but on the contrary uncultivated, somewhat boorish, and what was more intolerable, cruel in high office".
45. The failure of his army to take Aquileia during a civil war against the Roman Senate had contributed heavily to the murder of Maximinus Thrax in 238 (Herodian VIII.1.6–5.9; *SHA Maximinus* 32).
46. *CTh* I.6.1, 28.1; VI.4.12, 13; VII.8.1; XI.1.7, 15.1, 23.1; XII.1.48; XIII.1.3; XV.1.7 all issued in one law from Gephyra on 3 May, 361; *CTh* VII.4.4 from Doliche on 29 May 361; the bridge at Capersana had earlier been targeted for destruction by Ursicinus in 359 (Ammianus XVIII.8.1) so the presence of a bridge of boats for Constantius to cross in 361 (Ammianus XXI.7.7) might suggest that the bridge had be destroyed.
47. Ammianus XXI.13.1–2.
48. Ammianus XXI.13.7.
49. Ammianus XXI.13.10–15.
50. Ammianus XXI.13.13.
51. Ammianus XXI.13.16.
52. Ammianus XXI.14.
53. Ammianus XXI.15.1.
54. Ammianus XXI.15.2.
55. Ammianus XXI.15.2; the idea of a journey helping a fever was not just some old wives' tale. "Rocking" was considered a precise medical treatment for several maladies in antiquity (Celsus, *de Medicina* II.15).
56. Ammianus XXI.15.2.
57. Mobsucrenae has gone through many name changes throughout its history – under the Seluecids it had been Seleucia on the Pyramus; Pliny the Elder, *NH* V.22 called it Mopsos, while it had taken the name of at least two emperors in the past, Hadriana and Decia; most Christian era sources refer to it as Mopsuestia; the Arabs knew it as al-Massiah, although it was perhaps most famous as Mamistra during the Middle Ages;

under the Ottomans, it became Misis before finally becoming Yakapinar in the 1960s; Malalas, *Chron.* XIII on Constantius' bridge over the Pyramus, with Procopius, *de Aed.* V.5 recorded Justinian repairing it.

58. Ammianus XXV.4.2.
59. Ammianus XXI.15.3; Barnes (1993b), 64f accepts Seeck's rereading; Matthews (1989), 101.
60. Ammianus XXI.16.7, 5; Although Ammianus suggests that such "abstinence from dissipation and luxury have this effect on the body is shown by repeated experience, as well as by the statements of physicians", made it that while Constantius rarely suffered from poor health, when he did it was of "dangerous character".
61. Murdoch (2003), 94–95.
62. Ammianus XXI.16.21.
63. Ammianus XXI.15.4.
64. Ammianus XXII.1.1.
65. Ammianus XXII.1.2.
66. Ammianus XXII.2.2–3.
67. Ammianus XXII.2.4; Zosimus III.11.2.
68. Philostorgius VI.6; Gregory of Nazianzus, *Or.* V.16–17; Libanius, *Or.* XVIII.120; Zonaras VI.6.
69. Murdoch (2003), 98.
70. Ammianus XXII.4.
71. Ammianus XXII.3.4.
72. Ammianus XXII.3.7.
73. Ammianus XXII.3.9; Ammianus XXII.3 on the tribunal of Chalcedon.
74. Ammianus XXI.12.17.
75. Ammianus XXI.12.18.
76. Ammianus XXI.12.20.

Epilogue: Constantius II, A Good Emperor Lacking a Publicist?

1. Jones (1964), 116.
2. Whitby in Drijvers and Hunt (1999), 83.
3. Ammianus XXI.16.15; Matthews (1989), 234.
4. Whitby in Drijvers and Hunt (1999), 82.
5. Ammianus XX.2.4.
6. Ammianus XXI.16.15.
7. The specific motives behind Julian's Persian campaign, aside from his Alexandrian dream, are not recorded. There is some suggestion that Roman interests beyond the Tigris were being threatened (Matthews (1989), 136–38); however, the most likely explanation was that because the latest round with Shapur had not gone well, "a victorious campaign was doubtless desirable to secure a favourable peace" (Jones (1964), 123).
8. Zosimus III.12.5–13.1 Elton (1996a), 210–211 on Julian taking 65,000 men against Persia and left 18,000 with Procopius and Sebastianus; Jones (1964), 684 thinks that Procopius' 18,000 were part of the overall total rather than an addition. Ammianus states that Procopius and Sebastian were given 30,000 men (Ammianus XXIII.3.5), suggesting that 65,000 is the lowest estimate for Julian's army with 95,000 as the upper estimate.

9. Ammianus XXV.6.6 reports a rumour that Julian was killed by a Roman weapon while Gregory of Nazianus, *Or.* V.13, Sozomen VI.2 and Libanius, *Or.* XVIII.274 all suggest that it was a disgruntled Christian who dealt the death blow. However, Libanius later said, recorded by Philostorgius VII.15, that it was a Arab, possibly confirmed by Oribasius, who had personally examined Julian's wound; Bowersock (1978), 116–118.

10. Ammianus XXV.7.13.

11. Ammianus XXV.7.9, 12.

12. Ammianus XXV.7.13, 9.8–11; despite its unpopularity and its undermining of Roman Mesopotamia, the extricating of perhaps 50,000 men (Hoffmannn (1969), 306–308) went a long way to preventing the Roman position from collapsing. By 370 Valens could deploy sufficient forces to challenge the treaty and even defeat a Persian force at Bagawan in 371 (Ammianus XXVII.12.13, 16; Themistius, *Or.* XI.149b), although this masks how stretched the Roman military was. The removal of 16,000 men to Illyricum reduced Valens to making threats rather than taking action (Ammianus XXX.2.6; Lenski (2002), 311).

13. The *magister officiorum* Ursatius reportedly insulted the envoys of the Alamanni by giving them smaller and less valuable gifts than they were accustomed to (Ammianus XXVI.5.7).

14. Ammianus XXVII.2, 10.6–17; Heather (2009), 38–43; Drinkwater (2007) on the history of the Alamanni.

15. Ammianus XXVIII.2.1, 5–9; XIX.6.2–3; Halsall (2007), 143; Elton (1996a), 155–174; Southern and Dixon (1996), 127–147.

16. Ammianus XXVIII.5.1–3; XXX.7.8.

17. Constantine claimed to have reconquered Dacia in defeating the Goths in 332, although this was not the case (Blockley (1992), 8), while Theodosius annexed a section of Armenia in agreement with the Persians, although this was a political settlement rather than a military conquest (Blockley (1987)).

Bibliography

Abbreviations

AE	*L'Année épigraphique*
Anon. Val	*Anonymous Valesianus*
Athanasius Apol. ad Const	Athanasius, *Defense before Constantius*
Athanasius Hist. Ar.	Athanasius, *History of the Arians*
Athanasius Apol. c. Ar.	Athanasius, *Defense Against the Arians*
Athanasius Fug.	Athanasius, *Defense of His Flight*
Athanasius Hist. ac.	Athanasius, *Historia acephala*
Athanasius, Syn.	Athanasius, *On the Councils of Arminium and Seleucia*
CCL	*Corpus Christianorum*
CIL	*Corpus Inscriptionum Latinarum*
CJ Codex Justinianus	
CSCO	*Corpus Scriptorum Christianorum Orientalium*
CSEL	*Corpus Scriptorum Ecclesiasticorum Latinorum*
CTh	*Codex Theodosianus*
Firmicus Maternus, de err. prof. rel.	Firmicus Maternus, *The Error of the Pagan Religions*
Lactantius, DMP	Lactantius, *De Mortibus Persecutorum*
EOMIA	*Ecclesiae Occidentalis Monumenta Iuris Antiquissima*
FIRA	*Fontes Iuris Romani Antejustiniani*
ILS	*Inscriptiones Latinae Selectae*
ND	*Notitia Dignitatum*
NPNF	*Nicene, Post-Nicene Fathers*
P. Abinn	*The Abinnaeus Archive*
Pan. Lat.	*Panegyrici Latini*
P. Beatty Panopolis	*Papyri from Panopolis in the Chester Beatty Library*
P.Lond	*Greek Papyri in the British Museum*
PLRE	*Prosopography of the Late Roman Empire*
RIC	*Roman Imperial Coinage*
SHA	*Scriptores Historiae Augustae*

Primary sources

[Aurelius Victor], *Epitome de Caesaribus* (Banchich, T.M. translation, 2009).

[Hyginus], *De Munitionibus Castrorum* (Richmond, I.A. translation, 2004).

Acta Maximiliani (Musurillo, H. translation, *The Acts of the Christian Martyrs*, 1972).

Agathias, *De imperio et rebus gestis Iustiniani* (Frendo, J.D. translation, 1975).

Ambrose of Milan, *Epistulae* (Liebeschuetz W. translation, Translated Texts for Historians, 2005).

Ammianus Marcellinus (Rolfe, J.C. translation, Loeb Classical Library, 1939–1950; Hamilton, W. translation, Penguin Classics, 1986).

Anonymous Valesianus (Rolfe, J.C. translation, Loeb Classical Library, 1939).

Aphrahat, *Demonstrations* (Valavanolickal, K. translation, 1999).

Athanasius, *Against the Pagans* (Thomson, R.W. translation, 1971).

—— *Defence Against the Arians* (Atkinson, M., Newman, J.H. and Robertson, A. translation, *NPNF*, 1891).

—— *Defence before Constantius* (Atkinson, M., Newman, J.H. and Robertson, A. translation, *NPNF*, 1891).

—— *Defense of His Flight* (Atkinson, M., Newman, J.H. and Robertson, A. translation, *NPNF*, 1891).

—— *Encyclical Letter* (Atkinson, M., Newman, J.H. and Robertson, A. translation, *NPNF*, 1891).

—— *Epistula ad Afros* (Robertson, A. translation, *NPNF*, 1891).

—— *Epistula Catholica* (Robertson, A. translation, *NPNF*, 1891).

—— *Festal Index* (Payne-Smith, J. translation, 1892).

—— *Festal Letters* (Payne-Smith, R. and Robertson, A. translation, *NPNF*, 1891).

—— *Historia acephala* (Martin, A. and Albert, M. translation, 1985).

—— *History of the Arians* (Atkinson, M., Newman, J.H. and Robertson, A. translation, *NPNF*, 1891).

—— *Homily on Matthew* (Robertson, A. translation, *NPNF*, 1891).

—— *Letter to the Bishops of Egypt and Libya* (Atkinson, M., Newman, J.H. and Robertson, A. translation, *NPNF*, 1891).

—— *Letters to Serapion* (Shapland, C.R.B. translation, 1951).

—— *Life of Antony* (White, C. translation, 1998).

—— *On the Council of Nicaea* (Newman, J.H. and Robertson, A. translation, *NPNF*, 1891).

—— *On the Councils of Arminium and Seleucia* (Newman, J.H. and Robertson, A. translation, *NPNF*, 1891).

—— *On the Incarnation of the Word* (Thomson, R.W. translation, 1971).

—— *Orations against the Arians* (Newman, J.H. and Robertson, A. translation, *NPNF*, 1891).

—— *Tomus ad Antiochenos* (Robertson, A. translation, *NPNF*, 1891).

Augustine, *Against the Letters of Petilianus* (King, J.R., Hartranft, C.D. and Knight, K. translation, *NPNF*, 1887/2009).

Augustus, *Res Gestae Divi Augusti* (Brunt, P.A. and Moore, J.M. translation, 1967).

Aurelius Victor, *de Caesaribus* (Bird, H.W. translation, Translated Texts for Historians 1994).

Ausonius, *Commemoratio Professorum Burdigalensium* (Evelyn-White, H.G. translation, Loeb Classical Library, 1919).

Cassius Dio, *Historia Romana* (Cary, E. translation, Loeb Classical Library, 1914–1927).

Celsus, *de Medicina* (Spencer, W.G. translation, Loeb Classical Library, 1938).

Chronica Minora (Mommsen, T. edition, Teubner, 1892).

Chronicle of Arbela (Kroll, T. translation, 1985).

Chronicle of Zuqnin/ Pseudo-Dionysius of Tel-Mahre, *Chronicle* (Witakowski, W. translation, 1997).

Chronicon Paschale (Whitby, M. and Whitby, M. translation, Translated Texts for Historians, 1989).

Cicero, *Orations* (Sutton, E.W. and Rackham, H. translation, 1949).

Claudian, *De Bello Gothico* (Platnauer, M. translation, Loeb Classical Library, 1922).

Claudian, *Panegyricus de Quarto Consulatu Honorii Augusti* (Platnauer, M. translation, Loeb Classical Library, 1922).

Codex Iustinianus (Krueger, P. translation, 1914).

Codex Theodosianus (Pharr, C. translation, 1952).

Consularia Constantinopolitana (Burgess, R.W. translation, 1993).

Cedrenus, *Historiarium Compendium* (Bekker, I. edition, 1838).

Ephraem, *Carmina Nisibena* (Bicknell, G. edition, 1866).

—— *Hymni contra Iulianum* (Beck, E. edition, *CSCO*, 1957).

Epiphanius, *Panarion* (Amidon, P.R. translation, 1990).

Epistula Ammonis (Goehring, J. edition, 1986).

Eumenius, *For the Restoration of the Schools* (Mynors, R.A.B., Nixon, C.E.V. and Rodgers, B.S. translation, 1994).

Eunapius, *Historiarum Fragmenta* (Blockley, R.C. translation, *The Fragmentary Classicising Historians of the Later Roman Empire*, 1981).

—— *Vita Sophistarum* (Giangrande, I. (ed.), Rome (1956); *cf.* Wright, W.C. translation, Loeb Classical Library edition of *Philostratus Lives of the Sophists* (1921)).

Eutropius, *Breviarium ab urbe condita* (Bird, H.W. translation, Translated Texts for Historians, 1993).

Eusebius, *Vita Constantini* (Cameron, A. and Hall, S. translation, 1999).

—— *Ecclesiastical History* (McGiffert, A.C. translation, 1890).

—— *De Martyribus Palaestinae* (Cureton, W. translation, 1861).

Expositio totius mundi et gentium (Rouge, J. translation, 1966).

Festus, *Breviarium* (Banhich, T.M. and Meka, J.A. translation, Canisius College Translated Texts, 2001).

Firmicus Maternus, *The Error of the Pagan Religions* (Forbes, C.A. translation, 1970).

—— *Mathesis* (Bram, J.R. translation, 1975).

Flavius Polemius, *Itinerarium Alexandri* (Davies, I. translation, 1998).

Florus, *Epitome of Roman History* (Forster, E.S. translation, Loeb Classical Library, 1929).

Frontinus, *Strategems* (Bennett, C.E. translation, Loeb Classical Library, 1925).

Gelasius of Cyzicus, *Syntagma* (Hansen, G.C. edition, 2006).

Gregory of Nazianzus, *Orationes* (Daley, B. translation, 2006).

Gregory of Tours, *Historia Francorum* (Thorpe, L. translation, Penguin Classics, 1974).

Heliodorus, *Aethiopica* (Underdowe, T., Wright, F.A. and Roads, S. translation, 2006).

Herodian, *History of the Empire* (Whittaker, C.R. translation, Loeb Classical Library, 1969–70).

Herodotus, *Histories* (de Selincourt, A. and Marincola, J, translation, 2003).

Hilary of Poitiers, *Adversus Valentum et Ursacium* (Smulders, P. translation, 1995).

—— *de Synodis* (Pullan, L. translation, *NPNF*, 1898).

Hippolytus of Rome, *Apostolic Tradition* (Bradshaw, P.F., Johnson M.E. and Phillips, L.E. translation, 2003).

Homer, *Iliad* (Rieu, E.V. translation, Penguin Classics, 1950).

Hydatius, *Chronicle* (Burgess, R.W. translation, 1993).

Itinerarium Burdigalense (Stewart, A. translation, 1887).

Jacob of Edessa, *Chronological Canons* (Brooks, E.W. edition, CSCO, 1872).

Jerome, *Chronicon* (Donalson, M.D. translation, 1996).

—— *Vita S. Hilarionis* (Fremantle, W.H., Lewis, G. and Martley, W.G. Martley translation, 1893).

John Chrysostom, *Homily on St. Babylas* (Brandam, T.P. translation, *NPNF*, 1889.

John Lydus, *De Magistratibus republicae Romanae* (Carney, J.F. translation, 1971).

—— *De Mensibus* (Bandy, A.C. translation, 1983).

John of Antioch (Mariev, S. translation, 2008).

Jordanes, *Getica* (Mierow, C.C. translation, 1915).

Julian, *de Caesaribus* (Wright, W.C. translation, 1913).

—— *Epistulae* (Wright, W.C. translation, 1913).

—— *Misopognon* (Wright, W.C. translation, 1913).

—— *Orationes* (Wright, W.C. translation, 1913).

Julius Caesar, *The Civil Wars* (Carter, J. translation, 1997).

—— *The Gallic Wars* (Handford, S.A. and Gardner, J.F. translation, Penguin Classics, 1982).

Lactantius, *De Mortibus Persecutorum* (Creed, J.L. translation, 1984).

—— *Divine Institutes* (McDonald, M.F. translation, 1964).

Libanius, *Epistulae* (Norman, A.F. translation, Loeb Classical Library, 1992).

—— *Orationes* (Norman, A.F. translation, Loeb Classical Library, 1969–1977).

Livy, *Ab Urbe Condita* (de Selincourt, A. translation, Penguin Classics, 1965).

Lucan, *Belli Civilis* (Braund, S. H. translation, 1992).

Lucifer of Cagliari, *De sancto Athanasio, Luciferi Calaritani ofuscula* (Hartel, W. edition, CSEL, 1886).

Martial, *Epigrams* (anonymous translation, Bohn Classical Library, 1897).

Mauricius, *Strategikon* (Dennis, G.T. translation, 1983).

Michael the Syrian, *Chronicle* (Palmer, A. translation, Translated Texts for Historians, 1993).

Movses Khorenantsi, *History of Armenia* (Thomson, R.W. translation, 2006).

Optatus Milevitanus, *Against Parmenian* (Edwards, M. translation, Translated Texts for Historians, 1998).

—— *Against the Donatists* (Vassall-Phillips, O.R. translation, 1917).

Orosius, *Historiae adversum paganos* (Deferrari, R.J. translation, 1964).

Palladius, *Dialogue On the Life of St. John Chrysostom* (Moore, H. translation, 1921).

Panegyrici Latini (Mynors, R.A.B., Nixon, C.E.V. and Rodgers, B.S. translation, 1994).

Passio Artemii (Bidez, J. and Winkelman, F. edition, 1972).

Passion of Maximian and Isaac (Tilley, M.A. translation, 1996).

Passion of St. Sergius and Bacchus (Boswell, J. translation, 1895).

Paulinus of Milan, *Vita S. Ambrosii* (Kaniecka, M.S. translation, 1928).

Peter the Patrician (Reiske, J.J. translation, 1828).

Philostorgius, *Historia Ecclesiastica* (Amidon, P.R. translation, 2007).

Photius, *Bibliotheca* (Freese, J.H. translation, 1920).

Pliny the Younger, *Letters* (Radice, B. translation, Loeb Classical Library, 1969).

Plutarch, *Lives* (Perrin, B. translation, Loeb Classical Library, 1923).

Pomponius Mela, *Description of the World* (Romer, F.E. translation, 1998).

Procopius, *De Aedificiis* (Dewing, H.B. translation, Loeb Classical Library, 1940).

—— *De Bello Persico* (Dewing, H.B. translation, Loeb Classical Library, 1914).

Prosper Tiro, *Epitoma Chronicon* (Mommsen, T. edition, Teubner, 1892).

Pseudo-Kallisthenes, *Historia Alexandri Magni* (Stoneman, R. translation, 1991).

Rufinus, *Historia Ecclesiastica* (Amidon, P.R. translation, 1997).

Scriptores Historiae Augustae (Magie, D. translation, Loeb Classical Library, 1921–32).

Sallust, *Bellum Jugurthinum* (Handford, S.A. translation, Penguin Classics, 1963).

Seneca, *Medea* (Harris, E.I. translation, 1898).

Socrates Scholasticus, *Historia Ecclesiastica* (Zenos, A.C. translation, 1890).

Sozomen, *Historia Ecclesiastica* (Hartranft, C.D. translation, 1890).

Strabo, *Geography* (Jones, H.L. translation, Loeb Classical Library, 1917–32).

Suetonius, *Twelve Caesars* (Graves, R. and Grant, M. translation, Penguin Classics, 1979).

Sulpicius Severus, *Chronica* (Roberts, A. translation, 1894).

Symmachus, *Relationes* (Barrow, R.H. translation, 1973).

Tacitus, *Annales* (Grant, M. translation, Penguin Classics, 1957).

Tacitus, *Germania* (Mattingly, H. and Handford, S.A. translation, Penguin Classics, 1970).

Tertullian, *De Corona Militis* (Quain, E.A. translation, 1959).

Tertullian, *de Spectaculis* (Glover, T.R. translation, Loeb Classical Library, 1931).

Themistius, *Orationes* (Heather, P. and Moncur, D. translation (2001) *Politics, Philosophy, and Empire in the Fourth Century: selected orations of Themistius*, 2001).

Theodoret, *Historia Ecclesiastica* (Jackson, B. translation, 1892).

—— *Historia Religiosa* (Canivet, P. and Leroy-Molinghen, A. translation, 1977–1979).

Theophanes, *Chronographia* (Mango, C. and Scott, R. translation, 1997).

Thucydides (Warner, R. translation, Penguins Classics, 1954).

Vegetius, *De rei militari* (Milner, N.P. translation, 1993; Reeve, M.D. translation, 2004).

Zonaras, *Epitome* (Banchich, T.M. and Lane, E.N. translation, 2009).

Zosimus, *New History* (Ridley, R.T. translation, 1982).

Secondary sources

Alamannen, *Die Alamannen*. Stuttgart (1997).

Alföldi, A. *A Conflict of Ideas in the Late Roman Empire: The Clash between the Senate and Valentinian I*. Oxford (1952).

—— *The Conversion of Constantine and Pagan Rome*. Oxford (1969).

Arce, J. 'Notitia Dignitatum' et l'armge romaine dans la dioicesis Hispanarum,' *Chiron* 10 (1980) 593–608.

—— 'The Inscription of Troesmis (ILS 724) and the First Victories of Constantius II as Caesar' *ZPE* 48 (1982) 245–249.

—— 'Constantius II Sarmaticus and Persicus,' *ZPE* 57 (1984) 225–229.

—— 'La rebelion de los Judios durante el gobierno de Constancio Galo Cesar: 353 d.C.' *Athenaeum* 65 (1987) 109–125.

—— 'Frontiers of the late Roman Empire: Perceptions and realities' in Pohl, W., Wood, I. and Reimitz, H. (eds.) *The Transformation of Frontiers*. Leiden (2001) 5–13.

Ashrafian, H. 'Arius of Alexandria (256–336 ad): the first reported mortality from rectal prolapse,' *International Journal of Colorectal Disease* 29 (2014) 539.

Aujoulat, N. 'Eusebie, Helene etjulien. I Le Temoignage de Julien', *Byzantion* 58(1983) 78–103.

—— 'Eusebie, Helene etjulien. II Le Temoignage des historiens,' *Byzantion* 58(1983) 421–452.

Austin, N.J.E. *Ammianus on Warfare*. Brussels (1979).

Bagnall, R.S. *Reading Papyri: Writing History*. Ann Arbor (1995).

Banaji, J. *Agrarian Change in Late Antiquity: Gold, Labour and Aristocratic Dominance*. Oxford (2001).

Barbero, A. *The Day of the Barbarians*. London (2007).

Barcelo, P. *Das Römische Reich im religiösen Wandel der Spätantike: Kaiser und Bischöfe im Widerstreit*. Regensburg (2013).

Barchiesi, A. and Scheidel, W. (eds.) *The Oxford Handbook of Roman Studies*. Oxford (2010).

Barlow, J. 'Kinship, Identity and fourth-century Franks', *Historia* 45 (1996) 223–239.

Barnard, L. W. 'The Emperor Constans and the Christian Church' *RSA* 11 (1981) 205–214.

—— 'Athanasius and the Emperor Jovian,' *Studia Patristica* 21 (1989) 384–389.

Barnes, T.D. 'The Victories of Constantine,' *ZPE* 20 (1976) 149–155.

—— 'Sossianus Hierocles and the Antecedents of the "Great Persecution"' *Harvard Studies in Classical Philology* 80 (1976) 239–252.

—— 'Imperial Chronology A.D. 337–350', *Phoenix* 34 (1980) 160–166.

—— *Constantine and Eusebius*. Cambridge (1981).

—— *The New Empire of Diocletian and Constantine*. London (1982).

—— 'Two Victory Titles of Constantius,' *ZPE* 52 (1983) 229–235.

—— 'Constantine's Prohibition of Pagan Sacrifice', *American Journal of Philology* 105 (1984) 69–72.

—— 'Constantine and the Christians of Persia', *JRS* 75 (1985) 126–136.

—— 'Christians and Pagans in the Reign of Constantius', *L'Église et l'empire au iv siècle. Sept exposés suivis de discussions*, (1989) 301–343.

—— 'Praetorian Prefects 337–361', *ZPE* 94 (1992) 249–260.

—— *Athanasius and Constantius: Theology and Politics in the Constantinian Empire*. London (1993a).

—— 'Ammianus Marcellinus and His World'. *Classical Philology* 88 (1993b) 55–70.

—— 'Statistics and the Conversion of the Roman Aristocracy', *JRS* 85 (1995) 188–212.

—— *Ammianus Marcellinus and the Representation of Historical Reality*. Ithaca (1998).

Barnes, T.D. and Vanderspoel, J. 'Julian on the Sons of Fausta', *Phoenix* 38 (1984).

Bastien, P. 'Décence, Poemenius: Problèmes de chronologie,' *Quaderni ticinesi: Numismatica e antichità classiche* 12 (1983) 177–189.

Baynes, N.H. *Byzantine Studies and Other Essays*. Westport (1955).

Bidez, J. *La Vie de l'Empereur Julien*. Paris (1930).

Biers, W.R. *Art, Artefacts and Chronology in Classical Archaeology*. London (1992).

Bihain, E. 'L'epitre de Cyrille de Jerusalem a Constance sur la vision de la croix (BHG 413)', *Byzantion* 43 (1973) 264–296.

Bijovsky, G. 'Numismatic Evidence for the Gallus Revolt: The Hoard of Lod', *Israel Exploration Journal* 57 (2007) 187–203.

Bivar, A.D.H. 'The Political History of Iran under the Arsacids', in *Cambridge History of Iran* III.1, Cambridge (1983) 21–99.

Blockley, R.C. 'Constantius Gallus and Julian as Caesars of Constantius II', *Latomus* 31 (1972) 431–468.

—— *Ammianus Marcellinus: A Study of His Historical and Political Thought, Coll. Latomus* 141 Brussels (1975).

—— *The Fragmentary Classicising Historians of the Later Roman Empire*, Liverpool (1981).

—— 'Subsidies and Diplomacy: Rome and Persia in Late Antiquity', *Phoenix* 39 (1985) 62–74.

—— 'The coded message in Ammianus Marcellinus 18.6.17–19', *Echos du Monde Classique* 30 n.s. 5 (1986) 63–65.

—— 'The Division of Armenia Between the Romans and the Persians at the end of the fourth century AD', *Historia* 36 (1987) 222–234.

—— 'Ammianus Marcellinus on the Persian invasion of A.D. 359', *Phoenix* 42 (1988) 244–260.

—— *Eastern Roman Foreign Policy: Formation and Conduct from Diocletian to Anastasius.* Leeds (1992).

Boak, A.E.R. *Manpower Shortage and the Fall of the Roman Empire in the West.* Ann Arbor (1955).

Bodel, J. *Epigrahic Evidence: Ancient History from Inscriptions.* London (2001).

—— 'Epigraphy' in Barchiesi, A. and Scheidel, W. (eds.) *The Oxford Handbook of Roman Studies.* Oxford (2010) 107–122.

Boer, W. den. 'The Emperor Silvanus and His Army,' *AClass* 3 (1960) 105–109.

Bowersock, G.W. *Julian the Apostate.* London (1978).

—— 'Mavia, Queen of the Saracens' in Bowersock, G.W. *Studies on the Eastern Roman Empire: Social, Economic and Administrative History, Religion, Historiography.* Goldbach (1994) 127–140.

—— *Studies on the Eastern Roman Empire: Social, Economic and Administrative History, Religion, Historiography.* Goldbach (1994).

Boyce, M. *Zoroastrians: Their Religious Beliefs and Practices.* London (1979).

Brennan, P. 'The *Notitia Dignitatum*' in Nicolet, C. (ed.) *Les Litteratures techniques dans l'antiquité romaine.* Geneva (1996) 153–169.

—— 'The User's Guide to the *Notitia Dignitatum*: the Case of the *Dux Armeniae* (*ND Or.*38)', *Antichthon* 32 (1998) 34–49.

Brennecke, H.C. *Hilarius von Poiteris und die Bishofsopposition gegen Konstantius II.* Berlin (1984).

Brewer, R.J. (ed.) *Roman Fortresses and their Legions.* London (2000).

Brock, P. 'Why did Maximilian refuse to serve in the Roman Army?', *JEH* 45 (1994) 195–209.

Brown, P. *The World of Late Antiquity.* London (2006).

Brunt, P.A. 'Conscription and Volunteering in the Roman Imperial Army', *SCI* 1 (1974a) 90–115.

Bruun, P.M. *Roman Imperial Coinage, Vol. VII Constantine I–Licinius (313–337).* London (1966).

Buck, D.F. 'Some Distortions in Eunapius' Account of Julian the Apostate,' *Ancient History Bulletin* 4 (1990) 113–115.

Burgess, R.W. 'The Summer of Blood: The "Great Massacre" of 337 and the Promotion of the Sons of Constantine', *DOP* 62 (2008), 5–51.

—— 'The Chronograph of 354: its Manuscripts, Contents, and History', *Journal of Late Antiquity* 5 (2012) 345–396.

Burns, T.S. *The History of the Ostrogoths.* Bloomington (1984).

Cahn, H. A. '*Abolitio nominis* de Constantin II' in Huvelin, H., Christol, M. and Gautier, G. (eds.) *Mélanges de numismatique offerts à Pierre Bastien à l'occasion de son 75ᵉ anniversaire.* Wetteren (1987) 201–202.

Caldwell, C.H. 'Promoting Civil War: Rewards and Loyalty in the Danubian-Balkan Provinces 285–354' in Bragg, E., Hau, L.I. and Macaulay-Lewis, E. (eds.) *Beyond the Battlefields: New Perspectives on Warfare and Society in the Graeco-Roman World.* Newcastle (2008) 225–241.

Cameron, A. *The Later Roman Empire AD284–430*. Harvard (1993).

Cameron, A. and Garnsey, P. (eds.) *The Cambridge Ancient History Vol. XII*. Cambridge (1998).

Camodeca, G. 'Per la redazione del fasti delle province italiche: Fl. Romulus, consularis Flaminiae et Piceni nel 352(−3)', *ZPE* 28 (1978) 151–158.

Campbell, J.B. *The Roman Army 31BC–AD337: A Sourcebook*. London (1994).

Campbell, J.B. and Trittle, L.A. *The Oxford Handbook of Warfare in the Classical World*. Oxford (2013).

Carroll, M. *Romans, Celts & Germans: The German Provinces of Rome*. Stroud (2001).

Casey, P.J. *The Legions of the Later Roman Empire*. Cardiff (1991).

Chausson, F. 'Stemmata aurea: Constantin, Justine, Théodose. Revendications généalogiques et idéologie impériale au IVe s. ap. J.-C' (2007).

Chastagnol, A. *Les Fastes de la Prefecture de Rome au Bas-Empire*. Paris (1962).

Choksy, J.K. *Purity and Pollution in Zoroastrianism: Triumph Over Evil*. Austin (1989).

Coello, T. 'Unit Sizes in the Late Roman Army', *BAR Int. Ser.* 645. (1996).

Cohen, H. *Description historique des monnaies frappées sous l'Empire romain*, Vol. VIII London (1892).

Colledge, M.A.R. *The Parthians*. London (1967).

Crawford, P.T. 'Late Roman Recruiting Practices', unpublished PhD diss., Queen's University, Belfast (2011).

Crump, G.A. 'Ammianus and the Later Roman Army', *Historia* 22 (1973) 91–103.

—— *Ammianus Marcellinus as a Military Historian*. Wiesbaden (1975).

Curran, J. *Pagan City and Christian Capital: Rome in the Fourth Century*. Oxford (2000).

Cumont, F. *Études syriennes*. Paris (1917).

Dagron, G. 'L'empire romain d'orient au IVe siècle et les traditions politiques de l'hellénisme: Le témoignage de Thémistios', *T&MByz* III (1968) 1–242.

—— *Emperor and Priest: The Imperial Office in Byzantium*. Cambridge (2007).

Daly, L.J. 'The Mandarin and the Barbarian', *Historia* 21 (1972) 351–79.

Dark, K. and Dagron, G. 'L'empire romain d'orient au IVe siècle et les traditions politiques de l'hellénisme: Le témoignage de Thémistios', *T&MByz* III (1968) 1–242.

—— *Emperor and Priest: The Imperial Office in Byzantium*. Cambridge (2007).

Dark, K. and Özgümü, F. 'New Evidence for the Byzantine Church of the Holy Apostles from Fatih Camii, Istanbul', *Oxford Journal of Archaeology*, 21 (2002), 393–413.

Daryaee, T. *Sasanian Persia: The Rise and Fall of an Empire*. New York (2009).

De Blois, L. *The Policy of the Emperor Gallienus*. Leiden (1976).

De Clercq, V. C. *Ossius of Cordova: A Contribution to the History of the Constantinian Period*. Washington DC (1954).

De Hengst, D. 'Preparing the Reader for War: Ammianus' digression on siege engines' in Drijvers, J.W. and Hunt, D. (eds.), *The Late Roman World and its Historian: Interpreting Ammianus Marcellinus*. London (1999) 29–39.

De Jonge, P. *Philiogical and Historical Commentary on Ammianus Marcellinus XIX*. Groningen (1982).

De Ste Croix, G.E.M. *The Class Struggle in the Ancient Greek World: from the Archaic Age to the Arab Conquests*. London (1981).

—— *Christian Persecution, Martyrdom and Orthodoxy*. Oxford (2006).

Debevoise, N.C. *A Political History of Parthia*. Westport (1970).

Delbrück, H. *The Barbarian Invasions*. London (1980).

Dignas, B. & Winter, E., *Rome and Persia in Late Antiquity: Neighbours and Rivals*. Cambridge (2007).

Dihle, A. (ed.) *L'Église et l'empire au iv siècle. Sept exposés suivis de discussions*. Geneva (1989).

DiMaio, M. 'Zonaras' Account of the Neo-Flavian Emperors', unpublished PhD. diss., University of Missouri-Columbia (1977).

—— 'Zonaras, Julian, and Philostorgios on the Death of Constantine I', *GOTR* 36 (1981) 118–124.

—— 'The Antiochene Connection: Zonaras, Ammianus Marcellinus, and John of Antioch on the Reigns of the Emperors Constantius II and Julian,' *Byzantion* 50 (1980) 158–185.

—— 'Smoke in the Wind: Zonaras' Use of Philostorgius, Zosimus, John of Antioch, and John of Rhodes in his Narrative on the Neo-Flavian Emperors', *Byzantion* 58 (1988) 230–255.

DiMaio, M. and Arnold, D.W.H. '*Per Vim, Per Caedem, Per Bellum*: A Study of Murder and Ecclesiastical Politics in the Year 337 A.D.' *Byzantion*, 62 (1992).

Dodgeon, M.H. and Lieu, N.C. *The Roman Eastern Frontier and the Persian Wars, AD 226–363*. Cambridge (1993).

Downey, G. 'The Builder of the Original Church of the Apostles at Constantinople: A Contribution to the Criticism of the "Vita Constantini" Attributed to Eusebius', *DOP* 6 (1951) 51–80.

—— 'The Tombs of the Byzantine Emperors in the Church of the Holy Apostles in Constantinople', *Journal of Hellenic Studies* 79 (1959) 27–51.

—— *A History of Antioch in Syria*. Princeton (1961).

Drew-Bear, T. 'A Fourth-Century Latin Soldier's Epitaph at Nakolea', *HSPh* 81 (1977) 257–74.

Drijvers, J.W. and Hunt, D. (eds.), *The Late Roman World and its Historian: Interpreting Ammianus Marcellinus*. London (1999).

Drijvers, J.W. 'A Roman Image of the "Barbarians" Sasanians' in Mathisen, R.W. and Shanzer, D. (eds.) *Romans, Barbarians and the Transformation of the Roman World*. Farnham (2011) 69–76.

Drinkwater, J.F. 'The pagan underground, Constantius II's secret service and the survival and the usurpation of Julian the Apostate,' *Studies in Latin Literature and Roman History* 3 (1983) 348–387.

—— 'Silvanus, Ursicinus and Ammianus: Fact or Fiction?,' *Studies in Latin Literature and Roman History* 7 (1994) 568–576.

—— 'Julian and the Franks and Valentinian I and the Alamanni: Ammianus on Romano-German relations'. *Francia* 24 (1997) 1–15.

—— 'The revolt and ethnic origin of the usurper Magnentius (350–353), and the rebellion of Vetranio', *Chiron* 30 (2000) 131–159.

—— *The Alamanni and Rome 213–496 (Caracalla to Clovis)* . Oxford (2007).

—— Barbatio's Bridge: The Alamannic Campaign of 357, in Drinkwater, J. and Salway, B. (eds). *Wolf Liebeschuetz Reflected: Essays Presented by Colleagues, Friends, and Pupils* (2007) 115–123.

Drinkwater, J. and Salway, B. (eds). *Wolf Liebeschuetz Reflected: Essays Presented by Colleagues, Friends, and Pupils* (2007).

Duncan-Jones, R.P. 'Pay and Numbers in Diocletian's Army', *Chiron* 8 (1978) 541–60.

—— *Structure and Scale in the Roman Economy*. Cambridge (1990).

Duval, Y. M. 'La venue a Rome de l' Empereur Constance II en 357 d'apres Ammien Marcellin', *Caesarodunum* 2 (1970) 299–304.

Edbrooke, R.O. 'The Visit of Constantius II to Rome in 357 and Its Effect on the Pagan Roman Senatorial Aristocracy', *AJPh* 97 (1976) 40–61.

Edwell, P.M. *Between Rome and Persia: the Middle Euphrates, Mesopotamia and Palmyra under Roman control*. London (2008).

Elton, H. *Warfare in Roman Europe AD350–425*. Oxford (1996a).

—— *Frontiers of the Roman Empire*. London (1996b).

—— 'Defining Romans, Barbarians and the Roman Frontier' in Mathisen, R.W. and Sivan, H.S. (eds.) *Shifting Frontiers in Late Antiquity*. Aldershot (1996) 126–135.

Ensslin, W. 'Zu dem vermuteten Perserfeldzug des rex Hannibalianus', *Klio* 29 (1936) 102–110.

Epstein, A.W. 'The Rebuilding and Decoration of the Holy Apostles in Constantinople: A Reconsideration', *Greek, Roman and Byzantine Studies* 23 (1982) 79–92.

Erdkamp, P. (ed.) *A Companion to the Roman Army*. Oxford (2007).

Erim, K.T, Reynolds, J. and Crawford, M. 'Diocletian's Currency Reform: A New Inscription', *JRS* 61 (1971) 171–177.

Faulkner, N. *The Decline and Fall of Roman Britain*. Stroud (2000).

Ferrill, A. *The Fall of the Roman Empire: The Military Explanation*. London (1986).

Fitz, J. (ed.) Limes. Acts of the XI Limes Conference, 1976. Budapest (1977).

Frakes, R.M. 'Cross-References to the Lost Books of Ammianus Marcellinus', *Phoenix* 49 (1995) 232–246.

—— 'Ammianus Marcellinus and Zonaras on a Late Roman Assassination', *Historia* 46 (1997) 121–128.

—— 'The Dynasty of Constantine down to 363' in Lenski, N. (ed.) *The Cambridge Companion to the Age of Constantine*. Cambridge (2012) 91–107.

Frank, R.I. *Scholae Palatinae*. Rome (1969).

Freeman, C. *AD381: Heretics, Pagans and the Christian State*. London (2009).

Freeman, P. and Kennedy, D. (eds.) *The Defence of the Roman and Byzantine East*. Oxford (1986).

French, D.H. and Lightfoot, C.S. (eds.) *The Eastern Frontier of the Roman Empire: Proceedings of a Colloquium held at Ankara in September 1988*. Oxford (1989).

Frend, W.H.C. *The Donatist Church: A Movement of Protest in Roman North Africa.* Oxford (1952).

—— 'Athanasius as an Egyptian Christian Leader in the Fourth Century,' *New College Bulletin* 8 (1974) 20–37.

—— 'The Church in the reign of Constantius II (337–361): Mission, monasticism, worship' in *L'Église et l'empire au iv siècle. Sept exposés suivis de discussions*, (1989) 73–112.

Frye, R.N. *The History of Ancient Iran.* Munchen (1984).

Gabriel, A. *Voyages archéologiques en Turquie orientale.* II vols. Paris (1940).

Gaddis, M. *There is No Crime for Those who Have Christ: Religious Violence in the Christian Roman Empire.* Berkeley (2005).

Garnsey, P. 'Religious Toleration in Classical Antiquity', in Shields, W.J. (ed.) *Persecution and Toleration*: Studies in Church History 21.Oxford (1984) 1–27.

Gaudin, O. 'Remarques sur le texte "La peste d'Amida" (Ammien Marcellin, 19.4)' in Sabbah, G. (ed.) *Études de medicine romaine.* St. Etienne (1988) 39–41.

Geiger, J. 'Ammianus Marcellinus and the Jewish Revolt under Gallus: A Note', *Liverpool Classical Monthly* 4 (1979a) 77.

—— 'The Last Jewish Revolt Against Rome: A Reconsideration', *Scripta Classica Israelica* 5 (1979b) 250–257.

Geuenich, D. *Geschichte der Alemannen.* Stuttgart (1997a).

—— (ed.) *Die Franken und die Alamannen bis zur 'Schlacht bei Zu¨lpich' (496/97)* . Berlin (1998).

Goffart, W. 'Zosimus, the First Historian of Rome's Fall', *AHR* 76 (1971) 412–441.

Goldsworthy, A. *The Roman Army at War 100BC–AD200.* Oxford (1996).

Goodburn, R. and Bartholomew, P. (eds) *Aspects of the Notitia Dignitatum.* Oxford (1976).

Grant, M. *The Emperor Constantine.* London (1993).

Greatrex, G. *Rome and Persia at War 502–532.* Leeds (1998).

Greatrex, G. and Lieu, S.N.C. (eds.) *The Roman Eastern Frontier and the Persian Wars Part II AD 363–630: A Narrative Sourcebook.* London (2002).

Grosse, R. *Römische Militärgeschichte von Gallienus bis zum Beginn der Byzantinschen Themenverfassung.* Berlin (1920).

Guzmán Armario, F. J. *Los bárbaros en Amiano Marcelino.* Madrid (2002).

Gwynn, D.M. *Athanasius of Alexandria: Bishop, Theologian, Ascetic, Father (Christian Theology in Context)* . Oxford (2012).

Hadjinicolaou, A. 'Macellum, lieu d'exil de l'empereur Julien,' *Byzantion* 21 (1951) 15–22.

Halsall, G. *Barbarian Migrations and the Roman West 376–568.* Cambridge (2007).

Hamilton, H. *The Early Development of Canon Law and the Council of Serdica.* Oxford (2002).

Harries, J. *Law and Empire in Late Antiquity.* Cambridge (1999).

—— *Imperial Rome AD284 to 363: A New Empire.* Edinburgh (2012).

Heather, P. *Goths and Romans 332–489.* Oxford (1991).

—— 'Foedera and foederati of the fourth century' in Pohl, W. (ed.) *Kingdoms of the Empire: The Integration of Barbarians in Late Antiquity.* Leiden (1997) 57–74.

—— *Empire and Barbarians: Migration, Development and the Birth of Europe*. London (2009).

Helgeland, J. 'Christians and the Roman Army A.D. 173–337,' *Church History* 43 (1974) 149–163.

Henck, N. 'Constantius' 'paideia', intellectual milieu and promotion of the liberal arts', *PCPhS* 47 (2001) 172–186.

Henck, N. 'Constantius Ο ΦΙΛΟΚΤΙΣΤΗ & Sigma?', *DOP* 55 (2001) 279–304.

Henck, N. 'Constantius II and the Cities' in Drinkwater, J. and Salway, B. (eds.) *Wolf Liebeschuetz Reflected: Essays Presented by Colleagues, Friends, and Pupils* (2007) 147–156.

Hijmans, S. 'Sol Invictus, the Winter Solstice, and the Origins of Christmas', *Mouseion* XLVII (2003) 377–398.

Hoffmann, D. *Das spätrömische Bewegungsheer und die Notitia Dignitatum*. Düsseldorf (1969).

—— 'Wadomar, Bacurius und Hariulf', *Museum Helveticum* 35 (1981) 307–318.

Holum, K.G. *Theodosian Empresses: Women and Imperial Dominion in Late Antiquity*. Berkeley (1982).

Honoré, T. *Law and the Crisis of Empire 379–455AD: The Theodosian Dynasty and its Quaestors with a Palingenesia of Laws of the Dynasty*. Oxford (1998).

Hoover, J.A. 'The Contours of Donatism: Theological and Ideological Diversity in Fourth Century North Africa,' unpublished PhD diss., Baylor University (2008).

Howgego, C. *Ancient History from Coins*. London (2001).

Humphries, M. '*In Nomine Patris*: Constantine the Great and Constantius II in Christological Polemic', *Historia* 46 (1997) 448–464.

—— 'Savage humour: Christian anti-panegyric in Hilary of Poitier's 'Against Constantius'', in Whitby, Mary (ed.) *The Propaganda of Power: the Role of Panegyric in Late Antiquity*. Brill (1998) 201–223.

—— 'From Usurper to Emperor: The Politics of Legitimation in the Age of Constantine', *JLA* 1 (2008) 82–100.

Hunt, D. 'Did Constantius II have 'court bishops'?', in Livingstone, E.A. (ed.) *Studia Patristica XIX: Papers presented to the tenth international conference on patristic studies held in Oxford 1987: Historica, Theologica, Gnostica, Biblica et Apocrypha*. Oxford (1989) 86–90.

—— 'The Outsider Inside: Ammianus on the Rebellion of Silvanus' in Drijvers, J.W. and Hunt, D. (eds.), *The Late Roman World and its Historian: Interpreting Ammianus Marcellinus*. London (1999) 46–56.

Huvelin, H., Christol, M. and Gautier, G. (eds.) *Mélanges de numismatique offerts à Pierre Bastien à l'occasion de son 75ᵉ anniversaire*. Wetteren (1987).

Isaac, B. *The Limits of Empire*. Oxford (1992).

James, E. *The Franks*. Oxford (1988).

Jones, A.H.M. *Ancient Economic History*. London (1948).

—— *Later Roman Empire 284–602*. Oxford (1964).

Jones, A.H.M., Martindale, J.R. and Morris, J. (eds.) *Prosopography of the Later Roman Empire: AD260–395 Volume II*. Cambridge (1971).

Juneau, J. 'Pietas and politics: Eusebia and Constantius at court', *CQ* 49 (1999) 641–644.

Kaegi, W.E. 'Domestic Miltiary Problems of Julian the Apostate', *Byzantinische Forrschungen* 2 (1967) 247–264.

—— 'The emperor Julian at Naissus', *AC* 44 (1975) 161–171.

—— *Byzantine Military Unrest 471–843: an interpretation*. Amsterdam (1981).

Kagan, K. 'Spies Like Us: Treason and Indentity in the Late Roman Empire' in Mathisen, R.W. and Shanzer, D. (eds.) *Romans, Barbarians and the Transformation of the Roman World*. Farnham (2011) 161–173.

Kazuo E. 'The Origin of the White Huns or Hephtalites,' *East and West* 6 (1995) 231–237.

—— 'On the Nationality of the Ephtalites,' *MRDTB* 18 (1959) 1–58.

—— 'On the Date of the Kidarites (1),' *MRDTB* 27 (1969) 1–16.

—— 'On the Date of the Kidarites (2),' *MRDTB* 28 (1970) 13–38.

Kelly, C. 'Emperors, government and bureacracy' in Cameron, A. and Garnsey, P. (eds.) *The Cambridge Ancient History Vol. XII*. Cambridge (1998) 138–183.

Kelly, G. *Ammianus Marcellinus, the Allusive Historian*. Cambridge (2008).

Kent, J.P.C. 'The Revolt of Trier against Magnentius,' *Numismatic Chronicle* 19 (1959), 105–108.

Kienast, D. *Römische Kaisertabelle: Grundzüge einer Römischen Kaiserchronologie*. Darmstadt (1990).

Klein, R. *Constantius II und die Christliche Kirche*. Darmstadt (1977).

—— 'Der Rombesuch des Kaisers Konstantius II im Jahre 357', *Athenaeum* 57 (1979) 98–115.

Kulikowski, M. 'Barbarians in Gaul; Usurpers in Britain', *Britannia* 31 (2000a) 325–345.

—— 'The *Notitia Dignitatum* as an historical source', *Historia* 49 (2000b) 358–377.

—— *Rome's Gothic Wars from the Third Century to Alaric*. New York (2007).

Lane Fox, R. 'The Itinerary of Alexander: Constantius to Julian', *CQ* 47 (1997) 239–252.

Lee, A.D. *Information and Frontiers*. Cambridge (1993).

—— *War in Late Antiquity*. Oxford (2007).

—— 'Roman Warfare with Sasanian Persia' in Campbell, J.B. and Trittle, L.A. *The Oxford Handbook of Warfare in the Classical World*. Oxford (2013) 708–725.

Leedom, J.W. 'Constantius II: Three Revisions,' *Byzantion* 48 (1978) 133–136.

Lendering, J. and Bosman, A. *Edge of Empire: Rome's Frontier on the Lower Rhine*. Rotterdam (2013).

Lenssen, J. 'The Persian Invasion of 359: Presentation by Suppression in Ammianus Marcellinus' *Res Gestae* 18.4.1–18.6.7' in Drijvers, J.W. and Hunt, D. (eds.), *The Late Roman World and its Historian: Interpreting Ammianus Marcellinus*. London (1999), 40–50.

Lenski, N. 'Basil and the Isaurian Uprising of AD375', *Phoenix* 59 (1999a) 308–329.

—— 'Romanisation and Revolt in the territory of Isauria', *JESHO* 42 (1999b), 413–465.

—— *Failure of Empire: Valens and the Roman State in the Fourth Century AD*. London (2002).

—— 'Two Sieges of Amida (AD 359 and 502–503) and the Experience of Combat in the Late Roman Near East' in Lewin, A.S. and Pellegrini, P. (eds.) *The Late Roman Army in the Near East from Diocletian to the Arab Conquest. BAR International Series* 1717 (2007) 219–236.

—— 'The Reign of Constantine' in Lenski, N. (ed.) *The Cambridge Companion to the Age of Constantine*. Cambridge (2012) 59–90.

—— (ed.) *The Cambridge Companion to the Age of Constantine*. Cambridge (2012).

Lewin, A.S. and Pellegrini, P. (eds.) *The Late Roman Army in the Near East from Diocletian to the Arab Conquest. BAR International Series* 1717 (2007).

Liebeschuetz, J.H.W.G. *Barbarians and Bishops: army, church and state in the reign of Arcadius and Chrysostom*. London (1990a).

—— *From Diocletian to the Arab Conquest: change in the late Roman Empire*. Northampton (1990b).

—— *The Decline and Fall of the Roman City*. Oxford (2001).

—— *Decline and Change in Late Antiquity: Religion, Barbarians and their Historiography*. Aldershot (2006).

Lieu S.N.C. ' Captives, Refugees and Exiles: A Study of cross-frontier civilian movements and contacts between Rome and Persia from Valerian to Jovian,' in Freeman, P. and Kennedy, D. (eds.) *The Defence of the Roman and Byzantine East*. Oxford (1986) 475–505.

—— (ed.) *The emperor Julian. Panegyric and polemic (Claudius Mamertinus, John Chrysostom, Ephrem the Syrian)*. Liverpool (1986).

Lieu, S.N.C. and Montserrat, D. *From Constantine to Julian: Pagan and Byzantine Views*. London (1996).

—— *Constantine: History, Hagiography and Legend*. London (1998).

Lightfoot, C.S. 'The Eastern Frontier of the Roman Empire with Special Reference to the Reign of Constantius II', unpublished PhD. diss., Oxford University (1981).

—— 'Fact and Fiction: The Third Siege of Nisibis (AD350)', *Historia* 37 (1988) 105–125.

—— 'Sapor before the Walls of Amida' in French, D.H. and Lightfoot, C.S. (eds.) *The Eastern Frontier of the Roman Empire: Proceedings of a Colloquium held at Ankara in September 1988*. Oxford (1989) 285–294.

Livingstone, E.A. (ed.) *Studia Patristica XIX: Papers presented to the tenth international conference on patristic studies held in Oxford 1987: Historica, Theologica, Gnostica, Biblica et Apocrypha*. Oxford (1989).

Lorenz, S. *Imperii fines erunt intacti. Rom und die Alamannen 350–378* (Europäische Hochschulschriften, series 3, vol. 722). Berlin (1997).

Lucien-Brun, X. 'Constance II et le massacre des princes,' *Bulletin de l'Association Guillaume Budé* ser. 4 (1973) 585–602.

Luttwak, E.N. *The Grand Strategy of the Roman Empire*. Baltimore (1976).

—— *Grand Strategy of the Byzantine Empire*. (2009).

MacCormack, S. *Art and Ceremony in Late Antiquity*. Berkeley (1981).

MacMullen, R. *Soldier and Civilian in the Later Roman Empire*. Cambridge (1963a).

—— 'Barbarian enclaves in the northern Roman Empire', *Antiquité Classique* 32 (1963b) 552–561.

—— 'Some Pictures in Ammianus Marcellinus', *Art Bulletin* 46 (1964) 435–455.

—— *Roman Government's Response to Crisis AD235–337.* London (1976).

—— 'How big was the Roman Imperial Army?', *Klio* 62 (1980) 451–460.

—— *Paganism in the Roman Empire.* New Haven (1981).

—— 'What difference did Christianity make?', *Historia* 35 (1986) 322–343.

—— *Constantine.* New York (1987).

—— *Corruption and the Decline of Rome.* New Haven (1988).

—— *Changes in the Roman Empire.* Princeton (1990).

Mango, C. *Byzantium: the Empire of New Rome.* London (1980).

—— 'Constantine's Mausoleum and the Translation of Relics,' *Byzantinische Zeitschrift* 83 (1990) 51–62.

—— *Studies on Constantinople.* Aldershot (1993b).

Mango, C. and Dagron, G. (eds.) *Constantinople and its Hinterland.* Aldershot (1995).

Mann, J.C. 'What was the Notitia Dignitatum for?' in Goodburn, R. and Bartholomew, P. (ed.) *Aspects of the Notitia Dignitatum BAR Supp. Ser. I5.* Oxford (1976) 1–9.

Mann, J.C. 'Power, force and the frontiers of the empire', *JRS* 69 (1979), 175–183.

Mann, J.C. *Legionary Recruitment and Veteran Settlement during the Principate.* London (1983).

Maroth, M. 'Le Siege de Nisibe en 350 Ap. J.-Chr. d'aprts des sources syriennes', *AAS* 27 (1979) 239–243.

Martroye, F. 'La Repression de la magic et le culte des gentils au IVe siecle', *Revue historique du droit francais et étranyer (sér. iv)* 9 (1930) 669–701.

Mathisen, R.W. and Sivan, H.S. (eds.) *Shifting Frontiers in Late Antiquity.* Aldershot (1996).

Mathisen, R.W. and Shanzer, D. (eds.) *Romans, Barbarians and the Transformation of the Roman World.* Farnham (2011).

Matthews, J.F. *Western Aristocracies and Imperial Court AD364–425.* Oxford (1975).

—— *The Roman Empire of Ammianus.* London (1989).

—— *Laying Down the Law: A Study of the Theodosian Code.* New Haven (2000).

Mayor, A. *The Poison King: The Life and Legend of Mithridates, Rome's Deadliest Enemy.* Woodstack (2009).

McDonough, S. 'Were the Sasanians Barbarians? Roman Writers on the "Empire of the Persians"' in Mathisen, R.W. and Shanzer, D. (eds.) *Romans, Barbarians and the Transformation of the Roman World.* Farnham (2011) 55–65.

McNeill, W.H. *Plagues and Peoples.* New York (1998).

Millar, F. *The Roman Empire and its Neighbours.* London (1981).

—— 'Emperors, Frontiers and Foreign Relations 31BC–378AD', *Britannia* 13 (1982) 1–23.

Mommsen, T. 'Das römische Militärwesen seit Diocletian,' *Hermes* 24 (1889).

Mueller-Wille, M. *Opferkulte der Germanen und Slawen.* Darmstadt (1999).

Müller, W. (ed.) *Zur Geschichte der Alemannen (Wege zur Forschung, Bd 100)*. Darmstadt (1975).

Müller-Seidel, I. 'Die Usurpation Julians des Abtrünnigen im Lichte seiner Germanenpolitik', *HZ* 180 (1955) 225–244.

Murdoch, A. *The Last Pagan: Julian the Apostate and the Death of the Ancient World*. Rochester (2003).

Musurillo, H. *The Acts of the Christian Martyrs*. Oxford (1972).

Naudé, C.P.T. 'Battles and sieges in Ammianus Marcellinus', *Acta Classica* I (1959) 92–105.

Neufeld, E. 'Insects as Warfare Agents in the Ancient Near East,' *Orientalia*, 49 (1980) 30–57.

Nicasie, M.J. *Twilight of empire: the Roman army from the reign of Diocletian until the Battle of Adrianople*. Amsterdam (1998).

Nicolet, C. (ed.) *Les Litteratures techniques dans l'antiquité romaine*. Geneva (1996).

Nischer, N.C. 'The Army Reforms of Diocletian and Constantine and their Modifications up to the time of the *Notitia Dignitatum*', *JRS* 13 (1923) 1–55.

Nixon, C.E.V. and Rodgers, B.S. *In Praise of Later Roman Emperors: The Panegyrici Latini*. Oxford (1994).

Noethlichs, K-L. *Die gesetzgeberischen Maßnahmen der christlichen Kaiser des vierten Jahr-hunderst gegen Horetiker, Heiden und Juden*. Phd Diss. Cologne (1971).

Nutt, D. C. 'Silvanus and the Emperor Constantius II,' *Antichthon* 7 (1973) 80–89.

Oates, D. 'The Roman frontier in Northern Iraq,' *The Geographical Journal* 122 (1956) 190–199.

—— *Studies in the Ancient History of Northern Iraq*. Oxford (1968).

O'Brien, P. 'Vetranio's revenge? The rhetorical prowess of Ammianus' Constantius,' *Dialogues D'Histoire Ancienne 39 Supplément* 8 (2013) 221–258.

—— 'Ammianus Marcellinus, the Caesar Julian, and Rhetorical Failure,' *Cahiers des études anciennes* 50 (2013) 139–160.

Odahl, C.M. *Constantine and the Christian Empire*. London (2004).

Parker, H.M.D. 'The Legions of Diocletian and Constantine', *JRS* 23 (1933) 175–189.

Paschoud, F. *Zosime: Histoire nouvelle*. Paris (1971–1989).

Paschoud, F. and Szidat, J. *Usurpationen in der Spätantike: Akten de Kolloquiums "Staatsstreich und Staatlichkeit", 6.–10. März 1996, Solothurn/Bern*. Historia Einzelschriften 111 Stuttgart (1997).

Peeters, P. 'L'intervention politique de Constance II dans la Grande Arménie en338', *BAB* 5.17 (1931) 10–47.

Pharr, C. *The Theodosian Code and Novels and the Sirmondian Constitutions*. Princeton (1952).

Pietri, C. 'La politique de Constance II: un premier 'césaropapisme' ou l'Imitatio Constantini?' in Dihle, A. (ed.) *L'Église et l'empire au iv siècle. Sept exposés suivis de discussions*. Geneva (1989) 113–178.

Pohl, W. (ed.) *Kingdoms of the Empire: The Integration of Barbarians in Late Antiquity*. Leiden (1997).

Pohlsander, H.A. 'Crispus: Brilliant Career and Tragic End', *Historia* 33 (1984), 79–106.

Pollard, N. *Soldiers, Cities, ad Civilians in Roman Syria*. Ann Arbor (2000).

Potter, D.S. *The Roman Empire at Bay AD 180–395*. London (2004).

Pourshariati, P. *Decline of the Sasanian Empire: The Sasanian-Parthian Confederacy and the Arab Conquest of Iran*. London (2008).

Prioreschi, P. 'Contraception and Abortion in the Greco-Roman World', *Vesalius* I.2 (1995) 77–87.

—— *A History of Medicine: Vol.III Roman Medicine*. Omaha (1998).

Rees, R. *Diocletian and the Tetrarchy*. Edinburgh (2004).

Riddle, J.M. *Contraception and Abortion from the Ancient World to the Renaissance*. Cambridge (1992).

Robertson, A.S. *Roman Imperial Coins in the Hunter Coin Cabinet, Vol.V Diocletian to Zeno*. Glasgow (1982).

Robinson, O.F. *The Sources of Roman Law: Problems and Methods for Ancient Historians*. London (1997).

Rohrbacher, D. 'Why Didn't Constantius II Eat Fruit?', *CQ* 55 (2005) 323–326.

Rosen, K. *Studien zur Darstellungskunst und Glaubwürdigkeit des Ammianus Marcellinus*. Bonn (1970).

Ross, A. 'Constantius and the sieges of Amida and Nisibis: Ammianus' relationship with Julian's Panegyrics' *Acta Classica* 56 (2013).

Rostovtzeff, M. *Social and Economic History of the Roman Empire*. Oxford (1957).

Rougé, J. 'La pseudo-bigamie de Valentinien Ier', *CH* III (1958) 5–15.

Rüpke, J. *Fasti Sacerdotum*. Stuttgart (2005).

Sabbah, G. 'La "Peste d'Amida" (Ammien Marcellin, 19.4)' in Sabbah, G. (ed.) *Médecins et Médecine dans l'Antiquité*. St Etienne (1982) 131–157.

—— (ed.) *Médecins et Médecine dans l'Antiquité*. St Etienne (1982).

Salama, P. *Bornes milliares d'Afrique Proconsulaire: Un panorama historique du Bas Empire Romain*. Roma (1987).

Salzman, M.R. '*Superstitio in the Codex Theodosianus* and the Persecution of Pagans,' *Vigiliae Christianae* 41 (1987) 172–188.

Sasel, J. 'The Struggle between *Magnentius* and Constantius II for Italy and Illyricum,' *Ziva antika* 21 (1971) 205–216.

Sayers, D.L. *The Emperor Constantine: a Chronicle*. London (1951).

Schäfer, P. *The History of the Jews in the Greco-Roman World: The Jews of Palestine from Alexander the Great to the Arab Conquest*. London (2003).

Schäferdiek, K. 'Art. Germanenmission', *RAC* 10 (1978) 492–548.

Schmidt, H.-P. 'The Incorruptibility of the Sinner's Corpse', *Studien zur Indologie und Iranistik* 19 (1994), 247–268.

Seager, R. 'Perceptions of Eastern Frontier Policy in Amminaus, Libanius and Julian (337–363)', *CQ* 47 (1997) 253–268.

Seeck, O. *Geschichte des Untergangs der antiken Welt*. Stuttgart (1911).

Shaw, B.D. *Sacred Violence: African Christians and Sectarian Hatred in the Age of Augustine*. Cambridge (2011).

Sheridan, J.J. 'The Altar of Victor – Paganism's Last Battle,' *L'Antiquite Classique* 35 (1966) 186–187.

Shields, W.J. (ed.) *Persecution and Toleration:* Studies in Church History 21.Oxford (1984).

Simpson, C.J. 'Julian and the *Laeti*: a note on Ammianus Marcellinus XX.8.13', *Latomus* 36 (1977b) 519–521.

Southern, P. *The Roman Empire from Severus to Constantine.* London (2001).

Southern, P. and Dixon, K.R. *The Late Roman Army.* London (1996).

Speidel, M.P. 'The Rise of Ethnic Units in the Roman Imperial Army', *ANRW* 2.3 (1975) 202–231.

Stathakopoulos, D. *Famine and Pestilence in the Late Roman and Early Byzantine Empire.* Aldershot (2004).

Stein, E. *Geschichte des spätrömischen Reiches. Band I. Vom römischen zum byzantinischen Staate (284–476 n. Chr.).* Vienna (1928); Palanque, J.R. French translation, Paris, 1959).

Stephenson, P. *Constantine: Unconquered Emperor, Christian Victor.* London (2009).

Steuer, H. 'Herrschaft von der Höhe. Vom mobilen Soldatentrupp zur Residenz auf repräsentativen Bergkuppen', in *Die Alamannen.* Stuttgart (1997) 149–62.

—— 'Theorien zur Herkunft und Enstehung der Alemannen. Archäologische Forschungsansätze', in Geuenich, D. (ed.) *Die Franken und die Alamannen bis zur 'Schlacht bei Zu¨lpich' (496/97)* . Berlin (1998) 270–324.

Stevenson, J. (ed.) *A New Eusebius: Documents Illustrative of the History of the Church to A.D. 337.* Southampton (1983).

Stoneman, R. *Palmyra and Its Empire: Zenobia's Revolt Against Rome.* Ann Arbor (1995).

Stroheker, K.F. 'Die Alamannen und das Spätrömische Reich', in Müller, W. (ed.) *Zur Geschichte der Alemannen (Wege zur Forschung, Bd 100)* . Darmstadt (1975) 20–48.

Sutherland, C.H.V. *Roman Imperial Coinage, Vol. VI The Diocletian Reform–Maximinus II (294–313).* London (1967).

Sutherland, C.H.V. and Carson, R.A.G. *Roman Imperial Coinage, Vol. VIII The Family of Constantine I (337–364).* London (1981).

Swift, L. J. and Oliver, J.H. 'Constantius II on Flavius Philippus', *AJPh* 83 (1962) 247–264.

Syme, R. *Ammianus and the Historia Augusta.* Oxford (1968).

—— *Emperor and Biography: Studies in the Historia Augusta.* Oxford (1971).

—— 'The Ancestry of Constantine' in Straub, J. (ed.) *Bonner Historia Augusta Colloquium 1971. Antiquitas* IV.11 Bonn (1974) 63–79.

Szepassy, T . 'The story of the girl who died on her wedding day', *AAntHung* 20 (1972) 341–357.

Szidat, J. *Historischer Kommentar zu Ammianus Marcellinus Buch XX–XXI.* Wiesbaden and Stuttgart (1977–1996).

—— 'Die Usurpation Iulians. Ein Sonderfall?' in Paschoud, F. and Szidat, J. *Usurpationen in der Spätantike: Akten de Kolloquiums "Staatsstreich und Staatlichkeit," 6.–10. März 1996, Solothurn/Bern.* Historia Einzelschriften 111 Stuttgart (1997) 63–70.

Thompson, E.A. *The Historical Work of Ammianus Marcellinus.* Cambridge (1947).

—— 'Constantine, Constantius II and Lower Danube Frontier', *Hermes* 82 (1955) 372–381.

—— *The Visigoths in the time of Ulfila*. Oxford (1966).

Tilley, M.A. *Donatist Martyr Stories: The Church in Conflict in Roman North Africa*. Liverpool (1996).

Tomlin, R.S.O. '*Seniores-Iuniores* in the Late Roman Field Army', *AJP* 93 (1972) 253–278.

—— *The Emperor Valentinian I*. diss. Oxford (1973).

—— 'The Date of the Barbarian Conspiracy', *Britannia* 5 (1974), 303–309.

—— 'The Legions in the Late Empire' in Brewer, R.J. (ed.) *Roman Fortresses and their Legions*. London (2000) 159–178.

Tougher, S. 'The Advocacy of an Empress: Julian and Eusebia', CQ 48 (1998) 595–599.

—— 'In Praise of an Empress: Julian's *Speech of Thanks* to Eusebia' in Whitby, Mary (ed.) *The Propaganda of Power: the Role of Panegyric in Late Antiquity*. Brill (1998) 105–124.

—— 'Ammianus and the eunuchs' in Drijvers, J.W. and Hunt, D. (eds.), *The Late Roman World and its Historian: Interpreting Ammianus Marcellinus*. London (1999) 57–67.

Treadgold, W. *Byzantium and its Army 284–1081*. Stanford (1995).

—— *A History of the Byzantine State and Society*. Stanford (1997).

Trombley, F. 'Ammianus Marcellinus and fourth-century warfare: a *protector*'s approach to historical narrative' in Drijvers, J.W. and Hunt, D. (eds.), *The Late Roman World and its Historian: Interpreting Ammianus Marcellinus*. London (1999) 16–26.

Van Berchem, D. *L'Armée de Dioclétian et la réforme constantinienne*. Paris (1952).

Van Dam, R. *Rome and Constantinople: Rewriting Roman History During Late Antiquity*. Waco (2010).

Vanderspoel, J. *Themistius and the Imperial Court: Oratory, Civic Duty and Paidea from Constantius to Theodosius*. Ann Arbor (1995).

Vera, D. *Commento storico alle 'Relationes' di Q. Aurelio Simmaco*. Pisa (1981).

Vivian, T. *St. Peter of Alexandria : Bishop and Martyr*. Philadelphia (1988).

Vogler, C. *Constance II et l'administration imperiale*. Strasbourg (1979).

Wardman, A.E. 'Usurpers and Internal Conflicts in the Fourth Century AD', *Historia* 33 (1984) 220–257.

Warmington, B.H. 'Objectives and Strategy in the Persian War of Constantius II' in Fitz, J. (ed.) *Limes. Acts of the XI Limes Conference, 1976*. Budapest (1977) 509–520.

—— 'The Sources of Some Constantinian Documents in Eusebius', *Church History* and *Life of Constantine*', *Studia Patrisica* 18.1 (1985) 93–98.

Watson, A. *Aurelian and the Third Century*. London (1999).

Webb, M. *The Churches and Catacombs of Early Christian Rome*. Brighton (2001).

Whitby, M. 'Recruitment in Roman armies from Justinian to Heraclius (ca. 565–615)' in Cameron, A. (ed) *The Byzantine and Early Islamic Near East III: States, Resources and Armies*. Princeton (1995) 61–124.

—— 'Images of Constantius' in Drijvers, J.W. and Hunt, D. (eds.), *The Late Roman World and its Historian: Interpreting Ammianus Marcellinus* (London, 1999) 68–78.

—— 'Emperors and Armies AD235–395' in Swain, S. and Edwards, M. (eds.) *Approaching Late Antiquity*. Oxford (2006) 156–186.

Whitby, Mary (ed.) *The Propaganda of Power: the Role of Panegyric in Late Antiquity.* Brill (1998).

Whittaker, C.R. *Frontiers of the Roman Empire: A Social and Economic Study.* London (1994).

—— *Rome and Its Frontiers.* London (2004).

Wiesehöfer, J. *Ancient Persia From 550BC to 650AD.* London (2006).

Williams, S. *Diocletian and the Roman Recovery.* London (2000).

Williams, S. and Friell, G. *Theodosius: The Empire at Bay.* London (1994).

Wilson, A. 'Water-Mills at Amida: Ammianus Marcellinus 18.8.11', *CQ* 51.1 (2001) 231–236.

Wolfram, H. *History of the Goths.* Berkeley (1988).

—— *Das Reich und die Germanen. Zwischen Antike und Mittelalter.* Berlin (1990).

Woods, D. 'Two Notes on the Great Persecution', *Journal of Theological Studies* 43 (1992) 128–134.

—— 'Ammianus Marcellinus and the deaths of Bonosus and Maximilianus', *Hagiographica* 2 (1995a) 25–56.

—— 'The fate of the Magister Equitum Marcellus', *CQ* 45 (1995b) 266–268.

—— 'The Emperor Julian and the Passion of Sergius and Bacchus', *Journal of Early Christian Studies* 5 (1997a) 335–67.

—— 'Ammianus and some tribuni scholarum palatinarum c. AD 353–364', *CQ* 47 (1997b) 269–291.

—— 'Where did Constantine I die?', *Journal of Theological Studies* 48 (1997c) 531–535.

—— 'The Death of the Empress Fausta', *Greece and Rome* 45 (1998) 70–86.

—— 'Ammianus Marcellius and the *Rex Alamannorum* Vadomarius', *Mnemosyne* 53 (2000) 690–710.

Zotz, T. 'Die Alemannen in der Mitte des 4. Jahrhunderts nach dem Zeugnis des Ammianus Marcellinus', in Geuenich, D. (ed.) *Die Franken und die Alamannen bis zur 'Schlacht bei Zülpich' (496/97)* . Berlin (1998) 384–406.

Index